BUDAPEST

Also by Victor Sebestyen

Twelve Days: The Story of the 1956 Hungarian Revolution
Revolution 1989: The Fall of the Soviet Empire
1946: The Making of the Modern World
Lenin: The Man, the Dictator, and the Master of Terror

BUDAPEST

PORTRAIT OF A CITY
BETWEEN EAST AND WEST

VICTOR SEBESTYEN

Pantheon Books, New York

Library of Congress Cataloging-in-Publication Data
Names: Sebestyen, Victor, [date] author.
Title: Budapest : portrait of a city between East and West / Victor Sebestyen.
Description: First American edition. New York : Pantheon Books, 2023.
Includes bibliographical references and index.
Identifiers: LCCN 2023003244 (print) | LCCN 2023003245 (ebook) |
ISBN 9780593317563 (hardcover) | ISBN 9780593317570 (ebook)
Subjects: LCSH: Budapest (Hungary)—History.
Classification: LCC DB989 .S43 2023 (print) | LCC DB989 (ebook) |
DDC 943.912—dc23/eng/20230124
LC record available at https://lccn.loc.gov/2023003244
LC ebook record available at https://lccn.loc.gov/2023003245

www.pantheonbooks.com

Jacket photograph by Tanatat pongphibool/Getty Images
Jacket design by Oliver Munday

Printed in the United States of America
First American Edition
2 4 6 8 9 7 5 3 1

To Jessica

CONTENTS

Map   x

Introduction   1

Prologue   6

Part One: The Magyars

1   Aquincum   17
2   The Magyars   23
3   The Khans Invade   38
4   The Raven King   42
5   The Empire Strikes Back   57
6   Budun – A Turkish Town   64
7   Division of the Spoils   72
8   Buda Regained   78

Part Two: The Habsburgs

9   The Baroque – Gloom and Glory   89
10   Language, Truth and Logic   105
11   The Bridge Builder   116
12   The Great Flood   125
13   The Ides of March   134
14   The Revolutionary War   148
15   A Revenge Tragedy   159
16   Judapest   165
17   Empress Sisi   174
18   The Dual Monarchy – Victory in Defeat   184
19   Budapest Is Born   196
20   Café Culture   206
21   The Hungarian Pogroms   215
22   Illiberal Democracy   223
23   My Country Right or Wrong   230

Part Three: The World at War

24   The Beginning of the End   239
25   Lenin's Pupil   250
26   The Admiral Without a Navy   258
27   Marching in Step with Hitler   272
28   Madness Visible   281
29   The Siege of Budapest   292
30   Liberation   309
31   The Iron Curtain Descends   320
32   The House of Terror   331
33   Revolution – Again   340
34   Betrayal in Moscow   353
35   The Merriest Barracks in the Camp   358
36   The Last Rites   368

Conclusion   374
Notes   379
Bibliography   389
Acknowledgements   393
List of Illustrations   395
Index   397

BUDAPEST

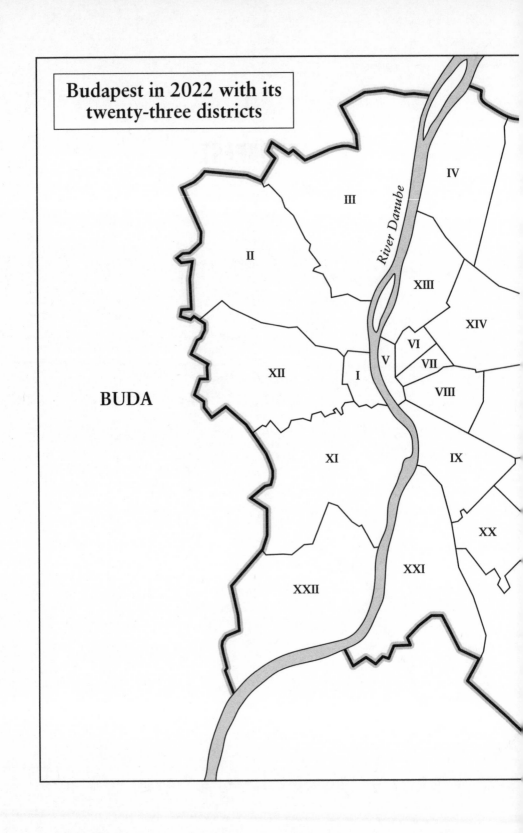

Budapest in 2022 with its twenty-three districts

III

IV

River Danube

II

XIII

XIV

VI

V

VII

XII

I

VIII

BUDA

XI

IX

XX

XXI

XXII

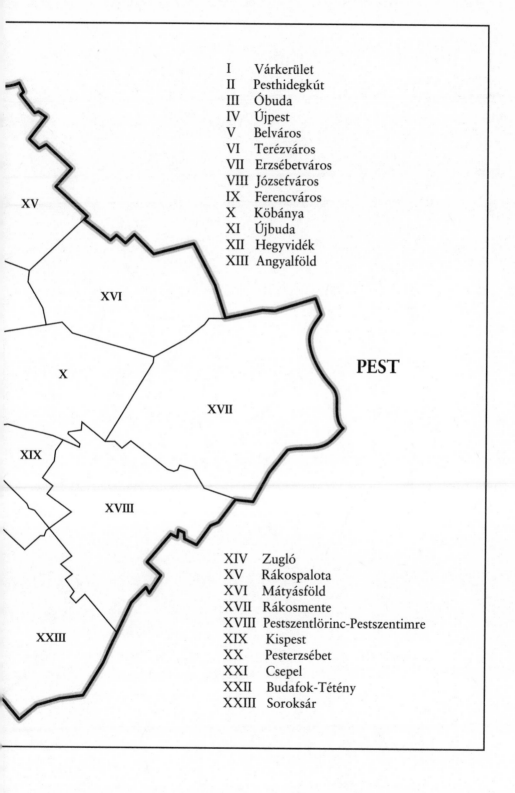

I Várkerület
II Pesthidegkút
III Óbuda
IV Újpest
V Belváros
VI Terézváros
VII Erzsébetváros
VIII Józsefváros
IX Ferencváros
X Kőbánya
XI Újbuda
XII Hegyvidék
XIII Angyalföld

PEST

XIV Zugló
XV Rákospalota
XVI Mátyásföld
XVII Rákosmente
XVIII Pestszentlőrinc-Pestszentimre
XIX Kispest
XX Pesterzsébet
XXI Csepel
XXII Budafok-Tétény
XXIII Soroksár

INTRODUCTION

As it flowed from my own heart in a spate,
wise was the Danube, turbulent and great . . .
whose waves embrace past, present and future.

Attila József (1905–37)

Towards the end of the Congress of Vienna in the spring of 1815, Klemens von Metternich, the Austrian Foreign Minister, took a young British visitor in his carriage to the eastern edge of the city. As the pair descended the steps, the eminent Habsburg statesman pointed his finger to the road towards Hungary and declared: 'Look, that's where Europe ends . . . out there, [Hungary] is the Orient.'

Half a century later William H. Seward, President Lincoln's Secretary of State, went on a journey around the world immediately after his term of office ended. In summer 1869 he arrived in Pest* from an unaccustomed direction, sailing from the Black Sea up the Danube through the Balkans. Most visitors came then, as they do now, from the west. He was surprised by what he saw. 'How striking is the contrast of European and Asiatic civilization,' he wrote later in his diary. 'Though Buda-Pesth is an inland provincial town . . . the tonnage in its port, altogether of steam, is greater than that of Cairo, Alexandria or Constantinople. We were not prepared for a scene of such activity . . . Here we feel, for the first time, that we have left the East behind, and have only Western civilization before us.'[1]

This is a constant theme, as alive in the twenty-first century as in the nineteenth. Throughout history Hungary and its capital have been a significant part of Western Europe yet at the same time apart from

---

* At this point Budapest was not yet a unified city but separate towns, Buda and Pest. The first bridge joining them, as we shall see, was not opened until 1849.

1

it – a point made repeatedly now by contemporary Hungarians. On the morning of 15 April 2016, in one of Budapest's grandest central squares, Viktor Orbán, Hungarian Prime Minister for more than a decade, made a typically pugnacious speech. 'Throughout history we Hungarians – more often than not all alone – have stood as the bridge between East and West and we suffered as a result,' he told a cheering crowd. 'Repeatedly we have saved Western, Christian civilization from catastrophe and destruction by invaders from the East.' In the Hungarian context this was an unremarkable comment, more a statement of fact than rhetoric. Most Hungarians of both Left and Right would see it as a self-evident notion expressing a deep-rooted idea about nationhood that has always resonated with people from Budapest – and still does.

Though much of it is similar to other lively, bustling European cities, the *sound* of Budapest is different. The unique, orphan language makes it so. The roots of Magyar, Finno-Ugric, originally – or so it has been assumed – derive from the steppes of Kazakhstan. Hungarian is unlike any other European tongue. Few outsiders, overhearing snippets of conversation at a coffee house or in the Budapest metro, would have any idea of what the people they were listening to were talking about. 'We are a lonely people,' the Hungarian national poet Sándor Petőfi wrote in the 1840s. This is equally true today.

A cursory look at a map shows why Budapest has always been an important place. It is close to Europe's geometric centre; it is at the crossroads of geographical regions and of civilizations, at the intersection of ancient trade routes. Mountains that gradually slope into gentle hills converge on a great river, the Danube, and a vast plain. Mediterranean Latin, Alpine German and Slavic peoples meet here. This is the focal point of Roman Catholic, North European Protestant and Greek Orthodox/Byzantine cultures.

Budapest became the capital of Hungary – and in many respects the centre of the Danube region – because of its favourable strategic location along a convenient traffic route. Modern Budapest grew along deliberately set, albeit repeatedly disputed and modified, plans. It is a city that was designed and built according to a scheme. Yet its most distinctive marks were left by involuntary forces – wars, revolutions, floods. Altogether Buda, over many periods the administrative centre of the Kingdom and then the Republic of Hungary, suffered thirteen sieges and was left in total ruins five times. Invaders have come and gone, empires have conquered, occupied for centuries or decades, and left a few footprints behind: the remains of a Roman bath house complete with wonderfully preserved mosaics stand next to a Soviet-style 'five-year-plan' apartment block that is already falling apart. As I hope to show, Budapest has grandeur, if faded around the edges, beauty in a gritty, lived-in sort of way. It is a city 'humbled by time and the ferocious moods of history', as the great poet George Szirtes put it.

Wallis Simpson, Theodore Roosevelt, Benito Mussolini, Hans Christian Andersen, the great tenor Luciano Pavarotti and the first man in space, Yuri Gagarin, were all agreed: the best thing about Budapest is its position. 'With the Danube, Budapest forms one of the most beautiful cityscapes that exists along a river,' the novelist Evelyn Waugh thought. 'It is the most beautiful in Europe.' Budapest is the place of my birth, and I do not pretend to be objective about its beauty and charm, though, as I shall also show, behind the charm lies much darkness and cruelty.

For much of my own lifetime, Budapest was the 'lonely' place described by Petőfi, cut off from the West, positioned unhappily behind the Iron Curtain during the Cold War, a colony of a tyrannical empire: the USSR. Physical reminders of the Soviet occupation, which ended only in 1989, are dotted around the city's skyline. Several public buildings are still pockmarked by bullet holes, deliberately preserved, to remind visitors and Hungarians alike of a trauma that was a defining moment in the history of modern Budapest: the 1956 Revolution, the event that took me from the city.

I was an infant when my parents, brother and sister fled Hungary as refugees immediately after the failed, tragic Uprising. I didn't return to Budapest until my early twenties; nobody in my family was allowed back there until then. I recall nothing from childhood about Budapest, yet I was steeped early on in Hungarian folk memory.

My parents loathed the ghastly turns of history that forced them from their home – the disastrous results of two world wars, fascism, Nazi German occupation, Soviet Communism. But they were never entirely happy in exile. Around our dinner table they talked wistfully of Budapest, rather as characters from a Chekhov play sighed the name 'Moscow'. My mother used to speak of entire days spent talking in coffee houses, surely the best invention, and perhaps the most long-lasting, of Habsburg *Mitteleuropa*. My father talked of music, Bartók, Kodály and evenings at the Vigadó, the wonderfully atmospheric Baroque concert hall by the Danube. My sister recounts winter days spent skiing – almost from the front door of the family home in the Buda Hills down towards the city centre, a run still just about possible if performed with care and skill, at dawn before the rush hour. My brother remembers a boyhood adventure, sitting atop the turret of a Russian tank captured by insurgents during the 1956 Revolution.

I started going to Budapest occasionally as a visitor from the late 1970s to see distant relatives who had remained in Hungary. Later, as a journalist covering the collapse of the Soviet Empire in the 1980s, I sometimes went several times a year on working trips. I then began to know the city intimately.

Budapest was the easiest place in Central/Eastern Europe in which to operate as a reporter. People were relatively free to talk, surveillance was almost non-existent – and the food and wine were better than anywhere else in what was then called the Soviet bloc. It was the merriest barracks in the camp. This book is the result of scores of visits to Budapest, including many months there researching my first book, written to mark the fiftieth anniversary of the 1956 Revolution. It is informed by using the knowledge of dozens of locals. It will be about the city's good days and bad, its sights and sounds, a portrait of the place and its people. It will take the story to the present day, when, once again, people in Budapest struggle with their identity and question how to be European and separate from Europe at the same time. It will look at Budapest's literature, its music, its history, its cuisine, politics and the essential role played by its Jewish population when Budapest was often referred to as Judapest. I will describe the ascendance of the city in the decades leading to the First World War – most of Budapest still looks like a nineteenth-century city – its decline into the maelstrom of the twentieth century, when it was all but destroyed, and its extraordinary rebirth in the twenty-first, when, after London, Paris and Rome, Budapest receives more tourists than any other capital in Europe.

A theme running through this narrative will be how, historically, the centre of gravity in Budapest and among Hungarians has shifted between East and West – culturally, politically, emotionally. Hungary is a country of extremes and the changes have repeatedly been violent, with battles won and often lost. Others were more peaceful, though the repercussions were no less significant, for example the fall of Soviet-style Communism in the 1980s. Hungary, now, is a small country that has often in history punched well above its weight. At many moments, events that began in Budapest have proved to be of world significance. This is an attempt to show how and why.

Victor Sebestyen
London, March 2022

PROLOGUE

Every nation has a Holy City which it thinks about with piety and pride.

Mór Jókai (1825–1904)

The life of the river is unceasing; and the whole warm, brilliant, animated picture is enlivening. Budapest! The very word names an idea which is big with the future . . . now at each forward step; it is the future opening up before a growing people.

Henri de Blowitz, The Times, 1894

From 5 a.m. until midnight on New Year's Day 1896 the bells of all the churches in Budapest rang every hour on the hour to signal the start of the biggest party in the city's history. It was Millennium Day, a monumental national event to mark the thousandth year since the Magyar tribes under their chieftain Árpád had ridden into the Carpathian basin from the Kazakh steppes to occupy what became Hungary. For a decade and a half the government, business leaders, architects, artists and artisans had been preparing for the occasion, designed to reflect the self-assurance and fast-growing prosperity of Hungary and its capital.

Large parts of the city had been turned into a construction site for vast new projects, showy and sophisticated in equal measure, embracing the look and style of modern Budapest. Two new bridges were built over the Danube to celebrate the millennium. The final section was completed of the Grand Boulevard (the Nagykörút), which became the new centre of the bustling city in Pest, the eastern side of the river. So was an enormous classical-style addition to the Royal Castle on the other, older, more sedate side of the Danube.

Continental Europe's first underground electric railway was opened just in time for the celebrations. It would take passengers from the old city centre by the river to the eastern edge of Budapest, where at the newly laid out City Park (Városliget) stood the most elegant building in town, the perfectly proportioned, Secessionist-style Gallery of Applied Art. So too, within sight, was the most vulgar: a reconstruction of an entire medieval Transylvanian castle (Vajdahunyad) by the shore of an artificial lake. Just a few metres along the city's main avenue, the Budapest Opera House had opened a few years earlier and Gustav Mahler had recently left after two controversial years as musical director.

In 1896 the grandiose Supreme Court was completed. Work was still going on to finish the Parliament building, one of the largest legislatures in the world, though its members were elected on one of Europe's smallest franchises – and not even on a secret ballot. As a British visitor to the millennium celebrations put it drily, in Budapest at that time, 'occasionally a disproportion between scale and function could be observed'. The previous year, the brash but impressive new Stock Exchange was opened, a huge pile designed by Ignác Alpár, whose hand can be seen in dozens of the public buildings of the period. It was the biggest of its kind in Europe, perhaps in the world at the time, but did a fraction of the business of the more modest-sized bourse buildings in London, Berlin and Paris – or even compared to the volumes of trade in the exchange at the other capital of the Habsburg Empire, Vienna.*

In Budapest, everywhere, expressions of faith in 'progress' and the future abounded, along with 'grandiloquent outbursts of national pride', as János Lukács, the brilliant historian of Habsburg Budapest, put it.[1] Often mere detail became lost amid the grand vision. The official date of the millennium itself was part of national myth, as nobody was (or is) entirely sure of the precise date of the so-called 'conquest'.

In 1862 historians from the Academy of Sciences were consulted by the Interior Minister, Ágoston Trefort, stoking a huge controversy. The academics couldn't agree on a date. Experts placed it 'sometime' between 888 and 900 but could not be more precise; in any case, the

---

* The Stock Exchange was closed after the Second World War and after a period as an empty shell reopened as the headquarters of Hungarian State TV. Alpár's work fitted with the times, but one critic saw then what was often remarked on: 'The ingredients of his style were strangely optimistic (strangely because the Hungarian national character tends towards pessimism, not optimism) and ... [were full of] myopic feeling about Hungarian omnipotence.'

migration was a process over a period of years, not one event. For the sake of convenience, they finally compromised and agreed the millennium date to be 1895 so that plans could be made for a giant celebration that year. But as early as 1893 it became obvious that the elaborate public works that were being planned, and the various large-scale events that had been proposed, were falling way behind schedule. So the jubilee year was put back until 1896.* It was a committee decision and slow work by building contractors that declared the official date of the Magyars' Carpathian crossing to be 896. In many cases that is how history is made.[2]

Originally plans were drawn up for a year-long programme of events, with a world fair and a huge permanent national exhibition in Budapest. Eventually the celebrations were scaled down, though still monumental in scope. International millennium conferences were held throughout the year – among others, of dentists, tailors, stenographers, geologists and art historians. There were press, mining and peace conferences in various towns across Hungary.

The biggest event by far was the Millennium Exhibition in Budapest's City Park, with 234 pavilions displaying 14,000 exhibits of Hungarian history, art and invention in an area covering 4,850 square metres, as many as at the 1851 Great Exhibition in London or the Exposition Universelle in Paris in 1878. It was opened with much pomp and ceremony on 2 May by the Emperor Franz Jozsef, never a popular figure in Hungary, and the Empress Elisabeth, 'Sisi', who on the other hand was loved in the country for her widely known support of Hungarian autonomy. Over the previous decade she had spent far more time in Budapest than in the royal court in Vienna. Even in the twenty-first century almost every town in Hungary has an 'Erzsébet' street, avenue or square named after the empress; Budapest has several.

The most important archdukes and archduchesses accompanied the monarch. His daughter-in-law, the Archduchess Stéphanie, widow of the tragic Crown Prince Rudolf, captured the occasion in a series of

---

* The grandest of the building projects was the Millennium Monument on Heroes' Square, by the City Park, a giant artwork next to a huge equestrian group of the seven Magyar tribal chieftains with the warrior Prince Árpád at the centre. It was not finished until 1929 and cost twelve times its original estimate.

charming photos taken with her Kodak box camera, the first ever to be seen in Budapest, which caused a sensation in the press the next day. So too did the absence of Prime Minister Count Dezső Bánffy's wife. It was said that she did not attend because she had been enjoying a long trip to the Italian Lakes, but in fact the real reason was that, although she was of noble birth, she was a trained schoolteacher and had held a job before she married. The leading aristocrats thought it was 'unacceptable' that such a person should play a part in such an occasion as Hungary's 'first lady', so she stayed at home. Though Hungary was in many ways a modern country, and new money was transforming the nation – as the Millennium Exhibition was designed to show – old ideas about power and rank remained. It was still a highly class-conscious and stratified society; aristocrats would remain in charge for some decades yet.*

The emperor spent more than two hours at the exhibition and seemed at ease. Normally stiff and exceedingly formal, he chatted amiably with everyone. At one exhibit of historical Hungary, a group of reconstructed straw huts and farms were on display to show agricultural life on the Great Hungarian Plain in the past century. A bearded peasant stood in front of one of them. Franz Jozsef approached him and asked, 'Do you live here?' 'No, thank God, your Majesty,' came the reply. 'Only for the millennium. Then I can go back home.'[3]

A week later, on 9 May, the royal couple celebrated a *Te Deum* in the coronation church, St Stephen's Cathedral, which had been magnificently renovated in the grand manner especially for the millennium. Most of the Viennese court was there, along with Hungary's leading nobles and business leaders. The Mass was conducted by the Primate of Hungary, Kolos Vaszary. The empress was visibly fighting back tears in the sermon when the cardinal gave thanks to her on behalf of the nation for 'having with her maternal, delicate hand once woven the golden bond by which the Magyar people and their dearly beloved King were inseparably bound together'. Even the aged emperor, who had

---

* A newspaper article in the Liberal daily *Pesti Napló* revealed what happened: 'The bluebloods are said to have given the Prime Minister the alternative in letters: either she . . . [the countess] went – or the whole millennium would go.' Countess Bánffy did eventually visit the exhibition, without publicity or fanfare, along with around 6 million other visitors that year, mostly from the Hungarian provinces.

succeeded to the throne nearly fifty years earlier when Hungary was at war with Austria, was moved.

Franz Jozsef and Sisi stayed more than a month in Hungary. The high point of the official celebrations was on Monday, 8 June, the anniversary of Franz Jozsef's coronation as King of Hungary, a gloriously sunny day. 'They had a sense of occasion, as did their hosts,' a contemporary witness recalled. 'Franz Jozsef wore a white Hungarian hussar's uniform. The melancholy Elisabeth, wan and beautiful, beloved by all Hungarians, smiled through a long day of parades. The day started with a ceremonial thunder of cannon from the Royal Castle. Green-trousered heralds were blowing silver trumpets.'

The emperor and empress rode in the front of the procession from the Royal Castle in Buda across the river to Pest in a crystal-paned Baroque coach dating from the time of Empress Maria Theresa in the mid eighteenth century. Behind them followed a huge procession of cavalry bands and regiments from the ancient counties of Hungary, some in seventeenth-century military finery. *The Times*'s Vienna correspondent could barely contain his excitement at the pageantry of it all. 'It would be a hopeless task to endeavour to give anything like a complete idea of the hundreds of uniforms and costumes of all colours of the rainbow of the procession that took nearly two hours to cross the Danube,' he wrote.

But when the king-emperor's party reached the still-unfinished Parliament building for the solemn part of the ceremony, there was an embarrassing hitch. The Crown of St Stephen, Hungary's first Christian king, considered a holy relic some 900 years old, was brought in an iron chest to be symbolically placed on Franz Jozsef's head. Time had rusted the lock and hasp of the chest and none of the noble 'guardians of the crown' could open it. Members of the royal household rushed to find a locksmith, who had to be fitted into a tailcoat before he could appear in public to solve the problem.

Meanwhile the emperor and empress sat patiently, boiling under the midday sun, while the crowd of thousands were getting restless. Wild rumours began circulating: the Holy Crown had disappeared, shouted some people. Something untoward had happened to the empress, said others. Mounted police formed around Parliament Square. Eventually a suitably attired locksmith arrived and broke open the chest. The ceremony proceeded as planned. But for a while the mood changed; many times in the past, large crowds in Budapest had made a habit of turning nasty – as they would in the future.[4]

For the next week Budapest was party city. In the Vérmező, by then a pleasant public park but formerly a place of execution known as the Field of Blood, the government provided all comers with free food and wine. Oxen were spit-roasted and bottles were cracked open. Five and a half thousand litres of wine a day were consumed and 32,000 links of sausages.

The authorities saw the millennium celebrations as a great success, but it left many prescient observers with a sense of anticlimax and fears of trouble ahead. The novelist Gyula Krúdy, one of the wisest observers of Budapest life around the turn of the century, saw the millennium as the defining moment when Budapest 'lost its virtue ... The bloated celebrations of Hungary's greatness wore thin.' He wrote of the old emperor's visit to a town

> that once consisted of small houses and modest citizens, of young, rosy, patriotic girls waving their handkerchiefs, of quiet antiquity ... But by the millennium year Pest had thrown off its mask of modesty; each year she put on more and more jewellery; the unassuming had become loud, the thrifty had turned to gambling; the virgins brought up in severe convents had begun to take pride in the fullness of their breasts. Pest had become unfaithful. This *raffiné* courtesan of a city had forgotten the triumphs of the young monarch upon whose bosom she had once thrown herself at the time of her innocence. She had become conscious of her developing charms; she discovered a new side that was both gamine and cosmopolitan; this once little wallflower had begun to appreciate herself; and the thrifty old gentleman was disturbed to find that the demanding cocotte that Pest had become no longer loved him.[5]

During the nineteenth century Berlin and Budapest were the fastest-growing cities in Europe, and from the millennium year to the start of the First World War Budapest was *the* fastest-growing one. In 1867 Buda and Pest – still two separate towns – had a combined population of 276,000; by 1913 it had nearly quadrupled in size to 933,000,

Europe's sixth-biggest city.* The speed of growth was spectacular and utterly transformed its people and its lifestyle. This was the period when modern Budapest was formed, planned to look more like Paris than a Habsburg town. Budapest around the millennium year 'was the world of the day before yesterday', as the Hungarian-born writer Arthur Koestler used to say, deliberately misquoting Stefan Zweig on the subject of Habsburg nostalgia.

Or, rather, half of it was. In the older and quieter part of the city, Budapest seemed to be from an even earlier era. A few rich families – the Zichys, Odescalchis, Esterházys, Pallavicinis – still owned their ancient vineyards in the Buda Hills overlooking the Danube, a frequent custom until the First World War. But from the 1860s a new agricultural population arrived in the city: a huge influx of peasants from the countryside to make better lives for themselves. This was happening in much of Western Europe too in the mid nineteenth century as the Industrial Revolution spread. But it was exaggerated in Budapest during the boom times, Budapest's golden period. Many peasants from rural Hungary went into fast-expanding industries and formed a new proletariat that would revolutionize the country and make significant history later. Big numbers would work in building the apartment blocks within the Budapest Ring for the new bourgeoisie – and the tenements in the expanding working-class suburbia to the south and east of Budapest.[6]

If cities tend to reflect the character of their residents, Budapest is a dramatic, theatrical kind of place. 'More than anything it resembles a stage set,' wrote Kati Marton, Budapest born but an exile who made a brilliant career as a journalist and historian in the US. 'There is Buda perched on steep hills, her sprawling Royal Castle and Citadel carved into jagged cliffs which plunge down into the Danube . . . Pest, on the flat plain on the other is all business, commerce and intellect, all conversation and art, music and a nightlife. Fantastic amalgams of Romanesque, Gothic and Byzantine straining to find a Magyar soul face the boulevards, which are unabashed imitations of Paris and Vienna.'[7]

In 1896 Budapest was the largest city of mills in the world (rivalled at that time only by Minneapolis). Wheat from the great plains of

---

* At the start of the nineteenth century, according to the 1808 census, the population was around 79,000.

Hungary and other parts of the Balkans was turned into flour in the mills of Budapest. Many of the successful entrepreneurs who began their business lives as grain traders became mill owners and then diversified. Budapest was by far the busiest port on the Danube. The (mostly nationalized) Hungarian river transport company, MFTR, had overtaken the Austrian equivalent more than thirty years earlier and was thriving. A pleasant daily Budapest–Vienna overnight journey on white paddle steamers was highly popular until the 1920s. Trains between the two cities were fast – four and a quarter hours in 1896. In 2022 it was three hours and thirty-five minutes.

Budapest finance caught up and surpassed the growth of agricultural and industrial production. By 1900 Budapest became the banking centre of Central and Eastern Europe. Between 1867, the date of the 'Compromise' which created the Dual Monarchy of Austria-Hungary, and 1914 the number of Hungarian banks grew from eleven to 160 and their capitalization increased fivefold. A few of them – the First Hungarian Commercial Bank and the Hungarian Credit Bank – rivalled the biggest Viennese and German banks in size and prestige, as their palatial headquarter buildings in downtown Budapest, designed by the most renowned European and Hungarian architects, showed. Their owners, such as the Wolianders, the Wahrmanns, Hatvany-Deutsch and Chorins, joined the European super-rich.

Sixty per cent of the Hungarian manufacturing industry was based in Budapest, from small enterprises to the giant Manfréd Weiss works, which employed more than 5,000 workers by 1913 in a vast factory complex on Csepel Island in the Danube, just north of the city. The factory exported munitions to Spain, Mexico and Britain, whose forces would soon be using them in a war against Austria-Hungary.

Little suggested that the unprecedented boom would not continue. Tekla Szilard, the mother of the Nobel Prize-winning physicist Leo Szilard, who would later flee Budapest from fascism and work on the Manhattan Project that designed and built the first nuclear bomb, described her mood on her wedding day, 25 April 1897, and 'the boundless optimism we all feel . . . The city was growing by leaps and bounds. I felt as though this was my progress . . . my development.' But some prescient people were more wary about the pace of change and thought of what was left behind. Krúdy wrote in 1900 about his beloved Budapest:

13

'They kept on building every day, palaces topped by towers rising towards the sun; and at night it seemed there were endless burials . . . of the town's broken matter, of old people and old houses, of old streets and old customs.'[8]

Within a generation much of this new wealth, optimism and confidence would disappear. In the millennium year Hungary was nearly three times the size it would be just twenty-five years later and its population around 50 per cent higher. Most of present-day Croatia and Slovakia, a third of Romania and a large slice of Serbia were all part of Greater Hungary. It possessed a busy seaport on the Adriatic with a busy merchant navy. Then the disaster of the First World War struck and Zweig's World of Yesterday came to an end. Hungary has never recovered from the shock.

PART ONE

THE MAGYARS

1

AQUINCUM

Look back over the past, with its changing empires that rose and fell, and you can foresee the future too.

Meditations, Marcus Aurelius (121–180)

A pair of fossilized footprints of a Paleolithic woman and a child, left around 30,000 years ago, were found in the summer of 1994 beneath one of the principal thoroughfares of Buda, Főutcá (Main Street), by the Danube. It was unearthed by a contractor digging up the road and prompted a wave of interest and debate among Hungarians about the far-distant past. For children educated under forty-five years of Communism, and to earlier generations brought up under regimes of the Nationalist Right, the history of Hungary began in the ninth century AD when the nomadic Magyar tribes, who originated from the Kazakh steppes, wandered west and began settling in the Danube basin. Before that, the narrative went, the area was almost empty, virgin territory. The stones of Budapest have always been political; each new discovery of life before the Magyar 'conquest' has begun a new round of culture wars about who was a Hungarian, when and where. Over the years, various archaeologists made finds nearby of a Bronze Age civilization along the Danube, locating tools, weapons and pieces of gold dating from more than 3,000 years ago. During the eighth to the fifth century BCE the nomadic Scythians, originally from central Asia, built temporary villages in present-day Budapest. One of their offshoot tribes were the Pannons.

Proof of the first semi-permanent settlement was made in the mid 1990s: a fort built around 550 BCE on what is now Gellért Hill, on the northern reaches of Buda, by a Celtic tribe known as the Eravisci. It had a commanding view of the great sweep of the river. Little is known about

17

the Eraviscans or their language, but it is believed they called their tiny settlement, on mineral springs perfect for bathing, 'Ak-Ik',* meaning warm water. Budapest has always been a spa town. The land further east, present-day Pest, on the other side of the river was occupied by the Sarmatians – the Danube was a natural border, hard to cross. But they built no permanent settlements in the region.[1]

In the early part of the first century AD the legions of the first Roman Emperor, Augustus, made short work of conquering and subjugating the Eraviscans. The Roman army arrived in force from around the year 50 and began work on building a defensive line of forts along the river to patrol the empire's newest province: Pannonia. One of the first of the camps, originally occupied by a corps of cavalry, was named Aquincum – because of the hot and cold water springs below what are now the Buda Hills. Around the year 90, the Romans reinforced the settlement and began to build a significant camp for the legions. Aquincum was the headquarters of the Legio II Adiutrix, the main army of defence against 'barbarian' raids from the North and East. A large civilian town grew a kilometre or so from the camp comprising a variety of traders and artisans to serve the military – along with a large number of slaves.

In 106 the Emperor Trajan made Aquincum the new capital of the province, which he renamed Pannonia Inferior – Pannonia Superior was further west, where its principal town was Vindobona (now Vienna). An enormous 120-metre square palace for the governor was built on the Danube island opposite, now Óbuda island. The first of the Aquincum proconsuls to live in the new palace, governor from 106 to 108, was Publius Aelius Hadrianus, who a decade after he left Aquincum would become the Emperor Hadrian. Almost nothing, sadly, remains of the building. In the late 1940s the Soviets, during the early days of their East European empire, laid the concrete foundations of a shipyard over it, but from surviving drawings, a few mosaics, and models it must once have been an extraordinary building.[2]

---

* This might have been what the Romans believed the Eraviscans called their settlement, as it is so close to a Latin equivalent. But some recent evidence suggests it was indeed the Celtic name. For a brief outline of Roman Buda, I have drawn extensively from original work in the invaluable *Blue Guide: Budapest* by Annabel Barber (London, 2018).

When troop numbers increased over the next decades, a second legion was stationed there. Eventually, by the third century, there were four – to quell the rising number of barbarian raids. The Emperor Marcus Aurelius stayed frequently in the military fort at Aquincum and the best evidence is that he began writing his *Meditations* in 167, while in the town but not actually on battle manoeuvres at the front. He certainly wrote parts of the work at Aquincum – perhaps even the aphorism so appropriate to the history-conscious Hungarians: 'Look back over the past, with its changing empires that rose and fell, and you can foresee the future too.'*

Aquincum grew into a large settlement, with central areas designed by well-known Roman architects. It became a significant Danube port, the centre of large-scale river transport. It had an enormous amphitheatre for games that could seat around 12,000 people. It was bigger in area than the Colosseum in Rome though its seating capacity was much smaller. (The Colosseum could seat 80,000.) It had animal pens to supply lions and other beasts for sacrifice and, for the time, a state-of-the-art watering system so it could be flooded for the mock sea battles with model boats that the Roman audiences loved so much.†

Disaster struck Aquincum around 170 when the Antonine Plague reached the town. Hundreds of thousands of people throughout the Roman empire perished from a pandemic of an unknown disease (now thought to be a variant of smallpox) that 'ate up the body, causing coughing fits, destroying the lungs and other organs' according to the Greek physician Galen, who treated many victims during three waves of the plague. The pandemic hit Aquincum hard. Perhaps as many as a quarter of the fort's legionaries died in the pandemic. But because of constant enemy incursions and its proximity to Italy, the garrison was

---

* Marcus Aurelius spent in aggregate more than a year in Aquincum, and was away from Rome for most of the last dozen years of his life, on assorted border fortresses along the Danube, fighting back various 'barbarian' tribes – the Marcomanni, the Quadi, the Iazyges, and others of the first wave of the tribes that would eventually overwhelm the Empire. He was there shortly before he died in 180 in Vindobona.

† After the Romans abandoned Aquincum it was turned into a fortress and used by various tribes during the early medieval period. From the twelfth century it was covered by earth and the huge mound was known as Királydomb (King's Hill). In the late nineteenth century workers' housing was built on it for the nearby Óbuda textile mills. Excavation didn't begin until the 1930s.

thought to be of such strategic importance that reinforcements were sent as a priority.[3]

Pannonia possessed significant political clout in the empire as a springboard for gifted and ambitious men. In 193 – the so-called 'year of five emperors', as civil war nearly ripped Rome apart – it was the Pannonian legions' declaration for the Senator Septimus Severus as Emperor that filled a political vacuum and began a reign of eighteen years which brought renewed prosperity and a measure of stability to the empire.

Septimus Severus had been governor of Pannonia a decade or so before ascending the throne and a year later, as a reward to his supporters in the province, he upgraded Aquincum into a *colonia*. This meant much more than mere status. It turned the town into a major provincial capital city and made an increasing number of its formerly Celtic population into full Roman citizens. For the following century, Aquincum boomed. A civilian area a couple of kilometres from the military base, nestling by the banks of the Danube, grew fast. At its high point the population was around 40,000, large by Roman standards, mostly comprising army veterans and their families and Romanized Celts. This was Hungary's first full-scale city. It would be around 1,500 years before as many people lived there again.

If one looks, there are still plenty of reminders of Roman Buda.* At one of the city's major transport hubs, Flórián tér (Square), amidst a bus terminus and a spaghetti junction of roads and underpasses, are the remains of a huge thermal baths complex that must have been as impressive as anything the Ottomans or the Habsburgs built later. There is a reminder, too, of an earlier musical city. Near the baths in the 1990s archaeologists found a richly decorated tomb chest of Aelia Sabina, the wife of the military camp's chief water organist, one of the most important musicians in the town, that bore a moving inscription: 'Enclosed within this stone lies Sabina, dear and faithful wife. Excelling in the arts, she alone surpassed her husband. Her voice was sweet, her fingers plucked the strings. But she fell silent, suddenly snatched away. She lived three decades, five years fewer, alas . . . She herself lives on.

---

* Nobody seemed to take much interest in Aquincum at all until the end of the nineteenth century when excavations began, and for decades most of the stones and tablets which would later become the Aquincum museum were stored in a side room of Buda restaurant, Frindt's Tavern, known for its fish delicacies.

She was a queen among the water organ players. May all who read this be happy. May the gods keep you and with a pious voice may you proclaim Fare thee well, Aelia Sabina. Titus Aelius Justus, water organist and stipendiary of the Second Auxiliary Legion erected this monument to his wife.'* Franz Liszt and Kodaly would surely have appreciated her work.[4]

Altogether, forty-eight governors and proconsuls ruled Aquincum, most of them relatives of the emperor. One of the most successful was Caius Septimius Castinus, brother-in-law of Septimius Severus, who was governor of Pannonia between 209 and 211 and then went back to Rome to a hero's welcome as the most senior consul in the empire. Cassius Dio had a less happy time. He was governor from 226 to 228, and when he got back to Rome wrote a major history of the empire in which he described his miserable time in Aquincum. He was accustomed to the Mediterranean and never came to terms with the rigorous climate of this northern frontier province, or the uncouth army life. It was an 'extraordinary experience for a man of my upbringing to see that the Danube should freeze over in winter', he said.

Other governors were far less fortunate and never survived their Aquincum years. Aelius Triccianus, who was born in Pannonia of plebeian origin, rose in the army and became governor of Pannonia Inferior in 217. He was a great friend of Emperor Macrinus. When the ruler fell, murdered in a coup, his successor, Heliogabalus, arranged to have Triccianus killed. His name was removed from the milestones erected during his Pannonian governorship.[5]

Recent excavations, which revealed major collections of silver, gold and jewels, show that some of Aquincum's inhabitants were clearly very wealthy and many were reasonably well off. The Sevso Treasure, fourteen pieces of extraordinary silver dating from around 210, was found in the late 1970s, some of it among supplies in a Buda bar. The find introduced evidence of a new page in Aquincum's history. One item is an enormous silver platter with an intricately designed engraving of diners at a table bearing the inscription: 'May these vessels remain with you for centuries, Sevso, and serve your descendants worthily'. Sevso

---

* For this translation from the Latin I am indebted to *Blue Guide: Budapest* by Annabel Barber.

owned a huge villa near Aquincum around the middle of the fourth century and the evidence suggests he was a Christian, as at least the previous three generations of his family had been. Christianity began spreading fast in Pannonia from the early third century – a basilica for worship was erected around 260, when gladiatorial games were forbidden in the amphitheatre.

Roman power in Pannonia began to dwindle during the fourth century. So too did Aquincum's fortunes and population, driven out by raiders from various tribes from the East and North who, piece by piece, exhausted the ability and determination of the Romans to cling on to their empire. By the end of the century both the military and civilian towns had become all but deserted. Instead of four well-equipped legions the Roman military presence was no more than 200-strong, and there were fewer than 2,000 civilians. When the Huns sacked the Aquincum settlements in 437 hardly a building was left standing. This was the first time, of many, that Budapest was destroyed.[6]

2

THE MAGYARS

Save us, O Lord, from the arrows of the Hungarians.

Common prayer in tenth-century psalters in
Germany and Lombardy

For two generations in the early tenth century the Magyars were regarded as the scourge of Europe. In scores of raids between 900 and 950 into the German lands, northern Italy, central and southern France – even across the Pyrenees into Spain as far south as Córdoba – they overran all that stood in their way, plundering, burning, killing. They are known to have pillaged present-day Bremen and Basel, Orléans and Otranto. They were mercenary troops employed by warlord princes from the Baltic to the Mediterranean coasts. They fought in turn both for and against the Italian King Berengar, for and against Arnulf of Bavaria, first in the interests of the rulers of Byzantium and then against.

In the Old French *Chanson de Roland*, the Magyars are, along with the Muslim Saracens, described as 'breeds of Satan' who left a trail of blood in their wake. Other early medieval chronicles confuse them with the Huns, an entirely separate if equally violent tribe. In oral tradition, which continued for a long period, they were 'horrifyingly cruel' and 'bloodthirsty man-eating monsters from Scythia' spreading fear and panic.

One atrocity in the spring of 926 is worth mentioning because it is the earliest surviving written account of the Magyars. They attacked the monastery of St Gallen, in what is now north-eastern Switzer-land, razed the abbey to the ground and murdered dozens of monks and nuns, including Wiborada, a noblewoman who had taken the veil a decade earlier. She had managed to move her priceless collection of manuscripts to safety just in time before the raid on 1 or 2 May. When the marauding band of Magyars arrived at the undefended abbey she was axed to pieces. But her holy books survived – hence she was canonized in 1047 by Pope Clement II and is the patron saint of libraries.* The chronicle by the monk Ekkehard the Younger described how the 'heathen barbarians . . . advanced like lightning' through Bavaria and Swabia. 'The onslaught increased from day to day . . . The barbarians with drawn swords pushed the neighbourhood of Lake Constance to the brink of disaster, killing countless people and burning all the houses.'[1]

Around the same time, marauding bands raided areas of Lorraine. Regino, Abbot of Prüm, recorded the emergence of the Magyars, who he said were 'Pechenegs who advanced from Scythian plains'. He wrote of an attack on monks at his monastery and of their 'horn-tipped arrows against which it is scarcely possible to find protection . . . These Magyars are not men but live in the manner of wild beasts.' For a century, prayers were routinely offered in German, Italian, French and Spanish monasteries: *'De sagittis Hungarorum libera nos, Domine'* – 'Save us, O Lord, from the arrows of the Hungarians'.

Yet there are other accounts, again by Ekkehard from the tenth century – still preserved at the Abbey of St Gallen – that show another side to the Magyars' character and demeanour. According to Heribald, one of the monks who survived a second raid on the abbey after Wiborada was killed, they looked ferocious but behaved no worse than other warriors of the time. They allowed some of the monks, including Heribald, to attend a feast in the inner courtyard of the building, which had not been destroyed. As he told it many times in the years ahead, the Magyars 'consumed half-raw pieces of meat, tearing at them with their teeth . . . they drank deep of the monastery's wine'. For entertainment they tossed 'gnawed bones as sport at one another and sang robustly . . . giving release to their high spirits, they danced and wrestled with each other before their captains'. When the monks and friars who had managed to escape the raid returned to St Gallen, they interrogated Heribald about what he had seen. He gave a surprising answer. 'They were wonderful,' he said. 'I have never seen such cheerful people in our monastery. They distributed plenty of food and drink before they left.' He then went on

---

* She was also the first woman to be canonized by the Catholic Church. Ekkehard's chronicle was probably written around 970–1000 and preserved in the rebuilt St Gallen Abbey as the *Vita Sanctae Wiboradae*.

to describe a group of loud, merry, hard-drinking but open and jovial men, the type common in Hungarian epic literature throughout history. Both sides – vicious at times, jolly at others – were probably true. As the French historian Fernand Braudel said: 'Until the late Middle Ages all states claimed to be the ancestors of rapacious beasts . . . Europe's map has never shown so many white patches as before the year 1000.'[2]

After the Romans left, the once-prosperous province of Pannonia had to fend for itself. A long struggle for power in the area continued for more than 400 years: 'a succession of bloody skirmishes were fought on horseback, with one band scarcely distinguishable from the next', one seventh-century chronicle despaired. The Roman fortress formerly known as Aquincum fell to rack and ruin and the civilian city that had been all but destroyed by the Huns became a settlement of wooden huts. On the other side of the Danube, a few buildings in what is now Pest never grew bigger than a small village. The river 'was wild and untameable' – much faster-flowing then – and it was difficult to cross. The Christians had gone, as the Romans had – either west for sanctuary, or killed by the pagan tribes relentlessly at war with each other for land to settle. This was the era of the Great Migrations, when successive tribes surged west from central Asia. They and their ancestors formed modern Europe.

The Huns remained the main power in the region for around fifty years – forced out by the Suebi, then the Vandals, the Goths, Visigoths, Herules and the Sarmatians. For just under 100 years from the seventh century the Gepids seemed to be in control of most of the area, displaced by the Avars, from the plains of Eurasia. None of these left much physical mark; no buildings in stone were erected in what is now Budapest from the fifth to the tenth centuries. But the Avars brought with them from Eurasia something lasting and useful: they can be credited with introducing the iron stirrup for riding horses, revolutionizing warfare.

The stirrup was easily exportable and the armies of Charlemagne learned to use the new invention to overcome the Avars early in the ninth century. The area around the Danube bend, including the remains of the ancient Roman settlements, was annexed by the Frankish Empire. The various tribes had intermarried for generations, and though the leadership changed several times over the centuries the best evidence suggests that a meld of peoples formed in the area generally labelled later as 'Slavic', if not correctly identified genetically. There were then probably no more than 75,000 people living in the entire region that would become Hungary and fewer than 1,500 in the settlements along the Danube in present-day Budapest.[3]

Around the 850s the tribes known as Magyar began entering the Carpathian basin. There is almost nothing definite recorded of their early history, before they began to appear in Europe; much is shrouded in myth and legend. What we do know is that they originated from the Finno-Ugrian people, from the eastern steppes of Kazakhstan. In the first millennium BCE they broke away from the main Ugrian tribes and began moving en masse south-west. How long this took – whether decades or even centuries – nobody knows for sure, but they were encountered along trade routes and one group of Turkic travellers around 1000 BCE recounted meeting a nomadic tribe of 'Ungars' or 'Onogurs' – in one Turkic/Bulgar language 'Onogur' means ten arrows. 'They are a race of Turks and their king rides out with horsemen to the number of 10,000 . . . They possess leather tents and they travel in search of herbage and abundant pasturage . . . These Ungars worship the sun and the moon.' They were polygamous and tribal custom was that a widow remarried her late husband's eldest brother.

Other traders, according to later Arab tradition, recall one of the ancient Magyar rituals – useful knowledge about the commodities in which they could conduct business:

> It is a custom when marrying that when a woman is sought in marriage, a dowry is appointed in accordance with the wealth in cattle, less or more, belonging to that man. When they sit down to appoint that dowry, the father of the maiden brings the father of the son-in-law to his own house and whatever he has in the way of sable and ermine and grey squirrel and stoat and the belly of the fox . . . and brocade, he collects all of these skins together to the quantity of ten fur garments and folds them inside a carpet and fastens them on the horse of his son-in-law's father and speeds him to his house. Then whatever is necessary for the maiden's dowry which they have agreed upon such as animals and money and goods is all sent to him (i.e. the maiden's father), and at that time they bring the woman to the house.[4]

For decades the Magyars – along with various Turkish tribes, Slavs and Alans – wandered in search of grazing land in a vast area between the Don, the Black Sea and the Danube which they called Etelköz, 'the area between two rivers'.

Towards the end of the ninth century, for whatever reason – some ancient accounts say they suffered defeats at the hands of an alliance of enemy tribes led by the Pechenegs, others that they could see an opportunity to take almost undefended land – they formed an army to cross the Carpathian Mountains and seize tracts of the Danube basin.

This is the point at which most published Hungarian histories begin and how the subject is taught in twenty-first-century schools, as though nobody had lived in the area before. Anything earlier is considered myth.* Whether it was an invasion, as Slav and Germanic historiography invariably calls it, or a 'land acquisition', as Hungarian historians have always euphemistically described it, has been a matter of debate for centuries and remains so even in the 2020s. The word 'conquest' is deeply concerned with legitimacy over disputed territories the Hungarians have always claimed inalienably as their own.

The invasion by a unified alliance of seven Magyar tribes was an easy task militarily. The Magyars were a formidably efficient fighting force and during their journey they developed iron discipline under talented generals. They were marvellous horsemen – and horsewomen too. Archaeologists as late as 2009 found decorated bronze bits for a woman's horse and it is clear that women joined the early Magyar raiding parties.†

---

* And very colourful myth too. A favourite of mine is that the discovery of Hungary (Magyarország, the country of the Hungarians) was predicted in a dream. Princess Emese, grandmother of the warrior chief Árpád, who led the Magyar tribe across the Carpathians, dreamed that she was impregnated on a divine command by a giant *turul* – an eagle – and the bird announced that her unborn infant and his descendants would rule distant lands. That is why her son was named Álmos (*álom* is dream in Hungarian). When he came of age, Álmos began preparations to lead his people to the promised land. The *turul* showed them the way until they reached their destination. Álmos died during the migration. A giant sculpture of an eagle now looks down across the Danube in pride of place from one of the highest points in Budapest at the top of the Royal Castle.

† That gender equality seems to have ended with the conversion to Christianity. Hungarian women, not entirely in jest, have said that it has never returned since.

They had overwhelmingly superior firepower. Units of 100 troops could loose off arrows at remarkable speed and accuracy in all directions; the iron stirrup enabled them easily to swivel 90 degrees in the saddle. A tactic developed over many raids, helped by the exceptional mobility of their forces, was the feigned retreat, which repeatedly confused enemies. Then it was easy to pick off the disoriented fleeing foe. 'The shrill, fearsome battle cries of the wild, shaven-headed warriors made the blood run cold,' according to one account.[5]

Initially the Magyars allied themselves with the Eastern Franks and remained on the periphery of the empire. But when one of the Frankish warlords died in the 890s the Magyars turned and saw an opportunity to take all the land in the Carpathian basin for themselves.

When the tribes moved along the Danube, they recognized the importance of the central location of the remains of Aquincum and of the surrounding warm-water springs. Five of the seven tribes settled there and two of the principal chieftains set up their camps around the site, including Árpád, the chief warrior. According to the earliest Hungarian chronicle, *Gesta Hungarorum*, attributed to Anonymous (it was signed only by 'P dictus magister' in the mid twelfth century, but has since been shown to be Péter, the Provost of Buda), Árpád's soldiers

> proceeded along the Danube to a large island mid-stream. They set up camp nearby, whereupon Chief Árpád and his noblemen marched on to it. When they saw the bounty and richness of the place and the advantage of the water on the Danube, they exceedingly rejoiced in it . . . They decided that it was to be hence and for evermore the island of the chief and that all nobles should be given a court and manor there . . . [he] hired artisans and had them build splendid houses for the chieftains . . . and he decreed that all horses be brought there to graze. He assigned a clever Cumanian, who was called Csepel, to oversee the grooms. As it was the home of the Master of the Horse, the island is named Csepel to this very day. Chief Árpád and his noblemen and their man and woman servants sojourned there in peace and power from the month of April until October.

28

Csepel Island still exists as a vast complex of factories and some down-at-heel apartment blocks.

One of the other principal chieftains, Kurszán, in charge of sacral matters, established himself in the remains of the Roman military lines of Aquincum in Óbuda. He used the amphitheatre and remaining outbuildings and it was known until the late Middle Ages as Kurszán's Palace. After Kurszán's death, Árpád took all power for himself, including the estates of his co-chieftains, and transferred his seat to Óbuda. The chronicle says he died in 907 and a 'white church' was built above his tomb, but the site has never been found despite the efforts of many generations of archaeologists.[6]

The Magyars far outnumbered the indigenous Slavic population. Accurate figures are impossible to come by, but the best evidence is that between 250,000 and 300,000 crossed the Carpathians. Árpád and the other warrior chieftains led the way and 'civilians' followed. These numbers allowed the Magyars to become different from the other horsemen of the steppes, who came and conquered and whose ways were absorbed into those of the indigenous population. The Avars, Bulgars, Franks and so on, who had settled there before, were expected, or forced, to speak Magyar – that is how 'a linguistic island was created in the German and Slavic sea', as Arthur Koestler would put it later – a fact evident to tourists in twenty-first-century Budapest.

The majority of the newcomers settled in the areas around the Danube and the River Tisza, but some of the tribes continued to make forays into Western Europe, where they gained their reputation for plunder and pillage during the fifty-year period that most Hungarian historians usually call, indulgently, 'the age of adventures' or ' the years of wandering'. Hungarian army commanders were often prepared to spare a region if it offered gold or silver, but would undertake punitive expeditions against those that would not – or did not volunteer themselves as well-paid mercenaries for hire. Lombardy was the first to pay the Hungarian raiders regular tribute. In 899 an army of Magyars said to be 5,000-strong massacred a smaller force of Berengar I, holding the king hostage. He was freed after a huge ransom was paid amounting, it is estimated, to 30 kilos of gold. Similar attacks continued into Germany and Lorraine until an alliance of Christian monarchs led by the Holy Roman Emperor Otto the Great was formed to end the raids by what he called 'heathen Hungarians'. On 10 August 955 the Magyars were decisively beaten at the Battle of Lechfeld, near Augsburg. Bulcsú, the third-ranking chieftain of the Magyar tribes (with the title *harka*) and Prince Lél, a leading figure from the ruling dynasty of Árpád, were hanged as common criminals from the gallows at Regensburg. Only seven survivors completed the return journey to Hungary, there to be reviled by compatriots for saving their own skins rather than giving their lives in battle.

The devastating defeat had momentous consequences for Hungary – and for the whole of Europe. The Magyars ceased their raids westwards, and in barely a generation they renounced a nomadic way of life and became settled peasants and herdsmen. Under Árpád's great-grandson Chief Prince Géza (who reigned 972–97) Hungary, between East and West, Rome and Byzantium, adopted Western cultural ways and Roman Catholicism.[7]

Géza I's decision to convert himself and his people to Roman Christianity was a political act, a secular choice. Though he was baptized in 973, he was essentially a pagan for the rest of his life. The conversion of the rest of the Magyars came at high cost. Most of them were performed by force; scores of recalcitrant *shamans* were tortured and murdered. Thononzoba, chief of one of the Pecheneg tribes who had sworn fealty to the Magyars, had a following among those who wanted to cling on to the traditional ways. He was buried alive and his entire clan was threatened with the same fate if they didn't convert to Christianity.

Géza ensured that his son, born with the pagan name Vajk, was brought up a Christian. He changed his name to Stephen (István) at his baptism and, far from being forced, he became genuinely, fervently pious.* Just before his death, Prince Géza arranged the marriage of his son to Gisela, sister of the young Bavarian Duke, later Holy Roman Emperor, Henry II, a major coup for a formerly 'barbarian', newly Christianized territory. The wedding took place in 996 and Géza died the following year.

---

* His birth date is not known for sure and is variously given as 967, 969 and, the least likely but still possible, 975. Neither is the date of his baptism clear.

Immediately Stephen had to fight for the succession – the first of many dynastic struggles over the next three centuries within the House of Árpád. His rival was Koppány, Prince of Somogy, great-nephew of Árpád, who ruled the lands south of Lake Balaton. He was still pagan and wanted to return to the traditional tribal customs and beliefs. Also, he had a better claim under the ancient family rules which granted inheritance to the oldest member of the clan. But Stephen based his claim on the idea that the conversion to Christianity changed the old rules and in future there should be a connection between the state and religion. The Roman Church favoured succession based on primogeniture.

This was a fight for a principle – and for the future. The crucial battle took place at Veszprém in western Hungary. Stephen had won the support of Bavarian armies loyal to relatives of Stephen's wife, Gisela. They crushed Koppány's forces; German knights sought the chieftain out after the battle and killed him. On Stephen's orders, his rival was quartered; the four pieces of his corpse were nailed to the gates of four fortress towns, including the castle gates at Buda, as a warning to other potential rebels. Stephen invited many German missionaries and monks to Hungary to hasten the conversion drive to Christianity – performed, as Bruno of Querfurt, whom the king had placed in charge of the campaign, described, 'by force and love'. The court was filled with German soldiers; all future Hungarian monarchs until the fourteenth century had Bavarian knights as their personal bodyguards.[8]

On Christmas Day 1000 (though some accounts put the date as New Year's Day 1001) Stephen had himself named King of Hungary, to differentiate his reign from the traditional title of chieftain, and his realm as a different kind of Christian state. He was a true visionary and remains – despite more flamboyant and martial successors – the founding symbol of Hungarian nationhood. His name lives throughout modern Budapest, in the city's cathedral, one of its central squares, countless streets and a giant shopping mall.

Stephen, who was canonized in 1083, half a century after his death, was responsible for ensuring that Hungary faced west rather than east. He could have brought Hungary into the Byzantine orbit and, like much of the Balkans, become part of the Orthodox Communion – overtures from Constantinople were made repeatedly to him, as they had been

31

earlier to his father. But he was determined to ally himself with Catholic Christendom and insisted on coronation by a papal legate, with a crown consecrated by Pope Sylvester II. Latin would be the language of official and legal Hungary, as it would remain until the nineteenth century.

Stephen moved the royal court from Buda first to Esztergom, about 45 kilometres north-west along the Danube, then to Székesfehérvár in central Hungary, which turned into a significant place of pilgrimage in Central Europe.

He retained Buda as a heavily guarded fortress and he would stay for short periods in the castle, mostly during spring and autumn. Twice a year he would personally hear legal cases there. But no more than 1,500 people lived permanently in Buda, a small town, and even fewer in the settlement of wooden huts on the plain opposite on the other side of the Danube, which was yet to be given the name Pest.

Hungary would be a land of many revolutions over the following millennium. It is no stretch to call King Stephen the first and arguably the most successful Hungarian revolutionary of them all. He centralized royal power in a unified state, as the Saxon and Danish kings in England, or Capetians in France, attempted but failed to do. He rooted out the ancient tribal customs of the Magyars and limited the powers of clan chieftains. He introduced a form of feudalism common for the period in Western Europe. Using various methods, he Christianized the Magyars. Hungary became a sizeable, relatively prosperous power in the centre of Europe, and when he minted new silver *dinars* the coinage quickly gained a good reputation as a currency in Europe, always the measure of relative success as a nation.[9]

Yet by his own admission Stephen's last years were sad and he feared for his legacy. His beloved son Imre died in a hunting accident in 1031, which prompted a bitter dispute over the succession. There was no other male heir, and as women were ruled out as monarchs the eldest surviving male Árpád should have been named as next in line. He was Stephen's cousin, Vazul, but the king hated him – he was a tribal traditionalist and it was widely believed that he was never a true believer but paid mere lip service to Christianity. Stephen nominated Peter Orseolo, son of the Doge of Venice, to succeed him. Strictly speaking, this was legal – the king was allowed, at that time, to name a successor. But it was always assumed that the heir would be a man from the ruling dynasty. Vazul claimed the title heir apparent and began preparations for a rebellion, with support from some tribal magnates. Stephen acted first and ruthlessly. He had Vazul blinded in both eyes and his ears filled with molten lead. His three sons fled into permanent exile. From 1034 the king retreated into prayer until he died in 1038.

Every 20 August, the date of St Stephen's canonization and a national holiday in Hungary, a casket containing what is believed to be the king's mummified right hand is carried in solemn procession around the basilica which bears his name in central Budapest.* This grisly celebration, followed by a Mass, took place even in the darkest days of the Soviet era when the Communists tried to suppress religion. Yet the holiest relic associated with Stephen is not a skeletal hand. One of the most popular tourist sights in Budapest – all Hungarian schoolchildren are encouraged to see it once in their lives – is the Holy Crown of St Stephen. It was for a long time the central symbol of royal legitimacy and has been venerated for centuries. The validity of a King of Hungary was coronation with the use of this crown, and no other, in the ceremony. The crown is shrouded in myth, like so much of ancient Magyar history.

It is certain that the crown on display in modern Budapest was never worn by King Stephen. The original was lost or stolen soon after the king's death and there are many theories about its fate. It is said that in 1044 it was found by soldiers loyal to the Holy Roman Emperor, Henry III, and he returned it to the Vatican. The lower half of the crown on display now, the so-called 'Greek part', made in 1074, nearly forty years after King Stephen's death, was a gift from the Byzantine Emperor Michael VII to the Hungarian King Géza I. The upper 'Latin' part was made in Hungary, probably at some point in the late twelfth century, to replace the lost original. The two halves were welded together around

---

* The rest of his body is in the burial tomb beneath the royal chapel at Székesfehérvár, last resting place of all the medieval Hungarian kings. Since 1988 he has been joined by the supposed remains of Queen Gisela which were brought from Passau to be reinterred with her husband.

1330, in order to make a solid base for a gold cross that surmounts the crown.*

Lost again and found in a series of centuries-long dramas and adventures, the crown was taken to Austria towards the end of the Second World War by Hungarian fascists – either, as one group said, to sell it on the black market or, as others claimed, to preserve it from the clutches of the Communists. Somehow it fell into the hands of the US army in Vienna in 1945. The Americans kept it in Fort Knox, to ensure its safety, until 1978 when it was ceremoniously returned to Hungary. The crown and other royal regalia thought to have belonged to Stephen or his immediate successors were then installed by a Communist regime aiming for national respectability in a large shrine in Budapest's National Museum under permanent armed guard. To mark the millennium of the Hungarian state, the first of Viktor Orbán's governments in 2000 transferred all the royal jewels, amid great solemnity and fanfare, to the Parliament building. In a republic, it seemed at first sight an odd place to move the crown jewels, but in the Hungarian context there was logic to it. For a nation that has been occupied by other powers for so many periods in its history, the crown has always been the symbol of independence and freedom, rather than of royalty. And besides, the crown jewels are magnificently presented in inspiring surroundings.

Stephen brought order out of chaos, stability and the beginning of a legal code. He is, rightly, one of the most revered figures in Hungary's history. He left a considerable literary legacy too: the *Exhortations*, written around 1015 as a guide to ethical kingship for his son Imre and other future rulers. It is a fascinating work, even if its insights are not always followed as examples by his people. 'Immigrants are of great benefit,' he wrote in one section. 'They bring with them different tongues and customs, different skills and weapons. And all that is an ornament to

---

* There is an excellent book, *A Magyar korona regénye*, about the adventures of the Holy Crown of Hungary by two history professors at Budapest University, Kálmán Benda and Erik Fügedi, who give an elegant reply to the obvious question that if the displayed royal regalia is a myth, how can it be called Stephen's crown: 'This belief over the centuries has proved indestructible . . . historians must have no choice but to admit that in this case it doesn't matter whether, as an object, it is Stephen's crown or not, but what is essential is the unshakeable belief in it.' An explanation for so many legends.

the country and alarms our enemies. So my son I advise you to face new settlers, and treat them decently. Then they will prefer to stay with you rather than elsewhere. A nation with but one tongue and one custom is feeble and fragile . . . if you destroy all that I have built, squander what I have collected, the empire will without doubt suffer.'[10]

Even before Stephen was buried, a crisis flared in the House of Árpád. Peter Orseolo was crowned king, but the family of his rival to the throne, the tortured, blinded Vazul, did not give up their succession claims. Within two years Peter was ousted by one of the claimant's cousins, Sámuel Aba. But he was loathed within the court of Stephen, and with the help of a German army led by the Emperor Henry III, King Peter was restored to the throne – though this time as Henry's vassal, which would become an important factor in the future. Aba, in turn, was blinded before being axed to death by German knights. Peter's second reign was no happier than his first. In 1046 he was ousted again* – this time by court officials and powerful groups of barons, who called back one of Vazul's exiled sons, Andrew, and made him king.

The Árpád dynasty continued for nearly 300 further years – under twenty-two monarchs – but although Hungary became in many ways a more important place within Central Europe, its territory expanded and the wealth of its nobles grew exponentially, it would seldom appear a stable, unified state. Repeatedly there were dynastic quarrels which had devastating consequences. Andrew was on the throne for fourteen years and tried to consolidate power centrally under the monarch, though the task was beyond him. He died on the battlefield against the forces of his brother Béla, who succeeded him until he himself was overthrown (though he did retain the use of both his eyes). In the next thirty-nine years the country changed its ruler six times. Three kings died a violent death and one of them fled and relinquished his throne to save his life. Another was ousted twice and returned twice. The royal family's feuds brought the intervention of foreign armies nine times – Bavarians, Czechs and Poles. Hungary became a German dependency twice. Law and order was utterly destroyed and there were two pagan rebellions,

---

* Hardly a surprise, Peter Orseolo had his eyes gouged out before being sent back to Venice whence he came.

suppressed with the utmost savagery. The kingdom was partitioned for decades.[11]

On the other hand, from the twelfth century, mainly through adroit marriage contracts, large new territories were added to the kingdom, for example tracts of Dalmatia, which gave Hungary access to the Adriatic Sea. Major deposits of gold, silver and other precious minerals were found from the middle of the century and the finds went directly to the royal coffers. Apart from any other benefits, fighting for the Crown was a potentially valuable enterprise for a claimant and his supporters. The wealth of Hungary in the medieval period was substantially the result of these rich mineral reserves. Historians of the period have estimated that of all the gold deposits in the known world before *c*.1420, at least 40 per cent came from Hungary, which supplied about three-quarters of the European demand. About a quarter of all the silver mined in Europe was from Hungary.[12]

There were two enlightened and sensible Árpád kings. The best of them was Coloman (reigned 1095–1116), who left writings which showed he was highly intelligent and forward-thinking for his time; he enacted laws against witch trials – 'since there are no witches' – and for the first time allowed Jews to live in the country legally.* He and his ablest successor, Béla III (1172–96), tried to limit nobles' powers of life and death over serfs and to halt warlords pillaging at will over Crown lands. But, as elsewhere in feudal Europe, the power of the king was not as absolute as it appeared. Seven years after the barons and the King of England reached a compromise about the separation of powers in the Magna Carta, enshrining baronial rights in law, the high nobility in Hungary forced King Andrew (András) II to sign a similar charter. But the Golden Bull (named because its seal was in gold leaf) of 1222 gave the nobility far more extensive rights than its English predecessor. They retained most of these rights until the middle of the nineteenth century, with enormous consequences for Hungary's future. Nobles

---

* There had been some Jews in Aquincum in Roman times, and some accounts record a handful of Jews living in Buda – even at the time of the conquest. But this was the first known Jewish community in Hungary during medieval times. Jews were subject to various regulations: they had to wear distinctive signs on their clothes in public and were barred from marrying Christians, but for the most part they were treated better in medieval times than co-religionists in Germany, France or England.

were excused from paying any kind of taxes, but unlike in feudal England or France they did not have to raise armies in 'foreign wars' if they didn't want to. This left a giant black hole in royal finances, filled by taxing peasants. The nobles were granted the right of armed resistance against the king if the monarch 'acted illegally' – legality was judged by the peers. The king was barred from debasing the currency. The few Jews who lived in Buda and two other Hungarian towns were banned from owning property and were forced to pay extra exorbitant taxes. There was not a single word in the Golden Bull about the 'people' (as there wasn't in Magna Carta). It related only to 'free men' or 'the nation' – and these were defined only as the nobility.[13]

During much of the early medieval period Buda consisted of the castle and a small settlement mostly of German squires, their servants and their families, a few artisans, some traders and a handful of Jews permitted to live only on the edge of the settlement, the oldest part of the town Óbuda. It was a sleepy, out-of-the-way place. Kings continued to visit the fortress and hold legal hearings there, but it was not the capital and the royal court had not been established there since the early days of Stephen's reign. There was no other building of importance apart from the castle, where Buda's provost lived, a high dignitary of the land who occasionally, if he had the king's favour, could claim to be effectively the Hungarian Chancellor. The year after the Golden Bull was signed, Buda was awarded sole fishing rights along both sides of the nearby stretch of the Danube, including the right to levy customs duties along much of the river. It grew in prosperity and population into a modest-sized medieval town. Andrew II came to like it; in 1230 he moved the court there and turned Buda back into the royal seat. It now had great influence in Hungary and importance throughout Europe. Then, in 1241, came catastrophe.

3

THE KHANS INVADE

Among all the peoples who in the course of history have passed before
our eyes there were none so unlucky as the Hungarians ... Nature
brought forth their strong, handsome, clever men in vain.

Voltaire (1694–1778)

Heaven grant us its peace, but not the King of Hungary's.

William Shakespeare, *Measure for Measure*, Act 1, Scene 2

'In this year, after existing for 350 years, the Kingdom of Hungary
was annihilated by the Tatars.' It was a simple statement of fact by
the Benedictine Abbot Hermann of Niederaltaich in Bavaria, who had
Hungarian relatives and recorded it in the annals of his monastery immediately on hearing the news in April 1241. The Emperor Frederick
II – technically still liege lord of Hungary – wrote to Henry III, the King
of England, around the same time: 'That entire precious kingdom was
depopulated, devastated and turned into a barren wasteland.' In Hungarian history books even now this period is known as 'the devastation'.
Contemporary chronicles, witnesses and monarchs called the invaders
'Tatars', though they identified themselves as Mongols.

The Mongol army, known throughout a terrified Europe as the
Golden Horde, had been one of the most successful military forces in
history, leaving a wave of destruction under Genghis Khan through
China, northern India and central Asia. When the great Khan died in
1227 his son Ögedei continued the Mongol advance west, ordering his
army commander Batu to seize the Russian steppes, Ukraine, Poland,
continue into Eastern Europe and take control over the whole known
world. The Hungarian King Béla IV understood the threat and appealed
to other European monarchs, and the Pope, in their own interests to
repel the invaders. He heard nothing. By spring 1241 the advance guard

of Batu's forces reached eastern Hungary. King Béla's army of Hungarians and German mercenaries outnumbered the Mongols but on 11 April it was routed at Mohi, on the Sajó River. The cream of Hungary's military leadership was slaughtered, though the king and a few of his young knights managed by luck to escape.

Half of Batu's force followed Béla – in the Mongols' eyes a territory was not entirely beaten while its rightful ruler was still alive. They almost captured him at the monastery at Klosterneuburg near Vienna, but again he got away. They followed his tracks all the way through southern Austria, Slovenia and Croatia to the Dalmatian island city of Trogir, which they blockaded and besieged. Béla again made desperate pleas for help against what he wrote were 'the heathen barbarians threatening Christendom'. All he received were a few words of consolation from the emperor, the Vatican, Louis IX of France and other Christian monarchs.[1]

The rest of Batu's army crossed the Danube and marched towards the royal seat, which the Hungarian king had left lightly defended. The Mongols had sophisticated siege engines, though they weren't needed. They were the first army in Europe to use the Chinese invention of gunpowder, though in taking Pest and Buda little of that was needed either. Their main method of attack was similar to the Magyar strategy that had advanced into the Carpathian basin: using maximum speed by charging en masse on horseback while releasing a shower of arrows on an enemy. This had proved successful even against well-fortified towns. Nobody had managed to stop them for long. The attack on Buda began on 16 April 1241 and lasted just a few hours. No contemporary Hungarian accounts have survived, but the prelate Thomas, Archdeacon of Spalato (now Split in Croatia), left an account allegedly from eyewitnesses later.

> The Tatar army, after setting up camp all around, began to attack the town from every direction, shooting arrows relentlessly and showering it with spears . . . the hapless Hungarians took up the fight against them and tried with all their might. They strained their catapults and crossbows, hurled innumerable spears and arrows into enemy ranks, and propelled many rocks with their ballistae. But the Tatars' deadly arrows struck their targets with precision and caused certain death to

the defenders. No cuirass, shield or armour could resist the arrows launched by Tatar hands ... So great was the blight befalling the town ... as God's vengeful sword wallowed most profusely in Christian blood ... the water of the Danube was red with human blood. When barbaric death had raged to satisfaction and they withdrew from the town, they set fires of every sort and before the enemies' eyes the greedy flames devoured all.'[2]

Buda was almost totally burned to the ground. Even in the twenty-first century archaeologists encountered a 30-centimetre layer of ash and charred wood where some Pest settlements had once stood in the thirteenth century; carbon dating has measured the destruction of the town precisely.

The whole of Hungary was open to the Mongols, and much of Western Europe was within their reach. But, suddenly and unexpectedly, they turned round and the huge Mongol army raced back east, taking cartloads of booty and enslaved people with them. The Hungarians were perplexed by the speed of the retreat. And the reason. Soon they heard that Ögedei Khan had died. Batu returned to the Mongol Empire's capital, Karakorum, and a vicious struggle for the succession consumed the empire in civil war for a generation. The West was saved.

King Béla returned home to a desolate land, a country in desperate straits and a population decimated. Master Rogerius, an Italian cleric who had somehow managed to survive the destruction of Buda, found only 'ruins, corpses and desolation all around'. The medievalist György Györffy, writing in the 1980s, said that Hungary did not recover from the Mongol invasion for a century and a half. He calculated that around 60 per cent of the lowland settlements in east and central Hungary were destroyed. For a long period afterwards, survivors of the massacres suffered from starvation and disease. Failed harvests caused by the destruction of thousands of fields and pastures made the catastrophe worse. The western areas of Hungary and Transylvania, some of which the Mongols had not occupied before their retreat, fared better:

---

* Archdeacon Thomas wildly overestimated the death count when he wrote: 'Over one hundred thousand men died a terrible death in a single day and in an area not at all large.' A more accurate figure would be roughly 10,000, most of them from the army King Béla had managed to leave guarding his principal fortress.

the population loss was lower than 20 per cent. Most historians of the period estimate that around half of Hungary's 2 million population in 1240 were direct victims of the Mongol invasion.

For the following twenty-eight years of his reign Béla wrote a barrage of letters to other kings, successive popes and noble families throughout Europe bitterly complaining about the indifference of the Western world to the plight of Hungary. In a letter to Pope Vincent IV in 1253 he wrote: 'We have received from all sides merely words ... We have received no support in our great affliction from any Christian ruler or nation in Europe.' These thoughts have been a constant theme throughout Hungarian history, echoed repeatedly – when the Turks occupied the country in the sixteenth century, the Austrians suppressed an independence movement in the nineteenth century, when the Soviet Union savagely put down a revolution in the twentieth. 'We are the most forsaken of all peoples on this earth,' said the poet Sándor Petőfi, with a hint of characteristic Hungarian pessimism. In the 2020s many Hungarian politicians strike a chord when they say similar things. The feeling of being endangered and defenceless, the idea of the nation alone have deep roots among Hungarians.[3]

4

THE RAVEN KING

The grim wars that our ancestors were waging
Have melted into peace in memory's sight;
A general settlement, past wrongs assuaging,
Is now our task to make; it is not light.

Attila József, 'By the Danube', 1936

Hungary survived the Mongol invasion and in time would prosper again, but it became a different country. King Béla IV rebuilt the castle and town of Buda, and in the remaining quarter-century of his reign erected a string of fortress settlements along the Danube and eastern Hungary to guard against a repeat attack by the Khans. He restored royal fortunes and reached an accommodation with the powerful noble families, some of whose lands had been left relatively unscathed by the Mongols and were as wealthy as the king. Old habits died hard though. The Árpáds resumed their family feuds which would soon destroy the dynasty.

For the last ten years of his reign Béla fought a series of wars with his son and heir, Stephen, who would not wait for his turn to be king. Having plotted, battled and killed his way to the throne, Stephen V, as he became, reigned for less than two years before he died from a mystery illness, though some contemporary accounts suspect he was poisoned.

The remaining Árpáds brought the court at Buda into disrepute throughout Europe for wild excesses. The most depraved, and violent, was Stephen's son Ladislaus IV (László in Hungarian), who was remembered for a lifetime of uninterrupted scandals, intrigues and bloody settling of scores with his own family and the richest magnates in Hungary. Before he could produce an heir he had his wife, Princess

Isabella of Anjou, locked up in a convent, where she died. The rest of his life was given over to 'luxury, idleness and debauchery', as one contemporary recorded.[1]

He had a string of mistresses from pagan tribes on the periphery of eastern Hungary, known as Cumans. The court was shocked. Even some other European monarchs whose own private lives were not entirely blameless were outraged, and the king received an interdict from the Vatican. His response, according to Philip of Felső the papal legate to Buda, in a letter to the Pope was a threat 'to have the Archbishop of Esztergom, all the other bishops, and the whole bunch in Rome decapitated with a Tatar sabre'. Ladislaus had sex with one of his Cuman concubines during a royal council meeting at Buda Castle in front of high clergy and some powerful noble dignitaries. That was the last straw for many in the court. In the winter of 1290, two hired assassins in the pay of one of the magnates murdered him.

Ladislaus left no heir and anarchy followed for the next decade and a half. Groups of warlords, along with established barons who possessed long-held lands and spheres of interest, fought for a country that was falling apart. None of the last Árpád rulers could re-establish central authority. When Andrew (András) III died in 1301, leaving only an infant daughter, the dynasty died with him.* Rivals from various royal houses in Europe laid claim to the crown of Hungary and battled for it over seven years – 'a series of foreigners killing and dying for what is Hungary's', remarked Thomas II, Archbishop of Esztergom, Prince Primate of Hungary. Eventually the Angevin Charles Robert, grandson of Ladislaus IV's sister, Mary of Naples, won a decisive victory: he was crowned King of Hungary towards the end of 1308 as Charles I. Foreign monarchs, some from far away and others who seldom lived within the borders of Greater Hungary, would rule for the following 225 years, among them four Neapolitans from the House of Anjou, a Luxembourger, two Habsburgs and three Jagiełłos from Poland and Bohemia. There was just one locally born Hungarian king among them, Mátyás

---

* Hungary had an equivalent of the medieval French Salic law that barred women from ruling in their own right (though they could act as regents for their sons before maturity). This remained the law until the mid eighteenth century, when constitutions had to be amended to allow the Habsburg Empress Maria Theresa to be Queen of Hungary, a process known as the Pragmatic Sanction.

Hunyadi, who reigned as Matthias Corvinus and became, even ahead of St Stephen, the most revered Hungarian monarch of all.[2]

In the 1350s vast new gold and silver reserves were found in northern Hungary and Transylvania – one rich mine was sunk just along the Danube near Esztergom, less than 60 kilometres from Buda. It fuelled, literally, a golden age in Hungarian history. Out of the chaos of constant civil wars between rival warlords and their mercenary armies rampaging through the land, the building blocks of a centralized state emerged; law and order were restored, the economy and the population boomed. Around 1400 Hungary's population was about 3.5 million, large by late-medieval standards. Due to its size and position, its trading connections between East and West, with the Danube as a transport hub, Hungary grew in importance. Early in the fifteenth century royal income from granting gold-mining leases and taxation amounted to at least twice that of the King of England at the time, around the same as that of the ruler in France. The biggest landowners – including the Church – became vastly wealthy.

Buda had little to recommend it, apart from the castle and the court. It was tiny compared to Paris, London or the Italian city states. There were probably around 8,000 people living there in 1400, mostly dependent on the king and his officials, or the increasingly busy river port. A French visitor from Paris familiar with more opulence described it as a 'homely town of two-storey stone houses, overshadowed by ramparts and battlements of the castle'. The skyline showed the spires of two churches: the Church of Our Lady, which was later renamed the Matthias Church (the original parts of which were still standing in the 2020s), where court officials worshipped, and the Church of St Mary Magdalene, destroyed in the sixteenth century, where the native Hungarian town dwellers went. It was a varied community of mostly Germans, Hungarian artisans, servants and traders, and a small number of Jews.[3]

Charles I was not much liked but he was highly effective, not least in the way he managed by stealth and luck to extend Hungarian territory and influence throughout the courts of Europe. He was married and widowed four times and each new marriage extended his diplomatic reach. His first wife was a Russian princess from Galicia, the second a Luxembourger princess from Bohemia, the third the sister of King John of Bohemia and the fourth, Elisabeth, the daughter of the Polish King Władysław I Łokietek, which ensured his family's claim to the Polish throne, potentially uniting the Kingdoms of Hungary and Poland to form a huge Central European empire from the Baltic to the Adriatic. His alliances gave Hungary influence in most of the major capitals of the continent.

His court was not without one major scandal, though nothing to compare with the excesses committed in the days of the former dynasty. It is a story remembered for one of the great works of Hungarian literature by the poet János Arany, a contemporary of Tennyson and often favourably compared to him. It's a ballad about Klára Zách, a famed beauty and Queen Elisabeth's lady-in-waiting, who was allegedly raped by the queen's brother Casimir, the future King of Poland. In revenge Zách's father, Felicián, one of the most powerful nobles in Hungary, burst into the great hall of the castle when the midday meal was being served to the royal family, drew his sword and hacked off four of the queen's fingers before he was killed by palace guards.[*][4]

His successor Louis (Lajos) I was the only Hungarian monarch known in Hungarian history books as 'the Great'. He spent almost his entire forty-year reign (1342–82) on campaigns of war and he deserved the sobriquet if judged only on territorial expansion. By the end of his reign he managed, temporarily, to gain dominions stretching throughout the whole of Dalmatia – with the coastline from Dubrovnik to Fiume – Wallachia, present-day Romania, Bosnia, Serbia and northern

---

[*] The epic poem has stood the test of time and is a delight, taught to generations of Hungarians in school. A taster here:

> Your fingers are bleeding.
> But not bleeding in vain:
> What is your wish, royal lady,
> What your deserved claim?
> For my index finger
> His beautiful young daughter,
> For my lost thumb his
> Oldest son's slaughter.
> For my other two fingers
> Whose blood ran and ran
> The lives of his whole clan.

Bulgaria. Hungary was master of the Balkans. For a while, following a series of battles on the Adriatic coast, even the Venetians acknowledged Louis I as their suzerain. 'No enemy trod on Hungarian soil,' the king boasted. He brought in large numbers of foreigners to help him protect his expanded empire, who would in future form major communities in the Hungarian lands: the Szeklers, a Turkic group originally from the Balkans, Christianized by the Hungarians, well known as fierce fighters; and Germans, mostly from Saxony, brought to Transylvania in their thousands to build fortresses against invaders from the East.*

In 1360 Louis the Great expelled all the Jews from Hungary, hardly an unusual event in the Christian world during the Middle Ages. King Edward I had thrown out all Jews from England seventy years earlier, when hundreds drowned in shipwrecks as they tried to escape to France. Throughout Central Europe there was a wave of anti-Semitism (or rather, even more violence than usual) in the fourteenth century, when Jews were often blamed for the Black Death. Savage pogroms were common in the few places in Hungary where Jews had been permitted to settle, for example in Óbuda, where a sizeable Jewish community had formed and two synagogues had been built. At first Louis I attempted to convert the Jews to Christianity by offering them protection – full equal rights under the law if they could make a big one-off payment in lieu of exemption from future taxation. But he had few Jewish volunteers and the clergy objected to the deal, so the king issued an edict of expulsion instead. Most found their way to Austria, Bohemia or Poland, where they were persecuted again as the pandemic continued to ravage Central Europe.

Less than a decade later, though, the king's finances and those of other nobles in the court at Buda began to suffer; as elsewhere, Jews proved useful as moneylenders and were necessary as a source of tax revenue. Louis invited all those he had thrown out to return – at least to Óbuda, if nowhere else in Hungary – and most went back. 'Hungary's indigent kings took good care of the geese that lay the golden eggs,' as one historian put it. Louis ceased persecution of the Jews, and attempts at conversion. He instituted the position of 'Jew Judges' who swore oaths

---

* His arrangement of a marriage between his daughter Margaret and a Habsburg would later, with enormous consequences, lead to Hungary becoming part of the Austrian Empire.

of impartiality, though for the first 100 years or so of their existence they were noblemen who adjudicated disputes between Jews and Christians, with royal orders to ensure, or appear to ensure, a modicum of fairness for Jews. In 1371 Louis appointed the first 'Jew Judge' for the whole kingdom with the status and power equivalent to a royal judge.[5]

Yet Hungary faced an existential challenge, not just to its status as a power in Europe. Again it came from the East, this time from the Ottoman Turks, who over the previous four centuries had seized most of central Asia and the Middle East, and much of North Africa, and were threatening the destruction of the Byzantine Empire. Hungary lay in the direct path to the Ottomans' ultimate goal: the takeover of Europe. They had made repeated raids into the Balkans, and launched several attempts to capture Constantinople, the capital of what was left of the Orthodox Christian state. In the summer of 1453, after a long siege, the Turks finally succeeded. The fall of Constantinople provoked a panic in Europe. In Scandinavia, far from the Bosphorus, there was terror. The King of Denmark and Norway, Christian I, declared that 'the grand Turk is the beast rising out of the sea described in the Apocalypse'. The sacking of the city itself was savage, even for a brutal age. Old people were murdered and women were raped in their thousands; the ancient churches were desecrated.

European monarchs felt menaced by the fact that the Sultan Mehmed II, who led the Ottoman army in the siege, adopted the title 'Sultan I Rum' – ruler of Rome, a direct threat to the Holy Roman Empire. He moved his own capital from Adrianople (Edirne) to Constantinople, which the Prophet Muhammad had said was the centre of the world. He retained the name of the city, for all that it meant in European and Imperial mystique. It seemed only a matter of time before the sultan would despatch more armies through the Balkans in pursuit of his claim to the Roman Empire and achieve control of Europe to vindicate his empire's mission to spread Islam throughout the world. The Hungarians, who had themselves been 'bloodthirsty heathen Scythians' and 'wild barbarians', were now rebranded as soldiers of Christ. Two months after Constantinople fell Pope Pius II called Hungary 'the bulwark and shield of Christianity'. Charles VII, King of France, said Hungary was 'the shield, the citadel, the rock'.[6]

Hungary was saved from occupation for seventy years – and the Ottoman advance into Europe halted – largely through the efforts of one enigmatic man, a brilliant military commander. János Hunyadi has hero status in his own country but is little known outside of it. He came from a minor noble family, originally known as Vajk, which moved from Wallachia to Transylvania at the urging of the Hungarian King Sigismund. They adopted a new Magyarized name, taken from the castle the king gave the family as a reward for generations of military service – Vajdahunyad.* The rumour has held that János Hunyadi (born in 1407) was Sigismund's illegitimate son, though that was never proven. It would explain his stratospheric promotions, accompanied by his accumulation of fabulous wealth as Hungary's richest landowner. But so would his undoubted genius as a general, and the hope and optimism he inspired among his troops. Hunyadi had led Hungary's armies in numerous campaigns in Croatia, in the Czech Wars against the Bohemians, in Dalmatia against the Venetians. He made his name in wars against the Ottomans as they began – slowly at first – to advance into Europe.

After Constantinople fell, the Turks poured into the Balkans in massive force and at first overwhelmed all resistance. Again, the Hungarians complained that they were being left, alone, to defeat the invaders from the East. The other Christian monarchs, and the papacy, raised some relatively small sums of money to help the defence of Hungary, but no armies. At speed, Hunyadi recruited and trained a professional army and devised a strategy to roll back the Ottoman advance. In 1456, at the Battle of Belgrade, the Hungarians were heavily outnumbered by the Ottomans – including several regiments of the sultan's crack troops, the Janissaries – yet won a decisive victory that kept the Turks at bay.

There are endless legends and epic poems about Hunyadi in Hungarian folklore; in parts of Romania, Serbia and Croatia songs are still sung about his deeds in the Balkans today. The Greek historian of the Byzantine Empire, Doukas, compared him to Achilles and Hector from classical fable. But Hunyadi was a practical man. He accrued more power,

---

* This was the original of the replica of a fantasy Transylvanian castle built in Budapest for the Millennium Exhibition of 1896.

land and titles after Sigismund's death. In a deed of gift to some estates in 1454 Ladislaus V stated that 'what others accomplish with foreign help and with the legal title of their forebears . . . [Hunyadi] achieves through his own sweat, virtue, talent and labour'. He was given a newly minted title with more powers than any other Hungarian magnate, Governor of Hungary, as well as Captain General of Belgrade, Voivode (Prince) of Transylvania and many more. After each victory he received royal gifts. At the peak of his career he owned more than 2.3 million hectares of land, twenty-eight castles, fifty-seven towns and around 1,000 villages. Then, just months after his great victory in the Battle of Belgrade, at the height of his powers, he died during an outbreak of the plague at his camp. King Ladislaus died almost immediately afterwards and Hungary was again plunged into a series of civil wars.[7]

Throughout most of Hungary and in many courts of Europe, Hunyadi was deeply and genuinely mourned. But a group of aristocratic magnates had always seen him as a 'bastard', an upstart, and resented the power and wealth he had accrued. An anti-Hunyadi party formed in the court, joined by the new, sixteen-year-old king, another Ladislaus, who saw potential rivals in Hunyadi's two surviving sons, László, aged twenty-five when his father died, who had already proved himself as a soldier, and the fifteen-year-old Matthias (Mátyás). The king had both brothers arrested, along with their advisers, and sentenced to death. László Hunyadi was beheaded in the main town square at Buda in March 1457, but Matthias, his uncle, Mihály Szilágyi, and their advisers were kept in jail, first in Vienna and later transferred to Prague.

Just a few weeks later the young king died from the plague and everything changed. There was no male heir to the crown and the two rival factions at court worked out a temporary truce. Matthias and his uncle were released. Szilágyi and Matthias's mother, Elisabeth, schemed, bribed and intimidated a path to the throne, but it was the allure of the Hunyadi name that presented Matthias with the opportunity. He was crowned outside Prague Castle in the autumn of 1458 and Szilágyi was named regent for five years. The young man, rather still a boy, grew up fast. He would prove that he was cast from the same mould as his father. He had been provided with the best education money could buy; he was steeped in history and the classics, spoke six languages fluently and soon displayed obvious gifts of leadership. In quick time he far surpassed the older Hunyadi as a politician, diplomat and statesman. He became a true Renaissance prince who could be merciless and forgiving, vengeful or chivalrous and had the intelligence to surround himself with talented people who knew how to present their master to the outside world as the very model of a philosopher king. 'He was the most cosmopolitan ruler Hungary has ever had,' according to Paul Lendvai, one of the most clear-sighted of modern Hungarian historians.[8]

Within a year the young monarch showed he could also be extremely ruthless. He removed his uncle from the regency, claiming that Szilágyi had treasonously plotted with the opposition faction to replace Matthias as King of Hungary with the Habsburg Holy Roman Emperor Frederick III, which was partially true. From then, still a teenager, Matthias ruled as an absolute monarch. His priority was to reduce the power of the barons and centralize the state under one authority – a similar nation-building process to that which was happening at around the same time in France, England and Spain. In 1463, around his twenty-first birthday, he was crowned again, to reinforce his right to the throne – in the same square in the centre of Buda where his older brother had been beheaded. He named himself Matthias I Corvinus – a spurious, made-up title but a brand that has stuck. His blue-tinted face stares out from Hungary's most commonly used 1,000-forint banknote. In modern Budapest there are streets, boutique shops, apartment blocks and a luxury hotel all named 'Corvinus', after the raven in the Hunyadi crest. Antonio Bonfini, a court historian, invented a bogus pedigree to accompany the name and traced Matthias's ancestry to a Valerius Corvinus, supposedly a Roman knight from the time of the Republic, who is said to have fought a Gallic giant – the descendant of Jupiter – with the help of a raven. It was an attempt, according to a contemporary, to make a parvenu as 'legitimate as a Habsburg or a Jagiełło', and it worked.

Matthias stamped his image on his era, within Hungary and abroad. By the end of his reign he ruled a European superpower – a state large enough, or so it then seemed, to form a mighty dam against the expansionist designs of the Ottomans.

He was a supreme realist, some would say a cynic, and abandoned his family's crusading tradition. Matthias came to the conclusion – to

the distress of several consecutive popes – that there was no alternative to reaching détente with the Turks. The fall of Constantinople
had changed the balance of power permanently. He wanted to contain
the Ottomans in the Balkans – and then negotiate with the Sublime
Porte, the Ottoman court, from a position of strength. He argued that
if the other European powers would not send armies to push back the
Ottomans – and the Pope would not raise the necessary money – there
was no reason the Hungarians should do so on their own. Instead they
would learn to live with the Turks.*

Matthias was a benefactor of Jews, relatively tolerant if in a self-
serving way. He expanded the role of 'Jew Judges' and in 1476 created
the new office of Prefect of Buda Jews, which carried with it considerable prestige: a place at court – unprecedented in Central Europe at the
time – a small militia to enforce his rulings and a private prison where
he could incarcerate the disobedient or malcontents. He appointed
Jakob Mendel to the job, a wealthy trader whom he had known since
childhood. But the post had practical benefits for the king, which for
Matthias was the main attraction. It was the prefect's role to assess the
tax owed to the royal treasury by the town's Jewish community – a sum
that would rise enormously as Matthias's reign went on. Matthias was
friendly with other Jews too, and interested in Hebrew. He invited the
scholar Peter Schwartz, a Dominican friar but renowned as an expert on
the Talmud, to live at the Buda court.

He stamped down hard on anti-Semitic violence, which had been a
common occurrence and would be again after he died when life for the
Jews returned to something like the default position in Hungary. The
year after Mendel's death in 1495 a pogrom erupted in Buda. Mobs
ransacked the Jewish area of the town, smashed windows, burned down
houses and killed innocent men, women and children. Bonfini was there
and, appalled, described the scenes: 'The crowd grew from hour to hour.
They smashed doors and windows, stole their [the Jews'] belongings, all

---

* In an age characterized by religious bigotry he stood out often and publicly for
religious tolerance, another reason the Church was disappointed with him. It was often
claimed that he was in fact an atheist, but this was almost certainly an exaggeration.
His main belief, like many rulers of his time, was in astrology and he employed several
court astrologers. He was deeply cynical about religion: once, he appointed a seven-
year-old as an archbishop, just to show the world that he could.

the gold and silver, dishes and silk dresses. Moreover the servants of the better-off Jews started plundering themselves.'

Matthias's fame among his contemporaries rested on other achievements besides diplomacy and statecraft. In Buda, he presided over an intellectually brilliant court. The arts, science and culture of Renaissance Italy, of Florence in particular, found a more appreciative audience in the Hungarian capital than anywhere else outside Italy. The royal library, perhaps numbering around 2,500 Greek and Latin volumes and about 6,000 works in all, was one of the great libraries of the known world, a testament to his inexhaustible thirst for knowledge – and desire to show off. Probably only the Papal Library in the Vatican was larger. Visitors came from far and wide to see it. He mastered the public-relations skills of his time. He invited well-known European intellectuals to Buda, paid them generous retainers and they united in a chorus of praise, hailing him for his brains and glamour. In 1472 Matthias bankrolled András Hess to set up a printing press in Buda, which produced a history of Hungary in Latin, five years before Caxton published his first book in England.*

Buda was small by comparison with Paris, London or Florence – still there were only 10,000 inhabitants at the most – but in Matthias's day it was as cosmopolitan as any of them. 'Pontiffs of Italian culture live in the neighbourhood of noblemen used to the rough life of soldiers. Swiss ambassadors open their doors to Turkish aristocrats,' wrote Bonfini, who assisted the king as a collector and tracked books for him to acquire for his library throughout Europe.

He was a child of twelve when he was first married, to a Serbian princess of the same age; she died a few months after the wedding, before the marriage was consummated. His second wife, from the Bohemian ruling family, died in childbirth and the child did not survive either. He was married for the third time in 1476 to Beatrice, Princess of Naples,

---

* The library was one of the wonders of the medieval world – and remains the legacy that has kept Matthias's name immortal. After the Turkish occupation the collection was scattered far and wide and over the years some of the books turned up in Constantinople, several in Venice – and then centuries later in the Low Countries, France and England. Huge efforts have been made to bring the volumes back to Hungary, but only a few score have been located and it has proved an impossible task physically. But in the twenty-first century a project has begun to reunite the scattered library digitally.

a cultivated woman of taste and sensibility, who brought with her to Buda a retinue of Italian artists, musicians and architects. Matthias had already spent large sums on an opulent court, but after Beatrice arrived in Buda the spending became, to many, reckless, paid for mostly by taxing the towns and the peasantry. At the wedding feast, twenty-four courses were served from 983 dishes.* 'For pomp . . . the court at Buda was not far behind the luxury of the Romans,' one contemporary Hungarian noble recorded with displeasure. The Renaissance brilliance of Matthias's Buda depended on the presence of many foreigners – native Hungarians became virtual spectators at their own court, and jealous ones at that.

Foreign visitors were impressed, though, which to Matthias was the point. As Bonfini wrote:

After the arrival of Queen Beatrice, the king introduced arts to Hungary that had hitherto been unknown here, and at great cost invited notable artists to his court. He engaged painters, sculptors, engravers, carpenters, goldsmiths, masons and builders from Italy at big salaries. Singers from Germany and France enhanced the services in the royal chapel. He called to his court ornamental gardeners, fruit growers and expert agricultural workers who made cheeses in the Italian, French and Sicilian manner. To these were added jesters and actors, of which the queen was especially fond, as well as players of wind instruments, zither players and other musicians. His court attracted poets, orators and linguists. Matthias loved and supported all these arts with admirable munificence. He strived to make Hungary into a second Italy. The Hungarians, however, condemned his great extravagance and daily accused the sovereign of playing thoughtlessly with money, of squandering on useless things taxes intended for other purposes . . . of neglecting the strict old traditional mores and customs which he replaced with Italian and Spanish pleasures and depraved practices. However, like any patron of the arts and supporter of talent,

---

* When Matthias and Beatrice married they were escorted into Buda by the Jewish prefect Jakob Mendel at the head of twenty-four other Jews on horseback and 100 on foot, all sumptuously attired. The Jewish community presented the couple with gifts – including two huge stags and a bag of ten pounds of silver, suspended from the end of Mendel's sword.

the king tried gradually to introduce culture to the country. He encouraged the higher and lower nobility to live in a cultivated manner, obliging them to build splendidly according to their wealth, to live like burghers, and to behave better towards strangers, whom on the whole they outrageously despised. He spurred everyone on by his own example.[9]

The cultural enthusiasm never extended far beyond the famous bronze doors of the Royal Castle in Buda. Many among the nobility remained strangers not only to the glories of ancient classical writings but to the skill of writing at all. In 1491, a year after the end of Matthias's reign, three Hungarian barons who held important offices of state were unable to sign their own names to an important international agreement, the Treaty of Pressburg, which detailed the line of succession to the Hungarian throne. A great awakening, perhaps, but as an elite undertaking the Hungarian Renaissance had limited appeal.*

To the resentment of many at court, for fifteen years Matthias employed as his master builder the Florentine Chimenti Camicia to create a new palace in the Gothic style. For the south wing he designed a hanging garden modelled on the one at the palace in Urbino. The main courtyard was given a Florentine facelift. He commissioned or bought works of art from the best Italian painters: a Madonna by Leonardo da Vinci, one work by Botticelli, and pieces by Mantegna and Filippo Lippi.

By the time it was completed the palace was a lavish masterpiece. Foreign diplomats waxed lyrical about its grand entrances, audience chambers, bronze statues, marble fountains and extraordinary hanging gardens. The papal legate wrote to Sixtus IV in 1483 about the sheer volume of the 'gold, pearls and precious stones' in Buda. He described 'so many woven tapestries, so many finely wrought gold and silver vessels that I believe fifty men would not be able to carry them away . . .

---

* This prompted Sándor Petőfi to parody a medieval lyric on the early modern Hungarian nobility:

> I don't know how to read
> I don't know how to write.
> I'm a proud Hungarian noble;
> And I am always right.

[there were] more than 590 great bowls, 300 golden tankards and basins without number. It can scarcely be estimated. I have seen . . . so many . . . costly vessels and such brilliant chambers that I do not believe Solomon in his glory can have been greater.'

Bonfini was equally eloquent: 'There were spacious dining rooms, very grand chambers and everywhere diverse gilded ceilings adorned with a great variety of emblems. One treads everywhere on chequered and vermiculated floors and many are tiled; all about are hot and cold bathrooms.' In the courtyard were enormous statues of Matthias, his warrior father and brother. 'Matthias, in a helmet, leaning on his spear and shield, thoughtful, on his right his father, and somewhat sad, on his left László,' he wrote.

Another ambassador described a bronze fountain placed within a marble pool over which a statue of Pallas Athena in helmet and girdle towered. He described the great twin staircases of purple marble that led to an audience chamber, at the foot of which stood two large bronze candlesticks. At the top of the stairs visitors passed through great bronze doors whose panels were decorated with the Labours of Hercules. The rooms of the upper storeys were decorated with fine paintings of the stars. In the principal dining room he stared with wonder at the ceiling: 'one looks up not without astonishment at its decorations with the twelve constellations of the sign-bearing sphere [i.e., the zodiac]'.

Bonfini explained how the magnificent gardens were maintained:

The water for the well of the Royal Castle comes from some seven miles hence; through tarred pipes and leaden taps. Below the castle are pleasant grounds. Here he had a marble villa constructed – on the garden side it has a covered porch. In the garden densely planted trees constitute a maze. Cages contain an assortment of foreign and domestic birds. The garden contains shrubbery groves, arbours and all sorts of trees. There are pillared corridors, halls, lawns, gravel paths and fish ponds. Above the upper storey and the attic rise turrets, one wall of the dining room has mirrors, one cannot imagine anything pleasanter and more beautiful. The roof of the villa is covered with silver plate.

An hour upstream by barge along the Danube, the king's summer palace at Visegrád was equally fabulous. It was in a wonderful position, with views east and west to the bend in the river. It was described by a historian of the time as a luxury and showy complex of some 350 rooms designed around a vast courtyard dotted with fountains and ancient Greek and Roman sculptures. Miklós Oláh, who later became the Archishop of Esztergom and the Prince Primate of Hungary, said the courtyard 'had enough room for four kings and all their retinues . . . like a hanging garden, situated over vaults of extensive and magnificent wine cellars . . . plated with lime trees too that breathe forth a sweet perfume'. The centerpiece of the courtyard was a magnificent red-marble fountain embellished with reliefs of the Muses and topped with a sculpted Cupid, from which wine flowed at times of celebration – the vintage being 'cleverly introduced into pipes at the foot of the hill higher up the estate'.*

Oláh's descriptions of the palace was for a long time written off by historians as 'exile's fantasy' – he fled from the Ottoman armies when they later invaded Hungary. But in the 1940s, when archaeologists began digging at a nearby site, a finding turned up that seemed to suggest he was probably not exaggerating by much. They unearthed broken but recognizable pieces of a magnificent octagonal red-marble fountain, executed in classic *quattrocento* style, possibly by the artist Duknovic. The panels were decorated with the lion of Bohemia, the arms of the town of Beszterce in Transylvania (Matthias's birthplace) and the familiar raven motif. All very lavish – all very Matthias. They also found a headless figure of Hercules, which had crowned the fountain.

For three decades after Matthias died in 1490 there were no changes or improvements in Buda. The fame of Matthias's court kept some humanist scholars and artists going there, but more as tourists than anything else, not to work. 'There was a weary lull' in Buda, according to Oláh.

---

* The Ottomans destroyed the palace when they occupied after 1526. Little was left, but when a fire razed the nearby town 'it returned to nature', as one historian put it. A German traveller at the end of the sixteenth century found 'goats grazing among the walls'. A century and a half later German settlers repopulated Visegrád. They stripped away whatever was left of the palace and used the rubble as stones for their new houses. In the 1890s a block of limestone was found decorated with Matthias's shield and distinctive raven emblem in a nearby church at Kisoroszi.

5

THE EMPIRE STRIKES BACK

Since the campaigns of Matthias, Hungary has seen many victorious battles but not a single victorious war. We have had only losses from the fifteenth century on . . . The successes of various generals were, when all is said and done, victorious battles in the course of a permanent war we lost.

Jenő Szűcs, *The Three Regions of Historical Hungary,* 1978

Matthias left no legal heir when he died in Vienna from eating a bad fig. He had been in agony for six days before his death, though on this occasion it seems there was no foul play involved in the demise of a Hungarian king. Everyone knew that with his long-term mistress, Barbara Edelpők, he had an illegitimate son, János, whom he educated with the best tutors available. To the fury of the queen, the boy was brought for long periods to live at court in Buda. Matthias had showered his son with wealth, lands and titles, and groomed him as heir to a 'Corvinus' dynasty. But in the eyes of the old baronial oligarchs, the Hunyadis were still low-born outsiders. The young János, eighteen when his father died, had few supporters – least of all his stepmother, Beatrice – and the leading faction at court turned to a familiar ruling family. They offered the Hungarian crown to Ladislaus Jagiełło, who had been joint King of Bohemia with Matthias. János Hunyadi was allowed to keep most of his land and given the title King of Bosnia if he agreed to go quietly to the Balkans and renounce any claim to the throne. He accepted the deal.

In the next three decades all the efforts Matthias had made to build centralized authority and a nation state were undone. Hungary retreated back into rule by warlords fighting each other – at a time of increasing threats from the Ottomans, who were rebuilding their forces for a renewed invasion westwards under an ambitious new sultan, Suleiman I.

The Turks were biding their time, waiting for the opportune moment to strike.

This time there was no disciplined and determined warrior like Hunyadi with a strategy to hold back the Turks. In Buda the court seemed determined to ignore the threat. They partied hard, as though there were no tomorrow – which for many there would not be. One foreign ambassador to Buda remarked regularly on the 'bacchanal and boisterous feasting that sometimes got out of control'. And the regular taunting of the Muslims.

In 1501 the envoy from Medina wrote to his prince that

In Buda, at the Corpus Christi procession – which his Majesty at-tended before a huge crowd – I witnessed an interesting spectacle. A prophecy has it that the Muslim creed shall die out if Muhammad's coffin is shattered. Following the prophecy they erected before our house Muhammad's mosque containing a coffin surrounded by dummies of the sultan and many of his pashas. As his Majesty and the procession reached the mosque, they hurled a flare into it and the coffin along with the 'Turks' around it. Anything the fire did not consume, throngs of Hungarians assaulted with sticks and stones, smashing it to pieces, even tearing it up with their bare teeth.[1]

The squabbles between the Hungarian nobility and their inability to reach agreement about tactics to deal with the Ottomans infuriated other monarchs. The ambassador to the Holy Roman Emperor Charles V, the most powerful ruler in Europe at the time, whose territories in-cluded Germany and Austria, Spain, the Netherlands and most of Italy, reported:

If the Hungarians were united, we are told, the richness of their coun-try would enable them to defend it in the face of any enemy. But they are of the worst type in the world. Everyone is seeking his own profit and, if he can, lives on the fat of public property. They have no esteem for other countries . . . Though they feast together as if they are all brothers, surreptitiously they fight each other. There is no case so evil that it should not be won by the bribing of two or three men. They are haughty and proud, unable to command and to obey but unwilling to accept advice. They work little as they spend their time with feasting and intrigues.[2]

Finally, in 1514, after Ottoman troop movements into Serbia, the Pope, Leo X, and Tamás Bakócz, the Archbishop of Esztergom, declared a crusade against the Ottomans and money was raised from most of the European capitals to finance an army to halt the Turks' advance. King Louis II of Hungary raised a force reported to be 40,000-strong, mostly peasants untrained in warfare, under an experienced soldier from the lesser nobility, György Dózsa. He was joined by a number of evangelical priests and friars. Most of the Hungarian barons had no appetite for the campaign, resented the loss of the serfs' labour on their land at harvest time and were deeply suspicious about permitting a peasant army to roam around Hungary. Rightly so as it turned out.

The majority of the peers in the royal council pressed the archbishop and the Vatican to call off the crusade even before it had properly begun. But Dózsa's army refused to disband and the crusade against the infidels turned into the biggest peasants' revolt in Hungarian history.

There had occasionally been eruptions of unrest among peasants, but Hungary's feudalism was among the most entrenched anywhere. In the sixteenth century, when in most of Western Europe serfdom had all but disappeared, it remained strong in Hungary. Dózsa was a skilful soldier and titular leader of the rebellion. But the real inspiration that under Catholic dogma would condemn the rebels' souls to eternal perdition were revolutionary priests, the best known of whom was a fiery preacher, Lőrinc Mészáros. After months of savage fighting, burning and looting on the way, Dózsa's army seized control of the Great Hungarian Plain and a few towns in south-eastern Hungary and in Transylvania. For months they lay siege to Temesvár (present-day Timişoara in Romania), but never managed to capture and hold the town. That was the high point of their success. They were finally beaten in the autumn of 1514 by an army led by János Zápolya, the *voivode* (chieftain) of Transylvania.

The magnates, safely back in untrammelled power, exacted vicious revenge. Dózsa was hauled to Buda in chains, enthroned on a flaming stake and a red-hot crown was placed on his head – as 'King' of the peasants. Several of his leading supporters were forced to eat his roasting flesh before they too were executed, as a warning to any others who might want to 'destroy the natural order', as the Archbishop of Esztergom put it. Several of the priests who took part in the rebellion were hanged, including Mészáros.

The direct consequences of Dózsa's revolt lasted well into the nineteenth century. Extreme measures were taken by the landlords and gentry against the peasantry 'to punish them for their faithlessness'. They were condemned to 'perpetual servitude', banned from any right to migration, any access to legal rights and denied the right to own land. A new tax was imposed of one gold florin, twelve chickens and two geese a year as compensation for the damage the rebellion had caused. Landlords were given the right to claim one day a week's unpaid labour. Serfdom continued in Hungary until 1848.[3]

Suleiman, who would soon be called 'the Magnificent', took years to prepare his full invasion force. Hungary was one stage, though a vitally important one, towards reaching his main goal: to take Vienna, the principal seat of the Habsburgs, whom he regarded as the secular leaders of Christendom. The Hungarians were entirely unequipped to face the Ottoman army on their own, which they would be. No other forces came to support Hungary – even though Louis II's wife Maria, a far more intelligent and strong-willed character than her husband, was the sister of the Holy Roman Emperor, Charles V.*

From 1525 the Turks swept through the Balkans almost unopposed, easily recapturing most of the territory once taken by János Hunyadi in Serbia, Bosnia and northern Bulgaria. Louis II could muster just a paltry army against one of the best military commanders of all time. The Battle of Mohács on 29 August 1526 was a disaster, a catastrophe for Hungary. The Hungarians raised a hastily assembled, amateurishly led force of 25,000 poorly trained troops against a professional force of experienced soldiers four times their number, with far superior armaments and equipment. The Hungarians had almost no artillery; the Ottomans were famed for their guns and skilled gunners. Technically and tactically, the Turks far surpassed the Hungarians. Reinforcements

---

* This was the alliance that finally cemented the Habsburgs' claim to the Hungarian throne.

of around 15,000 more men were due to arrive in a matter of days from one of his nobles, but the king thought the best form of defence was attack. At around 3 p.m. the Hungarians charged the Turkish positions. It was all over in little more than an hour. Hungarian accounts record that most of the best-known knights and dignitaries, seven bishops and 15,000 mainly Polish, Czech and German mercenaries were killed. The king fled the field in full armour but his horse fell in a cloudburst and he drowned in the fast-running Csele River.*

The Ottoman historian Ahmed Kemalpaşazâde, travelling with the Turkish army, wrote: 'The wretched king, having seen the mass of his troops cut into two by a blow of the sword and feeling his position was hopeless, fled from the battlefield . . . deceived of all hope, abandoned by all his men . . . the rebel hurried with his horse and his armour into the river, so adding to the number of those who perished by water or by flame.'[4]

Sultan Suleiman kept a detailed war diary, but his entry after the battle was simple and terse. 'Massacre of two thousand prisoners . . . [after the battle]. Rain fell in torrents,' he wrote on 31 August. His entry for 2 September read: 'Rest at Mohács. Twenty thousand Hungarian infantry and four thousand of their cavalry are buried.' He was exaggerating. If his figures were accurate, the entire Hungarian force would have been wiped out, which did not happen. He stayed on the battlefield for a few days, expecting the arrival of the main Hungarian army – which didn't happen either. He could not believe that 'this once great and rich nation', one of his empire's principal enemies in Europe, which had managed to defeat Turkish forces before, could put such a comparatively small force against him.

Three days later an advanced guard of the Ottoman army, led by the sultan, reached Buda. Queen Maria had packed up and left the moment she heard news of the defeat and, together with the Lord Chief Treasurer and Bishop of Veszprém, the papal legate and the castellan, fled to Pozsony (now Bratislava, the capital of Slovakia). Fear and panic had

---

* Soon after the calamitous battle conspiracy theories mounted and a rumour held that the fleeing monarch was killed by nobles who wanted to offer the throne to his brother-in-law Ferdinand, the Habsburg emperor. This is highly plausible, but has never been proved.

61

spread among the better-off inhabitants of Buda, most of whom had left, or tried to leave. 'There remained in Budun* only the people of low condition who wished to throw themselves at the mercy of the sultan,' wrote Kemalpaşazâde.

When the sultan reached the capital's gates 'the 'pitiful remnant' came out with the keys to the city, hoping to avoid punishment. Suleiman moved into King Matthias's palace – and that was preserved intact, for the time being. But the rest of the city was sacked and pillaged by the sultan's troops. Suleiman tried to halt the savagery of his battle-weary men when they began to burn Buda. Suleiman did not order the assault, as his war diary shows, but he couldn't do much to stop it. 'Fire breaks out in Buda,' he wrote on 14 September, 'in spite of the measures taken by the Sultan. The Grand Vizier hastens to check it; his efforts are useless.'

Suleiman wandered around the palace for the next week, assessing its treasures, admiring the statues and leafing through some of the books in the library. He was an educated man and appreciated them. When he looked in awe at some of the abandoned rooms he told one of his generals: 'Oh if this stood in our Istanbul it should be our seraglio.'[5]

The Ottomans began to depart the city on 21 September. The Janissaries took almost everything they could carry, and the sultan took some of the biggest prizes of all. The Turkish traveller Evliya Çelebi recorded later that 'Suleiman has the treasures of King Louis packed into seven leather chests, and the many military supplies, objects of rare beauty, thrones laid out with precious stones, hundreds of window shutters and doors containing precious stones, bronze and gilded shining angel figures, the statues of old kings, and splendid candlesticks and several similar objects . . . carried away and hauled to Constantinople by ship.'

The palace candelabra went back to decorate the mosque that had once been the Cathedral of Hagia Sophia. Two great cannon which Hunyadi had captured from the Turks at Belgrade in 1456 and kept as trophies went there too. Pashazde wrote that the army stripped the city bare: 'The king's palace, which with all its riches resembled a garden abounding in flowers and fruit, was stripped of all its valuables. Everything down to the last object was taken and loaded on to ships

---

* As Buda was now called.

with greatest care and taken to Belgrade. In front of the palace of the cursed king were two monstrous cannon and three statues of marvellous work . . . [both] taken as glorious trophies and loaded with the other baggage on the boats for transport.'[6]

Statues of Hercules, Apollo and Diana were shipped east along the river; Vizier Ibrahim placed them on pedestals inside the Hippodrome in Constantinople. This shocked many among the faithful. It was heresy in the eyes of traditional Muslims to display figures of pagan gods, and some people vociferously complained about the showiness and the idolatry of it all. But Suleiman sided with his adviser. The well-known poet Sighani wrote some satirical verses objecting; the sultan had him ridden around the city on a donkey and then strangled to death.

The famous Corvinus library was scattered far and wide. Many of the books had been looted soon after Matthias's death; Queen Beatrice took a few. Louis II's Queen Maria left with several more when she fled after the Battle of Mohács. Miklós Oláh believed the Turks took the rest, after tearing off the silver clasps on the bindings. He described the library as he had seen it when he escaped from Buda a few days before Mohács. It had been an awesome spectacle: 'Two vaulted rooms . . . one of them was full of Greek scrolls which King Matthias collected there with much care and exertion . . . while in the other room were codexes in Latin. Each of them was bound in coloured and gold embroidered silk . . . the scrolls were mainly papyri covered in silk with studs of precious stones and clasps of silver gilt.' After Mohács, he lamented, 'they [the Turks] tore up some of the books, while others they scattered . . . after stripping them of their silver and using it for other purposes.'[7]

6

BUDUN – A TURKISH TOWN

Fog before us, fog behind us, and beneath us a sunken country.
                                        Mihály Babits (1883–1941)

Almost every time I visit Budapest, the first place I go is a quiet, out-of-the-way section of old cobbled streets, halfway up Rózsadomb (Rose Hill) on the Buda side of the river. Here is the graceful white mausoleum of Gül Baba, a Dervish Muslim holy man of the sixteenth century, a favourite of Suleiman the Magnificent, who oversaw the Bektashi order of monks entrusted with the spiritual welfare of the Janissaries. Mid-morning there is usually nobody about in the surrounding lanes – Ankara utca, Mecset (mosque) utca, Török (Turk) utca, Gül Baba utca – one of the most expensive residential neighbourhoods in Budapest. In April, after the frosts have melted away, the graceful stone tomb is surrounded by the scent of violets. A month or so later come the roses of Rózsadomb, pink damascenas mainly, said to have been brought to Buda by Gül Baba. Whether that is true or not, the flowers and their scent, along with bath houses, paprika – and of course coffee – are the few remaining physical reminders of the 150-year-long occupation of Buda by the Turks. Not a bad legacy when you consider the ways other imperial masters who conquered Hungary have left their mark on Budapest – Hitler's Nazis, say, or Stalin's commissars. Sitting on a bench at Rózsadomb gazing at the sweep of the Danube is a healthy place for a historian to loaf and think.*

                                        *

---

* Gül Baba died in 1541 and his mausoleum was erected soon afterwards, with money donated by the sultan. The tomb is still impeccably maintained, by grants given to the Hungarians by the Turkish government. It is the northernmost place of pilgrimage for Muslims.

After the storming of Buda and the pillaging of the palace, the Ottomans retreated temporarily and left the town alone. They installed a poodle ruler, János Zápolya, one of Hungary's richest landowners, as a kind of viceroy who was nominally independent but swore fealty to the sultan and promised to cause no trouble. Suleiman returned to Constantinople, the army to Serbia and the area around Belgrade to plan their next step towards reaching the Ottoman goal of conquering Europe: the assault on Vienna. With a force of around 100,000 men and the most up-to-date artillery and equipment they were halted in 1529 after a bitter fifty-day siege.

Western Europe could breathe a sigh of relief. The rest of Hungary, and particularly the town of Buda, could not. In 1540 the Turks arrived back in force, took over Buda without a fight and stayed to build a fortress impenetrable against attack. Buda remained an occupied Ottoman town for a century and a half. When the Janissaries entered the conquered city, as Evliya Çelebi recorded, 'they held victory celebrations lasting seven days and seven nights'. Suleiman himself returned, with Gül Baba close by his side, in September 1541 for a triumphal march into Budun and a thanksgiving ceremony in the Büyük Cami (Great Mosque), which had until recently been the Matthias Church.

Most of the German burghers and Hungarian artisans had fled after the town was sacked fourteen years earlier, taking their belongings with them. The poor stayed behind. Buda was resettled by a few Muslims, Serbs, Greeks and other Orthodox Christians. The Jews had originally left after Mohács but later returned, with some others from Galicia and the nearby Habsburg lands. Little was left from what Matthias had called just a few years earlier his 'invincible triumphs'. His palace was stripped of its books, its ornaments and luxurious fittings. There were bare walls and crumbling plaster and paint. It was no longer a royal court but a barracks. It was called by the Ottomans a castle, deliberately not a palace.[1]

The adventurer Peter Lambeck, originally from Hamburg but a restless traveller throughout Europe, visited Buda for a few weeks early in the seventeenth century and was deeply depressed after he was given a tour of what was left of the palace. He had read earlier accounts of it as one of the wonders of the world, but only a small part of the building reminded him of how it might once have been:

In the Palace at Buda are several courts and in one a fair fountain of marble with a Bason, or huge shell of brass, with the Armes of the kings of Hungary ... On the right are the stairs which have rails and ballestries of porphyry. The Dining Room is prodigiously great and the windows proportionable with jambs of red marble, as the chimney-piece is, which is curiously carved and rich and at the end of said dining room is a noble square chamber.

But the rest of the palace was dismal,

in ruins, and Buda was in so tattered a condition that could Suleiman the Magnificent return from the dead he would change and recant his opinion of thinking it the fairest city in the world. And as for the famous Library ... formerly the glory of the world, for it had a thousand or more volumes of rare and choice books, of excellent authors, how poor a thing it is now and how much disagreeing with the fame and ancient lustre it had, since the few books it hath are of little and no use, being almost consumed by moths, dust and rats.[2]

At first glance a visitor approaching the walls of Buda would be impressed and see the town as a graceful and romantic place, nestling elegantly on the banks of the Danube, with minarets and Byzantine domes. But up close the town was falling apart. The Turks didn't care about the appearance of their Budun – nor did they have money to spend on it. To them the occupied territory of Hungary was barely integrated into the Ottoman empire. For Constantinople, it was simply a field of military occupation, an area of land with some heathen people it could fleece with taxes and tribute in kind. The minarets were hastily built additions to existing churches transformed into mosques and the domes new roofs to bath houses built over existing thermal springs.*

---

* There are warm springs throughout Buda – twelve of them alone beneath Gellért Hill, known in Ottoman times as Gürz Elyas Hill after a Bosnian war hero, killed while he paused to pray during battle. The Turks called the springs *atchik ilidja* 'the bath of the virgins', and built a structure around the source to keep the virgins safe from prying eyes. It was destroyed by bombardment when the Habsburgs captured the town in 1686 but was rebuilt over the centuries and can be seen in the 2020s.

Maintaining the baths was one of the few municipal services the Turks took seriously; they had a religious, aesthetic as well as a hygienic function and have always remained an important part of the town's infrastructure and charm. The Ottomans built fifteen of them, most of which were in constant use ever since the 1540s and five of which were still in operation in the 2000s.*

All the other services ceased to function, even what once had been a relatively efficient system of fire-watching. Fires were common; a huge blaze caused serious damage to large parts of the town in 1578, when the powder house exploded. Buildings were left to decay. Often visitors reported that they had seen bodies left unburied in the streets. Buda was nominally autonomous – up to a point. There was still a town council and a system of municipal government. But they simply administered the Turks' orders. Hans Dernschwam from Saxony wrote in a letter home in the 1580s: 'Houses collapse one after the other. Nothing new is built, except for a few shelters against rain and snow. Larger halls or rooms are subdivided into cells with walls improvised of stone, clay or wood to resemble a stable. They filled up the cellars with rubbish . . . No one is owner and master in his house.'[3]

The Turks had contempt for Christianity and the Christians, but they tolerated them. Protestants and Catholics shared the Church of St Mary Magdalene, though all the statues were removed. The Turks didn't understand the intricacies or care about the split that was violently tearing Christendom apart during this period. The Reformation was a mystery, much as few Westerners in the twenty-first century know or care about the differences between Sunni and Shi'ite Islam. When Lutherans and Catholics disputed in the 1580s about who had a right to use St Mary Magdalene, the ruling pasha – the *begler bey* – gave the right-hand nave to the Catholics and the left to the Protestants.

Christians and Muslims (for much of the time the majority of the Hungarian population left in the town) rubbed along reasonably well. In the market, pork and wine were sold in the Christian-owned stalls,

* The 'Turkish baths' in Buda and elsewhere in Europe are not the same as traditional baths found in Turkey itself, in the Levant or North Africa. The layout is quite different: the central space is not a steam or sweating chamber but a hall of several pools that change in temperature from cold to very hot – the Rudas, the earliest of all the Ottoman bath houses in Budapest, still in regular use, is the best example.

lamb, sherbet and coffee in the Turkish ones. The latter was one of the few things that the 'infidel' non-Muslims took a liking to straight away, though at first it was expensive; this was the birth of the Middle European coffee house that later would become so supremely important in the culture of Budapest.

In general, trade in everything was poor, for demand was so low. Vineyards in the Buda Hills rotted, so locals learned to use varieties of vegetable, for example corn, which flourished from the sixteenth century on. The main problem was that Buda's population fell continuously over the 150 years of Ottoman occupation: the birth rate went down sharply, and over generations families left in order to better themselves, whether to Royal Hungary or to Transylvania. The drop was dramatic immediately after Mohács, and continued. Turkish figures registered a fall in tax-paying households throughout their Hungarian domains from 58,742 in 1577 to only 12,527 in 1663. At one point in the 1620s the German and Magyar population of Budun was not much more than 2,000. The Turkish garrison rose and fell depending on military operations in the Balkans, but the average was around 4,000. There were never more than 1,000 Turkish officials, traders and craftsmen living in the town. Besides the pashas, who were army commanders, magistrates and chief executives rolled into one, the most important Turkish official was the *defter* – the tax collector. As time went on, during the occupation they learned to be flexible. They did not wish to destroy the westernmost and most prosperous colony in Europe, but wanted to profit from it. They had no interest in overturning habits and customs.

One group benefited greatly from Ottoman rule. The Turkish occupation brought benefits for the Jews. Many sought refuge from the neighbouring Habsburg lands, where pogroms were common – or Transylvania, where Calvinism grew strong and the Jews were treated equally badly, if not worse. Many families had come from much further away in the Balkans, which were even poorer. In the 1580s the Jews formed around 20 per cent of Buda's 'Hungarian' population. By the 1680s there were more than 1,000 Jews in Buda. The Turks allowed them freedom to worship – there were three synagogues in Buda by the middle of the seventeenth century – freedom to form communal groups and a measure of legal autonomy. The Ottomans, though, demanded high taxes, even higher than the Christian rulers had imposed. The

Turks used the Jews for commerce; they ran the lucrative trade routes along the Danube eastwards from Buda across Turkish domains. The pashas of Buda often intervened on the side of Jews in cases where they had been wronged by Hungarian Christians. Jews would repay the Turks by aiding their defence of Buda against the Habsburgs in sporadic attempts to retake the town. And when the Austrians eventually succeeded, the Jews would pay a heavy price.[4]

The Ottoman colonial system of governing their domains in Europe (less so in the Middle East) was never to keep their top officials in one place for long. All they were really interested in was suzerainty and collecting tribute in the form of exorbitant taxes. On the whole, the higher the rank of the official, the shorter time he spent in Hungary; the main reason was to prevent the growth of personal relationships between conquerors and the conquered. During the century and a half of occupation there were ninety-nine pashas in the highest positions.

For the first decades of Ottoman rule the pasha lived in a down-at-heel villa in the gardens below the palace. A Bohemian aristocrat on a diplomatic mission to Buda in the 1580s recounted how on Fridays 'the Pasha would conduct processions to the mosque . . . Leading the train were hundreds of Janissaries followed by several hundred *spahis*, or Turkish cavalrymen, and finally the Pasha himself, garbed in splendid gilded attire . . . He remained in the temple for some two hours, when the procession would return in the same order.'

Later, from around 1610, the pashas established their residence, with some luxury, in the former Franciscan monastery of St John in the castle. But apart from a few public buildings such as the Mustapha Jami, a complex of baths, and a madrasa south-west of Castle Hill, built by the eminent architect Mimar Sinan who designed the Great Suleiman Mosque in Istanbul, Buda presented a sorry sight, as described by an emissary of the German emperor in the 1650s:

In Hungary's capital, the royal seat, many houses and mansions stood that are now fallen to ruin, in most places propped up by poles, because the Turks care for nothing, only to have a place for their horses; and aside from that, rain may leak in wherever it will . . . They do not mind that mice, lizards, weasels, snakes, or scorpions install themselves in the houses . . . they use houses only in the way a pilgrim uses shelter, merely to protect themselves from frost, heat, wind and snow. If the emperor so commands they must move on directly. The noble lords surround their houses with fine gardens and in the gardens they have baths . . . otherwise they build nothing at all but allow the houses to fall utterly to decay.[*5]

They did support Buda's upkeep as a fortress, though. Its principal function was to protect the Ottoman Empire's Balkan territories and Buda was ready for battle even in the long periods of peace. As Evliya Çelebi recorded:

Vienna Gate has several iron gates, the spaces between them vaulted and the sky cannot be seen hence. In July they are refreshing places. The gates are fifty paces apart. Here thousands of weapons of all sorts adorn the walls and the soldiers of the castle stand armed and ready at any moment. Over each gate on the vaults are iron grids ingeniously set, with halberds and spears below them, and the iron grids are suspended on chains in such a manner that they may be released over the enemy in time of battle, and spears are capable of piercing several of them and obstructing the entrance.

The fire that damaged so much of Buda in 1578 was caused by an explosion in the once-magnificent Friss building, the heart of the old Royal Castle, dating from King Sigismund's time in the thirteenth century. It had been turned into a massive arsenal and gunpowder warehouse. Lightning struck during a summer storm, causing a huge explosion that threw stones into the air which destroyed the pontoon bridge across the river, most of the docks at the port and much of the castle.

---

* Few of the Buda pashas left any mark. The exception, and the best known, was Sokollu Mustafa, who held the position for an unprecedented dozen years from 1566 to 1578. By all accounts he was a relatively benign governor, fabled for his rotund figure, who built six mosques and a dozen bath houses. The last of them was Abdurrahman, who died defending the town against the Habsburgs. A small memorial plaque to him is still standing, originally put up by an Austrian general to 'a valiant foe. Peace be with him'.

Turkish occupation and (the much shorter) Soviet one-party-state rule are often compared, and in some ways they were similar. But apart from periodic assaults the Ottomans operated a system of relative tolerance and multicultural diversity. The freedoms permitted by the pashas would have been unimaginable for a Party boss under the Communist dictatorship 400 years later.[6]

7

DIVISION OF THE SPOILS

I'm being hunted and chased by those boastful Germans,
I have been near trapped and snared by those pagan Turks.
When, pray, shall fair Buda be once again my dwelling?
I have been so wearied by those Hungarian nobles,
They have rendered our homeland forsaken and godless.
When, pray, shall fair Buda be once again my dwelling?

Péter Bornemisza (1535–84)

After the Battle of Mohács, the old Hungary split into three. The Turks kept direct control of Buda, the other fortress towns downriver along the Danube, and a broad swathe of central and southern Hungary (Transdanubia) that gave them an unimpeded route back through the Balkans to Constantinople. Transylvania – then comprising a vast area much bigger than Hungary now – was semi-independent, but the Ottomans demanded ultimate authority and large amounts of money and goods every year as tribute. If the Ottomans received those, they left the Transylvanians alone to govern themselves. The third part, so-called Royal Hungary, was Habsburg-ruled and comprised most of western Hungary, Slavonia, around two-thirds of Croatia, Slovakia and part of eastern Hungary, including the ancient city of Debrecen – altogether about 1.2 million people.

In the Turkish areas the population declined catastrophically over the century and a half of occupation, devastating the countryside and the peasant way of life. In one area of previously fertile farmland, Somogy County, the 11,200 households in 1571 were reduced to 106 by 1671. Hungary suffered five major epidemics of plague and smallpox during the seventeenth century. The neglect of drainage and flood control on the Danube and the other major river, the Tisza, created vast areas of

marsh and swamp in what had been agricultural land a few decades earlier. Hungary became a breeding ground for disease, including malaria.
The Turks frequently used mass abduction of serfs – to the fury of many
landowners – to use as slaves in other Ottoman lands. In 1596 around
10,000 peasants in Szabolcs County, neighbouring Pest, were rounded
up and taken south into slavery to the Middle East. Ten years later
around the same number were seized around Sopron, 100 kilometres
from Buda. Gradually some of these areas were reoccupied by groups
of Serbs, Greeks and Wallachians from eastern Romania. Almost all the
wealthier aristocrats had left Turkish-occupied Hungary soon after the
defeat at Mohács. But some of the lesser nobles had stayed. 'Would that
the Lord had not let me live . . . [at this time] and I could have departed
this loathsome world long ago,' wrote the Catholic landowner István
Illésházy from his ruined manor house. 'Happy are those who have died
in the Grace of God and have not experienced these horrors.'[1]

Life was no better for most of the people in Royal Hungary. Under both
the rival empires survival was a struggle, as 'Habsburg mercenaries
and their Turkish adversaries marched and counter-marched through
the borderlands, leaving devastation in their wake', as a contemporary
historian recorded. In some ways it was worse in Royal Hungary than
in Buda, where at least the Turks left people to worship as they pleased:
all Christians were infidel, though as 'people of the book' they were
tolerated. But Hungary became one of the chief battlegrounds in the
series of religious wars that split Christian Europe apart during the sixteenth and seventeenth centuries. The Reformation had gained ground
in Hungary with astonishing speed – for obvious spiritual reasons, and
liturgical ones because of the use of the vernacular language in worship
and especially as an expression of resentment against foreign domination, whether Habsburg or Turkish. By 1600 more than three-quarters
of the Hungarian population had embraced one or other of the reformist
Churches – mostly Lutheran in Royal Hungary and in Transylvania a
version of Calvinism, though not quite as rigorous. After Geneva the
Transylvanian town of Kolozsvár (now Cluj in Romania) had the earliest Calvinist university in the world.

The Habsburgs saw themselves, in the words of Emperor Charles V,
as the 'spear point of the faith' and they led the fight for the true Church:

the Counter-Reformation. For the Austrians, the Holy Roman Empire, unity in Christendom under the papacy (and of course the Habsburgs) was more important than crusades against the Ottomans.

The Hungarians were regarded not only as heretics but as rebels against the Empire who needed to be put in their place. The prelate placed in charge of re-Catholicizing the troublemakers, Péter Pázmány, boasted of how he 'would make of the Hungarian first a slave, then a beggar and finally a Roman Catholic'. The soldier put in charge of pacifying them was a famous Italian mercenary and Imperial general, Raimondo Montecuccoli, who loathed the Hungarians: 'It is impossible to keep these ungrateful, unbending and rebellious people within bounds by reasoning with them, nor can they be won over by tolerance or ruled by law. One must fear a nation that knows no fear. That is why its will must be broken with a rod of iron and the people sternly kept in their place ... After all, the ferocity of a restive steed cannot be controlled by a silken thread, but only with an iron snaffle ... these Hungarian rebels, robbers are dastardly.' It was a view shared by the majority of the Austrian Habsburgs and all the members of the Imperial council.[2]

All of the wealthiest Hungarian magnates, who owned most of the land, abandoned Turkish-controlled Hungary and threw in their lot with the Habsburgs. In reward for staying loyal and Catholic they were given more lavish Imperial titles and allowed to keep their feudal prerogatives. The emperor made around sixty of them counts and turned some into super-magnates with the title 'hereditary prince', like the Pálffy, Nádasdy, Esterházy, Wesselényi, Forgách and Csáky families. This new upper class would be in charge in Hungary, apart from a very brief interlude of revolution, into the twentieth century. They paid no taxes, continued to own serfs and some increased their wealth vastly during the division of Hungary. The emperor gave the nobles rights to claim increased labour dues, or *robot*. Back in the time of Matthias this was limited to fifty-two days a year; by 1550 it was two days a week. In 1570 until the end of the Ottoman period it rose in many areas of Royal Hungary to three days a week. The peasantry was impoverished and there were several decades of repeated famines from the 1580s to the 1690s. István Petrőczy, one of the few nobles in Royal Hungary who remained Catholic but hated the Habsburgs, wrote: 'Our eyes are full of tears, when watching the sorrowful nightfall of our decaying dear fatherland and nation, since there has never been on earth another strong enough to have defeated our beloved one . . . Understand, true Hungarians, make yourselves believe that the Germans hate the whole Hungarian nation regardless of religion.'

The showy splendour of the big names of the Hungarian aristocracy shocked some outsiders. A Swedish visitor to the capital of Royal Hungary, Pozsony, was invited to a party given by Count Miklós Esterházy – an ultra-loyalist to the Habsburgs – in the 1650s. He remarked on the irony of the event when he saw the count display a huge silver jug made in Nuremberg by the engraver Tobias Seidler in which members of the Esterházy clan were presented as descendants of Adam with kinship connections to the Magyar tribal chiefs of Örs, Árpád and Hunor: 'Three out of four Hungarians had reached the stage of regarding the Habsburgs and the Austrians as their mortal enemies. This peculiar and eccentric nation harbours an unbelievable hatred of the . . . Germans and wants to elect a king of its own. Hungarians complained that the Emperor's soldiers committed just as many atrocities as the Turks – all the worse in Hungarians' eyes as they call themselves Christians.'[3]

One outstanding figure of the time, famous as a patriot, soldier, statesman, lover, politician – and, most influentially in the long run, a poet – was Miklós Zrínyi (1620–64), Bán (governor) of Croatia and doughty general against the Ottomans. He disliked the Habsburgs and much of his own class – 'We are lazy drunkards who hate each other . . . There is no nation which boasts so much about its titles of nobility as the Hungarians and who, as God is my witness, does so little to preserve and prove his nobility,' he said often. But he loathed the Turks far more and was convinced there was no future for Hungary to restore itself as an independent nation until the Ottoman occupation was ended. Many say that all wars, revolutions and national events in Hungary are inspired by poems, so his wonderfully atmospheric epic work *The Siege of Sziget* – as so often in Hungarian history about a battle heroically lost, this time against Suleiman I's Janissaries in 1566, where Zrínyi's great-grandfather was killed – is emblematic and reveals much of his wit and character:

I, who in times before, with youthful mind
my pleasure the verse of sweet love would find,
and battled with Viola's depriving cruelty
would sing this time a louder, martial poetry.
Of weapons and men, the might of Turks I sing,
Of him who bravely faced the Sultan, expecting
The wrath of arms of the great ruler Suleiman,
Who all over Europe held in terror the hearts of men.

The third part of divided Hungary, Transylvania, was the stronghold of Hungarian sovereignty. A succession of strong rulers remained independent of the Ottomans as long as they caused no trouble to the Sublime Porte and paid the tribute on time. Equally, they stayed separate and different from Royal Hungary, unwilling to unite with it but also happy that, with Buda and the Ottoman army in the way, the Habsburg forces were unable to reach the principality. In any case the Turks insisted the two would never be unified. In the 1570s the sultan's chief viceroy in the Balkans, the Grand Mufti, told the Prince of Transylvania, István Báthory – the biggest landowner in the territory – that 'we shall never allow you to be unified with Hungary. Transylvania is Sultan Suleiman's invention and the property of the Mighty Sultan . . . we do not give to anybody else what belongs to us.'[*][4]

The Transylvanians fiercely protected freedom of worship, unusually tolerant in Europe at the time. Calvinists formed a small majority, but

---

* Báthory may have had other things on his mind too. He became King of Poland and was constantly troubled by family squabbles. The Báthorys were among the best-connected families in Europe at the time, related to innumerable royal clans. But they were scandal-prone. Zsigmond, as was his brother Gábor, was known for wild sexual indiscretions and outbursts of irrational violence. He would be prince and then lose the title five times. One of his trickiest decisions must have been what to do with his cousin, Erzsébet (Elisabeth), who was arguably the most prolific female serial killer in history. She is said over a career spanning thirty years in the mid sixteenth century to have tortured and murdered scores of her servant girls – some accounts put the number at hundreds. This being Transylvania, legend has it that she bathed in the blood of her victims. Accusations against her were made repeatedly, but because she was related to so many of the families in the *Almanach de Gotha* she got away with it until finally she was arrested, tried and convicted. She spent her last days locked in a room at her castle in present-day Slovakia, but then part of Royal Hungary, 75 kilometres from Buda.

there were also many Catholics, a large number of Saxon and Szekler Lutherans, and in the east of Transylvania many Orthodox Christians among the Wallachian Romanians. In 1568 a law was passed in the Diet declaring that 'everyone should keep the faith he wishes . . . a village shall be allowed to keep any preacher whose preaching appeals to it . . . because faith is the gift of God.'

Most of the period from the sixteenth century to the end of the seventeenth century was a time of misery in the Hungarian countryside even for the gentry – especially the Protestant gentry – many of whom were reduced to peasant status. It took more than 100 years to recover. Lady Mary Wortley Montagu, who travelled through Hungary in January 1717 on her way to Constantinople, where her husband was British ambassador to the Ottoman Empire, wrote to her sister during the journey:

We continued two days travelling between . . . [Komárom] and Buda, through the finest plains in the world, as even as if they were pav'd, and extreme fruitful, but for the most part desert and uncultivated, laid waste by the long war between the Turk and the Emperor, and the more cruel civil war occasioned by the barbarous persecution of the Protestant religion . . . Indeed nothing can be more melancholy than travelling through Hungary, reflecting on the formerly flourishing state of that Kingdom and seeing such a noble spot of earth almost uninhabited.[5]

8

BUDA REGAINED

Not even the child in his mother's womb was spared ... All those who were caught had to die. I was utterly stupefied by what happened there, by the fact that humans could be much more cruel to one another than the wild beasts are.

Johann Dietz, surgeon in the Brandenburg army (1665–1738)

The Habsburgs had made several attempts to 'liberate' Buda from the Turks since the 1560s. None were entirely serious – more for show than with any substantial military heft behind them. For a brief period in 1602 the Holy Roman Emperor's army captured Pest, but then it was an almost undefended village, comprising mostly a few wooden buildings, not a heavily fortified stronghold like Buda and its castle. The Austrians were forced back again after a few weeks. Finally in 1683 there was a breakthrough, caused mainly by the hubris of the Ottomans. Suleiman the Magnificent had failed to capture Vienna in 1529. He and his immediate successors pragmatically accepted that the Austrian border with Hungary would most likely be as far west in Europe as their empire would reach. There had been repeated skirmishes between the Ottomans and the Habsburgs since then, but essentially it was a long Cold War which only occasionally, and in a few places, flared hot.

After a century and a half of stalemate, in 1683 Sultan Mehmed IV, 'the Hunter', despatched a huge force of more than 100,000 men, with the most up-to-date siege equipment, in a fresh attempt to capture Vienna. He had visions of equalling and surpassing the feats of his 'Magnificent' forebear. They were repelled by a brilliant defensive campaign led by the Polish King John III Sobieski, and the Turks retreated to their fortified bases in Hungary. This was the end of Ottoman expansion and the start of a long, slow decline. The Holy Roman Emperor,

Leopold I, encouraged by Pope Innocent XI, saw what his military advisers thought was an opportunity to press on their advantage and try to recapture Buda. But the army they raised was nowhere near strong enough and the siege of Buda in 1684 was a lamentable failure that cost at least 6,000 dead and despoiled the neighbouring crops and countryside. The Habsburgs retreated, but immediately started planning for another attempt.

Two years later the emperor and the Vatican put together a 50,000-strong force for a renewed effort under the experienced general Duke Charles of Lorraine, who could claim that he had never lost a battle against the Turks. The Pope declared that this time the crusade would drive the infidel from Christian lands throughout Europe. The army was composed mainly of Imperial troops: there were Austrian, Bavarian, Brandenburger, Saxon and Swabian units, along with volunteers and mercenaries from Italy, Spain, France, Sweden, Scotland and England. The volunteers included aristocrats, professional soldiers and ordinary men who, 'at the bidding of Pope Innocent, or from a thirst for adventure, had come to . . . gain a martial reputation or to acquire the latest skills in the art of war', according to one of the best accounts of the campaign, *A Journal of the Siege of Buda*, by the English privateer Jacob Richards. Among them was a sixteen-year-old illegitimate son of King James II of England, James FitzJames, who at the request of his father left off his studies in Paris in order to take part in the siege.* What was lacking in the campaign to 'free' Hungary were substantial numbers of Hungarians. There were fewer than 8,000 in the Duke of Lorraine's entire army, and many of those were mercenary soldiers or nobles who allied themselves with the Habsburgs. This was not principally a 'Hungarian' liberation army.[1]

Though they were realistic about what they knew of Buda's defences – Sultan Mehmed's Grand Vizier, Abaza Sivayuş, claimed that the castle 'is and will prove to be impregnable' – there was optimism within the army assembled in the spring of 1686 at Párkány, around 70 kilometres north-west of Buda (now Štúrovo in Slovakia). When the huge flotilla of barges set sail slowly along the Danube, and the troops marched along

---

* The young man distinguished himself several times during the siege and in the following year his father created him Duke of Berwick.

both sides of the river, the invasion force was formidably well equipped. Jacob Richards recorded that there were 188 cannon and mortars, the equivalent of 560,000 kilos of gunpowder, 300 kilos of fuse, 25,000 kilos of lead, 112,000 cannon balls, 54,000 grenades, vast stocks of food and medical supplies, and more. A further 15,000 English, French and Spanish mercenaries joined the force before it reached the walls of Buda at the beginning of June and set up their main camp in Pest.[2]

The Turkish defenders amounted to no more than 12,000 (down from around 15,000 the previous year). They were led by the 99th Pasha of Budun, Abdi Abdurrahman, aged sixty-eight, a highly experienced military commander of Albanian descent trusted by the sultan. Though the Turks knew that no relief force would come to their aid any time soon, they had the protection of a highly efficient system of fortifications and were confident they were well enough supplied to withstand a long siege. Between 1,000 and 1,200 residents of Buda were Jews, and they were the most ardent supporters of Ottoman rule. All Jews had been expelled from Vienna in the early 1600s, banned from holding land in most of the Habsburg regions and grown used to pogroms. They knew what to expect if the Austrian Empire regained control of Buda.

The strength of Buda Castle as a fortress 'was due not to the work of men but to its own natural qualities', the Ottoman historian Mustafa Naima wrote in the 1690s soon after the siege. It was built on a plateau rising 45–55 metres out of the surrounding valleys; the eastern and western slopes of the hill were steep and the Danube to the east also provided protection. Those who had besieged the castle in the past, almost without exception, attempted to approach the walls from the north and the south. This is why the Turks fortified the section in the north between the Esztergom Round Tower and the Vienna Gate in an old-fashioned but effective manner. They built three parallel walls with a rampart, which led to a deep ditch 20 metres wide and 11 metres deep. The old royal palace at the southern end of the fortress was protected by a clever layout of buildings and by the large number of separate courtyards and outer walls, which created a sort of labyrinth of structures which could be defended one by one. It was sheer force of numbers that defeated the Turkish defence, especially after a further 12,000 soldiers from Transylvania were finally persuaded to arrive to join the Habsburg forces, just before the final assault on the castle walls began. Those brought the number in the Habsburg army up to around 75,000.[3]

The siege lasted seventy-eight days. For seventy-five of them there was heavy bombardment of the castle and what was left of the palace that Matthias had built, which was being 'destroyed brick by brick', according to a Hungarian survivor of the fighting. On 16 June, Richards recorded, 'the Bavarians played very furiously against the castle . . . and shot in several bombs, which occasion'd a new Conflagration'. On 18 June, 'A great number of bombs were shot into the town, which did great Execution . . . and fire was seen to blaze out in several parts of the city.' On 22 July a mortar fired a bomb, directly hitting one of the town's main arsenals containing thousands of kilos of gunpowder. 'For a full hour the earth around Buda shook.' From the weight falling on the water the Danube rose over its banks, putting the garrison on the shore to flight, 'the surging waves in their pursuit. The air was brimming with large stones and over the opposite shore, too, a hail of rocks scattered.' The enormous detonation blew much of the Danube jetty into the air, along with hundreds of Turkish soldiers. Matthias's former palace had collapsed into pieces of rubble after the bombardment over the summer. Now the rest was consumed by fire.

The next day the Duke of Lorraine sent a message to the pasha, placed on the point of a pike. If they did not surrender the city 'you will all be put to the sword, Man, Woman and Child'. The pasha ignored it and the bombardment continued. A further final ultimatum was sent on 31 July, delivered by the duke's adjutant-general. 'The Turks received him with great ceremony . . . [and] he was presented with rice, a roasted pullet and little pastries with coffee . . . in a wooden lodging decorated with carpets,' one of the duke's aides-de-camp wrote later. 'The governor said he and his garrison would go down with the city if necessary. He would be willing to surrender any town in Hungary to Emperor Leopold, but not Buda. The adjutant-general said he had not come to negotiate peace terms but only to accept a surrender. The Pasha made no other answer but only shrugged his shoulders, remaining mute.' Abdurrahman knew that he still had two untouched powder stores at his disposal.[4]

The siege took a further month and was no walkover. At 3 p.m. on Monday, 2 September the heavy guns ceased fire and six small cannon thundered out the signal for the attack. This would be the final assault on the fortress. 'The walls at the north-west of the castle are breached,' Richards's journal reported. 'The slaughter was very bloody. Our soldiers, having driven the Turks from their defences, entered the city by main force, overrun the streets, put all to the sword that encountered their fury, sparing neither age nor sex, so that there was nothing to be seen but the dead bodies of the slain.'

Another account from a Habsburg commander at the north wall of the castle described the scene:

The attack was extremely fierce and bloody. It is claimed that the Turks were taken unprepared, because the alarm had already been sounded twice the same day with preparations being made to repel an attack which never came. The third time they did not believe the enemy was coming. All the same, the defenders of the second wall had already held their own for nearly an hour, when Colonel Oettingen with the right-flank column managed at last to mount the steep slope, and reach the breach in the . . . wall adjoining the Esztergom Round Tower. Those at the van marching through the barrage of the Janissaries bled to death; those in the second wave launched an attack on the flank of the defenders of the second and third walls. These then gave up their positions and withdraw behind trenches.

A Lieutenant-Colonel Fürstenberg with the Brandenburgers managed to

cross the deep moat running behind the first wall, broke through the defence on the breach between the Esztergom Round Tower and Siavus Pasha's . . . Duke Charles was watching from the Tower; he sent . . . reinforcement groups one after another. The best were dying on the walls: Lieutenant-Colonel Michele d'Asti at the head of the central column received two shots and several spear-wounds, Colonel Fritsch of Brandenburgers was killed . . . the Hungarian Colonel Ferenc Pálffy suffered a severe head injury. On the north wall the outcome of the siege was decided. The Turks fled panic-stricken: many of them rushed to the Danube bank and jumped into the water to seek safety . . . or they leaped from the castle wall.

Abdurrahman and his bodyguard withdrew to the eastern ramparts. 'He put up a stout resistance there,' wrote Richards. 'His courage prompted many fugitives to follow him and this small troop waged an unequal battle with the soldiers of Marshal Eugène de Cröy. Many took to flight and urged the grey-haired Pasha to flee. He would not hear of flight or surrender; giving an immaculate example, he shouts to heaven to entreat Muhammad for assistance. He chose to fall in battle. His body was later covered with a white cape; his sword was still in his hand.'

After Abdurrahman died, Richards recorded that, 'the Turks . . . are unable to further resist the pressure and just as they presage the destruction they become confused and tumble on open ground . . . few escape doom. Armed and unarmed men alike fall as the soldiers give free rein to their furore. The streets are swamped with barbarian blood and the town is tarnished with the slaughter.'[5]

By nightfall the whole civilian town was ablaze. It is unclear whether Buda was set on fire by the desperate Turks or by the Habsburgs. 'The victors went from street to street, from house to house, ransacking everywhere from cellar to attic in search of hiding Turks and of money, treasure and other valuables,' wrote Johann Dietz, a surgeon in the Brandenburg army. 'A great many people had to pay with their lives and possessions or freedom. Not even the child in his mother's womb was spared . . . All those who were caught had to die. I was utterly stupefied by what happened there, by the fact that humans could be much more cruel to one another than the wild beasts are.' Another eyewitness, Paolo Amerighi, a professional soldier from Italy, was 'horrified by what I have seen . . . Those who were unable to curb their anger by looting, mutilated the prisoners, tied them beside fires, cut out their eyes and bowels, and did things which propriety forbids me to talk about.' Hundreds of Turkish prisoners were tortured and killed, their skins flayed to be dried and sold to apothecaries in Germany – the powder produced from them was a sought-after remedy for boils, gout and male impotence.[6]

Jews fared the worst, specifically punished for the support many had given the Turks. The Hungarian Jewish chronicler Izsák Schulhof recorded that Buda's Jews were terrified when the Habsburgs began to attack the city. He and scores of others sought sanctuary in the synagogue:

Everyone was lamenting and weeping in despair, crying out for help, and the weeping rose into the skies . . . Such distress as our souls suffered had not been heard before . . . In my great torment I took my phylactery and prayer book, the Sion Kapuit, and, weeping to my wife and my son Simson, praised be his memory . . . While in the midst of the commotion a great many soldiers burst in, foot soldiers with destructive weapons in their hands, firearms, Hungarian hussars too, with their crooked swords in hand. And in the House of God they brought sacrifice, spilling innocent blood of the sons and daughters of Israel. Killing, pillaging, robbing and slaying . . . all befell us.

Less than half of Buda's Jews were left alive immediately after the siege. They were taken prisoner in chains and treated so appallingly in jail that a few weeks later only 200 or so remained. Eventually they were redeemed with enormous ransom money raised by Jewish congregations throughout Europe and a large sum from Samuel Oppenheimer, a banker whose family had been thrown out of Vienna.*[7]

Charles of Lorraine said later that 4,000 corpses were found below the castle walls after the siege was over and 6,000 people were taken prisoner. The Imperial force lost 500 dead and 400 wounded. Christendom celebrated, but the war was not over. The Habsburg army was heading south, along the Danube, to retake the rest of Hungary. It would be a further two decades before the Ottomans left entirely; each fortress and town had to be recaptured leaving behind a devastated country and a ravaged people. Johann Dietz, still with the Habsburg army, described the area around Buda:

The fields have been laid waste by the Imperial troops and their allies, as well as by the Turks . . . One cannot find any village or town intact for thirty miles around. The settlements have been pillaged, wrecked, devastated, set on fire. The families, chased out of their homes, live in caves or they have joined wandering hordes . . . The fields are no longer cultivated, so that often there is no food available. People are

---

* Sultan Mehmet was also a victim of the Turkish defeat at Buda. Within a few months of the siege he was deposed in a palace coup in Constantinople by his brother, who would become Suleiman II. Mehmet the Hunter was imprisoned in Topkapi Palace and died five years later.

feeding on berries and roots, they cut off and eat the flesh of horses, mules and camels which had been driven to Buda and abandoned on the way. Weary people in rags on the verge of starvation are waiting along the roads for food out of the dead animals in order to stay alive . . . otherwise beautiful Hungary was ravaged, destroyed.

The population of Hungary looked on, frightened. They felt the same about the Turks and the Imperial forces. They could only expect trouble from both.[8]

PART TWO

THE HABSBURGS

9

THE BAROQUE – GLOOM AND GLORY

Once again, the ancient wounds of the Hungarian nation are open. Arise, all of ye, for your country and take up arms for the sake of the widows, the orphans and the helpless poor . . . take up arms against the cruel empire that has besmirched its honour and robbed you of salt and bread.

Prince Ferenc Rákóczi II, *Manifesto to the Hungarian People*,
6 May 1703

Liberation from the Turks in 1683 did not bring independence or freedom for Hungary. Occupation by the Austrian Habsburgs, claimants to the Hungarian throne, was at first no more benign than it had been under the Ottomans – in some respects, in the early years, for many people it was worse. Like most imperialists, the Austrians knew how to divide and rule. Some groups were offered glittering rewards and opportunities as long as they accepted colonial status. Others lost everything under an increasingly absolutist Habsburg Empire, determined to establish their notion of order and to reimpose Catholic orthodoxy. In Hungary, the Counter-Reformation was particularly brutal and continued long after the religious wars of the seventeenth century were over in Western Europe. 'Hungarians found themselves in a position where . . . [their] enemies, who could be stirred up . . . at any time over the centuries, were installed on its territory in a protected and privileged position,' the usually pro-Habsburg historian Gyula Szekfű wrote. 'One cannot imagine a greater debasement of Hungarian independence; none of the . . . [other] people of Western and Central Europe had to suffer anything similar.'

Hungarians had to pay crippling taxes for the so-called 'liberating armies' who fought against the Turks – estimated by the Austrians at around 60 per cent of the total cost, but at more than 75 per cent according to Hungarians at the time. Most of this fell on tradespeople and peasants, as nobles were exempt from any taxes. This was on top of the plunder seized by the notoriously greedy armies. Around 50,000 troops – mostly mercenaries – were billeted in Hungary over the first thirty years of the occupation, more often than not in peasant villages and in the few towns. By the admission of Pál Esterházy, the palatine imposed on the Hungarians – a uniquely Hungarian title meaning a sort of Imperial viceroy with plenipotentiary powers – the price was heavy. 'In 150 years, Hungary had not paid as much to the Turks as it had to pay in the first two years to the Imperial armies,' he told the Emperor Leopold I.[1]

Some of the mercenary generals instituted a reign of terror in Hungary at the same time as the Turks were retreating back to the Balkans, with vicious reprisals against any perceived 'disloyalty' to the new colonial masters. The most notorious was General Antonio Caraffa, from an ancient Neapolitan family whose sons had served the Habsburgs for generations. With the title 'General Commissioner for War' he extorted enormous amounts of money and food from people throughout many towns in eastern and southern Hungary, using elaborate methods of torture to extract information of where valuables may have been hidden – including a portable 'rack' he transported with his troops wherever he went. In the small town of Eperjes, 185 kilometres south of Budapest, he had twenty burghers publicly tortured in the market square until they confessed to stashing away money, executed them by hanging and quartering – and then confiscated all their property.

There was no religious tolerance. Cardinal Leopold Karl von Kollonitsch, the emperor's chief adviser on Hungary, wanted to make Hungary a model province of the Catholic Empire. With the enthusiastic help of General Caraffa he held kangaroo courts which condemned hundreds of Lutheran and Calvinist pastors to long prison terms or death. 'Many "liberated" Hungarians longed for the return of the Turks,' one Protestant priest wrote in the early 1700s.

Kollonitsch was born Hungarian but he served the Habsburg aim of Germanizing the country. He established a commission with the stated purpose of restoring estates to historic owners from pre-Ottoman times. But in reality – as documentary proof of ownership was often missing and the original owners could not pay the exorbitant fees demanded to pursue the legal process – the property was awarded to loyal supporters of the Empire. 'Hungarian blood, which makes people inclined towards unrest . . . should be mixed with German blood so as to assure trust and love towards their natural hereditary King,' Kollonitsch said. Germans were settled on Hungarian estates, which their previous Magyar owners were barred from reclaiming.[2]

Buda, now without a castle, did not regain its previous importance for generations. It remained a sleepy backwater as the Austrians exerted their authority over what was formerly Ottoman Hungary. There would be no Habsburg court there for three-quarters of a century after the Turks left it – and even then, from Vienna's point of view, it would be a minor town with a very limited 'season'. Pozsony, or Pressburg as the Austrians called it, a few hours away from Vienna by carriage or a pleas-ant short sail by barge along the river, became the capital of Hungary 'and the middle Danube was left to decay into a dull provinciality', as Count János Pálffy, one of the most influential of the Hungarian courti-ers in the early days of absolute Habsburg rule, noted drily. Twenty-five years after the Turkish occupation ended the population of Buda was around 12,000 and that of Pest 4,000. The two towns were separated by the wide and ungoverned Danube, connected for just over half the year by a hastily assembled and then disassembled pontoon bridge.[*] 'Five centuries after its medieval origins, Pest was still not much more than a semi-Oriental river village; Buda consisted of clusters of small houses and vineyards,' as the expert on Habsburg Hungary János Lukács ex-plained. Throughout the eighteenth century the majority of the people in both towns was German-speaking, though gradually increasing numbers of people moved to Hungary from other Austrian Crown lands, like Polish Galicia or eastern Bohemia. The revival of a Magyar consciousness grew slowly.[3]

Freed from one occupier, many Hungarians were intent on liberating themselves from another. For a generation after the siege of Buda there were repeated Hungarian rebellions against Habsburg rule, though

---

[*] Half the year because until the mid nineteenth century – and this climate change has not properly been explained by either historians or scientists – the Danube at the area around Budapest reliably froze over entirely for much of the period between December and March, and large ice floes were often seen as early as November and as late as April.

Buda and Pest stayed aloof from the conflicts, avoiding the bloodshed and consequent Austrian reprisals. Leopold I's armies comprised mainly mercenary troops from the Low Countries, Italy and Spain, but that didn't stop most of the Magyars from regarding them as Germans, as nearly all the contemporary histories of the struggle from the Hungarian side show. Every revolt was ruthlessly and easily crushed, except one, the war of independence led by Ferenc Rákóczi II, Prince of Transylvania (1676–1735), a reluctant and unusual rebel whose extraordinary life is a quintessential Hungarian story of heroic defeat. There is a wonderful, vivid portrait of him by Ádám Mányoki in pride of place at the Hungarian National Gallery in Budapest that's reminiscent of Frans Hals's *Laughing Cavalier* at the Wallace Collection in London – with just a hint of a smile below the bewhiskered, handsome mouth: confident, assured, entitled, as if the idea of failure, even on so grand a scale, is impossible to contemplate.

He escaped dramatically from jail, disguised as a prison guard with the help of his beautiful wife Charlotte; he lost and won, and again lost and won vast fortunes at cards; he had a string of love affairs; he ruled a principality with benign tolerance, a Catholic amid a majority of Calvinists, and remained respected by both sides. All this was before his twenties, when he led the revolt of a smallish band of mostly peasant rebels against one of the great European powers.

He had often been asked by Protestant nobles in eastern Hungary and Transylvania to lead previous anti-Habsburg revolts but refused. Then in 1703, aged twenty-seven his patience snapped against the intolerance of Cardinal Kollonitsch and, according to his racy *Confessions of a Sinner*, in protest at the emperor's insistence on replacing the Hungarian nobility's constitutional right to elect their own king with the Habsburgs' insistence on a hereditary monarchy. He wrote that it was God's will that he should lead the struggle, 'because of the desire for freedom in the hearts of Hungary's Youth . . . and to teach the kings of the House of Austria that the Hungarian nation could not be led by servile fear, but would willingly accept the yoke of paternal love'. He thought, naively as it turned out, that if he could get some foreign help and funds from other European powers he had a chance of winning.[4]

He was by all contemporary accounts a spellbinding orator who could extemporize in Hungarian, Latin, Greek, German, French, Italian and

Turkish. 'Once again, the ancient wounds of the Hungarian nation are open,' he wrote in his *Manifesto* of May 1703, urging his supporters to rebel against the Habsburgs. 'Arise, all of ye, for your country and take up arms for the sake of the widows, the orphans and the helpless poor . . . take up arms against the cruel empire that has besmirched its honour and robbed you of salt and bread.' He had the absolute loyalty of his soldiers and the support of his home base in Transylvania. He was a cosmopolitan Hungarian, a frequent visitor to Louis XIV's court at Versailles – the French for a while supported Rákóczi's revolt until it became useful to seek a peaceful settlement with the Austrians, when the Sun King betrayed him. 'The Hungarian Prince Rákóczi is a great personality,' the Duc de Saint-Simon wrote in his memoirs of the French court. 'He is wise, modest, thoughtful . . . not very witty, but he has rare dignity . . . not haughty, principled, loyal and generous.' But one thing became obvious: despite all his other talents, Rákóczi was not a great military leader. He had poor strategic sense and often used his addiction to gambling as a tactic in war. He was no match against experienced professional generals. Yet for eight years he kept a large Habsburg army in check and gained a few scattered victories in battles in eastern and southern Hungary before the greater resources and professionalism of the Habsburg army relentlessly began to crush his forces in the autumn and winter of 1710.

Rákóczi was clear and honest about what went wrong:

The nobles and the great numbers of soldiers' families who had re-mained loyal to us and who voluntarily left the counties occupied by the enemy to follow us made the situation worse for the distressed people. Winter raged and enormous masses of snow covered the ground, so even horsemen could only use the roads. The fleeing masses with their loaded peasant carts wandered from village to village searching partly for sustenance and partly for security in the mountains . . . and the swamps. Soldiers deserted the flag in order to save and feed their families and the sorrowful laments of the people and the refugees constantly sounded in my ears. Forced by the cold, the almost barefoot soldiers abandoned their posts, some took their weapons, others their horses, all took their pay. They made justified complaints to me: they had not given up because of disloyalty or ill will but because the situation had become intolerable. I was worried and saddened by the miserable fate of those who, in the course of my life, have remained true to me.

Rákóczi's lieutenants begged him to give up the fight. Reluctantly he accepted a deal with the Austrians, but he would not sign the Peace of Szatmár that ended the war of independence in April 1711. Around 80,000 men had died in battle over the years and 400,000 civilians had perished from starvation or the plagues during Rákóczi's campaigns. Most of his supporters abided by the terms of the peace and swore allegiance to the new emperor, Charles VI, who had acceded to the throne just two weeks before the treaty was signed. Rákóczi could not stomach signing it. He went into voluntary exile, first to France, where King Louis initially welcomed him but soon cold-shouldered him when France formed a new alliance with the Habsburgs.

Then he accepted refuge from the Sultan of Turkey, Ahmet III. Again, at first he was feted and treated with deference in Constantinople, but after a while his presence in the city became inconvenient. He spent his last fifteen years in desolate exile, lonely 'but true to myself' as he wrote in his memoirs, in the small out-of-the-way Turkish fishing village of Rodostó, on the Asiatic shore of the Sea of Marmora.[*5] A pattern was set throughout the centuries of Habsburg rule: there would be periodic Hungarian revolts, and decades of passive resistance, followed by a reconciliation. Hungary was important to the Austrians; the multi-ethnic Empire was comprised of many kingdoms and provinces scattered throughout Europe, but Hungary was the largest unit and the Viennese court needed Hungary's taxes and soldiers to fight its wars.

*

---

* After Empress Sisi, there are probably more streets named after Rákóczi and statues honouring him than any other figure in Hungarian history. In Budapest, Rákóczi Avenue, one of the longest streets in the city, goes from the centre of town, near the Danube, to the southernmost suburbs, through some of the most impressive parts and, appropriately, some of the most raffish. Rákóczi's weaknesses were on the grand scale, like his personality. He was routinely, pathologically unfaithful to his wife and was with his mistress on the night that his first child was born. Chronically short of funds in his long exile, he commissioned a Parisian friend to open an illegal gambling den at the Hôtel de Transylvanie on the Quai de Malaquais which kept him afloat for many years.

The Habsburgs created a new aristocracy in Hungary, but left an ancient version of feudalism in place and the nobles' privileges intact. This was sound political sense and forged a settlement which helped to build a powerful layer of support for the Empire – an essential part of the 'divide and rule' policy that pacified Hungary. But in the long run it held back the development of the country by many generations. While serfdom had disappeared in Western Europe it continued as the way of life on the land in Hungary until the mid nineteenth century – much as it did in Russia and the eastern Balkans. The Agrarian Revolution passed Hungary by. There was no thriving middle class of merchants or professional people such as those in England, who created first a trading nation and then the 'workshop of the world' – or, in France, where the middle class launched a revolution that changed the dynamics of power.

The Habsburgs essentially appointed a new nobility, for the most part re-converted as Catholic and loyal to the Crown, that would run affairs in Hungary locally and stir no further rebellions. The biggest names of the Hungarian aristocracy, those who would hold all the power and own most of the land from the 1690s to the end of the First World War, were created by the Habsburgs: the Festetics, Andrássys, Odescalchis, Bánffys, Pallavicinis, Batthyánys, Esterházys, Csákys, whose names will recur time and again in the rest of this story. The new nobles retained unlimited power over their serfs and were exempt from any kind of taxation, even tolls on the roads and excise duties. Perhaps most harmful was the ancient system of land tenure under which estates were never owned by an individual lord but were entailed to the family and could only be inherited, not sold. This had a profound effect on the future, as it meant that only a very few of the biggest and richest owners could borrow money on their property, hindering investment needed to modernize farming. Agriculture languished in the Middle Ages.[6]

Few of the major magnates had town houses in Buda throughout most of the eighteenth century, though this began to change from around the 1780s. They lived mostly near the court in Vienna or when the Diet met – then a 'parliament' exclusively made up of nobles – in Pozsony/ Pressburg. They would make brief visits to their estates, scattered across a Hungary which was then three times the size it would be in the twenty-first century. Some possessed fabulous wealth. An English

95

visitor to one of the Esterházy palaces in western Hungary, around 75 kilometres from Buda, was in equal measure amazed and appalled by the luxury:

> Great is the splendour of some of our English peers. I almost fear the suspicion of using a traveller's licence when I tell of Esterházy's magnificence. Within three miles, he has three palaces of equal size . . . England is famous for her noble castles and her rich mansions: yet we can have little idea of such as Esterházy's . . . three hundred and sixty rooms filled with guests, its concerts directed by a Haydn, its opera supplied by Italian artists, its gardens ornamented by a gay throng of visitors; hosts of richly clothed attendants thronging its antechambers, and its gates guarded by the grenadiers of its princely masters. Its magnificence must have exceeded that of half the royal courts of Europe. I know of nothing but Versailles which gives one so high a notion of the costly splendour of a past age.

The Esterházy family did well out of the Habsburgs. They owned around a million acres of land, with more than 100 villages, forty towns and thirty castles/palaces.

The aristocracy was carefully and rigidly classified by the court, in a Baroque style that matched so much of the architecture. There were 108 'High Nobles' – members of the Magnates Table, without whose support no measure could be passed in the Diet: two princes (including an Esterházy), eighty-two counts and twenty-four barons, who between them owned more than half of the country. Most of the grandest families had changed their religion at least twice in the last 120 years and were newly created by a grateful Austrian Empire. But some of the old nobility, who had been Protestant during the Reformation, had kept their land and titles and with the promise of various inducements from the Austrians and the Church had become firmly Catholic once again. Many more were ennobled in the eighteenth century – 160 counts and barons and 249 'foreign' magnates with landholdings in Hungary were accepted into the list as Hungarian nobility, even if they barely visited the country.

Then there were between 25,000 and 30,000 *bene possessionati*, ranging somewhere between magnates and the petty nobility – equivalent to a *de* or a *von* – with landholdings of 1,000 hectares or more. Beneath them were the so-called 'sandalled nobles' (because they couldn't afford proper shoes), a mass of around 375,000 who were literally and figuratively stuck in the mud, most of whom fell on exceedingly hard times as the eighteenth century wore on. They owned tiny pockets of land, or perhaps merely a run-down manor house in the country – but possessed the title and the privileges of nobility. Technically, under the law, all nobles were equal, but some were a lot more equal than others. Many were worse off than the richer peasants who had managed to lease a few fields. Their lives were entirely different from those of the Esterházys and Andrássys, but just as different, too, from those of the peasants or the burghers in the towns. Hungary had the largest 'aristocracy' in Europe which, unlike almost anywhere else, comprised a sizeable chunk of the population.

Numerically, this made a big difference, lasting until the 1930s. In Bohemia around the end of the eighteenth century the ratio of 'commoners' to nobles was 828:1, in Austria 350:1, in Lombardy and the Veneto 300:1, in Poland 190:1; in Hungary it was 16:1 and among the Magyars 8:1.[7]

It was not just a class assumption but in fact the law that only the nobles formed the nation, the *natio Hungarica*. The serfs still had no right to leave the country and most needed permission to leave their villages; even most burghers and tradespeople in Buda or Pest barely had legal rights of property ownership. Only the nobles had the right of *habeas corpus* – subject to nobody but the legal monarch. Commoners could be arrested and jailed for long terms at will – and often were. 'It was the nobles who were permitted to wear swords, sit in the front pews at church and race their horses through the streets of Pest,' a shocked Scottish visitor passing through the town wrote back home. 'Only they have any political privileges. But what is the nation? Who constitutes the people? To whom do these rights belong? In this country, as in others where society is in its childhood, the nation – alas – is only the great aristocratic body of nobles and clergy . . . the productive part of the community, the citizens and peasants, have few or no rights . . . and no interference in public affairs, yet must submissively bear all of the burdens of the state.'

For the majority of Hungarians, 'commoners', the principal resentment was the exemption from tax of all the nobles. One of the early
economic reformers around the turn of the eighteenth century, Gergely
Berzeviczy, put it in simple terms: 'The nobility owns four-fifths of the
land for which it does not pay any taxes, the rest of the . . . [6.25 mil-
lion] inhabitants have no political rights and have to bear all the public
burden.' This was a reasonable observation, hardly the height of radicalism, but he was accused of treason for his criticism of serfdom and
threatened with arrest for sedition and jail.

Another critic of the Habsburgs, the writer Jenő Szűcs, pointed out
the hypocrisy of both the Austrian court and the Hungarian nobility:
'The dynasty avowed that it wanted to do the best by the Hungarian
"people", and only the rebellions had prevented them from doing this.
That was a lie. The nobility spoke of the incessant suffering of the
"Hungarian nation", which in time turned into a double lie because the
nobility, when speaking of the nation, meant exclusively themselves . . .
and they suffered little.'[8]

Visitors were often charmed by the hospitality and manners of the
aristocratic and gentry Hungarian families, but clearly saw the problems
in the country that would soon turn angry, violent and revolutionary.
'The besetting sin of the Magyar is vanity,' the doughty adventurer and
incessantly gossipy writer Julia Pardoe wrote in one of her popular travel
books:

He is proud of his nation, of his liberty, of his antiquity and above
all of his privileges. In short, he admits no superior, and scarcely an
equal, when he has high blood, a long pedigree and an apparent rent-
roll. I say apparent, for perhaps Europe cannot present collectively,
so pauperized a nobility as that of Hungary . . . There are not twenty
nobles in the country who are not de facto bankrupt . . . The Hungarian noble sacrifices everything to show, luxury and ostentation; and
thus his necessities ever outrun his income. 'The idea of a commercial
treaty with England is at best a bubble for the present,' said one of the
most intelligent of the magnates to me . . . 'We still have much to do
'ere it can be brought to bear.' The Magyars have not yet learned to be
traders; and as to the nobles – we one and all prefer sitting quietly on
our sofas, and disposing of our produce for a given number of years to

an accommodating individual who will pay down the price in *argent comptant*, even if it is at a loss of fifty per cent, to having the trouble of speculating, calculating and waiting.

An English traveller who fell in love with a Hungarian woman, married her, settled in Pest and became a Hungarian citizen was equally scathing:

No radical in England grumbles more about taxation than the Liberals in Hungary; but they mix the privileges of the nobility so peculiarly into their vituperations that it would be difficult to discover something of the principle in their opposition. In fact they do not clearly differentiate between right and prerogative. Some Hungarians speak with silly vanity of their *subjects* and their *souls*, forgetting that, instead of impressing a foreigner with an admiration for their greatness, such remarks fill him only with disgust at their injustice. What renders it still worse is that this language is sometimes used by men who talk loudly of the oppressions they suffer from Austria – of attacks against their rights and privileges. They may talk long enough before they excite the sympathy of an Englishman, when they utter in the same breath complaints of the disobedience and insubordination of their *vassals*. The nobility's exemption from taxes ... has serious consequences, as all public expenses were carried by serfs, subject to statute-labour. The lesser nobility preferred until recently to live in relative poverty rather than, like the burghers, to be subject to taxes, tolls and duties ... they interpreted their liberty as their privileges.[9]

The one Habsburg monarch for whom Hungarians of all classes seemed to hold a grudging respect was the Empress Maria Theresa, who reigned from 1740 to 1780. At the start of her reign, she owed her crown to the loyal support of the Hungarian nobles, who had benefited so much from her family's largesse. They repaid her – and she never forgot it. If the Hungarian magnates had not confirmed her as heir to her father Charles VI – a decision which for a while was touch and go – she might never have succeeded to the throne. They accepted the so-called Pragmatic Sanction, which changed Habsburg custom law to allow a woman to

99

be crowned – though, bizarrely, she retained the official title Apostolic King of Hungary.

Barely nine months later, at the start of the dispute that became the War of the Austrian Succession, she needed more men, arms and money to continue a battle with the Prussians that looked like it was ending in ignominious defeat for the Austrians. In a dramatic appearance at the Diet in Pozsony/Pressburg on 11 September 1741, the young monarch begged the Hungarians for help.* Her advisers warned her against going, fearful that if a Hungarian army was raised there was no telling what it might do or whom it might decide to fight – 'Your Majesty would do better to rely on the devil,' one of them told her. But, as so often in her reign, her sense of timing and of theatre were impeccable. In perfect Latin (only Latin was allowed to be spoken at the Hungarian Diet until almost a century later), she declared: 'I appeal to Hungarian courage and loyalty . . . I am a poor woman, a queen abandoned by all the world. The very existence of the Kingdom of Hungary, of our own person, of our children and of our crown is now at stake. Now that we are forsaken by all, our only hope is in the fidelity, arms and long-tried valour of the Hungarians.' The magnates thundered their applause with swords drawn – and voted through whatever funds, arms and troop levy she wanted.

Within Hungary there was peace and stability in her reign – an acceptance, for the time being, of Habsburg absolutism – and rising prosperity. The empress continued the Habsburg policy of rewarding the magnates with titles and binding them to the Vienna court; 'baubles, debauch and debt, along with cowardice, kept them from rebelling', as one of the eighteenth-century Pálffys noted. She travelled to Buda and Pest rarely – just four times in her forty years on the throne – though she liked to say, 'I am a good Hungarian.' Towards the end of her reign she wrote: 'Hungary is the nation to which I am beholden for preserving our throne . . . my heart is full of gratitude towards the people there.' On the other hand, she was often exasperated by the Hungarian gentry,

---

* The scene is remembered in several High Baroque paintings – the one in the Picture Gallery at the Royal Castle in Budapest is striking, if historically inaccurate. The empress is pictured as a great beauty and, as in many other images depicting the event, is shown clutching her baby son, the future Emperor Joseph II, to her breast as she spoke (which she wasn't: the infant boy was safely in his nursery in Vienna at the time).

particularly their attachment to the most ancient notions of feudalism. In 1764 she tried to persuade the magnates to end serfdom; hardly a single member of the Hungarian Diet supported her. She wrote in her diary that 'I do not want to be damned by God for the sake of a few noblemen', but made no efforts to do so in her remaining fourteen years on the throne.[10]

Maria Theresa was by any standards a remarkable ruler, politically astute, and a gifted picker of able advisers. But she was a mass of contradictions. She was deeply religious, 'an incorrigibly bigoted Catholic', yet for her time and place she was pragmatic. Occasional bouts of persecution aside, on the whole she tolerated Protestants – and she treated Jews more leniently than she did Lutherans and Calvinists. She started to relax laws against Jews, though she introduced a 'toleration tax': they could worship if they paid two florins a year per head, a hefty sum roughly worth £1,100 sterling in 2022. The tax did not prevent many Jews moving from further east where pogroms were routine – Poland and the Baltic States, for example – to Hungary. By the end of Maria Theresa's reign there were probably around 15,000 Jews in the two towns of Buda and Pest.*

She was highly intelligent, but culturally limited. She had no interest in science, literature or art but was well read in history. There were some inexplicable gaps in her education. She spoke German with a pronounced Viennese dialect; her French was mediocre, which was odd as it was the language of the Austrian court. She was a modernizer, but deeply attached to some profoundly conservative values. As Voltaire described her she was devout, maternal and marked by the contrasting traits of the Baroque, 'the spirit of the age . . . a mixture of mysticism, pathos and glitter'.[11]

Buda was still a sleepy small town by the end of Maria Theresa's reign and its population was static. Pest was beginning to grow, but still on the periphery of the Austrian Empire. They were decidedly two towns, now with a combined population in the region of 65,000, but with separate characters; the vast majority of people never went to the other side, which in any case could be a tricky business. The Danube was just over

---

* In 1783, three years after her death, the first kosher restaurant opened in Buda.

a kilometre wide between the two towns and flowed much faster then than in the early twenty-first century. After the Ottomans were expelled there was a 'flying bridge', a ferry that swung back and forth by a stout cable fixed to both banks. But this operated for less than half the year, from the beginning of May to mid October. In 1767 the empress, drawing on the royal treasury, paid for a pontoon bridge to be built by laying long planks over forty boats anchored on each side of the Danube.

Over the years the pontoon became a landmark of the twin towns; at one end, on the Pest side, there was a carved image in stone of St John Nepomuk, a fourteenth-century Bohemian saint martyred when he was thrown off a Prague bridge into the Vltava. Foreign visitors often wrote admiringly of the Buda to Pest pontoon – and of their fear of crossing it because often the planks sagged; there were several cases every year when they snapped and people fell into the river. That too was disassembled for most of the winter. When the Danube froze solid – most years until the 1830s – carriages and wagons could cross and watchmen were paid to keep an eye on the state of the ice. But that was safe for less than two months of the year.

The relative peace and stability of Maria Theresa's reign brought growing prosperity, and living conditions in the twin towns improved, though slowly. Some municipal services began running fairly well. From the 1770s the water supply in large parts of both Buda and Pest were built – first with wooden and then lead pipes. The first postmark in Buda dates from 1752 and the first post office opened in 1762, opposite the Matthias Church in Buda. A music conservatory, a veterinary school and a botanical gardens opened in Buda in the 1780s. In the 1730s in Pest there were very few stone buildings; most were made of puddled clay with thatched roofs. By 1765 453 of the 1,146 known buildings on the Pest side of the river were made of stone, and by 1790 around three-quarters of the 2,250 buildings were.

But there was no boom for business, and no lines of credit available to start one. The Hungarian nobles – the lesser and higher – had a disdain for commerce and trade that the British gentry had lost sometime in the seventeenth century. The few financiers, manufacturers, large-scale traders and better-off artisans of both Buda and Pest invariably came from non-Magyar families, which in any case formed the majority of the twin towns' population. The earliest, almost immediately after the siege of Buda ended, were a number of Greek families who saw an opportunity – as well as escape from Turkish rule – and established businesses in Pest. Their names, Magyarized from around the 1730s onwards, became well known: Haris, Sina and Nákó for milling and foodstuffs, Sacelláry, Lyca and Mannó for textiles, leather and timber, Agorasztó and Muráthy for the wine trade. Then more came from further afield: Gregerson (Norwegian) and Ganz (Swiss) for clothes; the Swiss traders Aebly, Haggenmacher and several Serbs – Petrovics, Vrányi, Grabowski, Bogosich, Mosconyi – for assorted trades from metalwork to carpentry. Few Magyars were setting up businesses. The real problem, in Buda especially, was that comparatively few people engaged in any kind of trade or industry – according to contemporary economists who studied census figures, just one in eighty-nine people in Hungary at the end of the eighteenth century, compared to one in fourteen in Austria and one in nine in the Lombardy region.

The British naturalist Robert Townson visited Budapest in 1790, as few of his compatriots did then. Pest and Buda were definitely not on the Grand Tour at that time. The Turkish baths of Buda fascinated him; they were not strictly segregated as they would be from the middle of the nineteenth to the twenty-first century, but were more gender-neutral. 'The greatest baths are Turkish remains,' he wrote:

There are large common baths for the lower order of the people and commodious private baths for those who can afford to pay for them. In a common bath I saw young men and maidens, old men and children, some in a state of nature, others with a fig leaf covering, flouncing about like fish in spawning time. But the observer must be just. I saw none of the ladies without a petticoat, though most were without their shifts. Some of the gentlemen were with drawers, some without; according, no doubt, to the degree of their delicacy, and as they thought themselves favoured by nature or not. But no very voluptuous ideas arise in these suffocating humid steams; and as a further sedative, the surgeon is seen hard at work cupping and scarifying.

The animal fights in Pest, involving bears, cocks and dogs, horrified him. His journal mentions many times how diverse the towns were, with Greek, Balkan and Jewish traders crowding the marketplace. He mentioned one type of business that as much as any other was the defining feature of the Habsburg lands, and crucial to the culture of the city that would become Budapest. Kemnitzer's was the progenitor of all the coffee houses in the golden age of Budapest and it became an instant success. It was the creation of Johann Kemnitzer, a master tanner, who had done well in his trade and built a large, three-storey house at the Pest side of the pontoon bridge, where Vigadó Square meets Deák Street today. In 1789 he opened the ground floor as a café and within a few months it was the most famous coffee house east of Vienna, with spacious rooms, marble columns, stucco on the arched ceilings, four crystal chandeliers, ornately gilded fireplaces and a fine kitchen.

Townson went there every day during his stay to listen and watch, surprised at the varied clientele who frequented the place: 'All ranks and both sexes may come; hairdressers in their powdered coats, and old market-women come here and take their coffee or drink their rosolio as well as Counts and Barons . . . it is an elegant house and very comfortable dinners may be had.'

Another thing that surprised him was that the main language he heard on both sides of the river was German, spoken by Hungarians, Germans, Slavs and Jews on the streets. He almost never heard the sound of Magyar.[*12]

* Buda was then generally called, among most people, by its German name, Ofen.

LANGUAGE, TRUTH AND LOGIC

It fell to the man of letters, and particularly to the poet, to say what the man of action was unable or reluctant to express. All that is articulate in Hungarian tends to be poetic.

Pál Ignotus (1901–78)

Without our language, our homeland will always be foreign, not a separate nation but a colony.

Ferenc Kazinczy (1759–1831)

It was barely dawn on Wednesday, 20 May 1795, but already hundreds of people – later some accounts exaggerated the figure to thousands – had gathered at the General Meadow, a grassy knoll a few hundred metres below Buda Castle. At 6 a.m. five wooden carts, each drawn by four horses and carrying a blindfolded man in chains and manacles, drew to a halt near the middle of the field. Public beheadings were rare in Buda, reserved only for the most serious criminals of the noble class – and this morning there would be five of them. The crowd grew excited.

The first of the condemned to be dragged to the block, on the dot of 6.30 a.m., was Count Jakab Sigray, a handsome twenty-four-year-old who, once he had collected himself, faced his fate calmly. But the executioner was drunk and botched the job. It took three strikes for the count's head to be separated from his body. Many in the crowd were horrified by the gruesome sight, turned and walked away. Ferenc Szentmarjay, another young aristocrat barely in his twenties, was next, followed by János Laczkovics, a former captain in the hussars who had won several medals as a brave and intelligent cavalry officer. The fourth was a lawyer and a senior local government official, József Hajnóczy, who had written a powerful pamphlet against serfdom. Last to face his death was Ignác Martinovics, the thirty-nine-year-old leader of the group, a Franciscan monk. His blindfold had been removed and he was forced to witness the incompetent executioner perform his handiwork. As guards tried to carry him to the block he suffered an epileptic fit and a physician had to be called to ensure he was well enough to be executed. By the end of proceedings, hardly anyone was there to watch; the crowd was disgusted and left. All the bodies were buried immediately afterwards in unmarked graves and ever since the meadow has been called the Field of Blood, the Vérmező.

After a five-month-long show trial designed as a warning against subversion, followed by the public executions, this was the bloody end of Hungary's home-grown Jacobin movement. The Austrians could complacently imagine that they had nipped a dangerous group of radicals in the bud; under a series of officials in Vienna and Buda, chiefly but not solely Klemens von Metternich, they would for the following four decades resort to increasingly reactionary measures of repression. But subversion would morph into different forms.[*1]

The Austrians were particularly nervous about the spread of revolutionary ideas. Marie Antoinette was a Habsburg, the youngest daughter of Maria Theresa, and two of her brothers would become Habsburg emperors. Austria went to war with revolutionary France even before the French king and queen were beheaded in 1793. Newspaper censors had banned any news from France after the first year of the Revolution in Paris. 'Hungary is overrun by spies, they are everywhere,' the poet János Batsányi wrote in a private letter to a friend in Buda that never reached its destination – we know because a copy was found some years later in a state archive in Vienna full of secret police files. 'It is easy to be labelled a Jacobin even when you are not one at all.' He was right there, too. The authorities watched closely for subversive activity. There was

* The following week two more Jacobins were executed for 'treason' at the same place; this time, though the event was public, almost nobody turned up to watch. More than a century and a half later the remains of all the dead Jacobins were exhumed by the Communist government in Hungary, reburied at Kerepesi Cemetery in Budapest, the most famous graveyard in the country, and a commemorative stone was laid for Martinovics near the Field of Blood. The short-lived Soviet Commune in 1919 issued a stamp bearing his features – valuable to collectors. The best memorial, though, to an intriguing chapter in Budapest's history, as so often in Hungary, is a rousing but sensitive poem by the twentieth-century poet Endre Ady titled 'A Hungarian Jacobin's Song'.

hardly any in Vienna, but in Pest Austrian secret police had identified a few signs of dissent and the existence of small groups reading the banned works of Voltaire and Rousseau (in Latin or German translations). The palatine in Buda, Archduke Alexander Leopold – effectively the viceroy – wrote to his brother, Emperor Leopold II, in the summer of 1792: 'I learned . . . that Pest maintains a club whose aim is supposedly an uprising of the burghers and villagers . . . [and] there are complaints that the French events are spoken about in the coffee houses and what is more, that in one of them they toast the French.'

Vienna launched a crackdown after it uncovered the Jacobin movement led by Martinovics, a curious and unlikely revolutionary – seriously intelligent and idealistic in some ways, a cynical conman in others. 'From the beginning to end, the . . . diabolical and brilliant Martinovics stood at the centre of the movement. His turbulent life seems like a mixture between a psychiatric case study, a detective story and a stirring tale of the French Revolution,' as one of his biographers put it. He knew better than anybody about the number of Austrian spooks spying on subversives in the Habsburg lands. He had been one of them himself for several years.

Originally from Croatia, a part of Hungary for centuries, Martinovics had trained for the priesthood, became a devout monk, but grew increasingly fascinated by the sciences. Frustrated by the life of his order, he asked to be released from the monastery. The abbot asked him to stay – he never renounced his vows – but let him leave the cloisters and study physics and chemistry. He travelled widely in France, England and Switzerland, gained a European-wide reputation as a scientist and teacher and was given a prestigious post: Professor of Natural Science at Lvov (then Lemberg) University, a Crown appointment made by Leopold II.

Somehow or other – the details are so contradictory they have never become clear – he made the acquaintance of Ferenc Gotthardi, the emperor's chief spymaster, who in the spring of 1790, just months after the French Revolution began, brought Martinovics to Vienna. Under the cover of his post as court chemist he worked as an intelligence agent, running a ring of informers encompassing the whole of the Empire, but with particular responsibility for Hungary. Martinovics produced dossiers full of dramatic reports – preserved in the royal archives in

Vienna – detailing a wide range of anti-Habsburg plots by Jesuits, Freemasons and Jacobins, each more vivid and disturbing than the last – until the new emperor who had succeeded Leopold, his young son Francis I, grew suspicious. He discovered that Martinovics had invented them all from a vivid imagination. The monk was fired.[*2]

He returned to Buda and transferred his loyalties almost overnight to radical causes. He translated Rousseau's *Social Contract* into Latin and passed it to groups of mainly young intellectuals, in a late-eighteenth-century version of Soviet-era samizdat, underground literature. He declared himself to be an atheist and the Catholic Church one of history's great evils. In early 1794 he published the first of his so-called *Catechisms on Social Reform*, similar to some of the early Jacobin pamphlets, calling for Austria and Hungary to become separate but federated republics. The second, a few weeks later, was considered yet more outrageous and revolutionary and called for 'a holy insurrection against the kings, nobles and priests'. He launched two societies, modelled on the original Jacobin 'clubs': the Society of Reformers, designed to attract young nobles who were interested in moderate change, which met in Buda, and the slightly more radical Society of Equality and Liberty in Pest, for the bourgeois intelligentsia: young lawyers, doctors, students and writers. Both, on Martinovics's orders, adopted the elaborate conspiratorial trappings of a secret society, separated into small groups who knew only the names of the members of their same 'cell' and the next person up the chain of command in their hierarchy. They read and wrote radical material aimed at each other, but they never took any real subversive action. At most there were never more than 300 members in the whole of the Habsburg Empire – far fewer in Buda and Pest. There was never a 'Martinovics plot' as the Austrian authorities claimed.

In July 1794 fifty-three people were arrested and imprisoned in the Franciscan monastery in Buda, charged with subversion. Even under torture some of the ardent young radicals refused to implicate their comrades. Unsurprisingly, without suffering any torture, Martinovics gave the authorities lists of names, including some entirely innocent ones. At the trial, the case for the defence was barely permitted a hearing.

---

* As Holy Roman Emperor he was Francis II, last in a line that spanned 1,200 years before Napoleon.

Eighteen death sentences were recorded, but only the seven at the Field of Blood were carried out. All the others were jailed for terms ranging from eleven months to nine years. The impact of the crackdown spread far wider than the meagre ranks of the Hungarian Jacobins. In Pest, ten professors were removed from their posts at the university. Even stricter new censorship was introduced against the press and a longer list of books were banned, including some ancient Greek texts in favour of democracy. The moderate reformers were effectively silenced on any political action for a generation.[3]

In 1801, after serving 2,387 days in jail for a minor walk-on part in the Jacobin movement, Ferenc Kazinczy was released from prison. He felt no bitterness. 'Examples had to be made to frighten the people,' he wrote to a friend shortly before he was freed. He was forty-one, an erudite polyglot – translator of, among others, Shakespeare, Goethe, Molière and Schiller – and proprietor of a modest estate close to Buda. He still burned with a zeal for radical change in Hungary, but during his years of incarceration he abandoned an overtly political programme and any ideas of rebellion against the Habsburgs as impractical gestures that were bound to fail. From prison he had been corresponding with a group of like-minded Enlightenment figures, who came to the conclusion that the way to modernize Hungary, to create a new nation, was through its language and culture. Out of prison, he withdrew to his estate, Széphalom, and for the thirty years up to his death he devoted himself to a single passion: the renewal of the Hungarian language and literature. There were many others involved in what amounted to a cultural revolution, but Kazinczy was the practical genius and chief organizer of the so-called 'Revival Movement'. Antal Szerb in his magnificent *History of Hungarian Literature* described him as 'a dictator of literary life' – though another twentieth-century admirer, the writer László Németh, called Kazinczy 'the telephone switchboard'.

The revival of the language was the focus of his life. Kazinczy was the leader of the 'neologists' who invented modern Hungarian. They transformed the grammar, standardized the syntax, enriched the vocabulary, produced dictionaries and lexicons, and gave new life to a moribund tongue. A twenty-first-century Hungarian would be hard-pressed to understand the archaic, formal and inflexible Magyar used in the eighteenth century – they would feel it was almost entirely foreign, rather as though Chaucer's English were still being used today. 'Magyar is half dead, atrophied . . . worn out. It has lost all vigour and freshness of the centuries long gone,' he said when he embarked on his undertaking.

There had been a few brilliant exceptions from the Early Middle Ages onwards, but Kazinczy and his collaborators knew that in reality, at this point, there was very little literature in Hungarian. The literary language was German. Few in the poorer classes were literate. Most of the nobles and the tiny middle class, those who *were* literate, read in German and spoke in German within their family or social circle – and governed in Latin. Alone in Europe, Latin was the official language in Hungary, used in the courts and the bureaucracy. In the rest of the Habsburg Empire, from the Baltic to the Adriatic, the official language was German – 'We don't *govern* the Empire, we administer it, and we do so in German,' said Metternich. In Buda and Pest, Hungarian was the language of the poor and of some townsfolk – which gave them access, if they could read at all, only to a limited and largely folkloric literature.* Hungarian was also the language of the minority of the 8.5 million people living in Hungary; only about 37 per cent of the population, according to the first census conducted in Hungary in 1787, were ethnic Magyars.[4]

Kazinczy and his collaborators created new words based on Hungarian roots, borrowed foreign words and 'Magyarized' them, or used image association. For example, the word secretary (*tiktár* or *titoknok*) was derived from an existing word for secret: *titok*. The Hungarian word for theatre was taken from two existing ancient words for 'colour' and 'house'. The word for revolution came from the existing word to boil, '*forr*', so revolution – a rather useful word in Hungarian as the country lived through so many of them – became *forradalom*, which translates as 'on the boil'. The Hungarian word for isolation is taken from the ancient Magyar word for island. A beautiful Hungarian word for wife or female partner was invented: *feleség*, which literally means 'my halfness' – a

---

* One language reformer, the writer Izidor Guzmics, was a well-known salon wit in Pest and sent a note to the palatine, reminding him of one of his distinguished Habsburg forebears, the sixteenth-century Emperor Charles V, who according to legend spoke French to his friends, German to his horse, Italian to his mistress, Spanish to God and English to the birds. 'Had he known Magyar doubtless he would have spoken Hungarian to his enemies,' Guzmics wrote.

noun, not an adjective. More than 8,000 new words came into common usage in colloquial and literary Hungarian within a generation. Kazinczy and his friends – the poet Batsányi, who had also spent time in jail for his involvement with the Jacobins, was his best friend – knew that the language had to adapt to modern life. How could industry be forged without a word to describe it? How could trade be promoted if there was no word for it in Hungarian? The old language, brought up to date, 'had an astonishing capacity to bring forth a national identity', Kazinczy said towards the end of his life.*5

All along the revivalists had understood that theirs was a 'project of patriotism', of nationalism, though the word had not come into use, carefully crafted to sound non-political, part of spreading culture in the vernacular. But the early reformers were well aware of their goal and the logic of the path they were taking. The lexicographer and writer György Bessenyei, one of the earliest of the revivalists, believed they would be spreading Enlightenment values to all groups of people in their own muscular language. 'All nations gained their education in their own language, not a foreign one,' he wrote. 'The basis and instrument of a country's welfare is culture. The key to culture is a national language . . . and the cultivation of a national language is the first duty of the nation.'

They believed that Hungarians would become like the Irish or Welsh, who at this point had almost entirely lost their 'national' languages. The philosopher Johann Gottfried Herder – originally German, but a cosmopolitan traveller who settled in Pest – was highly influential. As early as 1791 he wrote that the Magyars would soon disappear 'into an encircling sea' of Slavs and Germans and within three or four

---

* One of my own favourites was brought to my attention by the incomparable historian of Habsburg Budapest János Lukács. It is the useful and atmospheric word characteristic of a Hungarian view of the world – *délibáb*, a kind of Fata Morgana, or illusion; something that Freud's great friend, the psychoanalyst Sándor Ferenczi, called magical thinking, a talent for daydreaming and pretending, but which en masse turned into herd instinct that took hold of the general populace in times of crisis quite often in Hungarian history. Ferenczi described it as 'The readiness to see the world through rose-coloured glasses, which induced Magyars to exaggerate their grandeur, while they ignored the misery of subject peoples . . . a capacity for dreaming has made Magyars superlative advocates for lost causes and ever ready to defend Hungary as an exception among nations.'

generations the Hungarian language would never be heard again. 'The cause of Magyarization is, simultaneously, the cause of unification in our country,' he wrote. 'Hungary, in terms of language, is a true Babel. If we cannot change the course of things ... sooner or later our nation and even our name will be forgotten.'

Many others agreed. The Pest history professor Miklós Révai said: 'If the Magyar nation loses its own language, it will also be lost and the Magyars will no longer be Magyar.' Kazinczy wrote that 'without our language, our homeland will always be foreign, not a separate nation but a colony'.

The publisher István Kultsár, heir to a sizeable fortune, opened his magnificent house in Pest to an intelligentsia of writers, academics, lawyers and doctors that began to grow in the twin towns around the turn of the nineteenth century. He supported publishing of all kinds, raised money to open a theatre for plays in Hungarian, and in 1799 launched and edited the first Hungarian language newspaper, *Hazai és Külföldi Tudósítások* (Reports from Home and Abroad), which ran to several issues before the Imperial censors became too interested in it, closed it down and threatened the proprietor with prison.[6]

Many hardliners in Vienna warned of the dangers to the Empire of the linguistic revival, which in a small way by the end of the 1780s was spreading to some of the Slavic nationalities – for example Croatia and the Czech lands. They wanted tougher censorship, bans on national language teaching and arrests of 'troublemakers'. Sporadic crackdowns were tried, but failed. Most Austrians, led by Emperor Joseph II, who succeeded his mother Maria Theresa in 1780, were more mystified than perturbed by the fuss about language the Hungarians were making – and it was not lost on them that the argument was raging in either German or Latin. Why not simply get on in German, as the vast majority of people in Buda did and most of the inhabitants of Pest had done for generations?

The emperor saw himself as the true modernizer and in his ten-year reign attempted to introduce a series of changes to sweep away the archaic institutions and customs long preserved by the Hungarians, particularly the privileges of the nobility. In Hungary Joseph II is referred to as 'the hatted king' – because he was never crowned ruler of

Hungary, hence the hat. He refused to take any part in a coronation at which he would be expected to swear to uphold a constitution he was determined to abandon – honourable, if naive.

In 1784 he decreed that German would be the official language throughout the Empire, used in the courts and offices of state instead of Latin, and that no other languages should be taught in schools. He told Count Pál Eszterházy on 27 April 1784: 'The use of a dead language such as Latin is surely a disgrace to a nation for its enlightenment, as it tacitly proves that either the nation does not have a proper mother tongue, or that . . . [almost] no one can speak or write it. If Hungarian were relevant in all of Hungary, then it could serve on it own . . . [however] it is not. Therefore no other language besides German can be chosen as that of the Monarchy from both the military and political viewpoints.' He had his supporters and others put it more succinctly. 'Latin is useless because so few people know it. To make Hungarian the official language would be a catastrophe,' Samuel Kohlmayer, a well-known ethnic-German lawyer in Pest wrote at the time. 'It is a language which is only good for swearing in.'*[7]

The nobles were in uproar. They were never consulted and the decree was not put before the Diet – had it been, naturally, it would have been debated in Latin. They thought the use of Latin was part of their identity, separating them from the commoners. The linguistic

---

* A note on language: Hungarian is difficult and its complexities of syntax and sentence structure, not to mention pronunciation, are daunting. Just as an example, verb endings depend on whether they are followed by 'the'; vowel changes depend on the verb's tense. Most importantly, every syllable is pronounced, even those of one letter. Most people not brought up with Hungarian from childhood – and I am one, despite my background – find the intricacies hard to master. The poet George Szirtes, who has written wonderfully in two languages, described the language to me as 'an island of sound in a sea of Teutonic, Slavic and Romance languages . . . its structures, its modes and its sounds remain its own, incomprehensible to anyone else, even to the Finns to whom Hungarians are distantly related. Hungarian is, to begin with, a language without genders or diphthongs. Its consonants are flat, clear and unremitting. The mouth adopts a range of rigorous positions, as in some light military drill, and moves abruptly from one to the other in short, low staccato bursts. The vowels, too, are more crisply defined than their English equivalents, each syllable enjoying fuller articulation . . . This might suggest that the language is unyielding, resistant to lyrical effect, but that is not the case. Its clarity is wedded to great softness and liquidity.'

revivalists were furious because it would set back their cause and could swamp entirely the use of Hungarian. This was the first appearance of the aristocratic class uniting with the reformers and middle class in a nationalist cause – the politics that would define Hungary from now until the First World War. Previously, very few aristocrats had stood up to encourage the use of the Hungarian language. From this point it was the modern, 'enlightened' and chic thing to do. There was another explanation, too. Most of them could barely speak Hungarian or read it. 'The magnates, I suspect, have a better reason than mere courtesy for not speaking Hungarian,' a British visitor to Pest wrote in his diary. 'This is simply because they cannot do so. A large part of the higher nobility is denationalized to such an extent that they understand every European language better than their own national language.'[8]

Among the most enthusiastic people in the twin towns about extending the use of Hungarian were the Jews. Many had moved to Buda and Pest at the encouragement of successive Habsburg monarchs for economic reasons, fleeing from extreme persecution further east in Galicia and the Russian Empire, or a mixture of both. Jews were at the forefront of the linguistic revival. Few by the early nineteenth century spoke Yiddish and the 'modern' idea was to use the Hungarian language as a means of assimilation to Magyar life. As Marton Diósy, a well-known writer of Jewish extraction who was close to intellectuals in Vienna as well as Buda and Pest, explained:

Jews are not swept away by the idea of an old nationality but want to be Hungarians. It is enough of a problem . . . [for Jews] that the prayers are conducted in a language that the worshippers hardly understand; but under these circumstances, we hope that if the Hungarian language becomes more widespread, then enlightened views will win wider acceptance and Hungarian Jewry will adopt reforms that have already been introduced in many foreign temples . . . then Hungarian will be used in everyday life. Let friend speak to friend in this language, lover to beloved, children to parents. Let us complain to our God of our earthly woes in this language; and let us be confident that we will soon sing out our thanks in this tongue for the relief we have won and for our complete emancipation.[9]

Emperor Joseph was defeated in his attempt to outlaw Latin and Hungarian. The local dignitaries were deliberately slow to implement the decree in their areas, and the Diet rarely met. A month before he died suddenly and unexpectedly in 1790 the emperor repudiated all his reform measures, but the struggle for the Hungarian language had only just begun.

11

THE BRIDGE BUILDER

Who was the greatest Hungarian? Without a doubt, definitely, that's Széchenyi.

Lajos Kossuth (1802–94)

It's true he is no rebel against the dynasty, he is a moderate and charm-ing. But Széchenyi is the most dangerous type of reformer because he shields subversion with respectability.

Klemens von Metternich (1773–1859)

In the winter of 1820–21, in a hurry to reach Vienna for his father's funeral, the dashing twenty-nine-year-old cavalry officer Count István Széchenyi was stuck in his town house in Pest and forced to wait a week to cross the Danube to Buda. He recorded in his diary that he arrived on 29 December after a long and exhausting journey from distant Transylvania, 'my feet frozen because my boots were too tight'. The pontoon bridge had been disassembled two and a half months earlier and the river was impassable by boat because of ice floes, though not packed solid enough to cross by cart as was sometimes possible in the depth of winter. It was not until 5 January that he could get his carriage transported over to Buda on a grain wagon. The previous evening he had written: 'I would give a year's income to build a bridge between Buda and Pest, even if I myself never derive a single groat of profit from it.'

Széchenyi was certainly not the first person to have thought of the idea of a permanent bridge, nor the first to have been infuriated by the lack of one in the twin towns. Increasingly often as the population grew, people got stuck on the wrong side. In January 1801 the entire magistracy of Pest went to Buda for the wedding of the Austrian governor and were stranded, unable to cross back home for some weeks.*

Even in summer the drawbacks of the pontoon bridge had become clearer as Pest grew in bustle and wealth. It had to be partially closed when other river traffic used it and it sloped dangerously when the water level dropped; in strong currents and storms it frequently broke apart and was out of service for weeks. The pontoon also became a politically divisive issue: as a middle class grew in Pest and the number of businesses increased, complaints mounted in intensity that commoners had to pay the tolls but nobles didn't. 'Many people came to see the pontoon as an impediment rather than an instrument to progress,' Széchenyi said.[1]

But while others complained and talked about the problem, the energetic and industrious young count, well known as a decorated war hero in the campaigns against Napoleon – and also around the *ton* for his amorous dalliances and his astronomical gambling debts – was the first to do something about it. First, he tried to use his aristocratic contacts to persuade the Habsburg government in Vienna to build a bridge as a state project. He got nowhere. Then he attempted to press the worthies of both towns to pay for one. They delayed for years and did nothing. Széchenyi was invariably told it was impossible with the technology available at the time to build a stone-and-wood bridge a kilometre long across a fast-flowing stream like the Danube. Széchenyi, from knowledge of British engineers, many of whom he had met, knew otherwise.†

It was a long process but he never gave up. For Széchenyi the bridge had obvious practical benefits, but it was equally important as a symbol of the creation of a new city, a capital for a nation. In 1832 he founded the Budapest Bridge Association – the first time the name without a

---

* For a few years after 1750 there had been an 'ice bridge' solid enough for people and horses. The authorities checked the crossing points and if needed reinforced them with extra ice or straw. The frozen Danube was a popular place for balls and fairs. But they were banned after a disaster when the ice cracked during a ball held by the Greek Orthodox Church. The frozen dance floor collapsed and thirty-six people drowned.

† Some biographers of Széchenyi have suggested another, altogether less high-minded motive for his determination to build the bridge, which makes a good and plausible story though there is no hard evidence for it. Apparently at one point he had two mistresses, one living in Pest and the other in Buda, and the logistics of getting across the river for trysts was becoming tiresome.

hyphen appeared on any sort of official document. He provided significant funds himself and formed a committee to raise a lot more. The banker György Sina (from the Greek Sinas family) became chairman of the Chain Bridge joint-stock company in 1837. He, along with Solomon Rothschild in Vienna and the Pest financier Samuel Wodianer, bought most of the shares. But it was Széchenyi who commissioned the English engineer William Tierney Clark to design the bridge and the Scot Adam Clark (no relation; they barely knew each other) to supervise its construction.[2]

Széchenyi was closely involved in the project every step of the way – the scores of long letters between him and both the Clarks show how he interested himself in minute details of the scheme. William Tierney Clark did well for himself from the Budapest Chain Bridge (Lanchid in Hungarian, but just as often called Széchenyi Bridge). He got paid twice for essentially the same work, though it is indeed an elegant structure that still dominates the Budapest cityscape. It is practically identical to the suspension bridge over the Thames at Marlow, 45 kilometres west of London, completed in 1832 and still standing in 2022– though it is substantially longer – and is very similar to Hammersmith Bridge in central London, completed in the 1820s. He spent no more than a few weeks in Pest, as Széchenyi's guest, and returned to England. Adam Clark was chief engineer and project manager. He stayed in Pest as the work was being completed and remained after it finished. He married a Hungarian woman and was chief engineer on many other projects in Hungary – including the tunnel under Castle Hill, named after him, which transformed Buda, halving travel times in the town. He lived in a huge villa in the Buda Hills which he built for himself. He died in 1866 much feted and was buried in Kerepesi Cemetery, the graveyard of the most famous Hungarian figures – one of the very few foreigners interred there.[*][3]

---

* Hungary had an unusually good reputation among the British during the Reform Age, and vice versa, particularly after Széchenyi's exploits popularized England among Hungarians. 'For there is scarcely a European country in which Anglomania rages more fiercely than in that slighted land,' wrote the playwright and novelist Catherine Gore in 1829. 'There is scarcely an event of English life, a folly of London fashion, or an invention of British industry, which does not find admirers and commentators and imitators, among the Hungarians of respectable degree.'

Rows continued over the project and several times it looked doomed. There was a bitter dispute between the Buda and Pest municipal authorities about who should 'own' the bridge – Pest worthies at one point wanted to go ahead and build it on their own. Then there was a long delay in getting final approval from the emperor in Vienna, who did not want to give any money or Imperial resources for the project, but looked for ways of getting the credit. The foundation stone was laid on 24 August 1842. The discovery soon after construction began that much of the building material was brought over from England caused a rumpus. Then it became known that some specialist foreign workers were employed on the project. There was a big demonstration in Pest in protest, amid demands for their removal, which halted any work on the bridge before a compromise was reached. Then there was a revolution, a war and a bloody siege of Buda before it was finally completed in 1849.[4]

The controversy about the toll for crossing the bridge continued for years. The nobility saw it as a tax and believed they were exempt. Some refused to pay point blank on principle, including Chief Justice of Hungary Cziráky, who said he would never cross the bridge if it meant paying a tax and would prefer to take a two-day detour, travel 60 kilometres out of his way south and cross the river by ferry. The emperor stayed out of that row, and so did the courts. By a handful of votes, the Upper House in the Diet passed a law in 1836 that everyone must pay the toll. The legislation referred only to the Chain Bridge between Buda and Pest, but the nobles saw it as the thin end of the wedge before all their privileges disappeared. For Széchenyi, that was the point. Those 'zwei Groschen [tuppence] would start the process of dismantling the feudal system that held Hungary back', he said. The writer Gyula Krúdy put it neatly: 'It was under the soaring vaults of the Chain Bridge that old Hungary marched into new Hungary.'

The bridge was a vital first part of Széchenyi's vision of unifying the two towns, known even by locals as Pesth-Buda or Buda-Pesth, depending on which side of the river one lived. 'We cannot overcome time and must be patient in waiting to see what time may bring,' he wrote in Vilag (World) in 1831. 'But it is in our power to stand in the right place. And for Hungarians the right place cannot be but in Buda and Pest, which nature has so designated, because this is the heart of the nation – it must be in order and beat with all its vigour ... into the nation's arteries.'[5]

Széchenyi was the most gifted and romantic figure among Hungary's Enlightenment reformers, a *grand seigneur* who developed the common touch, and arguably the man who did more than any other to create the city that became Budapest. Written off early in his career as a lightweight and a dandy, he became a serious thinker and a doer. He was a passionate man with a troubled, pessimistic personality who could inspire a generation of Hungarians with optimism. His tragic final years and desperate end – a grisly suicide – added to his mystique and made his achievements more remarkable.

He had been born in 1791 in Vienna into an old aristocratic family, devoutly Catholic, which had included a cardinal, several archbishops, many generals and distinguished officers. They had made their fortune during the seventeenth century through faithful service to the Habsburgs. His father, Ferenc, was a generous patron of the arts and of scholarship. He founded the National Museum and established the National Library in a beautiful neoclassical building in Pest that bears his name.

István was the youngest of five children, all brought up to be ultraloyal to the dynasty and the Church. He joined a cavalry regiment aged eighteen and fought in the Napoleonic Wars, where he received a bravery commendation at the Battle of Leipzig in 1813. He rode into Paris with the Allies at the end of the war – and then, as the handsome 'Count Stefi', became, in the Duke of Wellington's phrase, 'the darling of the Congress of Vienna'. He wound up in a series of scrapes involving gambling and women. One of his early flames was Melanie, Countess Zichy, who many years later married Metternich.[6]

Soon after the war he began a long series of travels. He did the Grand Tour but tagged on the Middle East too, accompanied by two servants, a chef and a landscape painter. In Italy he danced with the Queen of Naples and in London the Prince Regent's daughter, Princess Charlotte. He met King William IV, Wellington again, Palmerston, Peel and Nathan Rothschild, who wanted to make Széchenyi his son-in-law through a marriage with his daughter, Charlotte – a failed attempt: the Hungarian count believed he was rich enough already. In Paris he met Talleyrand, Chateaubriand and Lamartine; in Berlin he became a confidant of Wilhelm von Humboldt. Tsar Alexander I admired him immensely. He accompanied Alexander to Buda when, at the end of the Congress, the Austrian emperor, Francis I, took the Russian tsar to show him the twin towns. The monarchs crossed the Danube in a coach from Buda Castle to Pest and the pontoon bridge was festooned with 1,000 lamps – thick candles on long poles: 'as magnificent [a] scene as one would ever see', Metternich wrote.[7]

Julia Pardoe, the author of romantic novels as well as travel books, met Széchenyi often, in Hungary and in England. She was charmed and impressed: 'He has a dark, keen, eagle eye, softening, however, at intervals almost into sadness; heavy eyebrows finely arched and in perpetual motion, giving a character of extraordinary energy in his countenance; and one of those full, deep-toned sonorous voices to which you cannot choose but to listen. In common conversation he is fluent and demonstrative rather than logical . . . he is earnest, very rapid and impassioned, very graceful in his attitudes and movements.'

Széchenyi was an enthusiastic Anglophile. His first visit to England in 1815 made a lasting impression on him and he returned often. He admired Britain's political institutions, its industrialization and, by Hungarian standards at least, its social mobility. He developed a fascination with the gadgetry of the Industrial Revolution. His style was a mixture of visionary zeal and obsession with practical details. In England his interest was aroused as much by perforated soap holders and the water closet as by Adam Smith's ideas about economics or Jeremy Bentham's or John Stuart Mill's thoughts on liberty. He loved horse racing and regularly went to Newmarket and Epsom. After his first visit he said his time in England had been 'a revelation . . . There are three things to be learned in England: the constitution; the machines; and horse-breeding.'

His restless travels changed him. The main lesson he learned from seeing the world was how backward Hungary remained. 'We are behind others in everything,' he wrote in his diary in 1820. 'The century is on the march, but unfortunately I live in a country that is dragging one leg behind. Poor little Hungary, how filthy you are!' He became far more serious and religious, though never fanatically. He fell in love and had a decade-long platonic relationship with a married woman, Countess

Crescence Seilern, with whom he found lasting happiness. They married only when her much older husband died.*

On 12 October in Pozsony/Pressburg he made history with a speech in the Diet – not for what he said, or even how he said it. He spoke in Hungarian, the first time one of the more important magnates had used a language other than Latin in the House. He caused a tremendous scandal that shocked his fellow peers and sent reverberations throughout the Empire to Vienna, where Metternich and Emperor Francis were enraged. Some people in Buda quipped that his gesture had nothing to do with politics, but simply because his Latin was even worse than his Hungarian. But from that moment Count Széchenyi took centre stage within the Reform Movement and for the next decade and a half others deferred to him.†

For anyone who got past the language issue, the speech put him directly at odds not only with the Austrians but with his own class: 'Is Hungary a free country? Good heavens No. The nobleman is free – the peasant is his servant, a slave. Defending this anti-liberal constitution is not a noble endeavour. We see 400,000 souls who want to assert their privileges, against 10 million who have no rights, who are not even mentioned . . . And we then speak of the emancipation of mankind, of freedom, of Christian philosophy . . . First we have to reform ourselves. We have to go through the school of humility, of self-denial.'[8]

Less than a month later he caused another sensation when he declared he would donate a year's income from his 50,000-hectare estate – worth 60,000 gulden, an enormous sum equivalent to more than £2.5 million sterling in 2022 – to establish an Academy of Sciences to advance learning in all branches of culture and academic study. 'But my

---

* After his marriage he changed his will, directing his secretary to remove anything in his diary or papers about any named women apart from his wife, however innocent and platonic.

† For much of his life Széchenyi could not speak or write fluent Hungarian – indeed, he didn't seem to have one language in which he wrote or thought. He wrote his diaries and some of his books in German, though there were paragraphs in French and English. He had Latin, as did all the Hungarian magnates, though a snobbish Austrian secret policeman in one report said that 'his Latin is poor, not good enough for him to have a career in the public service'.

dear, what will you live on?' his mother Julianna asked. 'My friends will provide,' he replied. And they did. One of the academy's first tasks was to establish a linguistics research department, which employed a second generation of 'neologists' and philologists to work on creating new Hungarian words and language.

Széchenyi had phenomenal energy as a practical modernizer and a long list of Budapest societies, institutions, companies and organizations were started by him. Though he may have thought little of the Hungarian nobility, he knew he needed them to further his various causes and that little would change politically in Hungary without them. 'In Hungary, even a revolution has to be started by an aristocrat,' as the early Communist thinker, Friedrich Engels, noted drily some years later.

He was loathed by the poorer 'sandalled nobles' for his high-handed ways and as the elite of the elite, particularly after the 1831 publication of his book *Hitel* (Credit), which supported the end of serfdom and the nobles' tax exemption. The biggest shock to them was his call for an end to the *aviticitas* which for 600 years had declared the landed estates inalienable. Owners had to inherit and couldn't sell. Sales of the book were huge by contemporary Hungarian standards, which added to the fury of the more conservative nobles. In many provincial Hungarian counties piles of the book were ceremonially burned by the landlords and Széchenyi was treated like a class traitor.[9]

He was popular among the more liberal circles in Vienna. Metternich tolerated him and liked him personally, but as the court grew increasingly reactionary the ageing Austrian statesman became more suspicious of him politically. 'It's true he is no rebel against the dynasty, he is a moderate and charming. But Széchenyi is the most dangerous type of reformer because he shields subversion with respectability,' he said. Széchenyi complained to a friend that 'in Vienna I am considered too Hungarian, in Pest I am considered too Austrian'.

He was the most famous man in Hungary in the 1830s and into the early 1840s. The writer Karl-Maria Kertbeny – the first to coin the words heterosexual and homosexual – knew Széchenyi well: 'He was a spirited, hurrying, gesticulating figure who would bound forward wherever he went, usually deep in conversation with one or often two companions, but often greeting people from all sides, sometimes crossing the street to accost someone to talk to them. Passers-by greeted him with reverence, gazing at his strange quicksilver-like appearance. Then one would say to another, "That is Széchenyi" . . . He talked to everyone on the street, treated every burgher as his equal.'[10]

THE GREAT FLOOD

Everywhere else I play for the audience, but in Hungary I play for the nation.

Ferenc Liszt (1811–86)

In Buda and Pest there had been warning signs for weeks, during an unusually cold winter. By early March 1838 thick blocks of ice further downstream had slowly choked the flow of the Danube. Buda, which had no protection of any kind, had flooded three times between 20 February and 10 March, though the damage had been limited because few people lived on the lower slopes on that side of the river. Some inhabitants had fled from Pest, but the vast majority had stayed in town.

On the evening of Tuesday, 13 March, despite news that there had been flooding in some towns and villages upstream, the coffee houses in Pest were thriving and two theatres were full. At around 8 p.m. news broke that the river had spilled over the dyke protecting the Inner City and one of the dams upstream had burst, but there was no immediate panic. At the German Theatre close to the Danube embankment the performance was halted and the audience evacuated. But at the National Theatre, slightly further from the river, the show went on. The water rose so quickly that spectators in the upper gallery seats were unable to leave and spent the night there.[1]

From around midnight thunderclaps roared overhead from a tremendous storm and there was torrential rain for three hours. Nobody was prepared for the devastation in Pest from the early hours on the following morning when the Danube burst its bank in Pest's worst flood, before or since. As soon as dawn broke, a few brave people did what they could to help. Baron Miklós Wesselényi – one of István Széchenyi's best friends, who lived in an elegant town house close to the river – kept a vivid account of the disaster in his diary:

I found Kigyó Street [several hundred metres from the riverbank] almost completely under water so first I inched forward to the swirling water up to my knees, then up to my waist without wanting to retreat, until I reached the city market area immersed in water up to my neck where I could not locate a single barge. When I reached dry land, my clothes began to freeze on to my skin and by the time I reached Helmeczy's residence in the Trattner-Károlyi House, which was only a few hundred steps away, my clothing was covered with a layer of ice. At that point, I had to shed my clothing and jump around a little bit, until my limbs thawed somewhat. Later, János [his valet] arrived with a barge to get home. I immediately got dressed into dry clothes and went to look for barges at the Sebestyén market, where I found heavy traffic and barges coming and going.

By around 9.30 a.m. much of Pest was under two metres of water, even more in some places:

Among the debris, there were ruined houses, ice floes, furniture, beams and every other obstacle. One could scarcely pass through the narrow streets and only with the most intense effort . . . everywhere the tottering buildings and collapsing roofs threatened destruction. Only the screams and hoarse cries for help from those in despair occasionally overwhelmed the thunderous, cracking rattling noise. One wanted and needed to go in ten directions at once, but could only go in one. I could see hundreds of people in danger but only help one-third and leave the others in the mouth of death; one had to turn back fathers and husbands whose children were already in the boats filled to overflowing and listen to their howls and sobs.

Some of the people who were tireless in their efforts to aid the flood victims were, he admitted, 'intoxicated a bit, which was helpful as it gave them extra courage to reach places they would not have dared to go while sober'. He was appalled by bystanders who did nothing to help – a Baron Csekonics, who tried to save his beloved horses instead of people, and some of the grandest of the aristocrats like Albert Prónay, 'who smoked their pipes sitting on their secure masonry roofs' instead of taking part in the rescue attempt.*

The redoubtable Julia Pardoe, fearless traveller, was in Pest at the time researching one of her adventure books. She, too, noticed that not everyone was selfless. She recorded eyewitness accounts of boatmen ignoring poor people in danger while they 'hurried off to rescue some wealthy sufferer who could pay them every inch in gold'.[2]

The Danube at Budapest is relatively tame today, but in the first part of the nineteenth century the river was wild and unpredictable. Floods were common. Every decade or so the river would burst its banks in low-lying areas close to Pest, and on the other side of the river as far as Esztergom. In the spring of 1775, when the ice melted, the embankments on both sides of the river were flooded. After that, a series of dykes and dams were built upstream and they did a reasonable job in protecting both towns. Prompted by the flood of 1838, there was general agreement that much more needed to be done – though, predictably, that prompted endless negotiation between Vienna and the municipal authorities in Buda and Pest about what exactly to do and who should pay for it. In the immediate aftermath, the waters began to recede by 19 March. One hundred and fifty-three people had died and at least five times that number were seriously injured. Between 35,000 and 45,000 people were made homeless, nearly half the population; 2,281 buildings had collapsed completely and 827 were badly damaged. Throughout Budapest in the twenty-first century there remain reminders of the Great Pest Flood – plaques that show the level the Danube waters reached on that devastating night. Most of them comprise a brass or marble plaque of a pointed finger with the word *vízállás* (water level).

---

* Wesselényi was hailed as a hero for his flood-relief efforts, even by the court in Vienna. The emperor personally praised him. All that was forgotten the following year when he was arrested and held in the dungeons at Buda Castle for operating a printing press that produced 'seditious' books and pamphlets. He was released after a few months and permitted to go abroad for treatment for an eye complaint that rendered him almost totally blind. He never recovered his sight. The poet Mihály Vörösmarty wrote a moving 'Ode to the Boatman of the Flood' honouring him, and in 2022 there was still a charming memorial plaque commemorating Wesselényi's deeds on Lajos Kossuth utca, opposite the beautiful, peaceful Franciscan Church in the heart of Pest.

The most dramatic is on the façade of the St Rókus Church on Rákóczi Avenue, more than a kilometre from the riverbank, which shows that at the height of the flood the water reached the top of the door at the main entrance to the church.

The flood was a catastrophe, the worst natural disaster in the history of Pest. But in the longer term it created an opportunity. New building regulations – strict for the time – were introduced and large-scale water management schemes were begun, with modern river-drainage technology and strengthened embankments on both sides of the Danube. The best-known architects were commissioned to draw up ambitious plans to rebuild the existing town and extend it dramatically to create a new city. Much of the look and feel of twenty-first-century Budapest dates from the period immediately after the flood.[3]

Donations for flood relief poured into Pest from most of the capitals in Europe. The Vienna court gave generously, led by Emperor Ferdinand I (known as 'The Benign'), who dug deep into his own pocket, as did many Austrian financiers led by the Rothschilds. The emperor also persuaded the state bank, then a private company, to lend Pest a million crowns – worth around £375 million sterling at 2022 values – at zero interest. A series of charity events were organized to raise money for the victims, thousands of whom remained homeless for months. For many people in Buda and Pest the biggest and most important fundraising event by far was the return to Hungary for the first time in years of the megastar music performer of the day, Ferenc Liszt.

Aged twenty-seven, Liszt was then the most famous pianist of the age, a sensation wherever in Europe he gave concerts. The poet Heinrich Heine coined the word 'Lisztomania' for the effect he had on audiences, particularly young women. He was probably the first pop star to be followed by bands of groupies.* For Hungarians he was every inch a Hungarian, though he had barely set foot in Hungary since he was aged

---

* One Liszt biographer recounted the story of a hysterical lady-in-waiting to a German princess. After one concert Liszt threw away an old cigar stump in the street under the watchful eyes of the infatuated young woman, who reverently picked the offensive weed out of the gutter, had it encased in a locket and surrounded with the monogram 'F.L.' in diamonds, and went about her courtly duties unaware of the sickly odour it gave forth.

nine. He had been educated mainly in France and had grown up as a citizen of the music world. As a young man, briefly, he had trained for the Catholic priesthood, but he was not destined for a life of sermon-making and celibacy. He had a long relationship with Countess Marie d'Agoult and fathered several illegitimate children with her – as well as children by various other mistresses. Later, he lived for years with the Polish Countess Carolyne zu Sayn-Wittgenstein. His reputation as something of a roué obviously increased his allure. 'Sinner or saint, his triple personalities of the musical, the erotic and the sacerdotal inflamed the public imagination,' a biographer wrote of him.

Even before the Pest floods, he had begun to rediscover his roots under the influence of the most powerful ideology of the time: nation-alism. The flood stirred his conscience. Soon after he heard about its impact on Hungary he wrote to the *Gazette Musicale*: 'Through this innermost tumult and feeling I learned the meaning of the words "my fatherland". Oh my wild and distant country! Oh my unknown friends! Oh my great far-spreading family! Your cry of pain has brought me back to you. Touched to the depths, I bow my head, ashamed that I have for-gotten you for so long.'[4]

Shortly afterwards he was invited by Count Leó Festetics to give a series of concerts in Hungary, with the proceeds going to flood relief. Liszt agreed with alacrity straight away. After three rapturously received nights in Pozsony/Pressburg he finally descended on Pest, accompa-nied by a '*caravane aristocratique*', as he put it in a letter to a friend, of Hungary's nobility, as well as the odd bourgeois music lover.

As Julia Pardoe described it, Liszt

stirred not only the aristocrats (male, and especially female), the press, nationalist politicians, and music lovers but also Budapest's tradespeople into activity. Every hotel prepared a suite of rooms in the fond hope that theirs might be the proud roof destined to shel-ter him. Print-sellers sent to Vienna for engraved portraits of all dimensions of their gifted countryman; extemporaneous antiquar-ies made researches to verify his genealogy; and even the pastry cooks . . . unwilling to be excelled in a patriotism, which moreover promised to be highly profitable, invented a new . . . sponge pudding, shaped like a grand piano, and graced with the name 'Liszt' in spun-sugar.* At length he came ... Daylight had no sooner merged into night than he was greeted by a serenade – and what a serenade! Nothing out of Germany could be compared to it.[5]

The concert at the Pesti Vigadó (House of Merriment), a splendid Baroque building that had miraculously survived the flood, on 12 February 1839 was a huge success; tickets changed hands for fantastical prices and an enormous sum was raised for flood victims. Liszt played for an hour and a half without a break – Beethoven, Schumann, some of his own pieces – and then conducted the orchestra until late into the night. Soon after the concert the poet Mihály Vörösmarty composed an hyperbolic 'Ode to Liszt':

> Oh freeman of the world
> And yet our kinsman everywhere you go
> Have you a word for this ailing land?

From then on he returned frequently to Hungary and eventually he was made the first head of the Hungarian Academy of Music, where for years he wielded vast influence in music and the arts generally in Hungary. He was given a grand mansion on Pest's principal avenue, Andrássy út, where he lived for around three months of the year during the winter. The civic authorities and ambitious politicians from the Reform Movement were using him cynically, and Liszt was willing to be used. The height of his national acclaim – or of absurd hypocrisy, depending on one's view – was a ceremony in January 1840 when he was made an honorary citizen of Pest and with great solemnity 'was presented with a sword [a sabre] of honour: a souvenir from the martial race to its noble-hearted and world-famous son', as the official programme for the event portentously declared. Many people had not yet realized it – neither his admirers nor his few critics – but Liszt could barely speak a word of Hungarian. This became obvious to everyone during the sword ceremony. He could have spoken German, which would at least have been understood by almost everyone in the Pest of those days. But the point about the event – and the National Theatre itself, where

* It is worth mentioning that the word *liszt* in Hungarian means flour.

130

at that time German was not allowed to be spoken on stage during a performance – was to emphasize the critical importance of Hungarians speaking Hungarian. He ended up making an impassioned Hungarian nationalist speech in French. 'At the very climax of his Hungarianization . . . his alien reality was revealed most fully,' one of his critics wrote angrily.*

Liszt had tried a few times to learn Hungarian and employed as language tutor a young academic reputed to be a brilliant teacher who had managed to get several dignitaries from the court in Vienna to at least utter a few sentences in Magyar. But, as he once admitted, he gave up the effort after five lessons when he encountered the word for unshakeability – *tántorithatatlanság*. Many of those trying to learn the language would have lost the will to carry on well before then. Liszt wrote to a newspaper after the National Theatre debacle: 'Notwithstanding my lamentable ignorance of the Hungarian language, I am and shall remain until my end, a Magyar heart and soul.'

And he meant it. To a Hungarian friend in 1842, while on a Europe-wide concert tour, he wrote: 'Sometimes my heart beats faster even at the sight of a postal stamp from Pest. It gives me such pleasure to be in your company. What is loud applause and endless acclaim worth compared to what all of you give me? Everywhere else I play for the audience, but in Hungary I play for the nation. And this is a noble and great thing, to make emotional contact in this manner with a nation such as ours.'[6]

Similar difficulties with forging a national identity were faced by Hungarians of all classes during this period. Expressions of nationalism included small gestures as well as grand visionary projects such as Széchenyi's. People wanted to show they were Magyar in a multitude of ways large and small. From the early 1810s there was a vogue for christening children with Hungarian names drawn from the distant and often imaginary past, as some of them were bogus. Like the philologists

---

* Later some cynics reminded Liszt of the event – and that when the War of Independence broke out he made sure he was far from the front lines, or even active on the 'home front'. He quietly disappeared 'to the safety of the court of a minor German prince and his sword remained in its sheath', as Heinrich Heine reminded readers in his poem 'Im Oktober 1849'.

inventing new words, parents were choosing fake Magyar names to give their children: the most popular for girls, like Jolán, Csilla and Tünde, had rarely been heard before around 1800, when some writers had invented them; the same went for Zoltán as a boy's name.

There was a big increase in Hungarian wine production and sales; some wealthy figures associated with the Magyar cause promoted them – for example Széchenyi. The aristocratic András Fáy, well known as a generous Pest host with a salon for writers and artists, refused to serve anything except Hungarian wine at his table. Pest hoteliers began serving Hungarian wines as well as French ones. Organizations, shops and some private houses flew the Hungarian national red, white and green colours on their shop fronts and homes and began putting the word 'National' in their names – 'the First National Swimming School', 'the National Tie Shop'.[7]

From the late 1820s an organization known as Pest Youth – comprising students, lawyers, doctors and writers – began a noisy and well-publicized nationalist campaign to force traders to change their shop signs as a sign of their patriotism. Those in Pest who still maintained '*Schuster*' signs for their shoe shops, '*Schneider*' for clothes shops and '*Tischelmeister*' for furniture shops were branded traitors, greedy businessmen without any national convictions. Mostly, Pest Youth attempted persuasion. Occasionally zealots went further and resorted to intimidation. Some traders who stood fast found their shop signs removed overnight. Many faced more violent threats, as Teréz Karács, a friend of one of the Pest Youth activists explained: 'They threw stones wrapped in paper into the "offending" shops, usually through the window. The paper read: "If there is not a Hungarian sign up here within 48 hours, not a stone of this building will remain." Most traders complied.'

A series of street names were changed – unofficially, as the Austrian authorities would not accept the changes. All the Buda Hills had German names, some of them commemorating the Habsburg victory over the Ottomans in the seventeenth century. They were all transformed overnight in 1830. Some were simple translations of the German name; for example, Adelberg (Eagle Hill) became Sashegy. Others were given the names of Hungarian kings from the Árpád dynasty instead of Austrian emperors. As the Buda town council explained, the new names would be 'public memorials that link the past with the present and speak to the future'.

Nationalism reached absurd levels. The academic István Horvát (1784–1846) became a highly popular historian – a kind of 'disco don' of the time – when he came out with a series of articles in which he claimed to have 'proved' that the Magyars were directly descended from Adam and Eve and that the ancient Hungarian language was Greek in origin. He insisted on the basis of no evidence that the Magyars had ancestors in Persia, Greece and Italy. The Magyars had been of such stature 'that they were giants and titans', he wrote. His books were as widely read as his articles and for twenty years he remained a respected and award-winning history professor at Budapest University. He inspired an entire generation. 'His historical myth-making surpassed even that of the medieval chroniclers,' one of his chief antagonists at the time wrote.[8]

13

THE IDES OF MARCH

Do you not feel the earth of Europe trembling once more? Do you not
feel the wind of revolution in the air?

Alexis de Tocqueville, 1 January 1848

Those were times that change one's soul.

Mór Jókai (1825–1904)

'We still don't know exactly what happened in March–April 1848, but
there is a national consensus that it was something magnificent,' István
Deák, the best and most original historian of the Revolution has said. 'It
has become all things to all people in that country.'

The 'Springtime of Nations', as historians many years later started
calling that extraordinary year of revolutions, started in Palermo and
Naples in January 1848, when a series of violent demonstrations forced
the Bourbon ruler of the Two Sicilies from the throne. On 23 February
in Paris the so-called 'bourgeois' king, Louis-Philippe, abdicated, Chief
Minister François Guizot was ousted and fled, and France's Second Republic was declared. Riots broke out in Prague, Pozsony/Pressburg, in
Lombardy and the Veneto, all Habsburg lands where people had struggled for national independence for decades, if not centuries. There was
unrest in Munich and some of the other German princely states, and in
the Russian part of a divided Poland.

On 13 March revolution reached Vienna. University students rioted,
workers in the sprawling industrial suburbs went on strike, destroying machines and burning down the factories of some hated business
owners. Demonstrators inside the city walls clashed with soldiers,
leaving forty-six people dead. Metternich, who had been in power for
more than thirty years, was driven out of office and escaped for safety
to London; the Police Minister, Count Josef Sedlnitzky, was fired.

Emperor Ferdinand was forced to make a series of concessions to a mob that demanded a constitution, a parliament with some real powers, the abolition of censorship, a raft of economic reforms – and an end to the reactionary politics that had marked the Habsburg governments since the Napoleonic Wars.[1]

News of the revolt in Vienna reached Pest the following day from passengers on the daily steamship. The first acts of the drama in Hungary were entirely peaceful – and, as one might have expected in Hungary, were played out in a coffee house, with the spark of revolution lit by the celebrated poet Sándor Petőfi. Groups of radical writers, students, journalists and lawyers had formed in Pest over the previous few weeks: 'March Youth' and the 'Society of Ten'. The wonderfully gifted twenty-five-year-old Petőfi was their inspirational figure. From Slovakian roots, he was the son of an innkeeper turned butcher. Since leaving school, where he had received the bare minimum of a primary education, he had made a meagre living as a bit-part actor with various provincial theatre companies. For a short period he was a mercenary soldier, but he had weak lungs and left the army because of ill health. He arrived in Pest at the start of 1844 and became an instant literary sensation. Poems had flowed from his pen since he was a child; in his brief life there were more than 850 of them, including *János Vitéz*, a brilliant long epic of around 25,000 words, as well as a novel and a play. His output was as varied as it was prolific. He wrote lyrical love poems – mostly to his wife Júlia Szendrey, herself an accomplished poet – and patriotic verses expressing, as the critic Pál Ignotus said, a 'bittersweet Hungarianness':

> I am Hungarian. Solemn is our race,
> Just like our violins when first they play.
> A smile may sometimes flit across my face,
> But sound of laughter rarely comes my way.
> When I am filled with joy, my eyes are sad:
> In high emotion, tears well up in me.
> But in the time of grief, my face is glad,
> For I do not desire your sympathy.

I am Hungarian, and my face is red
With shame, for shame it is to be Magyar!
For here at home no dawn is breaking yet,
Though sunlight streams on other lands afar.
Yet my country I never would leave,
Not for fortune or for fame,
For I cherish and adore
My nation even in its deepest shame.[2]

He is often compared to Byron and there are some obvious similar-
ities – dying for a lost cause is one – but the proletarian Petőfi would
most likely have loathed the aristocratic ways of Lord Byron. He revered the Jacobins, was an extreme socialist and an 'off with their heads'
republican, something the Right in Hungary, which has appropriated
his version of nationalism, tend to forget.* His brief but dazzling appearance on the revolutionary stage expressed the spirit of the first days
of the March Revolution.

The dissident radicals of March Youth and the Society of Ten frequented
the Café Pilvax, in central Pest near the Danube embankment. On the
afternoon of 14 March the two groups decided to call for a demonstration the following day in support of the revolutionaries in Vienna.
In one corner a group under the direction of a twenty-four-year-old
chemical engineer, János Irinyi, and a talented young writer, Mór Jókai,
twenty-three, set to work on preparing a list of demands which they
had been discussing for the last five days to the Austrian government.

----

* A week before the Revolution he wrote a poem outlining his policy towards the
nobility:

> The rich have waxed fat on us
> For long years past,
> But now it's our turn.
> Let our dogs on them grow fat.
> So toss them with your pitchforks
> In the dung and mud
> And there the dogs can make their meal
> Of their bones and blood.

They refined them to a dozen: the so-called Twelve Points, which put in simple, direct terms the founding ideals of Hungary's 1848 Revolution:

A free press
Abolition of censorship
An independent ministry residing in Buda-Pest
Elections by universal suffrage
Religious and civil equality for all
The establishment of a Hungarian National Guard
The establishment of an independent Hungarian army
Trial by jury
The establishment of a Hungarian National Bank
The withdrawal from Hungary of foreign (i.e. Austrian) troops
The release of all political prisoners
Union between Hungary and Transylvania*

In another corner of the Café Pilvax Petőfi was writing the poem for which he is probably best known, the work every Hungarian child for many generations has been taught to learn by heart, the rousing 'National Song' (but not to be confused with the official national anthem):

Arise Hungarians, your country calls you.
Meet this hour, whate'er befalls you.
Shall we be free men or slaves?
Choose the lot your spirit craves.
God of Hungarians we swear to thee
That slaves we shall no longer be.[3]

The following day, Wednesday, 15 March, was grey and chilly. Small knots of people had gathered at various parts of downtown Pest and in some of the town's other coffee houses, intent on going to the

---

* Irinyi later went on to invent the safety match, which prompted the joke around Pest that he had sparked the revolution that caused a conflagration and only much later devised a safety measure – 'too bad it wasn't the other way around'. Jókai was the prolific author of a series of highly popular novels from the 1860s onwards and has often been called the Magyar Dickens. In truth his work is a pale imitation, apart perhaps from *The Man with the Golden Touch*, which was much admired by Queen Victoria.

demonstration planned for later in the day at the National Museum; word was out that Petőfi would make an appearance there early in the afternoon.

The poet spent so much time at the Pilvax that he had his mail sent there. He once advised his fellow poet János Arany: 'If you write, then address the letter to the Pilvax. It would save time as I am more often here than at home.'* He usually turned up for breakfast at the Pilvax and a small crowd of the usual dissidents appeared at around 8.30 to wait for him. Jókai commented: 'A Magyar is no rebel early in the morning.' Nevertheless, at 9 a.m. on the dot, Petőfi arrived and immediately climbed onto a table, accompanied by cheers, to declaim his National Song and the Twelve Points. 'These are the demands of the people,' he said.

A small crowd followed him a few streets away to the workshop press of the well-known liberal printer Lajos Landerer. They demanded he publish the Twelve Points and Petőfi's poem immediately. His sympathies were with the demonstrators, but the law forbade it as neither had been approved by the censor. Then he suggested that the young radicals 'confiscate' the press 'in the name of the Revolution'. Irinyi put his hand on the press and solemnly declared: 'In the name of the people we herewith appropriate the press and demand the printing of the manuscript.' Landerer acceded to what he would tell the Austrian authorities later was 'a threat on my life' and ordered the presses to begin. Five typesetters worked non-stop and thousands of leaflets were distributed throughout large of parts central Pest by noon.

By 3 p.m., amid grey skies and steady drizzle, an estimated 20,000 people had turned up outside the recently opened National Museum building to hear Petőfi speak about the 'Revolution that is at hand – now, everywhere throughout Europe' that would bring an end to the feudal order and the 'rule of kings'. He read out the Twelve Points again and, taking the cue from Bastille Day 1789, announced the formation

---

* The Pilvax was opened in 1838, soon after the flood waters receded, as the Café Renaissance by a businessman called Ferenc Privorsky; Károlyi Pilvax was the well-liked bartender. Three years later the Austrian-born Pilvax bought the owner out and changed the name. The original Pilvax coffee house was pulled down in 1911, but there's a restaurant at roughly the original location (Pilvax köz) which keeps some archive pictures recalling the original nineteenth-century atmosphere.

of a Committee of Public Safety and a National Guard to 'protect the people'. As the population of Pest was no more than 85,000 at the time, this was an immense crowd, big enough to scare the Austrian authorities – although not everyone realized how significant the day would be. The director of the museum, Ágoston Kubinyi, a noted historian, wrote in his diary that evening: 'Some noisy mob had their hurly-burly outside which disturbed me in my work so I went home.'[4]

Thousands more joined the demonstration as the throng of people slowly crossed over the river via the pontoon – Széchenyi's bridge was only three-quarters completed – to Buda Castle, where they presented the 'demands' to the office of the governor general, who acted for the emperor. Petőfi described the scene. The leaders of the demonstrators 'stammered in all humility and trembled like a pupil before the teacher . . . Their magnificences the members of the Honourable council of the governor general were quite pale and deigned to tremble also . . . and upon holding council for five minutes agreed to everything.'

A crowd of teachers, journalists and lawyers at another café (Csiga, the Snail), in Sebestyén ter in the Inner City, heard the news just before 6 p.m. They rushed to the fortress adjoining the castle at Buda, overpowered the few guards on duty and demanded them 'to free all the political prisoners you are holding in there'. There was only one, as most had been released several years earlier; but he was Mihály Táncsics, an old romantic revolutionary, a weaver who had been locked up in the dungeon of Buda for writing subversive propaganda. They carried him around town on their shoulders. Petőfi wrote that night in his journal: 'Today Hungarian liberty was born, because today the shackles are broken from the press.'[5]

There had been no bloodshed at any point on the 'Glorious Fifteenth' but an intoxicating excitement of revolution, of melting into a crowd. The young lawyer Alajos Degré described the thrilling day: 'Now I too belonged to the tribe, without knowing what it planned or where it would go. I instinctively trusted my friends and blindly followed them – and would have followed them had they run straight into the jaws of death.'

For the two days the revolutionaries held Buda and Pest, as Jókai said, 'anything seemed possible'. Petőfi paraded through the streets of Pest wearing a long black cape, often accompanied by his radiant wife Júlia, who had cut her hair short in imitation of George Sand and proudly wore Hungarian national colours. The Pilvax Café was rechristened Revolutionary Hall. But soon the serious, experienced politicians took over and the radicals were shunted aside, having served their purpose.

On 17 March the court in Vienna – terrified of the likes of Petőfi, who they believed would inspire a peasants' revolt that could topple the Habsburg dynasty – did a deal with what one of Emperor Ferdinand's senior advisers called 'the more realistic opposition, the reasonable ones'. The Hungarians were allowed to form a government that would handle domestic matters, including finance and the military, but a new constitution would ensure that Hungary remained part of 'a common state'. There would be immediate elections, although on a limited franchise allowing only the nobility and a circumscribed number of wealthy townspeople to vote – around 11 per cent of the male population of Buda and Pest.

Count Lajos Batthyány, forty-one, one of the wealthiest landowners in the country, was made Prime Minister. For generations his family had been good Catholics and Habsburg loyalists, welcome at the Hofburg Palace in Vienna. Though he was a reformer and campaigner for Hungarian autonomy, he was no wild extremist or opponent of the Empire. His aim was never total independence from Austria. Reluctantly, Széchenyi accepted a position as Minister for Public Works and Transport, but he was deeply depressed at the prospect of a collision with the Habsburgs and wrote in his diary on the day the government was formed that 'the disintegration of Hungary is coming . . . and I have just signed my death sentence, heads will be on the block'. But the most powerful figure by far, the man who more than anyone else defined the Springtime of Nations throughout Europe in the tumultuous year of revolutions, was the new Finance Minister: Lajos Kossuth.[6]

Few political leaders have aroused such entirely contradictory verdicts as Kossuth, or so many conflicting passions. Queen Victoria wrote to one of her daughters, 'the fact is . . . that he is an ambitions and rapacious humbug'. Abraham Lincoln described him as 'a most worthy and distinguished representative of the cause of civil and religious liberty on the continent of Europe'. The poet Swinburne called him the 'Star of the unsetting sun' and several other poets – Walter Savage Landor,

Matthew Arnold and Heinrich Heine – wrote of him as a great romantic hero in the cause of freedom. But Petőfi thought he was a 'charlatan ... a schemer, a damned comedian', and the Hungarian novelist Zsigmond Kemény described him as a 'passion-driven fanatic ... who plunged his country into catastrophe'. Friedrich Engels was lyrical in his praise: 'For the first time in a very long while there is a truly revolutionary personality, a man who dares to take up the gauntlet of the desperate fight for his people – a Danton and a Carnot combined.' But Karl Marx was more dubious and thought Kossuth was too cynical an opportunist: 'It is permissible in politics to ally oneself with the devil in order to reach a certain goal – but one has to be certain that the devil is the one who is deceived, and not the other way around.' Széchenyi loathed him and thought Kossuth was 'the most dangerous man in Hungary'. Their bitter rivalry was one of the most interesting subplots in the drama of Hungary in 1848–9 – a personal story that illustrates broader points about the tension underlying so many revolutionary events throughout history. Széchenyi, who wanted to avoid bloodshed, believed in the art of the possible and urged evolutionary change unlike Kossuth, the idealist who refused compromise in the pursuit of doctrinal purity, even if the result was hopeless war and defeat.

In 1848 Kossuth was aged forty-six, around six feet tall, stocky, with a pale complexion and brown haired. Since early adulthood he had sported a long bushy beard that was his trademark physical feature. He possessed a mellifluous voice and over time became a mesmerizing speaker who by turns could be booming and gently lilting depending on where he appeared and in front of whom. All accounts of him attest to his charisma and presence, his charm and integrity, his phenomenal energy, his sharp intelligence and intellect; it was his judgement that was questioned, his occasionally arrogant manner, his colossal vanity and jealous rages.

The Russian reformer and exile from the tsars, Alexander Herzen, became a friend and wrote of him:

Kossuth is far better-looking than all his portraits and busts; in his youth he must have been a handsome fellow and the romantically pensive character on his face must have made him fearfully attractive to women ... Not only a powerful intellect but a deeply sensitive heart could be discerned through his gentle, melancholy expression; his musing smile and the somewhat enthusiastic manner of speech put the finishing touches to his charm. He speaks extremely well, but with a distinct accent, which is equally persistent in his French, German and his English. He does not try to carry things off with fine phrases, nor rely on commonplaces. He thinks with you, listens and develops his thoughts almost always originally, because he is much freer than others from pedantry . . . Perhaps a legal training can be detected in his manner of advancing arguments and objections but what he says is earnest and well thought out.[7]

Kossuth came from a landless family of the 'sandalled nobility' in the mostly Slovak-inhabited town of Monok in the Zemplén area of north-eastern Hungary. Habsburg loyalists in the nineteenth century, in an effort to smear him, suggested that he was ethnically a Slovak and felt Hungarian 'with the fervour of a renegade'. In fact he was able to trace his Magyar ancestry back to 1263, in the time of King Béla IV, when an ancestor was awarded a small land grant. The family name was ancient* but there was little money, even though his father was a lawyer employed as an adviser to the estate – or rather one of the estates – owned by the Andrássy family. Nevertheless Kossuth received an excellent education, at both Catholic and Lutheran schools. He qualified as a lawyer and worked in a series of local government posts – including in 1831–2 as a 'cholera commissioner' overseeing relief to victims of an epidemic that killed thousands of people in northern Hungary, Bohemia and Galicia but fortunately left Buda and Pest relatively unscathed.

He was active in local politics and had a practice as a moderately successful lawyer, known for high-flown oratory. But he was almost unknown nationally until the start of 1833 when he launched his *Országgyűlési Tudósítások* (Parliamentary Reports), which contained verbatim bi-weekly accounts of the debates in the Hungarian Diet and the Austrian Chamber, originally to a tiny circulation of subscribers and friends. Reporting on Diet meetings at this point was illegal, as was sending any 'published material' through the mail uncensored. Within a few months there were more than 150 subscribers, including one copy

* The word *kosut* means a billy-goat in Slovak.

for every Austrian government department, which was the most assid-
uous subscriber. At the end of the year he bought a lithographic press
to produce the reports, which is when the government stepped in. The
Master of the Horse, who was responsible for keeping order in the Diet,
confiscated the press and threatened him with arrest – though in a typically Austrian touch the authorities compensated Kossuth generously
for the financial loss of the equipment. Overnight he became a serious
political figure, a leading light in the liberal opposition as a campaigner
for press freedom.[8]

The following year Kossuth moved to Pest and started a new journal,
Törvényhatósági Tudósítások (Municipal Reports), a bi-weekly account
of the local governments in all the sixty-three counties of Hungary,
again financed by subscription. This too landed him in trouble with the
government, which from 1836 had begun a much more orchestrated reactionary campaign against any opposition, tightening censorship and
arresting 'radical elements stirring up the mob', as Metternich called
Hungarian liberal reformers.

Late at night on 5 May 1837 a violent storm raged in the hills above
Buda, 'as though the Gods were giving a warning something dramatic
would happen', according to Kossuth's account. Austrian soldiers and
a few Hungarian gendarmes surrounded an inn outside a remote village
called, appropriately enough, God's Eye. The Habsburg secret police,
which would later become known as the *Evidenzbureau*, had been told
by informants that the 'dangerously subversive journalist' Kossuth
would be staying for a few days working on his newspaper. He was arrested and charged with planning a rebellion and high treason.

A storm of protest followed, including from Count Széchenyi, whose
feud with Kossuth was already the gossip of Pest. Under Hungarian law
a nobleman could not be detained on remand but was allowed to stay at
liberty until trial. But the Habsburgs weren't interested in legal niceties
at this point. Kossuth was held in the castle dungeons in Buda. When
the case finally got to court he defended himself cleverly and became
an instant hero, a victim of Habsburg despotism. He was sentenced to
three years in jail, which a higher court increased to five years. In fact
he was released early on 10 May 1840 and given a pardon after serving
eighteen months.

At first he was kept in solitary confinement in the military barracks in Buda, but later conditions eased. His only visitor was his mother, but he was allowed to write and receive letters and read any books he wanted. He was treated with a mixture of brutality and relaxed leniency. Towards the end of his sentence he was even allowed a subscription to a newspaper, the *Augsburger Allgemeine Zeitung* – at the government's expense. It was in prison that he perfected his English to such an extent that he translated a large part of *Macbeth* into Hungarian before his release. Later he amazed audiences in Britain and the US with his fluency in English, which he learned from reading the Authorised Version of the Bible and Shakespeare in his cell.[9]

Soon after his release the printer Landerer set up Kossuth with his own newspaper, which became a highly effective mouthpiece and propaganda tool.* The twice-weekly *Pesti Hírlap* (Pest Journal) became an enormous success politically and financially for Kossuth and commercially for Landerer. Kossuth became a first-rate journalist and newspaper editor. He started with a pompous, overblown style, but he soon learned to be pithy and populist. The print run rose from sixty to 4,000 within three months and 5,200 within a year. Readership was reliably estimated at around 100,000 in a country where the voter roll was 136,000 (out of a population of 11 million) and there were fewer than a million literate people. In a reversal of policy that was now designed to appease moderate opposition, censorship was loosened. Only seven out of 200 editorials written by Kossuth were banned – the press under the Habsburgs in the 1840s was much freer than it would be in Hungary under the regimes of the far Right between the world wars or the Soviet-style Communist regime after 1948. Kossuth introduced the idea of placing the tub-thumping editorials (most of them written by him) on the front page – a practice often adopted later in France, Britain and the US.

---

* It turned out much later that Landerer was, off and on, a police informer and his offer came with the knowledge – and perhaps at the behest – of Metternich himself, who may have reasoned that the dissident lawyer, not a wealthy man and with a wife and three children to support, would keep clear of politics if he had a well-paid job he was scared of losing. It was also hoped that the radicalism of the new organ would be limited by Landerer as the printer/publisher. The Austrians got the wrong man, or two of them, if that is what they thought.

He campaigned for some progressive causes, like abolishing serfdom, an extension of religious freedoms, taking away the tax exemption privileges of the nobility and radical health reforms. But on the central issue which eventually led to the defeat of the Revolution and the War of Independence he was anything but liberal – either in a modern sense or as defined in 1848. Though he saw Hungarian nationalism as a glorious and romantic thing, he never understood the aspirations of other ethnic groups in a multinational country like Hungary. Kossuth filled his paper with ultra-nationalist demands that 'the nationalities' give up their demands for greater autonomy and that Hungarian must become the official language in the whole of the country, despite the fact that in much of Hungary the Magyars were a small minority. In eastern and southern Transylvania, for example, three-quarters of the population were Romanian, and in Croatia only around 30 per cent were Hungarian.

This was one of the main disagreements between Kossuth and Széchenyi, who consistently argued against a confrontation with peoples who far outnumbered the Magyars, even in Hungary. 'It is poor tactics if we, the lesser weight, ceaselessly collide with the boundlessly greater weight,' he wrote:

Do not force the Magyar language by flame and sword . . . otherwise you cannot prevent your destruction by flame and sword. Speaking a language is by no means a sentiment, the sounding of a tongue is by no means the beating of a heart . . . Do not do to others which you would not accept wholeheartedly for yourselves . . . This is the main reason why Hungarian patriotism is less respected on the stage of the world, why the purest Magyar civil virtue cannot excite sympathy and cannot form a favourable opinion outside Hungary . . . We must use moderation, caution and patience.'

This was entirely different from Kossuth. 'On the one hand we should demand the acceptance of our nationality, and on the other let us give the benefits of our constitution . . . All non-Magyar elements should be welded together with us by the flame which is ignited and kept alive by the Hungarian constitution,' he said in his first editorial as editor of *Pesti Hírlap*. The palatine, Archduke Joseph, told the Hungarian Diet in July

1843: 'When every fraction of the Hungarian people lays claim to a separate individuality, the general welfare of the country is threatened. I belong to those who think that every Hungarian, whatever his language may be, while he enjoys the rights, the privileges and the benefits of the Hungarian constitution, should consider himself a Magyar.' Kossuth thundered: 'I shall never recognize, under the Holy Crown of Hungary, more than one nationality and one nation, the Magyar.'

Kossuth wanted economic independence from Austria – trade barriers and tariffs and protection for Hungarian businesses. This was a bitter bone of contention with the Viennese court. Metternich in early 1844 ordered Landerer, as owner of *Pesti Hírlap,* to fire the editor-in-chief immediately. The publisher followed instructions. Kossuth at first thought the row with his proprietor was over the share of profits of the newspaper, but he soon realized that he was barred from access to the press anywhere within the Habsburg Empire.

In May 1844 Kossuth had a dramatic two-and-a-half-hour meeting with the Austrian Chancellor in Vienna. Metternich tried to buy off Kossuth. He would allow him his job back, or access to contribute elsewhere for other newspapers, as long as he moderated his attacks on the government and changed his vitriolic tone. The Hungarian refused. Kossuth wrote in a letter to Wesselényi, the hero of the Pest flood, a few days after the meeting that Metternich 'was a diplomat in the truest sense of the word, who does not believe in the honesty of a man's character, because he has probably not met ten honest men in his life. I hope that he has at least learned from me that not every Hungarian can be bought.'[10]

Following the meeting, Metternich told Széchenyi that the Austrians had made four mistakes in dealing with Kossuth: they arrested him – and then let him go; then they gave him a newspaper to run, and took it away from him. What, he asked, should the government do with him now? 'Use him or hang him,' replied Széchenyi. They did neither, but let him grow more popular. Széchenyi's reputation, meanwhile, diminished almost by inverse ratio. 'The count once praised to the skies for awakening the nation lost his popularity, while Kossuth, the first to have succeeded in moving the masses by emotion, carried the day and was propelled towards the role of national leader,' one of Széchenyi's earliest biographers in the 1860s, who knew both the count and Kossuth, noted.

The Austrians allowed Kossuth to run for the Diet in November 1847, which turned out to be the fifth mistake in dealing with him. He campaigned for the constituency of central Pest, which usually cost a lot of money for a candidate – it was the most expensive place in which to run for a seat. But Kossuth had plenty of rich backers, including Count Batthyány. Now increasing numbers could see and hear Kossuth and he shone more brilliantly the larger the crowd. It was no surprise when he won a thumping victory by 2,948 votes to his conservative opponent's 1,314.*

The worst fears of the Austrians were immediately realised. The chief of police of Pest County wrote to Vienna: 'Kossuth is an agitator and not a peaceful and quiet character as had been recommended by His Gracious Majesty when the Diet was convened. He is the kind of man who will cause more trouble on his own than all the rest of the Diet combined.'

One of his first speeches suggested as much. It was dubbed later as 'the inaugural address of the Hungarian Revolution'. On 3 March 1848 he declared: 'a pestilential air wafts out of the leaden chambers of the Viennese system, which depresses and poisons everything, paralyses our nerves and drags down our soaring spirit ... The dynasty must choose between its own welfare and the preservation of a rotten system.' Twelve days later the Hungarian Revolution had begun.[11]

---

* Only a small minority of those entitled to vote cast their ballot. Pest County, comprising the town and a 125-square-kilometre surrounding area, had 600,000 inhabitants, with 14,000 nobles allowed to vote.

14

THE REVOLUTIONARY WAR

The road of the new culture leads from humanity, through nationality, to bestiality.

Franz Grillparzer (1791–1872)

Kossuth is all things to all men . . . shouting Vive La République in
Marseilles and God Save the Queen in Manchester.

Friedrich Engels to Karl Marx, 1851

Over the next fifteen months of revolution and war, control of Buda and
Pest would change hands three times and the mood would veer from
triumph to disaster – and then to grudging acceptance of defeat. For the
first few weeks after 15 March there was euphoria in the twin towns. The
names of landmarks were changed overnight on both sides of the river.
Buda renamed streets in honour of Kossuth and Batthyány. In Pest signs
were quickly put up on 15 March Square, Freedom Square, Free Press
Street. In the first week of April Emperor Ferdinand officially approved
the deal struck with the Hungarians on the first day of the Revolution –
the April Laws. By then rebels had taken over Prague and burned parts
of the city, Austrian troops were desperately fighting in Lombardy
and the Veneto to hold on to Habsburg domains in northern Italy, and
the Balkans were in turmoil. Further riots had erupted in Vienna and
the court fled to Innsbruck, the original home centuries earlier of the
Habsburgs. The monarchy was in retreat and the dissolution of the
Empire seemed possible, if not probable. But in Buda and Pest it looked
like most of the demands of the less radical of the revolutionaries had
been met. Hungary would regain the kind of independence it had not
seen since the Ottoman invasion. The monarch would be a Habsburg,
but Hungary would essentially be autonomous. Kossuth was a national
hero – and would remain so into the twenty-first century.

The new government started work with extraordinary energy. Batthyány was nominally at the helm, from an office near the Royal Castle in Buda, but all the drive came from Kossuth. A long list of reforms first proposed in his former newspaper *Pesti Hírlap* came into law within a few days: serfdom, at last, would be abolished; a new currency, the forint, would be created, an independent army formed, and a commission was created to look at the financial consequences of ending the tax exemption of the nobles. But when the government announced that the new laws which gave equality to all religions meant unprecedented emancipation to Jews it encountered enormous opposition throughout the country. This would be the first time Jews were granted the same economic and voting rights as all other Hungarians, subject to similar property-owing qualifications. Opposition soon turned into a violent pogrom. On the day the terms of the proposed new legislation were announced in Pozsony/Pressburg, where the Diet sat, a dozen Jews were killed and more than fifty wounded in a riot aimed at throwing Jews out of the city. In Pest and Buda local artisans and traders tried to force Jewish businesses out of the marketplace; their shops were ransacked and their houses burned.[1]

On 19 April a group of angry youths attacked Jews on Király (King) Street, one of the principal thoroughfares into the main Jewish district of Pest. Soon they were joined by a large mob that ran wild through the Jewish quarter of the town. The crowd pushed aside the few National Guardsmen patrolling the area, beat Jews in the streets, and destroyed Jewish shops and houses. Julian Chownitz, a journalist for one of the revolutionary papers, the influential *Marczius Tizenötödike* (March Fifteenth), was on the scene: 'The crowd advanced in a rage from one place to another, at every moment assaulting solitary pedestrians . . . if someone had Jewish features . . . they shouted "Here's one! Smash his head."￼It was hours before the streets were again under control.' Prime Minister Batthyány appeared before the crowd to call for calm, more soldiers were despatched to the streets and order was restored, but it was instructive that this had happened once the moment of 'freedom' from controls was permitted.

The poet Vörösmarty was appalled and declared: 'the sacred name of equality has never been a more monstrous lie than now.' Albert Pálffy, editor of *Marczius Tizenötödike*, said the riots 'defiled this decent and outstanding city . . . were it possible this day should be erased from our history.'

Kossuth reacted to the pogroms with the cynicism and weasel words of a seasoned politician. 'Prejudice exists and against its reality even the gods fight in vain,' he said. He abandoned the proposed legislation in the face of the mob. 'To legislate now concerning the Jews would be throwing masses of these race-victims to the fury of their enemies.' The invariably decent and liberal-minded Széchenyi reacted similarly: 'The English and French can afford to liberate . . . the Jews because a bottle of ink will not spoil the taste of a great lake, yet it would certainly spoil a plate of Hungarian soup.'*

On the whole, as most Hungarians knew, Jews in the 1848 Revolution and the War of Independence that followed enthusiastically supported the nationalist cause, and Kossuth; they identified themselves with the uprising. They thought it was part of Magyarization and assimilation. Many played an active part, including bankers and financiers who backed it with money; large numbers of ordinary Jews fought and died in the war. Around 8,500 Jews joined the *Honvédség* – national army – when it was set up, proportionately a far higher number to Jews in the population. The novelist Mór Jókai, who was at the Café Pilax at the start of the Revolution, was ashamed at the way some of his own friends behaved to Jews. 'No nationality was more loyal to us than the Jews, and none did we treat more unfairly,' he wrote soon after the revolutionary war ended.[2]

The opponents of Kossuth and his idea of Hungarian freedom were not Jews but the Slavs who lived in Greater Hungary as – in their eyes – second-class citizens. Hungarians thought their own national-ism was a fine and romantic thing, part of the struggle for freedom and

---

* A few months later the head of the National Guard ordered the hanging of a Jewish peddler suspected of spying. There was no obvious reason; he had nothing on him besides a few needles, threads and thimbles. What sealed his fate was the discovery by the police of the *tefillin* around his neck, a small black box which many male Jews carry containing a few verses from the Torah. The box was assumed to hold military secrets destined for Hungary's enemies – a clear sign that the suspect was a traitor. True, no military plans were found in the box, but the prosecutor reasoned that they had either contained such plans in the past or would in the future. The peddler was duly executed.

independence which their poets wrote about so majestically. Many Romanians, Croats, Serbs, Ruthenes and Slovaks saw nothing romantic about living under Hungarian domination. Some saw the Revolution in Buda and Pest as an opportunity to put pressure on Hungary to grant more autonomy for the other ethnic groups in Hungary, or at least recognition of their nationhood. But the first Cabinet of the revolutionary Hungarians showed that they had little sympathy with the aspirations for independence of any others; nationalism was good for them, not for the Slavs. There was bound to be a clash.

On 14 April a delegation of Romanians from Transylvania, who formed more than two-thirds of the population there, was told by Kossuth not to expect anything 'beyond the freedom we Magyars ourselves have won for you'. A few days later Đorđe Stratimirović, the leader of the Serbs in Vojvodina, a southern province in Hungary, told the Hungarian Cabinet that if the new government in Buda would not look sympathetically at the Serbs' aspirations for autonomy, they would have to look for help from Vienna. Kossuth replied icily, 'in that case the sword must decide between us'. Kossuth dismissed the Slovak agitation for independence as a pan-Slavic plot, had the three most senior leaders of the nationalist movement jailed and appointed Magyar commissioners to administer the northern counties of Hungary in which Slovak representatives would have no say. Mihály Táncsics, who had been released from a Habsburg prison by revolutionaries on 15 March to a hero's welcome throughout Pest, described Kossuth's actions as 'just the kind of thing the Austrians would have done'. In the leadership, only Széchenyi saw where this might lead and warned that there had to be some form of accommodation with the nationalities who formed such a large majority of Hungary's population. He was ignored. In his diary he foresaw 'blood, and blood everywhere. Brother will be slaughtered by brother, one race by another . . .' This was the beginning of the series of breakdowns that would see him in hospital. Ill he may have been, but this was hardly a deranged insight.[3]

In Croatia a leader emerged who could articulate the national aspirations of Slavs as powerfully as could Kossuth for Hungarians. Josip Jelačić, the Bán, saw a way to play off the Hungarians against the Austrian emperor, to whom ultimately he was a loyal subject. He loathed Hungarian nationalism and Kossuth especially, even before the Hungarian leader had told him, insultingly, that he 'couldn't find Croatia on the map'. Kossuth badly underestimated Jelačič, a skilful politician and a talented general who had been effective on the Imperial General Staff. The Austrians encouraged him and, in a badly kept secret everyone in the twin towns knew about, helped the Croats raise an army to invade Hungary.

Emperor Ferdinand and his advisers had never accepted the deal they always regarded as forced on them under duress in the first days after 15 March. They were biding their time in the hope that the revolutionary fervour throughout Europe would ebb away or the Slav nationalities would make Hungary ungovernable by the likes of Kossuth. Despite signing the April Laws, the Austrians believed that Hungary was still bound inseparably to the Habsburg Empire as part of a 'common state'. The new Hungarian government interpreted the agreement differently: they thought Hungarians owed their allegiance to the King of Hungary, who happened to be the Habsburg Emperor of Austria. They acted as an independent state and, to the fury of the Viennese court, refused Austrian requests for money and troops to help fight the debilitating and expensive war in Italy that Vienna believed was so critical to the integrity of the Empire.

When the government in Buda set up the *Honvédség*, and to pay for it Kossuth established a Hungarian currency, the dispute with Austria deepened. The court claimed the Hungarians had gone too far. 'The existence of a Kingdom of Hungary separate from the Austrian Empire must be described as politically impossible,' the palatine, Archduke Stephen, said in August 1848. A month later an envoy was sent to Buda with orders to rein in Hungary and to negotiate a new deal with Kossuth. An Imperial general, Ferenc Lamberg, who in the past had shown some sympathy with Hungarian autonomy, was despatched. He arrived in Pest on 28 September. When he left his rooms that evening for informal talks and supper with Hungarian ministers a mob recognized him, forced him from his carriage and lynched him. His corpse was hacked to pieces with scythes. The conflict with Austria looked to be careering out of control and would soon turn into open warfare.[4]

A separate war had already begun on 11 September when 50,000 soldiers led by General Jelačič crossed the Dráva River in southern Hungary and marched towards Pest. They flew the Habsburg black and yellow insignia as the Croat general had sworn a renewed loyalty pledge to the emperor. This was a strange war in the often complex history of the Austrian Empire: Habsburg generals were fighting against Habsburg generals. As the Hungarian Count Majláth noted when it began: 'The King of Hungary had declared war on the King of Croatia while the Emperor of Austria remained neutral, and these three monarchs were one and the same person.'

The Croat invasion prompted a political crisis in Buda. There was a split within the government. One group – not including Kossuth – offered Jelačič independence for Croatia if he withdrew his forces. It was far too late for that; the Croat general refused and his army continued to march. Batthyány's government fell apart and Kossuth formed a Committee of National Defence, with him as governor and regent. Kossuth now had virtually dictatorial powers. In Vienna a month later a palace coup toppled Emperor Ferdinand V, technically on grounds of ill health but essentially because his weakness in the eyes of many court officials and the army had led to the real prospect of the collapse of the Habsburg Empire. The military replaced him with his nephew, the eighteen-year-old Franz Jozsef, and surrounded the inexperienced young ruler with tough advisers who would be determined to bring Hungary back to the status of occupied colony. The new Prime Minister was the arch-reactionary Prince Felix of Schwarzenberg, described by Széchenyi some years earlier after a dinner with him in Vienna as 'a cold-blooded vampire'.

The Hungarians refused to recognize Franz Jozsef as King of Hungary because he had not been crowned with the historic Crown of St Stephen and did not feel bound by the coronation oath of his royal predecessors. This was the pretext for the break with Austria and the War of Independence. The Austrians invaded Hungary in full force in December and initially the *Honvédség* had some success. But the Austrians regrouped. Kossuth and the revolutionary government retreated to Debrecen, 300 kilometres east of Buda and Pest. In early January 1849, without firing a shot, the Austrian army occupied the twin towns and imposed martial law.

The newspaper editor Károlyi Glembay, who soon after the Revolution had written a passionate piece that called on Hungarians to 'fight for the welfare and security of their beloved homeland with swords rather than pens', now wrote a column welcoming the return of the Habsburg dynasty. The Austrian military governor, Field Marshal Prince Alfred Windisch-Grätz, closed down most of the other newspapers, proclaimed a curfew and issued an edict warning Jews that he would hold them collectively responsible and fine them 20,000 crowns (a huge sum worth more than £15 million sterling at 2021 values) if any of them were found spying for the revolutionaries or sending them supplies. With great ceremony, Austrian troops disinterred and reburied General Lamberg, Vienna's royal commissioner who had been murdered by the Pest mob in September.[5]

The Hungarians looked defeated and few outside observers would have given them any chance against the combined Austrian and Croat forces. But Kossuth had performed miracles in recruiting an army from scratch. This had posed problems at first because many of the key officers didn't speak a word of Hungarian. Many were professional soldiers from abroad who had volunteered for the Hungarian cause. The officer corps of the *Honvédség* was around 25 per cent foreign – 15 per cent German and 5 per cent Polish. Despite the language difficulties, it soon melded into a highly effective fighting unit.*

In March 1849 Kossuth placed the Hungarian army under the command of a talented general, Artúr Görgey, who won a series of impressive battles and routed the Austrian forces in western and eastern Hungary. Along with his deputy, the highly regarded Polish General József Bem, the Austrians, against all the odds, were put to flight, at least temporarily. Görgey took the twin towns after a costly campaign. About 1,000 died on each side and at least 2,000 civilians in the siege. No defences had been built at Buda since the Habsburgs captured it in the 1680s; the castle couldn't be defended as a fortress – the gates were so rusty they could barely be lowered. General Heinrich Hentzi commanded 4,000

---

* One of the most popular officers was an English captain, Richard Guyon, who had fought in a Hungarian hussar regiment (in the Habsburg army). He had a Hungarian wife and became a Magyar patriot. Another well-known commander was General Count Karl Leiningen-Westerburg, a member of the Hessian ruling house, related to the Coburgs and cousins of the English royal family. He later became a Hungarian citizen.

Austrian troops against a much larger Hungarian army. But Görgey lacked heavy artillery to break down the Buda walls. The final assault on 21 May was bloody. Hentzi and seventy of his officers were killed, along with scores of enlisted men. Just before they left, as a last desperate measure the Austrians tried to blow up the almost completed Chain Bridge. Lieutenant-Colonel Alois Allnoch threw a burning cigar butt at a barrel of gunpowder near the Buda side of the bridgehead and ran. The explosion killed him, but the bridge was unharmed.*

The days following the fall of Buda were filled with a victory parade, a massive celebration in the centre of Pest and a burial procession for the fallen Hungarian dead in which an Austrian officer was thrown into a ditch and died. Kossuth re-entered Pest on 5 June 1849 in a gilded carriage, greeted by a huge crowd. One of his first acts was officially to create 'Budapest' for the first time from Buda, Pest and Óbuda. The decree announcing the decision was written by Kossuth personally. 'The Hungarian state can have only one capital, in which Pest chiefly provides the living strength and Buda chiefly provides the ancient historic memory. The splendour, strength, power and greatness of the national capital is dependent on its unity, of which our country, attacked in an unjust war, now stands in most particular need.'[6]

By then it was too late for Kossuth's dream of independence to live in the real world. The end was obvious once the Austrians begged for help from the Russians, who with great brutality had just suppressed a nationalist rebellion of their own in Poland. They saw a way of gaining extra influence in the Balkans among Slavs if they were seen to be enemies of Hungarian nationalism – and they wanted to show their power over 'small nations'. Franz Jozsef needed Russia's help, but Tsar Nicholas I made the new Austrian emperor, still a teenager, publicly make the appeal in a grovelling letter – published in the *Wiener Zeitung* – for armed assistance in 'the struggle against anarchy'. For added humiliation, Franz Jozsef was instructed to rush to Warsaw to genuflect and kiss the hand of the Tsar of all the Russias. The Austrian emperor

---

* The real hero was Adam Clark, the engineer who supervised construction of the bridge. When he realized the Austrians were about to be defeated and would very likely try to blow up the bridge, he thwarted their plans by having the chain lockers flooded, which would have minimized the damage.

recorded the occasion in a letter to his mother, Princess Sophie. 'He received me exceptionally graciously and cordially,' he wrote. 'At four o'clock I dined with him *tete á tete*. We travelled very fast and the Russian railways are especially outstanding for their good organization and smooth ride . . . Altogether, everything is so pleasantly orderly and calm here.'

The tsar's viceroy in Poland, Prince Ivan Paskevich, led a Russian army of around 190,000 troops to stamp out the rebellion. On 3 July Kossuth and his ministers fled south to Szeged, but after a final defeat in a battle outside Temesvár most of the 'rebel' Hungarian government escaped abroad. Kossuth fled, disguised as the servant of a Polish nobleman. He had shaved off his trademark beard, dyed his hair a lighter shade of brown and decamped to Turkey carrying two passports – one Hungarian in the name of Tamás Udvardi, and one English as a James Bloomfield. Petőfi had enlisted in the *Honvédség* soon after it was formed. He was almost immediately promoted to major under the Polish General Bem, but was killed in one of the last battles of the war, at Segesvár, by the time the Hungarians had to all intents and purposes already lost. His body was never recovered but his comrades in arms confirmed that they witnessed his death. He was barely twenty-six years old and became the stuff of legend. He is the national poet not just because of his skill as a writer, but for the high romance of his life and his early death on the battlefield. Even Byron didn't quite manage that, as the critic Pál Ignotus remarked: 'His picture is found on the walls of restaurants and cafés like that of Kossuth (whom he loathed). He is claimed as a figurehead by the extreme Right and Left. It is largely due to him that Hungarians thereafter could hardly conceive of a social Reform Movement, let alone a revolution or war for independence, not inspired by a poet.'

His last poem, written just a few days before he died, resonates in Hungary still:

> Amid the storm the Magyar stands alone.
> And I would join this nation, I declare it,
> If I were not Magyar from my birth.
> For they are friendless, and the most deserted
> Of all the peoples of this encircling earth.

*

As the Austrians acknowledged, they could not have prevailed without foreign help – and the only foreigners willing to come to their aid were the Russians. Captain Ramming von Riedkirchen, an aide-de-camp to the Chief of Austria's Imperial General Staff and of the Emperor Franz Jozsef, put it simply:

> The question is often raised whether the Austrian state, without Russian aid, would have been able to defeat the Hungarian uprising ... In order to attain a decisive military superiority, which would also be assured in all aspects of foreign relations, the Russian intervention was indispensable ... The mighty and imposing aid of the Russian army would inevitably lead to success, and result in the establishment of peace in Austria and the whole of Europe, even if Austria's performance was less energetic and successful.

The Austrians kept inadequate records and the Hungarians almost none. But the best evidence suggests that about 50,000 Hungarians died in the War of Independence and around the same number of Austrians. The Russian expeditionary forces lost only 543 killed in battle and 1,670 wounded.[7]

The Hungarians were isolated. When the Austrians returned to Buda soon after Kossuth decamped, Bertalan Szemere, the last Prime Minister of revolutionary Hungary, made a desperate plea to the people and leaders of Europe: 'The freedom of Europe will be decided on Hungarian soil. With it, world freedom loses a great country, with the nation a loyal hero.'

But nobody lifted a finger to help Hungary – a refrain that has echoed in history since the Mongol and Turkish invasions, and would again when the Hungarians revolted against their Soviet masters a century later. Worse, there was plenty of hypocrisy among European leaders. Lord Palmerston, Britain's Foreign Secretary, believed it was important for the balance of power that the Habsburg monarchy stay intact. 'The independence and liberties of Europe are bound up ... with the maintenance and integrity of Austria as a great European power,' he told the House of Commons on 21 July 1849. 'Therefore anything which ... tends to cripple or weaken Austria must be a great calamity to Europe.'

But popular sentiment in England was on the side of the plucky Hungarians. Publicly, in Parliament and outside, Palmerston often sounded sympathetic to their cause and often repeatedly said that he was deeply disturbed by Russian intervention in Central Europe. Privately he told the Russian ambassador in London that Britain would not interfere and that the tsar's army should get its job done quickly.

The surrender was eventually made by General Görgey. He had been hailed as a hero a few weeks earlier, but has since forever been labelled a coward and traitor – especially by Kossuth, who had made his getaway safely to neutral territory, and needed a convenient scapegoat for defeat and for his own errors of tactics and judgement. Many generations of Hungarian schoolchildren were taught that Görgey betrayed the Revolution. But he always claimed that the Hungarians had already been defeated by the time he surrendered, that it was futile to continue the fight, and he was trying to minimize bloodshed.

The failure of the Hungarian Revolution was the end of the Springtime of Nations that so many liberals had yearned for. In France the Revolution had burned itself out by the summer of the previous year; in the Balkans, too, and in most of Central Europe, after just a few months. Heine declared that with the defeat of Hungarian independence, 'thus fell the last bastion of freedom'. Prince Paskevich reported to his emperor at the end of July 1849: 'Hungary lies at the feet of Your Majesty.'[8]

15

A REVENGE TRAGEDY

No more hope . . . No more hope.

Mihály Vörösmarty (1800–55)

I am the man who will restore order. I shall have hundreds shot, with a clear conscience.

Baron Ludwig von Haynau (1786–1853)

Tsar Nicholas I – at least in public – urged the teenage Austrian emperor to show magnanimity to the defeated 'rebels'. But Franz Jozsef, or his chief adviser, Prince Schwarzenberg, was in no mood for leniency. The savagery of Habsburg retribution against Hungary shocked Europe.

At dawn on 6 October 1849 Lajos Batthyány, the first Prime Minister of revolutionary Hungary, was dragged to the courtyard of the main military barracks in Pest. He had been held prisoner since the end of July and was sentenced to hang for treason by a court martial – even though it was established at his trial that he had argued against Hungary declaring independence precisely on the grounds that it could be seen as treasonous. He was too weak to stand or walk so he had to be carried from his cell to the place of execution; three days earlier he had tried to cut his throat with a knife smuggled into the jail by his wife. It was seen as a dishonour for a nobleman to die by hanging, therefore he had done what he could to avoid the shame. The prison infirmary had saved his life so that he was fit enough to be killed. In what was described as an act of leniency, the court changed its sentence to death by firing squad.

He was shot sitting on a chair. He refused to have his eyes covered by a blindfold – and he himself gave the order for the execution squad to fire. Like a true Hungarian aristocrat, he spoke in words from three languages *'Allez Jäger, eljén a Haza'* (Long Live the Fatherland). His

159

body lay in public at the scene of the execution for a day and a half – in what is now Szabadság tér (Liberty Square) in the heart of Budapest opposite the US Embassy, almost exactly on the spot where a more than life-size, awkward-looking statue of President Ronald Reagan has stood since the 1990s. On the same morning in Arad, Transylvania, now part of Romania, twelve *Honvédség* generals and a colonel were hanged. The date is one of the most important public holidays in Hungary.[*][1]

General Baron Ludwig von Haynau was despatched to Budapest by the emperor and Schwarzenberg to teach 'the Hungarians a lesson they will never forget'. He took up the challenge with alacrity. 'I am the man who will restore order. I shall have hundreds shot, with a clear conscience,' he told the General Staff in Vienna. The illegitimate son of Elector Wilhelm I of Hesse-Kassel, he was more widely known as the 'Butcher of Brescia' for the atrocities he had carried out in Lombardy, including the public flogging of women and girls he had accused of sedition, and the execution of a priest who was dragged from the altar of his church by soldiers directly to the gallows. His immediate commander, Field Marshal Jozsef Radetzky, told the emperor: 'He is my best general, but he is like a razor that should be put back in its case after use.'

Von Haynau launched a reign of terror for the thirteen months he remained in Buda-Pest, where he was given virtual plenipotentiary powers. Around 130 other prominent revolutionaries were hanged or shot, many of them in public in the graceful garden of the National Museum. Originally his orders had stated that no executions should be carried out without approval by Vienna, but the emperor gave in to his urging that this would appear a sign of weakness and gave von Haynau the authority to do as he wished. Kossuth and a dozen others who had fled into exile with him were hanged *in absentia*, their names pinned to gallows built in the Castle district of Buda.

Courts martial laid down 1,765 jail sentences of longer than fifteen years and more than 2,400 prison sentences in all. Five hundred former Habsburg army officers were jailed, including twenty-four Imperial generals. Around 45,000 officers and rank-and-file soldiers of the

* After the Second World War the Soviets tried to ban it as a holiday because of its anti-Russian connotations, but the local Communists, usually subservient, protested that it would be counterproductive and lead to loathing of the USSR.

Honvédség were conscripted into Austrian regiments of the Imperial army.

Martial law lasted for two years and there were bans on all public meetings, on wearing the Hungarian national colours of red, white and green – and even for wearing long beards in the cut and style of Kossuth's. Censorship reached absurd levels and continued for many years: a decade later a production of Verdi's *Ballo in Maschera* was banned, unless it was reworked to make its central character, the assassinated King Gustavus III of Sweden, remain alive at the end. Stiff sentences were handed out to even the most minor 'law breakers'. The country was closed off; foreigners were kept out. Even in 1854 only five British visas were issued for entry to Hungary, one of them to the Andrássy family's governess, who was kept waiting in Vienna for several weeks while the Austrian government decided whether to grant permission for her to travel further. A range of high new taxes were imposed. Jews were forced to pay an extra 'indemnity' because of their support for the Revolution and for independence. Schools were purged of 'unreliable' teachers, newspapers were closed down or their editors replaced. The emperor declared that the silver plate looted from the *Honvédség* General Ernő Kiss's mansion by von Haynau was legitimate war plunder. 'Schwarzenberg and Haynau achieved a rare thing,' said one of the Hungarian revolutionaries who had managed to avoid jail or exile. 'They united French, English, German and even Russian popular feelings of revulsion against them.'[2]

Among the Austrians' first decisions was to rescind the amalgamation of Budapest as a single city; it would not be unified again for nearly a quarter of a century. The Chain Bridge, however – it could not be called the Széchenyi Bridge until much later – was finished soon after the war's end and was opened in November 1849. To the outrage of many people in both Buda and Pest, the first to 'officially' cross, amid much ceremony, was a squad of Austrian troops.

The Café Pilvax was renamed Café Herrengasse. German street signs were restored, shop fronts were written in German lettering again. Official state buildings were draped in Habsburg black and yellow once more. When the linguistics professor Pál Hunfalvy returned home near the end of the year he wrote in his diary: 'Pest is no longer ours. Pest is henceforth our grave.' Aabbi Löw, the wife of one of Pest's most famous rabbis, Lipót Löw, wrote to a friend: 'Pest, which I had seen so happy before, where a warm welcome had always awaited me, now seemed so ugly.'

The writer Emilia Kánya described the devastation of Pest following the siege: 'Oh Lord! What has become of our beautiful town? The banks of the Danube have become almost unrecognizable. The large Redoute Hall [now the Budapest Vigadó Concert Hall] is blasted to ruin, its columns lay scattered on the ground, its windows stare out blackly like the hollows of a giant's blinded eyes.' An American visitor to Pest in 1851, Charles Loring Brace, saw 'a cannon ball that still sat in a woman's parlour and a clergyman's shelled library . . . it will be long before Pest recovers from that fearful punishment.' Parts of Buda, which had seen so much of the fighting, were in worse shape: the Royal Castle was wrecked and had to be almost entirely rebuilt.

Von Haynau was called back to Vienna in the autumn of 1850, coolly thanked for his service to the state by the emperor and pensioned off. Extraordinarily, soon after he retired he bought a country estate in western Hungary. He never understood why his neighbours didn't invite him for dinner and wrote to friends at court in Vienna to complain about the rude and ungrateful Hungarians.[3]

Kossuth lived for a further forty-six years – half his lifetime – in exile after his escape. He became more famous throughout the world as an itinerant speaker and 'celebrity' than he ever was during his brief period in power in Hungary. On the day of his 'execution' in effigy in Pest a vast crowd turned up in Marseilles, where the American navy ship *Missouri*, taking him to refuge from Constantinople to England, was due to arrive. But the port authorities, bowing to pressure from the French government, refused permission for the 'dangerous visitor' to dock. A bootmaker called Jean-Baptiste Jonquil jumped in the water, swam out to the frigate outside the harbour, climbed on deck and, shivering from cold, threw himself at Kossuth's feet declaring: 'Now that I have set eyes on the saviour of humankind, I am ready to die.' In fact, he lived for many more years too.

Kossuth went on to England, where his ship was allowed to land. In a month-long tour during October 1851 he addressed huge crowds in London, Manchester and Birmingham to wild acclaim. 'He spoke in poetic English embellished with long quotations from Shakespeare,' as one witness recalled. He raised enormous amounts of money to help other refugees from Hungary and to buy arms for attempts to 'liberate my homeland', but nothing came of that. He met the leading political figures throughout Western Europe – Palmerston, Napoleon III, Cavour, even Bismarck – but could get no serious backing from any of them.*[4]

From Britain he went on a triumphant seven-month coast-to-coast tour of the US, where huge crowds would gather for hours before he was due to speak. Banners in his honour compared him to Jesus Christ, Moses and George Washington. In Washington DC he appeared at a rare event, speaking to the combined houses of Congress – an honour previously given to no other foreigner except Lafayette. There is still a bust of him under the domed ceiling of the Capitol, and a town in Wisconsin is named after him. His reputation among liberals in the North fell in the US, though, after he refused to be drawn when asked about slavery: many of his most important financial backers in America were from the South and he needed their money. As Marx noted on Kossuth's various speaking tours, 'Kossuth is all things to all men . . . shouting Vive La République in Marseilles and God Save the Queen in Manchester.'

Others have been even harsher as they looked back at his legacy for Hungary and elsewhere in Europe from considerably later on. Golo Mann, the historian son of novelist Thomas Mann, was no admirer: 'This rousing, far too self-admiring revolutionary . . . was the craziest nationalist who had emerged until then. He offered the non-Magyar people the choice between total subjugation without any political existence, or eradication.' The British historian Edward Crankshaw saw in Kossuth a prototype, 'a new kind of demagogue, without scruples . . . [who] awakened the pride and arrogance, the subterranean romanticism of Magyar nationalism. As Hitler wanted to be a German, as Mussolini wanted to be a Roman, so Kossuth wanted to be a Magyar.'

Széchenyi, by contrast – described by Kossuth, despite their differences, as 'the greatest Hungarian' – exiled himself to a mental institution

---

* By contrast, when von Haynau visited England in 1851 he was, according to *The Times*, 'set upon by the draymen of Barclay and Perkins Brewery, pelted with dung and chased down Borough High Street'.

in Döbling, on the outskirts of Vienna, where he lived his last sad years. His periodic depressions became continually worse, but his diaries show that he had long periods of sharp clarity. He shot himself in April 1860.*

Lajos Kossuth, for all his faults and failures, had an energizing effect on so many who came into contact with him, and Hungarians of all classes and political attitudes revere him. Almost every small village in Hungary has a street named after him or a monument. In Budapest, Kossuth Square, by the Parliament building, is where the most important national events and political dramas have been enacted for more than a century. In the Soviet years the Communists tried to appropriate his memory as a heroic campaigner for economic reforms, against serfdom and dynastic imperialism. For others he has stood unwaveringly for Hungarian independence and freedom – a figure of whom the nationalist Right claims ownership. Schoolchildren are still taught a song about him, which is often sung on national occasions:

> Lajos Kossuth – golden lamb,
> Golden Letters on his back.
> Whoever can read them
> Can become his son.
> Lajos Kossuth is a writer
> Who needs no lamplight.
> He can write his letter
> In the soft glow of sunlight.[5]

---

* Suicide rates in Hungary – and especially in Budapest – have traditionally been exceptionally high for a developed country, and many other well-known figures throughout history have died by their own hand. According to the last figures in 2012, Hungary has the sixth-highest suicide rate in the world – for men, 49.2 per 100,000 deaths, compared with 19.3. in the US and 11.2 in the UK; for women Hungary has the second-highest, at 15.6 per 100,000 deaths compared to 4.4 in the US and 3.3 in the UK. In most of the Communist years it had the second-highest rate, but the numbers were high in the Horthy years too and they are high in the 2020s. There is a vast amount of suicide literature in Hungary trying to explain the reason for this – by psychologists, historians, poets and novelists. Arthur Koestler wasn't referring specifically to suicide, but this is a plausible explanation: 'To be a Hungarian is a collective neurosis.' In Budapest, a favoured spot for suicide was for many years Liberty Bridge, a three-part steel structure which, until the authorities made access more difficult in 2003, was easy to climb.

16

JUDAPEST

Budapest – built by Jews, for the rest of us.

Endre Ady (1877–1919)

By the mid nineteenth century the Goldberger print-dyeing factory in Óbuda was home to one of the largest textile firms in Hungary. It was opened in 1784 by Ferenc Goldberg, in one small wooden building, at the height of the then fashionable trend of indigo printing on linen. But the company soon expanded to work on all kinds of fabric – cotton, calico, silk – opened three new buildings in stone along Óbuda's High Road and was employing around 125 people. The proprietor added an extra syllable to his name in 1800 and the company became Goldberger and Sons. His (only) son, Samuel, grew the business further and by 1848 it was one of the principal employers on the Buda side of the Danube.

The Goldbergers were proud Jews and proud Hungarians. In the 1848 Revolution they were enthusiastic supporters of Kossuth and of Magyar independence. The company was awarded a lucrative contract to supply the uniforms for the revolutionary army, the *Honvédség*. After Hungarian defeat in the war, Austrian reprisals hit Goldberger and Sons hard: it was one of the Jewish-owned firms that the vindictive von Haynau fined heavily for the 'crime' of backing the rebels and he requisitioned the factory's entire stock of materials and dye. But the Goldbergers weathered the storm, kept out of politics and prospered under the peace.

Many Jews had feared that losing the war would be especially hard on them, and that they would be blamed by both sides. But in fact, despite the early repression immediately after the war, the opposite happened. Soon after martial law in Buda-Pest ended at the start of 1852 the

165

Habsburgs, supported by the Magyar nobility, began a policy of welcoming increased Jewish immigration to Hungary and particularly to the twin towns. Families poured in from Galicia, what is now the Baltic States and from Russia's Pale of Settlement. They thought – rightly as it turned out – that Jews would be the engine of much-needed economic growth which would make Hungarians more content with their lot as an Austrian province. The Jewish population of Hungary had increased from just 250 families in the 1760s to around 120,000 people at the turn of the century, 170,000 in 1848 and 430,000 in 1860. About a half of them lived in Pest. The Hungarian nationalists welcomed Jews for a different, and in some ways contradictory, reason. Most of the Jews learned Hungarian quickly on arrival, or wanted to, and identified as Magyars, which the Slovaks, Romanians, Croats and Serbs had shown they were reluctant to do.[1]

The Habsburg emperor found a way of advertising his new alliance with Hungary's Jewry – and Jewish-run businesses were more than happy to be advertised. On 7 May 1857 Franz Jozsef, on one of his first visits to Hungary, toured the Goldberger factory with a radiant Empress Elisabeth at his side and made a long speech emphasizing that 'in my eyes all subjects are equal regardless of their religion'. The company was then being run by Samuel Goldberger's widow, Erzsébet Adler, and she spared no expense for the visit, designed to emphasize the company's patriotism and the relationship between Jewish-led industry and the monarchy. The walls of the two-storey factory were entirely covered in red, white and blue bunting and yellow and black fabric (the Habsburg colours).* A huge festive tent was erected where the Goldbergers greeted the royal family. An enormous papier-mâché two-headed Habsburg eagle was the centrepiece. Freshly planted evergreens surrounded the tent and, as the major daily newspaper *Pester Lloyd* reported, 'the pavement was richly covered with carpets and the workers were all dressed in blue uniforms. Standing in front of the workers the owner and the family welcomed the most graciously receptive Majesty.' Not long after the visit the next Goldberger to own the factory, Bertold, was ennobled

---

* The building was still standing in 2022 as a fascinating museum of the Budapest textile trade in general and the Goldbergers' business in particular – including its travails under the Nazis and during the years of Communist nationalization.

by the emperor and the family took the more Hungarian-sounding name Budvay-Goldberger.[2]

One of the earliest Hungarian Jewish jokes – a genre of humour that became famous in Central Europe – appeared in a guidebook to Buda-Pest in the 1860s written by an Austrian visitor to the twin towns, Franz Xavier Kempf. It was later told by gentiles as routinely as by Jews and became highly popular as the nineteenth century went on and the Jewish population of Hungary increased. A local from Pest is show-ing a visitor around town: 'Here, on Calvin Square, is the Calvinists' Church . . . over there, by the Danube, the Greek Orthodox Church . . . The crumbling one over there belongs to the Lutherans and the Basilica over there is the Catholic Cathedral.' The tourist chimes in: 'And the big one there with the twin towers?' 'Oh that . . . is the synagogue of the people of Pest.'

For the four years from 1855 while it was being built, the Great Synagogue on Dohány Street, on the edge of the Inner City, intrigued visitors and local inhabitants as they watched the progress of the work. It was so unlike anything seen in either Buda or Pest and, for the time, on a grander, more monumental scale. Only the National Museum, completed the year before the Revolution, remotely matched its size, but that was neoclassical in the West European tradition.* The huge synagogue was part Moorish with its two minarets, part Byzantine with a graceful dome and part Catholic with its basilica. Even before it was half finished it was dubbed 'the Israelite Cathedral'. It was designed inside and out by two non-Jews from Vienna – the exterior by Lajos

---

* It remains the biggest synagogue in Europe and can seat nearly 3,000 worshippers. The word *dohány* means tobacco in Hungarian and the synagogue is often called the *Tabakgasse shul*. There were three big synagogues in Pest by the 1860s. The main temple built for the traditionalists was in Rumbach Sebestyén Street (no relation to this author), designed by the well-known Viennese architect Otto Wagner. It was once, by all accounts, a fabulous building, also part Moorish and Byzantine, and from early photos it had a beautiful interior. It survived the Second World War largely intact, but post-war neglect in the Communist era led to the collapse of the roof in the 1970s. There were attempts to renovate it but they were incomplete in 2022. For a while in the early 2000s it was one of the most successful of Budapest's 'ruin pubs' – mostly temporary bars formed out of derelict buildings – but hasn't been used for worship for decades.

Förster and the extraordinary, hauntingly beautiful interior by Frigyes Feszl. Soon after it was completed Kempf's guide gushed, with just a hint of ahistoric hyperbole, that it 'surpassed even Solomon's Temple in Jerusalem'.

Its consecration on the morning of 6 September 1859 was a huge event that drew high-ranking officials of all faiths, including the Catholic Prince Primate, Cardinal János Scitovszky, the Protestant bishops and the emperor's representative from the Vienna court. A sprinkling of archdukes and archduchesses made an appearance. The mutually beneficial relationship between Hungarian Jewry and the Habsburgs was reinforced when the ceremony closed with a specially composed blessing for Franz Jozsef and the ruling dynasty. But the real highlight of the various opening celebrations attracted an altogether more popular celebrity than the loathed emperor or his stuffy courtiers. A few days after the consecration service Ferenc Liszt gave a concert and played 'unforgettably ... majestically', according to one witness, on the 5,000-pipe synagogue organ. A fortnight later, the French composer Camille Saint-Saëns played on the same instrument to huge applause.[3]

The following year the congregation reinforced its relationship with Hungarian patriots at a Festival of Jewish-Magyar Brotherhood that brought Jews and Christians together in a nationalist celebration. They sang 'Szózat' (Vörösmarty's Call)* and collected money to build a statue of Petőfi. Attempts at assimilation for Hungarian Jews have always involved walking a tightrope – and often the balance has proved impossible to maintain.

---

* A rousing national poem that is often sung at major public events – rather like 'Jerusalem' in England, or 'The Stars and Stripes Forever' in the US. It opens with the lines:

> Oh Magyar keep immovably
> Your native country's trust.
> For it has born you and at death
> Will consecrate your dust.
> No other spot in all the world
> Can touch your heart or home –
> Let fortune bless or fortune curse
> From hence you shall not roam

The synagogue was Neolog in persuasion, a uniquely Hungarian denomination that's a mixture between Orthodox and Reformed, but rather more like the latter. Neologs were on the whole less strictly observant of the Sabbath and of the kosher dietary stipulations.* As so few of Pest's Jews by this time regularly used Yiddish – or understood it – two years after the Great Synagogue opened the congregation elected a Magyar-speaking board headed by the reforming rabbi Dr Ignác Hirschler, a brilliant and imaginative scholar. By then most rabbis in the capital preached in Hungarian, not German or Yiddish – one of the causes of a schism in the mid 1860s among the twin towns' Jewish community into progressive and more conservative camps. Confusingly, there was a sizeable group, too, that rejected both sides and referred to themselves as the 'status quo antes', but over time the overwhelming majority in the city became Neolog and were keen to assimilate. There were very few Hassidic Jews in Pest, or ultra-Orthodox practitioners, though in provincial Hungary, especially in the east of the country, there were several Orthodox communities.

A raft of progressive legislation gave Jews civil rights they had never before possessed in Hungary – or virtually anywhere else in Middle Europe. In 1867 a royal rescript (decree) stated: 'It is hereby proclaimed that the Israelite inhabitants of the country are entitled to exercise all civil and political rights equally with the Christian inhabitants.' All discriminatory laws were repealed. Jews were allowed to marry Christians and to receive converts.

Franz Jozsef was eager to show his support; a few years later, on a visit to Budapest, he toured the Rabbinical Seminary in Budapest soon after it opened.

The novelist György Konrád, who later would hide in a Budapest basement to avoid deportation to Auschwitz and faced years of harassment as a dissident under Communism, wrote movingly of Hungarian Jews' longing for assimilation:

---

* The interior of the Great Synagogue is substantially different from a traditional Orthodox temple. For example, the *bimah* faces east rather than the centre of the building, where it traditionally would be, and looks similar to a raised pulpit in a Christian church.

The Jews living in Hungary became Magyars by preference. They adopted the language and made themselves at home in it. They wrote poetry, philosophized, chatted, traded, gave treatment, acted, sang, joked, made love, quarrelled, prayed in Hungarian, and all this came naturally to them quite quickly. Others celebrated an invasion, we the exodus. There were places . . . which the Jews were rather reluctant to leave. Hungarian Jews . . . clung tooth and nail to a Hungary of a motley national composition with a stubbornness beyond reason and an attachment bordering on the sensuous.

In 1863 a Pest rabbi, Sámuel Fisher, put it more prosaically but just as persuasively: 'The Israelites have suffered everywhere on the globe, but have only flourished in our homeland: Hungary. To recognize this is our duty, only in this way will we become Magyar-Israelites.'[4]

Though many modern guidebooks refer to Erzsébetváros (Elisabeth-town), just east of the Inner City, as the 'Jewish district', in fact there were many scattered areas around both Buda and Pest, where large Jewish communities thrived. The market still held in present-day Deák Square, close to the Great Synagogue, was dubbed in the mid nineteenth century *Judenmarkt*, but there was another big trading area for Jews in the northernmost suburb of Pest, District XIII, Újlipót-város. There was still a strong Jewish community in Buda, where for many centuries it was the only area in the vicinity Jews had been permitted to settle, and a small number in Óbuda, where for long periods some Jews were allowed to live, under the protection of the Zichy family.

The hub of Jewish life in the mid to late nineteenth century, though, was in the area around Király Street. Unlike elsewhere in Central Europe, very few of the signboards for the multifarious shops and traders were in Yiddish. Király Street was a bustling place with people 'buying, selling, bargaining, gossiping', one trader there for three decades from 1852 enthused. The poet József Kiss, in his 1874 book *The Secrets of Budapest*, called the area 'the nest of the proletariat and the Jews . . . Here the dirt of the Orient, the cacophony of Constantinople, Jewish resourcefulness and Hungarian laziness are blended into such a wonderful mishmash at which the Western tourist, seeing it for the first time, could hardly be more amazed.'

An entire block in Pest, designed by the well-known Pest architect Andreas Mayerhofer, was for generations almost a separate town within the town, mostly for Jewish traders – a kind of metropolitan *shtetl*, known as the Orczy House. Originally it was built in the 1780s by Count József Orczy, an enlightened nobleman, who saw a way of helping poor Jews settle in Pest, and also see a profit for himself. Soon it became a bustling centre of Jewish life. Orczy was happy to rent apartments and commercial space to Jews, who at the time found it hard to find accommodation or establish places for trade.*

It was a huge complex – a mixture of a giant mall and housing estate – with one side along Király Street. On one corner there was an ancient inn called the English King (hence the street name). It comprised forty-eight apartments, some of them on the first floor luxurious, and others higher up in the third and top (fourth) storey more modest for the poorer traders, many of whom worked in the nearby market. It included two small synagogues, one for the reformers, another for traditionalists, a Jewish school, a *mikveh* for ritual bathing, three kosher restaurants and various shops on the street fronts, and numerous inner courtyards. The building was often referred to as *Judenhof* (Jewish court) or alternately, because of its bazaar-like atmosphere, the Jewish caravansary. 'Orczy House offers everything . . . an Israelite may need all his life and under all circumstances, be that the Pascall flour or a savings bank, a pocket watch, a meal cooked according to Jewish law, a bookshop, or a kosher butcher,' wrote the popular art critic for the Viennese press, Lajos Hevesi. 'Orczy House is home to many people, and it is rare to see anyone moving out . . . The entire residence of the house has something patriarchal about it and I dare say one must give not half a year's notice but a quarter of a century's – grandfather gives notice when the grandson is to move

---

* The Orczy House was one of the biggest buildings in the city until 1936, when it was demolished and replaced by various hideous buildings in the fascist 'monumentalist' style, like something out of Mussolini's Rome. It provided a good income to the Orczys of Buda and Pest for generations (though not to one distant relative, the novelist Baroness Emma Orczy, author of *The Scarlet Pimpernel*, whose branch of the family left Hungary in the 1870s and ended up in London in 1880).

out. Thus this peculiar house confers on its residents a certain pride – it's a community within a community.'[5]

Nowhere in Middle Europe did Jews play such a prominent part in modernization as in Hungary – in industry, commerce, banking, the professions. Partly this was because Hungary was more feudal: the landowning magnates and petty nobility ran the country, but scorned being 'in trade'. This left a space greater than anywhere else for Jews to become the middle class, the professionals and the engineers of economic growth.

For rising Jewish capitalists the ban on owning land was, paradoxically, an advantage. Because their capital was not tied down and entailed in arcane Hungarian traditions about property ownership, they could look for investment elsewhere – and they did. At first the main trade was in agricultural products. The profits from grain, tobacco or coffee enabled them to lend to new enterprises and then launch their own financial business. This was the start of the Hungarian Commercial Bank of Pest, the first merchant bank in Hungary, founded in 1841 by Mór Woriadner and Móric Ullmann. The original capital came mostly from the tobacco trade, but they became the first Hungarian financial oligarchs. Ullmann was responsible for raising the money for the construction of the first railway line in Hungary in 1837. Heavy industry grew from its loans and commercial enterprise – directed by Leó Lánczy (a name Magyarized from Lazarsfeld). It changed the banking business itself. It was the first bank in Hungary to introduce savings accounts.[6]

The alliance seemed to work well for all sides: the Hungarian nationalists found an increasingly powerful counterweight against the majority of Slavs and Germans in Greater Hungary. Jews spoke Magyar and on national holidays the new synagogues were richly decorated with Hungarian national flags. The Habsburgs found a loyal group dependent on their patronage who would bring forward an economic boom. On their side, the Jews – at least the more educated and more ambitious among them – had every reason to subscribe to this unwritten contract with the political elite, and did so with enthusiasm. The outcome was an economic revolution in the latter part of the century and a rapid process of integration. The most successful gained fabulous wealth, and what seemed in such a caste- and class-conscious place as Hungary the ultimate reward: titles. Franz Jozsef ennobled 338 Jewish families during his reign, half of them to the highest baronial rank.*

But it all depended on extreme delicacy and minimal introspection if it was not to unravel. The poet and journalist Endre Ady – a liberal-minded non-believer – could see the tensions and sinister undercurrents in the new arrangement between Jews and gentiles in Hungary. In a famous essay he likened the relationship to a tribal dance among the native Aboriginals in Australia, the *Korrobori*. 'What cowardice it is to deny that for some decades we have been practising, dancing the *Korrobori* in the region of the Danube and Tisza rivers,' he wrote. 'Here two nationalities, equally foreign and devoid of pedigree, are making love to each other according to the rules of the dance. The Jews take their place here with their musical instruments copied from already established cultures. And we, who call ourselves Hungarians, are filled with a mixture of hatred and longing . . . Here, in our mutual love-strangle, we will either create a new nation – or after us the deluge.' Prophetic words.[7]

---

* There were some Orthodox Jews in manufacturing business, but few had large companies. Freudiggers, Hungary's biggest bed linen and underwear company, was based from the 1870s in a factory in Óbuda. It was difficult to stick to the Sabbath rules while operating factories on a Saturday. The Mayers, who owned one of the largest cotton mills in the country in Pest, found a novel, if comical, loophole. They 'sold' their factory on Friday afternoons to one of their Christian employees and bought it back again at dusk on Saturdays, to get round the rules. Arguably, they kept to the letter of the law, but hardly the spirit. They couldn't find an Orthodox rabbi in Pest to approve the trick, but they managed to locate a provincial rabbinate in eastern Hungary which agreed to it.

17

EMPRESS SISI

Empress Elisabeth ... She did not sit down, she lowered her body;
she did not stand up, she rose.

Kaiser Wilhelm I of Germany (1797–1888)

The crowd was already two deep along both sides of the Danube
embankment by 4.30 a.m. and huge numbers more were still stream-
ing in from the countryside as dawn broke. It was Saturday, 8 June
1867, coronation day, and the preparations had begun weeks earlier.
Police had rounded up the usual suspects and arrested any potential
troublemakers.

At 7 a.m. the procession set off from the castle the short distance to
the Matthias Church. Seven standard-bearers chosen from the high nobility, all on horseback, preceded the newly installed Hungarian Prime
Minister, Gyula Andrássy, who was carrying the Crown of St Stephen.
He was followed by the official bearers of the royal insignia resting on
red velvet pillows. Then came the emperor on a white stallion, dressed
in the uniform of a Hungarian general. But all eyes were on the queen-
empress, in a glass carriage drawn by eight white horses. She was dressed
in a gown made by Worth, the most famous couturier of the day, who
had adapted the Hungarian national dress into a skirt and train of white
and silver brocade embroidered in jewels, with the black velvet bodice
entirely laced in pearls. Press reports of her appearance were universally
purple in their gush, but the moderate German-language *Pester Lloyd*
was the most understated in tone: 'On her head was the diamond crown,
the glittering symbol of sovereignty, but the expression of humility in
her bowed bearing and the traces of the deepest emotion on her noble
features – thus she walked, or rather floated along, as if one of the paintings that adorn the sacred chambers had stepped out of its frame and

come to life. The appearance of the Queen here at the holy site produced a deep and lasting impression.'

At the hour-long service Franz Jozsef was anointed king by the Prince Primate of Hungary, János Simor – but the crown was placed upon his head by Andrássy, who until a few years before was a fugitive under a death sentence for fighting against the emperor in the War of Independence. According to ancient custom, the queen's crown was held over her right shoulder.

There were psalms and hymns, but the highlight was a coronation Mass by Liszt that had been commissioned by Cardinal Simor for the occasion – a piece 'bursting with nationalist fire', as one critic wrote afterwards. The composer had travelled specially from Rome for the performance, but was told when he arrived that he couldn't conduct the music because of 'protocol': the Vienna County Choir had to sing under the direction of an Austrian. Liszt was relaxed about the slight and his only comment on the event was to wax lyrical about the empress, writing to his daughter Cosima that 'Erzsébet is a celestial vision'.*[1]

No women formed part of the next scene in the theatrical production: a vast procession crossed the Danube along the suspension bridge from Buda to Pest, led by the emperor wearing the crown and a resplendent white cloak. All were on horseback, even several ageing bishops. Ludwig von Przibram, an eyewitness, reported:

What was offered here in the way of splendour or national costumes, in opulence of harness and saddles, in value of the gems and clasps, belts and pins, in antique weapons, swords studded with turquoise, rubies and pearls . . . corresponded more to the image of an Oriental display of magnificence than to the impoverishment and exhaustion of the country, Hungary. The overall impression was that of a feudal-aristocratic military review. One truly believed oneself transported to the Middle Ages at the sight of those national barons . . . laden

---

* Every report of the event describes at great length how radiant the empress looked on this day. She must have been a vision. Emperor Franz Jozsef was famously a man who seldom failed to master his emotions – if he had any. One court diarist recounted that when Franz Jozsef saw her just before the coach took them to the coronation Mass he was so enraptured by her appearance that, throwing off his usual reserve, he threw his arms around her and embraced her in front of all his attendants.

with splendour, followed in silent submission by the beweaponed vassals and men in their service . . . Most particularly the horsemen of the tribes, the Jazyges and Cumans, variously clad in hauberks and bearskins, their most striking adornment being animal heads and buffalo horns, recalling the times when Christian Europe was forced to defend itself against incursions from the pagan East. There was no trace of 'the people' in this pageant, of the bourgeois elements, of guilds or trades.

The opulence, or vulgarity, was breathtaking. Count László Batthyány had a massive ornate silver harness made specially for the occasion – his horse blanket alone weighed ten kilos. His brother Elemér commissioned the artist Karl Telepy to reconstruct his costume from medieval drawings. It comprised 18,000 links of chain mail, assembled painstakingly by hand over the previous three weeks. At a time of extreme poverty in Hungary – called in various parts of Europe 'the land of a million beggars' – Count Ödön Zichy wore his emerald jewellery, with some stones the size of hen's eggs.[2]

There were a few comic moments. Some of the older prelates had to be strapped on to their horses to prevent them from falling off: Countess de Jonghe, the wife of the Belgian envoy, observed: 'Now, when a horse became excited by the loud noise and commotion, or if a loose girth slipped . . . more than one of these riders anxiously threw his arms around his mount's neck, causing the towering headdress . . . to dangle from his nape, which contributed to the amusement of the public lining the route.' The pageantry of the event was spectacular and camouflaged some of the tawdriness beneath. 'The Hungarian costumes transform Vulcan into Adonis,' she wrote to a friend. 'But when I saw the handsome gentlemen in their everyday dress: boots, a sort of buttoned-up frock coat, an ugly little not so clean neckerchief, rarely a shirt, they seemed to me to present quite a spoiled appearance . . . In all that, there remained a remnant of barbarism.'

When the procession reached the platform on the Pest side of the river opposite the Chain Bridge, the emperor repeated the coronation oath: 'We shall uphold intact the rights, the constitution, the lawful independence and the territorial integrity of Hungary and her attendant lands.' Then he rode to the top of 'Coronation Mount', a mound of earth raised from soil gathered in every county in Hungary. According to ancient ritual devised by the Árpáds, he swung his sword to the four points of the compass as a sign that he would defend the nation against enemies from whichever direction they came. It was a swelteringly hot day and no easy task in the midday sun. Yet everyone could grasp the symbolism of the moment, after the centuries of subjugation, revolution, the War of Independence and the painful acceptance of defeat. This was the reconciliation, the time of compromise.

Some foreign observers were not altogether impressed, though. The Swiss envoy wrote back to his ministry: 'The pageantry . . . in spite of its splendour and genuine grandeur, nevertheless affected the detached observer somewhat like a carnival prank . . . This piece of the Middle Ages simply does not suit our times, neither our level of evolution, nor current political events.' The novelist Mór Jókai, erstwhile revolutionary and comrade of Petőfi, had mellowed with age and had turned into an Establishment figure, loyal to the monarchy – as had so many of his compatriots. He wrote of the day that 'such a splendid stageplay is to be seen only once in a lifetime, never to be forgotten'.

The people enjoyed the party that followed, through that night and the following day, though only one event, the Night Festival, was open to the general public, on the Vérmező. 'Oxen and mutton were roasted on the spit, or on veritable funeral pyres,' one reveller recalled. 'The wine flowed from butts, goulash simmered in giant vats . . . and was offered free.' Briefly Franz Jozsef made an appearance. 'The figure of the monarch, surrounded by a crowd of people, most of them in peasant dress and some on their knees, others with their arms raised high . . . and throughout the twittering fiddles of a gypsy band playing . . . the whole thing illuminated by the firelight of one of the pyres – truly a romantic sight.'[3]

The best-known woman in Hungarian history wasn't Hungarian at all. The longest section of the Grand Boulevard in Budapest, one of the city's prettiest squares, a bridge over the Danube and a charming statue on a promenade by the river are dedicated to the Empress Elisabeth, Erzsébet as she was called by most Hungarians, the beloved Sisi. She stands serenely above the city – literally. From the point atop János Hegy, the highest of the Buda Hills, there is a delightful white marble

Romanesque lookout tower bearing her name which offers a fabulous panorama of the city below. In Hungary, she is credited – even by the most hard-line Marxist historians of the Soviet era – with playing the vital role in bringing about a compromise with Austria which led to the establishment of the Dual Monarchy, often thought of as the high point of the Habsburg Empire. There were many geopolitical, economic, social and diplomatic reasons for the reconciliation between Austria and Hungary, the *Ausgleich*. As much of the Vienna court and Franz Jozsef could see, it made pragmatic sense to reach a deal with Hungary that would weld the country to the Empire. But certainly it would not have happened in the smooth and dignified way it did if Empress Elisabeth hadn't oiled the wheels. In this case, bedroom diplomacy really did play a part.

There is so much romantic gush and gossip mixed with mischief written about Sisi that it is difficult to separate fact from total fiction. Even a man as obtuse as Kaiser Wilhelm I of Germany could recognize her unique qualities and her extraordinary manner on entering a room. 'She did not sit down, she lowered her body; she did not stand up, she rose,' he told an official in Berlin. Her confidante, Marie Festetics, like so many close to her, was smitten: 'One never grows tired when one goes out with her. At her side it is delightful, and so it is behind her. Looking alone is enough. She is the embodiment of the idea of loveliness. At one time I will think that she is like a lily, then again like a swan, then I see a fairy – oh, no, a sprite . . . and finally, an empress! From the top of her head to the soles of her feet a royal woman . . . In everything excellent and noble. And then I remember all the gossip and I think there may be much envy in it. She is so enchantingly beautiful and charming.'[4]

But even Festetics could on occasions be more realistic and objective. Elisabeth had all the virtues, she wrote, but a wicked streak could in a trice transform each one into an opposite: 'Beauty! Loveliness! Grace! Elegance! Simplicity! Goodness! Magnanimity! Spirit! Wit! Humour! . . . And now the curse: for everything turns against you – even your beauty will bring you nothing but sorrow, and your high spirit will penetrate so deep – so deep that it will lead you astray.' There was endless meanness also within the Austrian court, which she encountered from the moment she arrived in Vienna aged just sixteen as Franz Jozsef's bride. 'She was a world away from being the ideal wife,' the emperor's valet put it succinctly. She loathed the strait-laced manners at the Hofburg and was at first terrified of her mother-in-law, Archduchess Sophie. But she was content to see all the legends being built up around her, within the court and the yellow press, even if so many of them were lies.

Having done her bit by providing a male heir, and daughters to be married off to the royal houses of Europe, she travelled, flitting between health spas, Corfu and England. There were visits in between to Monte Carlo, where she liked to play the tables, and long cruises in the Mediterranean – she sported an anchor tattoo on her shoulder to show her love for the sea. It is true that for most of her life she kept her waist measurement at 42 centimetres in diameter, but she was neither too thin for the corsets of the day nor did she suffer from an eating disorder as has been speculated. She had a healthy appetite – normally a large breakfast with wine, generally a meat dish for lunch, but a light supper. She chain-smoked, including in the state carriage.

She exercised vigorously, unusual for the time, but hardly unique or weird. She had a gym set up in the Hofburg – her high bar and balancing rings survive, and she was widely known to be a superb, near-obsessive horsewoman. In England she spent weeks of the Season riding with the Northamptonshire hunt, though the rumours that she had a long-running affair with a handsome Scottish huntsman, Bay Middleton, are way wide of the mark.

She had been educated in a haphazard fashion by her eccentric Wittelsbach parents, though the surprisingly interesting poetry she wrote in imitation of Heinrich Heine shows she had a sharp intelligence when she chose to use it. In contrast, Emperor Franz Jozsef may not have been entirely dim, but he was certainly unimaginative and a pompous bore – 'a stickler for etiquette, mainly because in its absence he did not know what was appropriate,' according to one courtier.

Most of his letters to Sisi survive, but just a few of hers to him. To Franz Jozsef she is 'my heavenly angel', 'sweet soul', 'darling', and he usually signs off 'the manikin' (*Männeken*). In his study he hung a portrait of Elisabeth in a loose robe with her hair cascading to her waist in which she had the faintest of smiles – looking more annoyed and petulant than seductive, which was perhaps the way he liked her.[5]

Her love of Hungary was genuine and came at first sight. But its principal attraction, which occasionally she let drop, lay in the fact that it wasn't Vienna or the fusty Habsburg court. The Hungarians in turn were willing – desperate – to be loved by the glamorous young empress. Franz Jozsef was hated for his suppression of the uprising, his alliance with the Russians and the brutal Austrian retribution against the revolutionaries, which was easing but still caused rancour. The mood 'was no longer rebellious, but one of sullen anger', as Jókai put it in March 1858 on the tenth anniversary of the Revolution. But the empress was different and intriguing; Hungarians gave her the benefit of the doubt from the start, particularly when word leaked out that she got on so badly with Archduchess Sophie, who was as loathed in Hungary as the emperor.

Sisi made a dramatic entrance when she first appeared in Buda on 4 May 1857, when she was nineteen. The emperor was riding a white horse wearing the red uniform of a Hungarian general; she was in a variation of Hungarian national dress – with a velvet bodice and wide lace sleeves, driven in a glass coach, accompanied by her two little girls. 'From the first moment they saw her even the bitterest memories of 1848 were dispelled,' one contemporary Hungarian diarist recorded. That night one of the wealthiest men in Budapest at the time, the banker Baron Georg von Sina, commissioned the Empire's most famous pyrotechnician to stage a firework display on a scale never seen in Budapest before and 'the Chain Bridge glittered with a thousand lights'.[*6]

Elisabeth's sympathies for Hungary may have had their roots in her opposition to the Viennese court and in her toxic relationship with her mother-in-law. But when she was allowed to meet them, she found she liked the easy charm of Hungarian men and the company of Hungarian women away from the formality of life in Vienna. The more she came to know about Hungary, the more her sympathies were aroused.

The Cult of Sisi was genuine – up to a point. But the affection for her in her lifetime, as the historian of Habsburg Hungary, András Gerő, put it, 'was enhanced by the fact that it provided public opinion with a reliable way that they could demonstrate their dislike for Emperor Franz Jozsef while maintaining the appearance of loyalty to the Habsburg dynasty . . . If Franz Jozsef had not been loathed so much in Hungary, Elisabeth would probably have received far less attention and affection.'[7]

---

* Which in the twenty-first century it does, resplendently, every night – but that was one of the first occasions the bridge was illuminated along its entire length.

*

Soon after she returned from Hungary after her first visit, out of the blue the empress decided she wanted to learn the Magyar language. It seemed an eccentric wish – particularly as she had previously been notoriously bad at learning other languages. She hardly knew any French, a requirement among cultivated royal circles in Europe, and had given up on learning Czech after a few elementary lessons which she said she had found altogether too difficult. Everyone knew that Hungarian was a much harder language to learn. Her first teacher was Count János Majláth, a Hungarian aristocrat who lived in Vienna and was a favourite at court, a devout Habsburg loyalist and the best friend of Maximilian, Emperor Franz Jozsef's brother (who was soon to come to a sticky end, executed by revolutionaries just three years after being imposed on Mexicans as their king). Majláth was a charming and interesting man who thought he was there for general conversation, but Sisi wanted something more systematic.

Franz Jozsef objected, but Sisi got her way and found a qualified teacher, a professor of linguistics and a priest, Father Homoky. But her progress in Hungarian had much more to do with the arrival into her inmost circle of a young Hungarian woman, Ida Ferenczy, in 1864. For the next thirty-four years – until Sisi's death – Ida was her closest confidante, knew all her secrets, was the go-between for most of her private correspondence and was 'indispensable not only as a servant but as a close friend', the empress said. Ida, two years younger than Sisi, came from a poor but well-connected gentry family with some contacts at court. Soon her close relationship with the empress predictably aroused the bitter hatred and jealousy of the courtiers in the Hofburg.[8]

The letters from Sisi to Ida that survive are much longer than any to her husband. They usually began 'My sweet Ida' and ended 'I think of you a thousand times a day'. Nobody has ever suggested any kind of romantic relationship between them, but Ferenczy had an enormous influence on the empress and was an essential part of her growing enthusiasm for all things Hungarian. Ferenczy's family had no money, but they did have some powerful friends, and she was close to the leaders of a new generation of liberal reformers and moderate Hungarian nationalists who sought a compromise with the Austrians – Gyula Andrássy and Ferenc Deák. The relationship was carefully cultivated by the two

Hungarians, and soon by another important player in the circle: the empress's next Hungarian 'tutor', the well-known journalist Max ('Miksa') Falk, who was living in Vienna as the correspondent for the Hungarian newspaper *Pesti Napló* (Pest Daily). When he heard about Falk's visits to his wife, the emperor was at first horrified. Not only was Falk a journalist, a liberal and a Jew, but he was also known to the police. In 1860 the Vienna constabulary searched his house and took away almost his entire correspondence in two flour sacks. Falk spent a few weeks in a Viennese jail for offences against the censorship laws and wrote several articles about the experience. He stayed out of trouble afterwards. The stuffier courtiers were dismayed. Countess Pauline von Königsegg complained that it was difficult fulfilling her position as Mistress of the Robes when the empress and everyone around her spoke Magyar all the time. Sisi was unsympathetic, and replied that whether the countess understood or not is 'a matter of complete indifference to me, but if she wished to remain in attendance it would be advisable to learn Hungarian as quickly as possible'. The empress's stock in Buda and Pest rose immeasurably when that story found its way into the newspapers. The emperor came round to Falk's presence, as he usually did after Sisi found a way of calming his grumpiness.

The Falk/Empress Elisabeth sessions were never really language lessons, rather seminars on Hungarian history, customs and literature. For homework he assigned translations of the classics from German into Hungarian. The meetings opened her eyes more broadly to Hungary. 'The lessons in the narrower sense of the term receded further and further into the background,' Falk said later. 'We began occasionally to discuss current events, then very gradually moved on to contemporary Hungarian affairs.'* Falk introduced her to the ideas of the reformers.

---

* Falk returned to Budapest in 1867, edited the German-language newspaper *Pesti Lloyd* and went into politics – he joined the Liberal Party founded by Ferenc Deák – and became one of the most influential men in Hungary until his death in 1908. His legacy offers a typically Hungarian example of how symbolic name changes of streets and removals or reinstatements of statues have always been at the forefront of politics – or (as it seems to me wrongly called) 'culture wars'. Soon after he died in 1908 a street in downtown Pest near the Parliament building was named after him. But at the height of the anti-Semitic times many streets named after Jews, or with any Jewish connections, were renamed, including his in 1943. At the end of the Second World War Falk was rehabilitated, or at least the street was given back its old name. But in 1953 it fell out of

This was the beginning of her entry into Hungarian politics – and her influence on the country that would last long after she was gone. As much as anyone, Austria-Hungary as an empire was the creation of Empress Elisabeth.[9]

favour again and it was renamed Street of the People's Army. Only after 1989 and the collapse of Communism did the street bear his name again. Curiously, there is a statue there, not of the great journalist and parliamentarian Miksa Falk, but of a very distant relation, the actor Peter Falk, who starred in the long-running TV detective series in the 1970s *Columbo*.

18

THE DUAL MONARCHY – VICTORY IN DEFEAT

Here in Hungary no one disturbs me, as if I were living in a village where I can come and go as I please.

Empress Elisabeth of Austria to her mother,
Princess Ludovika of Bavaria, 19 November 1868

The new generation of reformers in Buda and Pest had given up on any idea of formal independence from the Habsburgs. They aimed instead for more freedom over domestic affairs in Hungary, more influence within the Empire and less interference from Vienna. Von Haynau's brutal reprisals against revolutionary Hungary and Kossuth supporters were relaxed. In 1858 there was an amnesty for almost everyone jailed for political offences during the Revolution and the War of Independence.

Alexander von Bach, the Austrian Interior Minister for a decade from 1849, but essentially head of the Government, softened some of the censorship rules and abandoned the worst features of Austrian repression, even if careful monitoring of suspected 'subversives' by the *Evidenzbureau* remained. But colonial status still felt bitter. A moderate opposition was tolerated by the Austrians – led by figures such as Andrássy and Deák, who had played a minor part in the Kossuth government but later pledged loyalty to the monarchy. Deák developed a form of civil disobedience – or passive resistance, as he called it – that was within the law, just. It was described by Jókai in one of his novels: 'A raised tobacco tax was introduced . . . "right," said the count . . . "I'll give up smoking." Duty on wine? "Steward, get me beer." This is our attitude to the Austrians.'

Reaching an accommodation with the Hungarians was becoming more important for Vienna than it was for Buda and Pest. In time, a sullen, potentially disloyal population in Hungary mourning defeat could become a clear danger, especially by the 1860s, when the Habsburgs lost their provinces in Lombardy and the Veneto and a confrontation was looming with Prussia – the start of the process that had unified Italy and soon would do the same for Germany. The emperor was persuaded that Austria's place as a major European power was slipping, and a compromise deal with Hungary would help arrest the slide. The realists in the court – and Franz Jozsef himself – could see it made sense to begin discussing concessions to the Hungarians, as long as they could be made without losing face. But there was a strong group of reactionaries around the emperor, led by his mother, who still regarded the Hungarians, in particular the Hungarian nobility, as a nest of revolutionaries and traitors who could no longer, as before, be relied on to support the Habsburgs. The archduchess frequently railed against the Magyar aristocrats – 'rebels who through their excessive self-confidence and pride will never accept you as their ruler recognised as God's will', she told her son. But in the modern world, it was hard to hold the line on the idea of the divine right of monarchs. Left to his own devices Franz Jozsef might perhaps, over time, have come to terms with the Hungarian opposition. Equally, if it were not for the mediation of the queen-empress, all attempts at reconciliation could easily have broken down. It was her relationship with Andrássy that made the difference.[1]

Gyula Andrássy's forebears had been loyal, ultra-Catholic supporters of the Habsburg dynasty for centuries until his father, Károly, midway through his life, fell under the influence of the liberal-reform ideas and of Hungarian nationalism. Gyula, born in 1823, was a protégé of his father's great friend Széchenyi, but later joined the ranks of the more radical supporters of Kossuth, whose newspaper published his fiery pro-independence articles. He had fought in the War of Independence in 1849 against the Tsarist army at Schwechat, one of the Hungarians' most painful defeats. Then, as a colonel in the *Honvédség*, he was despatched to Constantinople to negotiate a deal with the Ottomans to prevent the sultan from returning to Austria a group of Hungarian exiles who had sought refuge with the Turks. After the surrender in the War of Independence, Andrássy was sentenced to death for high treason – his name was posted on the gallows by the hangman, next to Kossuth's.

By then, the twenty-six-year-old was in exile in Western Europe – 'an ebullient and robust grand seigneur', according to one of his French friends. His fame and romantic allure spread in the best salons. He was in popular demand in the society of London, his first place of refuge, and then in Paris, where women called him *le beau pendu* (the handsome hanged man).

He had plenty of money sent from his family in Hungary – his mother, Countess Etelka Szapáry, was fabulously rich in her own right. He had excellent connections among the aristocratic houses of Europe, charm, good looks and a fluent wit in four languages other than Hungarian. In England, as one of his friends there said jokingly, 'he could play with de-lightful elegance the homeless person on Derby Day'. In France he was an insider at the court of Napoleon III. It was in Paris that he met his wife, the Hungarian aristocrat and celebrated beauty Countess Katinka Kendeffy. It was a love match and they returned together to a huge man-sion in Pest in 1858 after an amnesty for most political prisoners. On his return he was a martyr of the Revolution and gained a leading position politically without having to work for it. He had his jealous detractors, but for the most part those who had struggled in Hungary during the bitter years after the failure of the War of Independence were glad they could attract to politics a man with such good connections in the West, with acumen, common sense and wit. 'The new Austria resembles a pyramid that has been stood on its head. No wonder, then, that it cannot stand up straight' was a *bon mot* that made even some of the stuffy die-hards in the Hofburg smile.[2]

He was a man of large, bold ideas, not good at grinding detail. 'Few men in public life deserve the epithet of "political sensualist" as much as Andrássy,' said one of his smarter followers. He was as vain as a prima donna, and assiduously cultivated the image of being irresistible: to his compatriots, who admired him, and especially to women, who chased after him.

But not everyone was taken in. Non-Hungarians – particularly Austrians – often saw him as a villain. Count Joseph Hübner, who had known him in Paris, recorded in his diary in 1866: 'Personally he is not unlikeable, he has a touch of the bohemian and the gentleman, the sportsman and gambler. He looks like a conspirator and yet at the same time like a man who says everything that is going through his mind. He is the boldest liar of his day and at the same time the most indiscreet of braggarts.'

Though they had been corresponding for a few months – all conducted in utmost secrecy through Ida Ferenczy as intermediary – Andrássy and the empress first met in March 1866; he was among a delegation from Pest despatched to invite the emperor and empress to visit Hungary. Officially Andrássy was there as vice chairman of the Hungarian Chamber of Deputies. Unofficially, he had been sent specifically to effect a meeting with Sisi. The first formal encounter was a piece of theatrical kitsch. The deputation to the Hofburg, preceded by Imperial court and chamber heralds, strode ceremonially through the anterooms and the ranks of the Royal Household Guards. In the last anteroom they were greeted by the empress's chamberlain, who led them into the audience room. Andrássy was wearing the gold-embroidered ceremonial dress of the Magyar aristocracy (known as the Attila) with a coat studded with precious stones, spurs on his boots and a tiger skin over his shoulders. In this ornate setting he still managed to stand out – 'by virtue of his casual, man-of-the-world appearance, his somewhat gypsy-like wild aura', according to one of the courtiers.

The empress presented herself as a fairy-tale princess, with her own take on a national Hungarian costume, a white silk dress, the black bodice trimmed with lace, diamonds and pearls. On her head she wore a Hungarian bonnet. She improvised a short speech that didn't say much – but it was in faultless Hungarian.

At the reception afterwards, it was noticed that she spoke to Andrássy for more than fifteen minutes, again in Hungarian. It was at this tête-à-tête, Andrássy said later, that she told him: 'You see, if the emperor's cause goes badly in Italy it pains me, but if it goes badly in Hungary it is death to me.'[3]

Later that month the emperor and empress went together for a five-week tour of Hungary. Normally she found official receptions in Vienna and elsewhere a burden, but in Buda and Pest she looked forward to every event and was a huge draw. The newspapers published special pull-out supplements covering her appearances, filled with gossip about her, some of it true. Sisi was an overwhelming success on that state visit wherever she appeared. Even the emperor noted it in a (for him) effusive letter to his mother: 'Sisi is of great help to me with her courtesy, her exquisite tact, and her good Hungarian, in which the people are less reluctant to hear some rebuke from lovely lips.'

Her affection for Andrássy was the subject of gossip in Viennese society. The most malicious of the rumour-mongers and one of Sisi's main enemies at court was Franz Jozsef's adjutant, General Count Franz Folliot de Crenneville, who wrote that at the Crown ball given by the emperor at the Royal Castle in Buda, halfway through the visit, she had been in deep discussion with him in Hungarian – 'so that nobody could work out what they were saying' – for a quarter of an hour, and emphasized the point to those at home by concluding with three exclamation marks. The gossip had an entirely different effect in Hungary; it increased Andrássy's renown and political importance domestically and increased the empress's wildly growing popularity. If the Empress of Austria could look with such favour on a Magyar, there must be something right with her. Sisi bloomed in the comparative informality and outward emotion on display in Buda and Pest, so different after the strict life in the Hofburg. 'All the liberality, all the elegance, all the charm of Hungary, crystalised, for her, in Gyula Andrássy,' as her best biographer, Brigitte Hamann, wrote.[4]

Rumours increased over the years. It was said that Sisi's youngest child, her favourite daughter (Marie) Valerie, born in April 1868, was Andrássy's – as it became known the empress was determined to give birth in Hungary. But that can be discounted. For one thing, Marie Valerie's paternity can be in no doubt; it is obvious from the husband-and-wife correspondence. 'Sisi and Andrássy loved each other, but they never had a love affair,' according to Hamann, who tried hard to find some evidence of one but failed:

In spite of the immense curiosity and almost criminal inquisitiveness of a great many Viennese court appointees in an effort to find an 'indiscretion' on the part of the Empress . . . such attempts have never succeeded. Both the Empress and Andrássy were under constant surveillance by innumerable court members . . . aside from the fact that Elisabeth was not a woman who found anything in physical love that seemed worth the effort, and that in any and every situation, Andrássy never stopped being the carefully calculating politician.

The empress was infatuated with him, but she put all of that emotion into serving his Hungarian cause. An adventure in the more ordinary sense was out of the question for a woman like her and in her position.[5]

After their first meeting the correspondence between the empress and Andrássy grew more intense, with Ferenczy continuing to act as postmistress. Parts of their letters were written with elaborate code words that are hard to decipher but become clear when read as a whole and in strict chronology. The letters were almost entirely about what the empress could do to persuade her husband to start negotiating a compromise deal with the reform leaders in Hungary, specifically with her favourite, Andrássy. Franz Jozsef was reluctant to go too far and alienate the conservatives at the Vienna court. From spring 1866, the 'Hungary problem' became significantly more urgent for Austria. The long-expected war with Prussia broke out and the Austrians were faring badly. They needed a settlement with the Hungarians to ensure peace on the home front – as well as their taxes, soldiers and arms.

Empress Elisabeth worked furiously when the moment seemed right for the Hungarian cause. She spent most of the period between May and August 1866 living in Buda Castle, away from the emperor. On 3 July Austria suffered a humiliating military defeat by the Prussians at Sadowa (Königgrätz) in southern Bohemia – a disaster for the Habsburg Empire, but an opportunity for the politicians in Buda and Pest. What the Hungarians wanted was, essentially, parity with Austria, much more so than any of the other parts of the Empire – far more than, say, Bohemia, which was more important economically at that time.

Sisi picked this moment to put maximum pressure on Franz Jozsef. Six days after the battle, while she insisted on remaining in Buda, she wrote to the emperor pleading not just for the cause of Hungary but the cause of Andrássy. She begged the emperor to make him the Hungarian Foreign Minister 'as a way of saving us all . . . I am convinced that if you will trust him and trust him implicitly we still may be saved – and not only Hungary, but the monarchy too. But you must talk to him yourself . . . I can assure you that you are not dealing with a man desirous of playing a part at any price or striving for a position . . . I beg you in Rudolf's name [their son] not to lose this one chance at the last moment.'

This was the beginning of the final round of negotiations that resulted in the Compromise agreement. Franz Jozsef gave way partially and agreed to meet Andrássy privately, though the audience didn't go altogether well for the Hungarian. Franz Jozsef was still deeply suspicious of him. Andrássy, the emperor later wrote to Sisi, 'spoke very frankly and cleverly, and developed all his views . . . For the rest, I found him, as always, too imprecise in his views and without necessary consideration of the other parts of the monarchy. He covets a great deal and offers too little at this crucial moment . . . I admire his great frankness and level-headedness . . . but I fear that he has neither the strength nor can find the means in his country to carry out his present intentions.'

The following day, at Andrássy and Sisi's urging, he met the 'sage' of Hungary, the chief strategic thinker behind the idea of passive resistance, the theorist as well as the tactician of the liberal Reform Movement, Ferenc Deák, now aged sixty-three. 'He is much clearer than A[ndrássy] and takes the rest of the monarchy much more into account,' the emperor reported to Elisabeth. 'But I gained the same impression from him as I did from A. They want everything in the widest sense and offer no guarantees of success, only hopes and probabilities, and they do not promise to hold out, and should they be unable to carry through their intentions in the country and are outflanked by the Left . . . I have great respect for his honesty, frankness and dynastic loyalty. However, courage, decisiveness and endurance in misfortune is not granted to this man.'

She lost all sense of being Empress of the Austrian Empire in her obsession with the cause of Hungary and never saw a wider picture, which for all his many faults Franz Jozsef at least tried to do. He reminded her that 'it would be contrary to my duty to adopt your exclusively Hungarian point of view and slight those lands which have endured unspeakable conditions with steadfast fidelity, and now if ever, require special consideration and care'.

The emperor was exasperated by her constant nagging about Hungary and her inability to let the subject drop. 'Although you have really been very tiresome and disagreeable, I love you so much that I cannot exist without you,' he wrote.[6]

Nevertheless, the emperor agreed to meet Andrássy again. The interview lasted more than two and a half hours in Franz Jozsef's private rooms at the Hofburg. Occasionally some of Franz Jozsef's principal advisers joined the talks and progress was made. Afterwards, he and Deák were asked to draft the wording of a document on reorganizing the Empire in the spirit of 'dualism' (rather than feudalism). This became the basis for the *Ausgleich* agreement, and after weeks of debate within the Austrian government it was finally approved by the emperor. Franz Jozsef knew it did not feel entirely right in principle – the Bohemians and the Slavs generally felt betrayed – but it was right on immediate pragmatic grounds.

On 17 February 1867 Andrássy was appointed Prime Minister of the new Hungary. Sisi visited a few weeks later to mark what she called the 'emotional reconciliation'. It was a triumphant return. An editorial in the daily *Pester Lloyd* declared: 'And who would underestimate that the nation's love is totally and collectively devoted to the Queen? This gracious lady is regarded as a true daughter of Hungary. Everyone is convinced that the sentiments of patriotism dwell in her noble heart, that she has acquired the Hungarian mentality along with the Hungarian language, and that she has always been a warm advocate of the Hungarians' needs.' The writer turned politician Baron József Eötvös, Minister of Culture in the Andrássy government, wrote to Max Falk, the queen-empress's erstwhile Hungarian teacher, who was still in Vienna writing columns:

> Your high-born pupil was received among us with flowers. Day by day the enthusiasm for her grows. Firmly as I believe that never before has a country had a queen so deserving of it, I also know that there has never been one so beloved . . . I am convinced that when a crown breaks, as the Hungarian crown broke in 1848, it can only be welded together again by the flame of feeling. For three centuries we have tried faith. Time and again we have tried hope, till only one possibility remained – that the nation should be able to love some member of the reigning house from the depth of the heart. Now that we have succeeded, I have no more fears for the future.[7]

By the day of the coronation only the most dissenting voices in the court were complaining about the Compromise. Most had come round to accepting it as a consummate act of outstanding diplomacy by the emperor.* In Hungary Andrássy and Deák were declared the presiding political geniuses and it was generally agreed that the Hungarians had received from the arrangement more than they had thought possible a few years earlier. 'Hungary won victory from defeat,' as Jókai once said. He meant it with a degree of irony, but the phrase has stuck and entire histories of Hungary have been written with the famous phrase as their titles.

Only the diehards close to Kossuth never reconciled themselves to the Compromise. He and all his exiles were amnestied on coronation day – and the still-revered old man was allowed back to Hungary safe from arrest or retribution, if he wished. But he said he would refuse until Austrian 'occupation' ended and Hungary was 'a free country'. He never set foot there again, though he lived into his nineties. From his place of refuge in Turin he wrote a series of articles around the time of the coronation predicting that the *Ausgleich* would be a disaster for Hungary.†

The old Hungarian constitution was re-established, giving the Hungarian nobles essentially the same rights they had before 1848, though technically serfdom was abolished. The Empire of Austria became the Dual Monarchy of Austria-Hungary with two capitals, two parliaments (both with limited powers) and two Cabinets. Only the Foreign Minister, the War Minister and the Finance Minister acted for both (and even then only for financial issues that affected the Empire as a whole). It was a highly complex structure that gave the Hungarians far more power as

---

* In Budapest the most absurd efforts were made after the Compromise and the coronation of Franz Jozsef as King of Hungary to 'prove' his Hungarian origins. Genealogists claimed (in news to Franz Jozsef himself and to other Habsburgs) that he was a descendant of Béla III, from the House of Árpád, the original Magyar royal family, and Anna of Antioch. A marble stone in a newly erected chapel of the castle in Buda showed the alleged bloodline. Later, in the millennium year, 1896, the emperor was presented on phoney evidence as 'the new Árpád'. At her coronation as queen, Sisi – born in Bavaria – was revealed as fifteenth in line of descent from the Hungarian Princess Erzsébet, who was canonized after her death in 1321. Part of the cult around the empress presented her as the new Saint Elisabeth.

† One of them was remarkably prescient. He predicted that Hungary's foreign policy would henceforth be bound entirely to Germany's, which in a generation or two would lead to a war in which Hungary would be catastrophically defeated and lose its territorial integrity. Which is precisely what happened following the war of 1914–18.

a proportion of their population. But Austria was far richer and paid 70 per cent of Imperial costs.[8]

The system worked, for the moment, by balancing and safeguarding the Magyars' sense of identity and the dynastic sovereignty of the Habsburgs. It was an intricate and fragile system, which worked for a limited period and gave rise, in Hungary at least, to an extraordinary spurt of prosperity and creativity. Essentially, modern Budapest is the product of the Dual Monarchy – and despite sporadic hostile reactions in Hungary, people were more satisfied with it than frustrated. It had plenty of absurdities: Hungary was under the king-emperor's rule but was not subject to the Austrian Imperial government, a fact that wasn't even mentioned in the Compromise Laws that brought the new empire into being and would cause severe problems later.

The construct was easy to mock: think of *The Good Soldier Švejk*, or some works by Joseph Roth. Nobody did so with such verve and irony as Robert Musil in his brilliant novel *The Man Without Qualities*, in which he christened Austria-Hungary Kakania:

> It did not consist of an Austrian part and a Hungarian part which, as one might expect, complemented each other, but of a whole and a part; that is of a Hungarian and an Austria-Hungarian sense of statehood . . . The Austrian existed only in Hungary, and there as an object of dislike; at home the Austrian calls himself the citizen of the Austro-Hungarian monarchy's kingdoms and countries as represented at the Council of the Empire – which comes down to saying one Austrian plus one Hungarian, minus that self-same Hungarian.

The nomenclature of 'dualism' had to be navigated with extreme tact for there were endless snares and traps. The joint institutions were called 'Imperial and royal' (*kaiserlich und königlich*), or *k.u.k.* The Hungarians had insisted on 'and' to signify that they were equal. The purely Austrian offices were called Imperial-royal *k.u.k.*, but the purely Hungarian ones just royal (*königlich*, or simply *k*). But in Budapest the term *magyar királyi* (Hungarian royal) was in general use, abbreviated as often as not on official signs in Budapest as *magy.k.*

Hungary was even more caste-conscious and hierarchical than Austria. Titles were important and there were highly complex rules about how to address different grades in the civil service. The first two grades were addressed as Gracious Sir (*kegyelmes*), grades three to five as Dignified Sir (*méltóságos*), grades six to nine as Great Sir (*nagyságos*) and grades ten and eleven as Respectable Sir (*tekintetes* or *cimzetes*). This was followed in various ways in a whole range of other managerial jobs and professions, and navigating proper usage was a minefield until after the Second World War.

For three decades after the Compromise the Liberal Party founded by Deák on the principle of cooperation with the Austrians, the party of Andrássy, retained an overwhelming majority in Parliament and could claim rapid economic and social advances – at least in Budapest, if not the rest of the country. For ten years its Prime Minister following Andrássy was a decent, humane moderate, Kálmán Tisza. But over time, waves of nationalism and social and religious conflict eroded its liberal foundations. Between 1867 and the turn of the century there were fifteen governments formed in Budapest – often they were basically the same with just a few portfolios changed. They were comprised almost exclusively of highest-rank aristocrats. The gifted comic novelist Kálmán Mikszáth, a friend of two of the premiers in the 1870s, who himself went into politics briefly, described how government business in 'Liberal' Hungary was conducted: 'The decisions to build railways and other public works were taken in between two games of tarot around the card table; policies regarding the nationalities were shaped between pre and post luncheon drinks.'[9]

While on various visits to Hungary in the 1860s before the *Ausgleich*, Empress Elisabeth had spotted a house she wanted as her own, as a base she could keep, far away from intrigues in Vienna. About 25 kilometres north-east of Budapest, now almost a suburb of the city but then an area surrounded by beautiful forest, she discovered a seventy-room mansion that had been built for Count Grassalkovich in the 1830s in Gödöllő. She coveted it passionately and in the summer of 1866, immediately after the Austrian–Prussian War, she begged the emperor to buy it. But Franz Jozsef vetoed the idea on the grounds of cost: the war with Prussia had left Austria to pay immense reparations and he said the Imperial royal family itself had to cut spending by at least 20 per cent.

She complained about it to Prime Minister Andrássy. As a 'coronation present' the new Hungarian government gave her the mansion, with around 10,000 hectares of woods – perfect for her passion of hunting. She travelled relentlessly, but she spent several months of each year there, substantially more time than in Vienna. As she once told Mór Jókai: 'Here, in Hungary, at last one feels eternally free.' Particularly so in Gödöllő. 'Here no one disturbs me, as if I were living in a village where I can come and go as I please,' she wrote to her mother. Before the coronation she had spent 114 days in Hungary. Afterwards, according to Hungarian historians who spent their time calculating such things, during other relentless travels she spent 1,549 days in Hungary, either at Gödöllő or in the castle in Buda.

Statues in Budapest come and go depending on the political climate. It is safe to say that the charming statue of Elisabeth on the Buda side of the bridge that bears her name – it has her seated, with a hunting hound by her feet – will never be removed. Even during the Communist years, when many symbols of Hungary as a monarchy were erased, the cult of Empress Elisabeth, friend of the Hungarians, thrived: she was the People's Empress.*

---

* Strangely, the statue did not appear until 1932, more than three decades after her death. When she was assassinated at Lake Geneva by an Italian anarchist, Luigi Lucheni, in 1898, aged just sixty, there was an outpouring of emotion in Budapest. The public appeal to erect a memorial to her was massively oversubscribed when it was announced in 1900. It was considered so important that successive committees appointed to vet the designs were never satisfied with the results. Recurring competitions could not come up with a winner. Finally in 1919, on the fifth attempt, the sculptor György Zala's design was approved, though it took another thirteen years before it was completed. Originally it stood on the opposite, Pest side of the river and was damaged when the Germans blew up all the bridges across the Danube at the end of the Second World War. But it was repaired relatively quickly. Then more damage was found and it was removed at the end of 1953. It reappeared, restored in its present location, four years later.

BUDAPEST IS BORN

The Hungarian state can have only one capital, in which Pest chiefly provides the living strength and Buda chiefly provides the ancient historic memory. The splendour, strength, power and greatness of the national capital is dependent on its unity, of which our country . . . now stands in most particular need.

Lajos Kossuth, 1 July 1849

The leftist radical Mihály Táncsics, who had been broken out of jail on day one of the 1848 Revolution – carried aloft through Pest and hailed as a martyr against Habsburg oppression – was aged seventy-three when he began his last political campaign. Like most of his previous battles, this too would end in failure. He was a venerable old idealist, the son of a serf, with a long grey beard and a deeply embedded loathing of compromise.

During the Revolution he launched a newspaper that railed against Kossuth for being too accommodating to the Austrians. He was sentenced to death *in absentia* after the War of Independence, as Andrássy had been; for eight years he was in hiding around various villages in Hungary, a wanted man. He was granted an amnesty in 1860, but was soon jailed again for three years for writing a series of articles attacking the monarchy and for trying to start a new opposition newspaper. Now, in 1873, the target of his anti-Establishment rage was his objection to the unification of Buda, Pest and Óbuda to form one city.

There were few open objectors to the idea of unity. It had been established policy by the 'reformers' since at least the 1820s. Széchenyi and Kossuth agreed on little, but were as one on this. In one of its last acts, days before defeat, the revolutionary government had decreed that the three towns would become one city. The Austrians rescinded this immediately after they regained control. But it was the aim of the new Liberals, as the Buda-born historian Béla Grünwald wrote a decade before the 1867 Compromise:

It is unique in the history of nations that there is one that does not have a capital where its language is understood. The Hungarian capital was so German that a Hungarian artisan, settled here fifty years ago, forgot his mother tongue within a few decades, as if he had emigrated to Germany. If the king or a member of the ruling house 'dons Hungarian trousers', or utters a word of Hungarian, the assembly where that occurs is moved to tears, forgetting that the Hungarian clothing and the few words appear only when the Hungarians are needed.[1]

There had always been a feeling by many people who lived on both sides that they lived in separate towns, divided not just by a river but by custom and attitude: Buda represented the feudal past, while Pest exemplified everything that was new, a future built on entrepreneurship, capitalism and commerce. The difference was obvious to any visitor in the eighteenth and nineteenth centuries, even at unification. A Russian courtier in the 1820s was surprised that 'a considerable part of the population of Pest are merchants while Buda . . . is the residence of the nobility. The industriousness of the former and the indolence of the latter is not acknowledged equally by the government . . . therefore the inhabitants of the two towns live in disharmony with each other and represent two utterly different societies, ways and philosophies of life.' The writer Antal Szerb put it more succinctly two generations later in his hilarious little book *A Martian's Guide to Budapest*: 'Here in Budapest, as in Paris – and many other cities, I believe – each bank is an entirely different world. As the chestnut trees close down for the night on the Buda side, the coffee houses open up in Pest, alive with music.'

For much of the nineteenth century Buda was still mainly German-speaking – even in the 1848 Revolution, many who lived there were fiercely Catholic, conservative and loyal to the Habsburgs. They did not entirely share the enthusiasm for Magyar nationalism and the radical notions of the revolutionaries in Pest, where the Revolution began and most of its leaders lived. Kossuth originally came from north-eastern Hungary, but made his name in Pest. Many of those who backed the

Revolution distrusted the conservatives of Buda – Mihály Táncsics, for example, who was vociferous in the campaign against unification from the Left. There were figures on the Right in Pest, including the former mayor Mór Szentkirályi, who argued that a mainly German Buda, incapable and unwilling to develop, would impede the modernization of *their* city. Some prominent and influential figures in Buda were also against the unification, but after the *Ausgleich* they could see their cause was lost and they were quieter about voicing their opinion.[2]

Demographics as well as politics were changing on both sides of the Danube, principally the rapid decline in the use of the German language – a victory for the cause of Hungarian nationalism. The German populations almost everywhere else in Central and Eastern Europe maintained their German heritage and their separation from the other, mainly Slavic, populations surrounding them – in the Czech lands, Galicia and parts of Romania. In Buda and Pest, if not the rest of Hungary, things progressed differently. The German-Austrian populations in Pest and Buda merged with, and then were absorbed by, the Magyars into a linguistic, political and cultural 'Hungarianness'.

Another big demographic factor was the rapid influx of immigrants, mostly Jews, into Pest, who adopted the Hungarian language to assimilate into Magyar life. The main political manager of the unification was a prominent son of immigrants whose family had moved to Pest in the 1820s, the vastly experienced (and wealthy) Moritz Wahrmann. In 1869 he was the first Jew elected to the Hungarian Parliament, for the Leopoldváros (Leopoldtown) district of Pest, an area of large town houses and a few commercial businesses in the finance sector, populated by many better-off Jews. A close associate of Andrássy and a moderate Liberal, he steered the legislation uniting the city through Parliament. By then, though, the population of Buda was in decline compared with that of Pest. In 1848 the population was nearly even, with 46 per cent in Buda. Twenty years later this proportion fell to 25 per cent. By 1900 only one in six of the city's inhabitants lived in Buda.*

There was snobbery and parochialism on both sides of the river for decades after the unification. The writer Sándor Márai could be

---

* Though this changed in the twentieth century after major development in parts of the Buda Hills and post-war housing estates in Óbuda. Pest in 2021 housed around 70 per cent of the 1.7 million or so population of the city.

happy only in Buda, close to the Castle district where he lived, until he emigrated to the US after the Second World War. A Pest loyalist profoundly disagreed: 'The Danube flows along the edge of Budapest, because Buda is not really one half of the capital city but merely a place for excursions,' wrote Adolf Ágai, founder and long-time editor of the humour magazine *Borsszem Jankó* and author of the classic *Travels from Pest to Budapest*. 'It is naturally right to rejoice in the dawn of tomorrow even while looking back wistfully to yesterday,' he wrote. 'Pest represents dynamism of the present and future . . . the other side is sleepy and secretive . . . I think highly of Buda but I am not familiar with it. My imagination remains baffled by its monotonous hills and valleys . . . I have travelled through all the great capitals of Europe but Buda remains a foreign place to me.'[3]

It is fitting that Budapest's spine, its 'avenue of dreams', is named after Gyula Andrássy. His crowning achievement, which lives on, was one of his early acts as Hungary's first Prime Minister under the Dual Monarchy. Budapest looks as it does in the twenty-first century largely because of his Act 1870:10 – on the face of it a dull piece of municipal legislation, but the spark that by the turn of the century created Europe's sixth-largest city. It set up a Metropolitan Board of Public Works that was charged with planning the future of the city, rather like Georges-Eugène Haussmann did in Paris, but with greater powers. It opened an international competition for a comprehensive plan to direct the long-term development of the city, which would serve as the blueprint for Budapest's development throughout the remainder of the nineteenth century. The best-known architects and town planners from all over Europe entered, but the vastly lucrative contract was eventually given to the Hungarian engineer Lajos Lechner, who made the detailed recommendations for the regulation of the river, the restoration of the Castle district in Buda – and, above all, the construction of the Ring and radial avenue of central Pest. Lechner's plan was followed with very few alterations over the decades, and any visitor can familiarize themselves with the topography easily. Look at Pest from a vantage point on a hill in Buda and one can see what the original planners had in mind, intending it to look more like Paris than a Habsburg city, although close up many of the buildings would not be out of place anywhere in the Empire.

On the Pest side, a broad semicircular Ring, the Grand Boulevard (Nagykörút), links the Margaret Bridge to the north with the southern Petőfi Bridge. The four and a half kilometres of the boulevard is divided into sections all bearing a Habsburg name – Theresa, Elisabeth, Jozsef, Francis – though over the decades of regime changes and whatever was politically correct at the time the names were changed. For a period a section of the Nagykörút was officially rechristened after Hitler, and for a generation following the Second World War there was a Leninkörút, but they were restored to their original names after the collapse of the Communist regime in 1989. Every 350 metres or so the Grand Boulevard is intersected with an elliptical curve of avenues.[4]*

When the Andrássy út was built, according to Lukács, 'it was typical of the grandiloquent verve of modern Pest', and it still is: geometrically straight and nearly 50 metres wide, though not quite as wide as the Champs-Élysées. Beneath the road runs the first underground metro line in mainland Europe, opened in 1896. As Lukács noted, it is characteristic and surely not coincidental, that its terminals were next to the most famous pastry shop in Budapest, then and in 2022 Gerbeaud, downtown in the Inner City – and by a famous restaurant near the zoo in the City Park, Gundel, which for many years in the 1990s and early 2000s had Michelin rosettes. The splendidly ornate original yellow coaches of the Franz Jozsef Line, as it was called, had polished wooden seats that lasted until the 2000s with their rickety clanking noise of barely oiled wheels.

As Gyula Krúdy described it in its golden period just before the turn of the century, the first section of Andrássy Avenue, near the Inner City, was initially the most elegant:

---

* In 1945 Andrássy út was renamed Stalin Avenue, then in 1956 the Avenue of the People's Republic, then in the 1980s it reverted to its original name. Landmarks along it changed too. A third of the way down the avenue there's a square where eight roads converge, including the main Ring. That was called Oktogon until 1934, when it was renamed Mussolini Circus, and changed back after the war. Further down towards the People's Park there's a pretty circus where four roads converge, originally called the Körönd. In 1938 it was renamed after Hitler, then after 1945 had its original name back, but since the 1970s has been known as Zoltán Kodály Körönd, after the composer who lived in a house on the avenue until his death in 1967.

On its three-fathom-deep asphalt every gentlewoman of Pest who could boast an immaculate toilette had the opportunity to present herself . . . Every burgher without any hope of entering the Hungarian nobility or a baronage was eager to obtain the rank that can be reached on one's own strength – a landlordship on Andrássy Avenue . . . Real Andrássy is where the asphalt is always immaculate, the parquet that is the carriageway is sprinkled with dust-repellent oil, the constable's frock coat is always pressed and his gloves white, the carriage wheels are red and have noiseless tyres, the cafés are bustling with life, in the restaurants they are always cooking, and the people forever smiling.[5]

In October 1888, the Budapest Opera House took a gamble when it appointed as its new musical director a twenty-eight-year-old Austrian-Bohemian composer, who was acknowledged to be a genius, but also known as a troubled and temperamental young man, a perfectionist who frequently found dealing with other people more difficult than making music. Gustav Mahler was given a ten-year contract worth 10,000 forints a year – a big sum in those days, worth around £120,000 sterling at 2022 values – plus a free apartment on Andrássy Avenue. The aim in hiring him was to put the Budapest Opera House, which had opened only four years earlier, on the musical map of Europe. A fine orchestra played, and a decent chorus sang in a wonderful new building, set back three metres from the avenue itself – 'near-perfect in its appearance as well as in its interior and even in the modesty of its perspective, forming a perfectly harmonious setting', according to a contemporary critic. It was the masterpiece of Miklós Ybl, the most interesting of the Hungarian architects of the golden period, who had by then made an international reputation.* Ybl based his design on the Vienna Opera House. But the Opera House in Budapest is much more graceful and elegant, and though it had 200 fewer seats, its interior was far superior – as it was backstage, with more modern equipment, more orchestra space

* Ybl was the fashionable architect picked by the aristocrats and the nouveau riche for their mansions in Pest and estates in the country. Count István Károlyi used him to rebuild his beautiful neoclassical palace in Pest, as did a host of the finance oligarchs of the period. But his public commissions included the Basilica, the new St Stephen's Cathedral, a stone's throw from the Opera House, and the near-complete rebuilding of the Royal Castle in Buda, including the Castle Garden, the Várket Bazár.

and a fire curtain inspired by the memory of the devastating blaze in 1869 that destroyed the Dresden Opera House.

The Budapest Opera and its company had made little mark in its first few years – hence the decision to employ the energetic new maestro, who had made a name for himself as a conductor, as well as a composer, in Vienna and Prague. Johannes Brahms, who generally disliked opera, admired his work after seeing his production of *Don Giovanni*, and Verdi praised his interpretation of Wagner. Mahler arrived in Budapest with much fanfare and on 1 October, his first day in his job, to the delight of his new hosts, he declared that he would learn Hungarian – 'I am sure I can be fluent within a year, or perhaps two,' he said. He assured his new employers that he would guarantee to mount more Hungarian works. But Mahler's two and a half years in Hungary were turbulent, themselves the stuff of grand opera, culminating in two tenors in the chorus challenging him to a duel.[6]

He left the post speaking barely a word of Hungarian and not a single home-grown work was performed in the Opera House while Mahler was there, though he did establish the practice that all the operas should be sung in Hungarian. After eight months he had staged two parts of Wagner's Ring cycle and conducted his own First Symphony. Audiences were enraptured and the reviews throughout Europe were exceptional. Every seat was sold, and on performance nights touts were standing on Andrássy Avenue offering tickets at double or treble the official cover price. The company was making serious money for the first time and foreign stars were anxious to perform there.* The Budapest Opera had arrived. But behind the scenes tempers were flaring and things were falling apart.

Mahler was loathed by the chorus and the orchestra. For both *Das Rheingold* and *Die Walküre* he had insisted on eighty full-length re-hearsals and he often worked the players and singers from early in the morning to late at night. 'Life under Mahler as conductor was like slow,

---

* Foreign performers who sang German, Italian or French parts in broken Hungarian, even when they misunderstood what they were singing, received enthusiastic applause and foot-stomping (and still do in the twenty-first century). Mahler was appalled that a professional singer would be so ill prepared. He hired Ede Újházi, an actor at the National Theatre, as language master to teach proper Hungarian pronunciation, not just to foreign stars but also to Hungarian performers who spoke with regional dialects.

painful torture,' one of the wind section of the orchestra remarked later. There were frequent rebellions and threats of strikes, which the administrative director, Ferenc von Beniczky, had to smooth over as best he could. Mahler had a final say in every aspect of the production. His technique was described later by one of his principal backers, the Liberal politician and future Education Minister Count Albert Apponyi, in a letter recommending him to the Vienna Opera House when the director there was thinking of employing him:

> Like other famous conductors, Mahler does not only conduct the orchestra but directs with a sovereign force the whole stage where the works he conducts take place, the performance of actors and chorus, their acting and gestures as well, so that a performance prepared and conducted by him will be perfect artistically in every respect. His attention embraces the production as a whole, the sets, the machinery and the lighting. I have never yet encountered such a harmoniously accomplished artistic personality. I ask Your Excellency to reinforce my judgement by asking Brahms for his opinion on the production of *Don Giovanni* conducted by Mahler, which he saw in Budapest . . . [he] will remember the experience as one not easy to forget.[7]

To make his problems worse, Mahler had alienated large sections of the press and from the summer of 1890 there was an orchestrated campaign against him in opposition newspapers. Stories about his treatment of musicians and singers seeped out at regular intervals, including the case of the two singers who 'called him out' for a duel, they claimed, on the political grounds that not enough Hungarian operas were being produced, though other members of the chorus said the whole thing was a publicity stunt. Mahler declined the challenge. Duelling, though quite common even at the turn of the century, was illegal in Hungary, but that did not prevent some of the ultra-nationalist papers accusing Mahler of cowardice. They accused him of importing foreign goods (meaning German operas, singers and musicians), and much of the anti-Mahler tone was clearly anti-Semitic. When von Beniczky was ousted as 'intendant' of the Opera House at the end of 1890 and Count Géza Zichy – with the help of his political connections and a press chorus – replaced him, Mahler could see his time in Budapest was almost up.

Zichy's first step was to draw up a new regulation in a parliamentary Bill, endorsed by the Interior Ministry, which gave him the power to take decisions on every detail of artistic management of the Opera House, from engagement of singers, the choice of operas and casting to programme design. The musical director only could 'submit suggestions'. The two had a row, Mahler lost his temper and Zichy reported the incident to the minister, his close friend Count Gyula Szapáry. The minister's response to Zichy is the voice of the philistine bureaucrat down the ages: 'Having learned of the unseemly behaviour that Gustav Mahler . . . yesterday displayed towards the intendant and the regulations of the Ministry of the Interior regarding the modification of the Opera House Bill, I herewith call upon you to summon . . . Mahler, and inform him that (1) I have learned about his unseemly conduct which I disapprove of, and (2) should this conduct of his be repeated, he would be immediately sent on leave and further disciplinary steps be instituted against him.' Mahler had by this time organized an escape route from Budapest. Early in 1891 he contacted the Hamburg Opera House and was appointed artistic director there, where he had a happier experience. But before his departure he negotiated a tidy 25,000-forint payoff.[*8]

Politics and music have always mixed in Hungary – occasionally with discord. Even the beloved Liszt landed himself in trouble towards the end of his life. In 1875 he founded and appointed himself the first president of the Hungarian Academy of Music and he had an immense influence on all the arts in Hungary. He kept a few chosen students well into his seventies. But when he began creating his most famous works and branded them as Hungarian, for example the series of twenty Rhapsodies, they caused an enormous political stir. Many of them mixed traditional gypsy music with Magyar folk themes. Was the music really 'Hungarian'? Magyar chauvinists were not pleased. Even the Prime Minister, Kálmán Tisza, was drawn into the controversy. 'At

---

* Mahler was not the last 'foreign' conductor to become musical director of the Opera House. After the Second World War the Communist regime appointed the great Otto Klemperer to the job. He had escaped Nazi Germany in the 1930s. He, too, was a brilliant success musically, who recreated the Opera House as an important venue with some exceptional musicians and singers. He established an excellent repertoire before he fell ill. He was hugely admired for his gifts but, as a Jew and a leftist, linked to a regime that was loathed; he was never a popular figure in Budapest.

a time when Hungary has lost almost everything but her music, Liszt chose to proclaim to the world that it was not Magyar music at all, but gypsy music,' he said. It occurred to few in high politics at the time that anyone from a Romany background could be a Hungarian.*

Liszt was not an uncritical admirer of the music scene in Hungary. If the nationalists had known his thoughts they would perhaps have taken a different view of him – as they might have done if they realized that according to his will, despite his protestations about being a Hungarian, he had insisted on being buried in Bayreuth. Shortly before his death in 1886 he wrote to the composer Ödön Mihailovich: 'If you were not chained to Budapest, your career as a composer would develop more freely. You can be certain that in a few years' time no Hungarian composer will make his mark anywhere but in his own country, where progress proceeds only in fits and starts.' Which is not entirely true: Think of Béla Bartók, Zoltán Kodály, György Ligeti and György Kurtág, to name four.[9]

---

* Bártók, on the other hand, disliked the works on musical grounds. 'The Hungarian Rhapsodies, which should say the most to us, are his least successful . . . (perhaps that is why they are so generally known and admired),' he said.

20

CAFÉ CULTURE

For ten years a married couple I knew sat every day for several hours quite apart in the coffee house. That is a good marriage, you will say! No. That is a good coffee house!

Alfred Polgár (1873–1955)

Among my favourite places in the city to sit and while away time is on the pedestrianized section of Ferenc Liszt Square, just off Andrássy Avenue, a stone's throw from the Opera House and the magnificent Liszt Concert Hall. In the 1990s a knot of coffee houses opened in the square, spilling over the paving stones under the plane trees, and from the 2000s they have been full of young people at tables using the free wi-fi. Occasionally they might even order a coffee. The technology may be different from the days of Austria-Hungary, but the way of life maybe not so much. Many things have changed in Budapest since the Dual Monarchy – and many have stayed just the same.

A hundred and thirty years ago the nearby coffee houses in downtown Pest would have been filled with journalists, writers or wannabe writers, artists, architects, fashion designers, a whole range of new middle-class people previously unfamiliar with urban living. If the country wasn't democratic, the coffee house was – up to a point. Entire novels were written there, newspapers were edited there. The most famous and the best of Hungary's *fin-de-siècle* and early-twentieth-century poets, Endre Ady, said he couldn't write anywhere other than a coffee house, 'with people's bustle and ideas and emotions all around'. The national Revolution of 1848 started in a coffee house and the words to the Hungarian national anthem were written in a Pest café on 22 January 1823 by the author, and later politician, Ferenc Kölcsey.*

In many of the literary coffee houses the waiters (some of them hopeful writers themselves, and knowledgeable about authors' ways) kept sheaves of paper called 'dog's tongues', available to those who wanted to write there. At a few, demijohns of ink were stored in the basement among wine racks. Head waiters were the source of gossip and, more importantly, a line of credit. As the Budapest saying went, 'Every writer had his own café and every café had its own writer.'

It is difficult to overstate the importance of the coffee house in Budapest's lifestyle and culture. Café life is of course ubiquitous in Paris, Rome and Vienna, but the coffee house in Budapest was different. To begin with its history was much longer. Whereas the Turkish habit of coffee-drinking came to Paris and Vienna early in the eighteenth century, the first coffee drinkers in Hungary were the Ottomans from the 1560s. Drinking coffee was one of the few things that caught on and remained popular after the Turks were ousted. By the mid 1700s a few big, established cafés were highly successful, as many accounts by visitors attest. There is a three-volume history of Budapest coffee houses covering 350 years by the noted historian Béla Bevilaqua-Borsody, which takes the story only up to the start of the First World War.[1]

Arguably, the last period of the Habsburg Empire – the Dual Monarchy – has left behind nothing more significant, and certainly nothing more delightful, than the coffee house. For all the bizarre trappings and failures of the late Habsburg Empire, this was a lasting and solid achievement – the living demonstration of an ideal that within a

---

* It is deeply pessimistic, and rather fuller of national self-pity than of national pride, more about defeats than victories. It concludes:

> Bless the Magyar, Lord we pray,
> Nor in bounty fail him.
> Shield him in the bloody fray
> When his foes assail him.
> He whom ill luck long has cursed
> This year grant him pleasure,
> He has suffered with the worst
> Time beyond all measure.

highly classified society, people of different status, race and sex, political persuasion and nationality could meet under one roof, without opening the floodgates to civil war and mutual destruction. In a coffee house everyone could coexist; when outside on the streets (or indeed on countless battlefields) there was so much hatred. This might seem straightforward, barely of note in the twenty-first century. But in an age that was on the precipice of descent into the horrors that would soon consume Europe, this was no simple or unimportant thing.

At the turn of the twentieth century, the comic writer and journalist Frigyes Karinthy performed a crucial – and typically Hungarian – social experiment. He once tried to measure how quickly it would take a joke to cross Budapest. His method: one afternoon he told a joke he had made up on the spur of the moment to some friends in a coffee house in Buda. An hour or so later, strolling into a café in Pest, he heard the same (by his own admission very unfunny) story relayed back to him.[*] This was why the future dictatorships in Hungary, fascist and Communist by turn, frowned on the subversive element in cafés – communication, the exchange of information and especially jokes, were seen as potentially dangerous. By 1900 there were more than 600 coffee houses in Budapest. After the Second World War, when the Soviet-style Communist regime began closing most of them down, there were fewer than twenty.[2]

Unlike Paris or London, Budapest had no tradition of literary salons, and there was just one fashionable 'gentlemen's club' along English lines, the National Casino, which allowed admission only to the nobility – and no Jews.[†] Coffee houses became the centre of Budapest's intellectual life.

---

[*] Karinthy, a satirist who saw Jonathan Swift as his guide to good writing, lived a large part of his life in a coffee house – and it was in a café in Pest that he realized he would soon be dead. He was sipping coffee in the Central Kavehaz in the Inner City when he suddenly lost his sight in one eye and suffered a piercing headache. As he recalled in his tragicomic novel *A Journey Round My Skull*, he knew at once, there in the café, that he had a brain tumour, which killed him within two years. Known to critics as a humourist, he characteristically refers to himself in the book as a tumourist.

[†] Although for twenty-five years in the late nineteenth century there was a highly exclusive salon run by two dashing sisters, both accomplished poets, Janka and Stefánia Wohl, whose home in a Pest mansion was a meeting place for artists, politicians and writers. But it was attended regularly by only a very few names.

Yet they were much more than that and fulfilled many roles: a respite for a hard day at work, a safe haven from a bad marriage or a cramped apartment – a sentimental and social education. 'Every intelligent person had spent a part of his youth in the coffee house,' recalled the theatre director Jenő Rákosi in 1926, when he was in his eighties. 'Without it the education of a young person would be incomplete.' They were cheap – even the flashiest ones on the Grand Boulevard or the Corso, the fashionable riverside promenade in Pest. You could sit for many hours with a cup of coffee and a glass of water and read a wide number of Hungarian and international newspapers and journals, hanging on bamboo racks. 'In such places you were not just *allowed* to linger over a coffee. You were *supposed* to linger,' the Nobel Prize-winning physicist Eugene Wigner, who left Hungary after the First World War and then worked on the Manhattan Project which built the first atomic bomb, remembered from his youth in Budapest.

Labour was cheap and a throng of young men (they were all young men, women did not work in coffee houses until after the Second World War) left the provinces to wait at tables in Budapest. Some coffee houses became famous for the after-supper nightlife, and especially dawn life, of Budapest. At 3 a.m. many cafés would be full of people drinking what became a Budapest specialty – the chicken and paprika-based pre-breakfast 'night owl soup', supposedly effective in preventing a hangover.

Gambling was illegal in Budapest coffee houses, but it was rife and the authorities did very little about it. Until the Communist takeover, card tables could be found in most of the coffee houses in the city – 'from the obscure hole-in-the-corner establishment to the elegant. In the former one finds professional card sharps, in the latter the impeccable gentleman who shoots himself in the head when he loses,' recorded Krúdy, an habitué of various Pest cafés, in his *Chronicles*. 'In the coffee houses of Andrássy Boulevard so-called frivolous women and young men with penetrating eyes converse about literature, music, painting and the foundation of banks.'[3]

At the height of the Budapest café culture, from the 1880s, the famous old names – the Crown, the Turkish Emperor, the Coffee Fountain, the White Ship and the ultra-select and elegant Seven Elector Princes –

gave way to far bigger and splashier establishments with vast plate-glass windows, elaborate terraces, gilt mirrors and chandeliers. Many were outstanding buildings architecturally.

The best-known and most sumptuous, the New York Café, was designed by one of the most famous architects in Hungary, Alajos Hauszmann, who had previously been in charge of reconstruction of the Royal Castle. A decade earlier he had also built another tea house, the Kiosk, on Elisabeth Square, which was highly fashionable among the theatre set.

The New York was grandiose, opulent and eclectic but art nouveau in style and full of elaborate gilding, marble ceilings, frescoes of putti and fine metal latticework. It was commissioned in 1894 as offices for the New York Life Insurance Company, but with the café on the ground floor in mind as the main attraction of the building. The lamps around the entrance are borne by bronze fawns. In its heyday, it was the most celebrated and glamorous coffee house of them all.

Particular spaces within the New York were reserved for different groups: writers, painters, publishers, actors. Other visitors sat in the area known as 'the deep end', where they could encounter anyone – a Cabinet minister, a gangster, a *grande horizontale*, an intellectually curious banker, even a royal personage from one of the ruling houses of Europe. As Budapest grew and attracted more visitors, increasing numbers of tourists went to the coffee houses. The New York was not notable as a pick-up joint, but aspiring actresses and young women of light virtue were often found at the tables in the upper gallery. When he was Prince of Wales the future Edward VII was a regular visitor to Budapest in the 1870s and 1880s, always travelling entirely incognito, enjoying its nightlife to the full. He was spotted in Budapest cafés several times, which caused a minor sensation in the Budapest press. But his presence was never mentioned in the British papers, which is one reason why he liked the city. 'There is no country in Europe in which I feel more at home than here,' he told a Hungarian acquaintance on one of his last visits in 1891. 'Heaven knows why I am so fond of Hungary. I am always happy to come, and I leave with a heavy heart. It seems to me that I can find many of the pleasant traits in the Hungarian nation that so captivated me during my travels to India with the gallant Rajputana people, but here the Eastern characteristics are combined with more than one splendid aspect of Western culture, all the more captivating to strangers.'*

Many a book deal or play was negotiated and signed at its tables. Many a literary feud was started there – and some were patched up. When he was a brash young film director on the make Sándor Kellner, who would become the movie producer Sir Alexander Korda, was at the New York 'almost every day', as he said later. He made his first big hire of a star there – by chutzpah and luck. One morning in 1916 he was at a corner table and spotted the National Theatre's leading man of the moment, Gábor Rajnay, who was also a regular. He approached the actor and said: 'My name is Korda . . . I'd like you to star in my new war picture . . . You'd play the hero, the captain who joins their ranks . . . We have money. We have cameras. We have everything.' In reality he had nothing at that point except the ability to talk and to persuade others. The actor was swept along by Korda's enthusiasm and agreed. The next day, when Rajnay arrived at the railway station which Korda had told him was the movie set, a company of real hussars was marching past. Korda told the actor to join them, ordered the cameras to start rolling and directed his new talent. This was the first reel of *The Officer's Sword-knot*, Korda's debut movie, starring Rajnay and 100 unpaid extras. Within a few months Korda's Hungarian career was established, and he had moved into a huge suite at Budapest's most opulent hotel, the Royal on the Ring – the first of many luxurious places where over the years he would live beyond his means.†

---

* The Prince of Wales was also known to favour a luxurious Budapest house of assignation in Magyar Street run by the city's well connected Madam, Róza Pilisy. It was not only British royals who could be found at that establishment. In 1907 a delegation of British MPs visited Budapest and two of them ran up a large bill there which they refused to pay, charging it to the Hungarian government. There was an unseemly scandal.

† From the 1910s the café was famous among film-makers and in the 1920s, when Hungarian actors, producers and directors made it in Hollywood, they often returned to show themselves at the café. Movie magnates like Adolph Zukor, William Fox, Korda, Jack Warner and Louis B. Mayer were regulars. Michael Curtiz (born Mihály Kertész Kaminer in Budapest) spent a large part of his formative years as a film director in the coffee house, though it is wrong, as some have suggested, that he based Rick's Café in the movie *Casablanca* on his beloved New York, which was altogether more flamboyant, more quintessentially *Mitteleuropa* than Rick's. Towards the end of his life, from Hollywood where he had been living for thirty years, he wrote to a Budapest

The poet and novelist Dezső Kosztolányi immortalized the New York in a story:

It felt so good to dip ourselves in that mist, in that hot pool, not think-ing of anything for a while, paying attention to how it is bubbling and wobbling, and it was a great feeling to know that all these people who are paddling here, are slowly being relaxed, being tied to each other, all will soon be melted into one single noisy soup . . . all were talking at the same time. The topics were: whether one has free will or not, what shape is the pest bacterium, how much are salaries in Britain, how far away can Sirius be, what did Nietzsche mean by 'eternal return', is Anatole France Jewish? They wanted to get the gist of everything, in a quick and thorough manner.

According to legend, and it may indeed be true, in order to ensure that it would never close the novelist and playwright Ferenc Molnár, an habitué of the coffee house but later an exile in New York City itself, where he lived in a suite at the Plaza Hotel, threw the keys of the café into the Danube as a dramatic gesture.* During the Communist years the New York was renamed the Café Hungaria, but everyone still called it the New York.

Within three blocks of the New York along Andrássy Avenue and the main Ring Boulevard there were at least five famous coffee houses popular among writers, artists and musicians: the Japán, beautifully decorated in Oriental style (the haunt mainly of painters, sculptors and architects), the Hall of Arts, attended mostly by painters (and many of their female models), the Opera, Dreschler and Abbázia, visited by a steady mix of journalists, bourgeois traders and flâneurs. A small group of painters who had two tables always reserved at the Royal were of course known as the Royalists. Older writers and the more conservative

---

friend that he was occasionally filled with nostalgia and homesickness for the café: 'I am sometimes overcome by a feeling that I am living not surrounded by American man-sions, but gazing at the hour hand of the New York Café through the mist, at dawn.'

* However, according to my friend Mátyás Sárközi, grandson of Molnár and author of a wonderful biography of the writer, the owner of the New York, Willy Tarjan, threw away the key. Nevertheless a portrait of Molnár still hangs in the coffee house, above the table where he invariably sat.

Aquincum. Roman 'Budapest', an important frontier post in the ancient world, and an inspiration for Marcus Aurelius, the emperor who is said to have written large parts of his *Meditations* there.

The Budapest statue of Stephen (István), the first King of Hungary, arguably the most radical – and successful – revolutionary in Hungarian history.

Matthias Corvinus, the Raven King, creator of a glittering Renaissance court in Buda during the fifteenth century and collector of the finest late-medieval library in Europe.

Ferenc Rákóczi II, Prince of Transylvania. A rebellious spirit whose revolt against the Habsburgs has been an inspiration to all revolutionaries in Hungary.

Suleiman the Magnificent, the Ottoman sultan who conquered Hungary and whose reign saw the start of the 150-year Turkish occupation of Buda.

Lajos Kossuth, leader of the failed Revolution of 1848 and War of Independence against the Austrians. Probably the most revered Hungarian, though reviled by some for his impractical ultranationalism.

Empress Elisabeth, the beloved 'Sisi', was the most popular of all the Habsburgs among Hungarians. There are more squares, streets, and landmarks in Budapest honouring her than anybody else.

Unlike Sisi, her husband Franz Jozsef, emperor for nearly sixty years after the War of Independence, was hated in Hungary as a symbol of an occupying power, but over time he came to be respected.

The 1916 coronation of the last Habsburg emperor, Charles IV, as King of Hungary.

Mihály and Katinka Károlyi, the Red Count and Countess. Mihály was the first President of a Hungarian Republic, a socialist, one of the richest people in Hungary, and 'the scapegoat for an entire era'. His aristocratic wife was an avowed Marxist – yet still loved wearing her extraordinary jewels.

Béla Kun, Lenin's pupil, who led a short-lived Soviet government in 1919 and launched a four-month terror in which thousands were killed.

Miklós Horthy, the admiral on a white horse, entering Budapest after his coup. He would be the reactionary authoritarian leader of Hungary for the next quarter of a century and left a legacy that is still hotly controversial in the 2020s.

Adolf Eichmann, architect of the 'final solution' in Hungary, during which nearly half a million Jews were murdered in Auschwitz in little more than 150 days.

Perhaps the most moving of all memorials to victims of the Holocaust. A line of sculpted shoes by the artist Gyula Pauer to remember those who were executed on the Danube embankment in the last year of the war and thrown into the river.

During the siege of Budapest in the last months of the war, the Nazis blew up all the bridges across the Danube and left much of the city centre in ruins.

Stalin's viceroy in Budapest, Mátyás Rákosi. Had he operated on a larger stage than Hungary he would have gone down with the likes of Hitler, Mao Zedong or Pol Pot as one of history's most monstrous murderers.

Imre Nagy, the Communist Party boss who led the heroic but failed uprising against the Soviet Union in 1956 and was hanged for his part in the revolt two years later.

The symbolic moment of the 1956 Revolution, when rebels tore down the statue of Stalin in the centre of Budapest. For a brief time it seemed as though the uprising might succeed, but then the Soviets invaded with overwhelming force and crushed it.

The reburial in 1989 of Imre Nagy in central Budapest, attended by hundreds of thousands of people – the event that marked the beginning of the end of Communist rule in Hungary.

The view of Budapest and of the Danube most visitors remember, a city still with two very different sides.

academics at the big universities frequented the Sódli on the Museum Ring, while Lloyd was the favourite of businesspeople and stockbrokers.[4]

The Japán, on Andrássy Avenue on the corner with Ferenc Liszt Square, was, like the New York, opened in the 1890s and a favourite of artists and, more important for them, collectors. The flamboyant architect Ödön Lechner, who designed some of the most imaginative buildings in Budapest's boom period, was a regular. 'The artists' table at the Japán was behind the window looking on to Andrássy [Avenue] to one side of the café,' one regular recalled. 'It was Lechner who decided that the table should be by a window ... Though continuously busy translating his artist's dreams into architectural designs on the marble table top, he would always keep an eye on the life of the street, the men, women and pretty girls and the forever changing view in general.' The writer Ernő Szép was often there. He remembers

> its walls covered with majolica tiles painted over with bamboos, chrysanthemums, vases and dream-like birds. We who went to the Japán are likely to have traversed a greater distance than we would have done if we'd gone to Japan itself. The coffee house was a more distantly exotic place than the world of white lotus, green tea and the Golden Buddha, because the Japan was the fairy land of youth. That was where I went in the afternoons, ignoring novels, horse races, and even love sometimes; such a sacred need of life that was in the time of amicable fraternization.[*]

In the so-called golden age of 'dualism' some prudes objected to everything that the coffee houses represented. Earlier than in Paris or Vienna, unaccompanied women started going to them in Budapest from the 1880s – not prostitutes, but bourgeois women with families to get out of poky apartments. Many coffee houses encouraged them, but to preserve their hair and clothing from the overwhelming smell of cigar

---

* In 1909 the Japán was bought by the entrepreneur Richárd Weisz, who maintained the tradition of attracting artists. After the First World War there was an outburst of anti-Jewish violence on the streets of Budapest. Weisz, who was heavily built and won a Gold Medal in wrestling for Hungary in the 1908 Olympic Games, walked on to the main Ring with a placard around his neck that declared 'I am Jewish.' Nobody touched him.

smoke women often chose to patronize the patisseries (*cukrászda*) instead, often connected to the bigger coffee houses.[5]

But to some people still the danger of sex loomed. 'Some women abandoned their children to the care of others . . . and exposed themselves to potentially undesirable acquaintances whom they would not have invited into their own homes,' declared a shocked rabbi attached to the Dohány Street Synagogue. Christian moralists were equally appalled and saw the coffee house apocalyptically as a threat to family life. 'Women go to them, showing a neglect of their duties as wives and mothers,' said the far-Right populist politician Győző Istóczy.

The writer Tamás Kóbor objected to Budapest café culture on aesthetic grounds. He said people went to coffee houses not for coffee, the newspapers or the company but for

the mysterious atmosphere of excitement . . . Yes, the coffee house has become an inescapable part of our lives. Smoke saturates its atmosphere and its characteristic beverage induces sleepless restlessness. It is a place where flirtation imitates love, where haggling pettiness accompanies the search for truth; where the division of labour and the fragmentation of ideas rule triumphant; where the four-penny literature and the sixteen-penny earthly paradise flourish. The Budapest coffee house . . . erased the distinction between truth and falsehood, art and kitsch, love and prostitution. The coffee house is where culture is bought and sold in the market for pennies . . . the writer has the same status as the waiters. Both live off tips and bow before the wishes of clients. They are the enemy of life, an ever-present danger to the family and the work ethic.[6]

21

THE HUNGARIAN POGROMS

I'll gladly resign my claim to the Hungarian Jews if only I were
certain that their patriotism would save them from the misery of anti-
Semitism . . . But the Jews of Hungary will also be overtaken by their
doom, which will be all the more brutal and merciless as time passes,
and wilder, too, the stronger they get in the meantime. There is no
escaping it.

Theodor Herzl, 1903

On 1 April 1882, a few days before Passover, fourteen-year-old Eszter
Solymosi disappeared from her home in the small village of Tiszaeszlár,
about 120 kilometres east of Budapest. Two weeks later, fifteen members of the district's Jewish community were arrested and charged with
her murder – but not just murder. The indictment was that the Jews
had used the girl's blood to make the unleavened bread prepared in the
traditional Passover feast: the original blood libel. The newspaper reports at the time alleged that the Jews had lured the girl back from the
village shop, where she was running an errand for her employer, to their
temple, where they cut her throat and collected her blood in a ritual urn.
Then, rumour had it, they placed her body on a cart, took it to the Tisza
River and floated the corpse downstream.

No body was found at the time, but among the men charged with
killing the victim were Salamon Schwarcz, the local kosher butcher,
Ábraham Buxbaum, a well-known schoolteacher, Lípot Braun, from a
nearby hamlet, and Hermann Volner, a day labourer. The eleven other
men were accused of various degrees of involvement in the alleged
crime. This episode was one of the first and most widely publicized
ritual murder trials in Central Europe. Every grisly detail of the case
was reported in the Hungarian and international press – written up

as a murder mystery and embellished with lurid Gothic fantasies and violent folk legends. The case collapsed when the main prosecution witness, Móricz Sharf, the son of one of the accused men, broke down in the witness box and admitted under cross-examination that he had been bribed by the presiding magistrate to give false evidence. Then the girl's body was recovered from the river, unmutilated; the most likely explanation for her death was that she accidentally fell into the fast-flowing Tisza and drowned. Eventually, after more than a year on remand, the Jews were acquitted, but the damage had been done.[1]

Immediately after the prisoners were released there was a wave of anti-Semitic demonstrations 'of medieval intensity' in many Hungarian towns, as one Budapest newspaper described them. In the capital, shops were looted in the Jewish quarter and at least a dozen Jews were lynched before the riots were quelled by troops. More than 100 were badly injured. On 11 August 1883 the Budapest local authority declared Budapest to be in a state of siege. Károly Eötvös, the lawyer who had defended the accused Jews, lived in central Budapest at the time and remembered some years later: 'there was no Jew, no matter how respected or socially prominent, who was exempt from the most callous insults . . . Sensitive individuals hardly dared to go out on to the street, into public places, or social gatherings . . . Those who could not, or would not, think for themselves, those who lacked all integrity, saw a murderer in every Jew.'[2]

The Tiszaeszlár case was unusual in its intensity and violence, but not exceptional for what it showed about deep-rooted anti-Semitism in Hungary. Occasionally it rose to the surface, encouraged by demagogues and populist politicians. Yet at the same time as there were pogroms on the streets, Budapest had become, according to the leading historian of Hungarian Jewry, Raphael Patai, one of the most welcoming cities in Europe for Jews, and 'by the end of the nineteenth century, Jews as a group had achieved a power position in Hungary unmatched by their co-religionists in any other country . . . in no period in their long history did Hungarian Jews feel as much at home in the *haza* [homeland], as much at one with their Magyar compatriots, as much part of the great national endeavour . . . to become an important cultural entity in Europe, as in the half-century after their emancipation.'

By the end of the nineteenth century Jews were the acknowledged leaders of the new capitalism in Hungary, in an era of extraordinary expansion. During the thirty years after the Compromise of 1867, the Hungarian economy quadrupled in size and Budapest became the city recognizable in the twenty-first century. Jewish business people and the professional class of doctors, lawyers and managers formed the backbone of the bourgeoisie. Most Magyar nobles still sneered at tradespeople, and the big Austrian landowners were too grand to sully their hands with business. Jews were the agents of modernization. By the turn of the century, 54 per cent of the owners of business establishments were Jewish, 85 per cent of the owners of financial institutions and 63 per cent of those who worked in them.[3]

Gyula Andrássy, Prime Minister until 1871 and then Foreign Minister of Austria-Hungary for almost a decade, frequently said he wished there were more Jews in Hungary, so important were they to the country's economy and culture. Kálmán Tisza, the long-serving premier from 1875, the high priest of Magyar liberalism, described Jews as 'the most industrious and constructive segment of the Hungarian population'. Even the generally anti-Semitic – and highly influential – *fin-de-siècle* historian Gyula Szekfű wrote that during the Dual Monarchy, 'without the establishment of factories by the Jews, Hungary would either have become a colony of Austrian capital, or stagnated at the agrarian level'.

Jews constituted about 8 per cent of Hungary's population according to the 1910 census, but around a quarter of Budapest's inhabitants were Jewish – the second-largest Jewish population in Europe after Warsaw (at around 36 per cent). By 1910 Jews made up half of Budapest's doctors and lawyers, a third of its engineers, and a quarter of its artists and writers. Jews were largely responsible for Budapest's transformation into a publishing hub: more than 40 per cent of the journalists working on the thirty-nine daily newspapers were Jews. The Mayor of Vienna in the 1890s, the rabidly anti-Semitic Karl Lueger, dubbed the city 'Judapest', an epithet that stuck.

The majority of the major industrial oligarchs were Jews, including the richest and most powerful of them all, Manfréd Weiss, who created and ran the country's largest manufacturing enterprise, the munitions plant on Csepel Island, which became a vast industrial suburb in southern Budapest and was the largest supplier of armaments to the

Austro-Hungarian army. Zsigmond Kornfeld dominated the transport and milling industries. Ferenc Chorin controlled mining – in Hungary and many parts of the Habsburg Empire. Leó Lánczy, along with several other Jews, was the most powerful banker. The leading figures in the Budapest Stock Exchange and the National Association of Manufacturers were Jewish. The professions were dominated by Jews. By 1900 more than two-thirds of young men at medical school in Budapest (there were no women there yet) were Jews. Large numbers were beginning to join the ranks of the major landowners. Nearly a fifth of the estates between 200 and 1,000 *hold* (a singular Hungarian measure of land amounting to around half a hectare) were Jewish-owned.[4]

Substantial numbers made the next step and converted to Christianity, including many prominent Jews, who took Heinrich Heine's cruel but honest advice to heart: 'The certificate of baptism is the admission ticket to European culture.'* Many Jewish families 'celebrated' the millennium year in 1896 by changing their surnames to make them sound more Hungarian. Increasing numbers of Jewish magnates joined the Habsburg nobility.

Jews had been careful about entering politics for fear of an anti-Semitic backlash. But by the early 1900s the sons and grandsons of the Jewish 'aristocracy' were beginning to enter Parliament and government. In 1910 a quarter of the Liberal Party in Parliament were from Jewish origin, and on the eve of the First World War there were five Jewish ministers in the Hungarian government, though they were all Christian converts.

Many Jews joined the Imperial *k.u.k.* army and some reached high rank. One of the three field marshals in the 1880s was the monumentally bewhiskered and bemedalled Hungarian Eduard von Schweitzer, who had never converted to Christianity. He regularly attended synagogue in Budapest, kept kosher and when dining with Emperor Franz Jozsef, who was fond of him, he requested special dispensation from the rabinnical authorities to be permitted to eat non-kosher dishes.

The most successful Jewish officer of them all served originally in the Hungarian army, the *Honvédség*, Baron Samu Hazai (born Kohn), the

---

* Including my great-grandfather on my father's side, who had been born Abraham Schwartz but changed his name to Mátyás Sebestyén – and my grandparents on my mother's side.

son of a well-to-do Budapest wine merchant. He and his two brothers joined the army as enlisted men in the 1870s, and he became one of the youngest officers in the service, at which point he converted to Catholicism. He became a colonel on the General Staff in 1900, still in his forties, a full general in 1907 and Hungarian Minister for Defence in 1910, which he remained until 1917 when Emperor Charles made him Deputy Chief of the Imperial General Staff. There were twenty-four other Jewish generals or senior staff officers.[5]

On the whole, Zionism didn't appeal to Budapest Jews and never attracted much of a following, though two of the founders of modern Zionism, Theodor Herzl and Max Nordau, were originally Hungarian. Herzl was born in the building adjoining the Dohány Street Synagogue, but he was a teenager when he moved from the city and his career as a journalist and his development of Zionism did not take off until he had left Hungary.* It was life in Vienna and Paris, as much as his upbringing in Budapest, which taught Herzl that assimilation for Jews was an illusion and undesirable because the roots of anti-Semitism in Europe were so deep. Neolog Jews were much more interested in becoming Magyars – until at least the 1930s, when increasing numbers, but even then a mere dribble, became interested in emigration to Palestine. 'Most of us thought we had found Zion, the Promised Land on the Danube, and had little interest in going to Palestine or anywhere else,' as Aabbi Löw, the wife of a rabbi, wrote at the end of the nineteenth century.

In 1912, for the first time a Jew, Ferenc Heltai, was elected Mayor of Budapest. He was Herzl's uncle, but that made no difference to the proto-Zionist's views. He warned Hungarian Jews against counting too much on assimilation. 'I'll gladly resign my claim to the Hungarian Jews if only I were certain that their patriotism would save them from the misery of anti-Semitism,' he wrote. 'But the Jews of Hungary will also be overtaken by their doom, which will be all the more brutal and merciless as time passes, and wilder, too, the stronger they get in the meantime. There is no escaping it.'

Crown Prince Rudolf, heir to the throne until his grisly death in 1889 in an apparent suicide pact with his teenage mistress, had several Jewish friends and was known to be a great supporter of Jews in the Austrian

---

* His birthplace is an excellent museum of the history of Hungarian Jews.

Empire – and also of Hungarian aspirations in general. He likened Budapest to London and thought it 'the England of the East, a similarly free haven of enlightenment and progress . . . In Budapest there is vitality, revival, self-assurance and confidence in the future, features which every liberal era can produce, and which can be observed here with pleasure and contentment, but which are unfortunately lacking on the other side of the black-and-yellow frontier posts.'

Budapest's Jews went into deep mourning when he died. The Neolog community turned his memorial service at the Dohány Street Synagogue into a monumental display of patriotism and loyalty to the monarchy. Ten thousand mourners crowded into a building designed to hold 3,000. Hundreds more stood in the courtyard outside. Inside the synagogue all the lamps, walls and sacred scrolls were draped in heavy black cloth. To a man and woman, all wore black. A choir of forty, led by the internationally celebrated tenor Mór Friedman, sang an emotional rendition of the *kaddish*, the prayer for the dead, and Psalm 19. The meaning of Chief Rabbi Samuel Kohn's sermon was clear to everyone: a passionate plea for Jews to integrate into Magyar life. 'Hungarian Jews assume a larger share in the general mourning and grief than any other religious group,' he said. 'Emperor Franz Jozsef is dearer to us than to any other religion; he is not only our lord, our king, but also our benefactor . . . the object of our most fervent prayers, of our heart's unending gratitude. It is under his rule that we regained what the dark centuries had deprived us of, our most precious treasure, our freedom and equality.' A short while later, in another sermon Kohn explained further the position of Jews in Hungary. 'We know ourselves to be Hungarians body and soul,' he said. 'And yet we are Jews. We identify as such. The Jewish word is an adjective to the Hungarian word and means this: we are Hungarians, what is more Jewish Hungarians – or Hungarians of the Jewish faith.'[6]

At times the backlash was severe and turned ugly. Various openly anti-Semitic organizations were formed, disappeared and re-formed from the late 1870s onwards. The most influential, which peaked around the time of the Tiszaeszlár Affair, was led by Győző Istóczy, a county magistrate who had bungled a case involving a Jewish plaintiff against the local district and lost his job as a result. He fired up resentment of Jews among the peasantry and poorer gentry (who had the vote) and he won a seat in Parliament on a viciously anti-Jewish ticket. He proposed, among other things, the creation of a Jewish state in Palestine, to which most Hungarian and other Jews would be deported.*

Istóczy's Anti-Semitic League appealed to the same support base as the fascist organizations a couple of generations later, and the rhetoric was more or less identical, including the chilling use of the phrase the 'final solution'. His rallying call was 'Wake up Hungary' against the dangers of Jewish assimilation. Well before Hitler was born he wrote:

I have come to the conclusion that the task of the final solution to the Jewish question has devolved on our generation. What is at stake here is not medieval Jew-baiting . . . In the Middle Ages the people of Europe faced Jews as individuals, whereas in our day we have to deal with Jews as a political and social institution. It is an undeniable fact that modern Jewry forms an internal Trojan horse within the European state, a distinct ethnicity, with political and social power, not simply a religious denomination, as Jews would like to claim.

His party split amid personal squabbles. But soon it was replaced by another extreme group, Awakening Magyars, which attracted many radical young people at the time. The group was inspired by an ul-tramontane priest, Ottokár Prohászka, and its more unruly members often beat up Jews on the Budapest streets.[7] Higher-crust anti-Semites disdained that kind of crude street violence. They looked down on those who went too far – or, as the poet Attila József put it, 'indulged in the vulgar sin of hating Jews even more than is necessary'.

The court in Vienna and the Hungarian government may have opened the doors to Jews, but the nobility and upper gentry on the whole would still have little to do with them. Jews were excluded – by custom if not by the law – in local county administration outside the capital and barred from membership of the social and political hub of Budapest, the National Casino. Yet in reality, despite superficial sophistication and the veneer of respectability, when it came to Jews they were little

---

* Istóczy's family lived a few blocks from Theodor Herzl in Budapest. His ideas may have predated Zionism as defined by Herzl, but Budapest Jews realized what his pur-pose was in sending Jews out of Europe. It was one of the reasons why Zionism never attracted much support among Hungarian Jews.

different from the lumpenproletariat. When in the 1880s the Prince of Wales, later Edward VII, went to Hungary to shoot and to enjoy himself amid Budapest's lively demi-monde, he stayed at the house of a Jewish banker. Count Miklós Pálffy, of ancient lineage, refused to attend a reception held for the prince because he would not set foot in a Jewish house.

On the other hand, the aristocrats who believed work was beneath them and were reluctant to meet people 'in trade' were happy to benefit from the capitalist boom after 1867, so much of it run by Jews. It was not beneath many of the best-born magnates to sit on the boards and lend their names to various banks and industrial conglomerates owned and run by Jews. In 1893 a researcher established that thirty-four Zichys, twenty-nine Széchenyis and twenty-seven Pallavicinis did so, plus a handful of Andrássys and Esterházys. As one of the most illustrious nobles of his age, Count Julius Károlyi, explained: 'Just as we keep the gypsies so they can play . . . [music] we keep the Jews so that they can work instead of us.'[8]

22

ILLIBERAL DEMOCRACY

There must be no place for caution, calculation and thrift. As the symbol of the constitution of Hungary, the Parliament building must be monumental and resplendent . . . to the eyes of our friends and foes alike.

Kálmán Tisza, Prime Minister of Hungary, 1883

From any hilltop view in Buda, as the broad sweep of the Danube gently bends through the city below, the focal point of the observer's eye will almost certainly be the Parliament building, magnificent in its pomp and grandeur, according to many admirers – Hans Christian Andersen, who knew a thing or two about fairy tales, admired its 'fantastical . . . unreal' beauty. It is not to everyone's taste, though. 'A Turkish bath crossed with a Gothic chapel' sneered Gyula Illyés, one of Hungary's finest twentieth-century writers. Whatever one might think of the aesthetics, nobody can deny that as a building it is monumental – or its demand to be noticed.[1]

It took seventeen years to build. When construction began, the architect, Imre Steindl, was a fit and healthy forty-five-year-old. By the time it was near to completion he was almost blind and so ill with heart and kidney disease that he had to direct work from a chair carried to the spot by contractors. By 1904, when it officially opened, he was dead. But, as ordered, he had designed the biggest Parliament building in the world, loosely based on Westminster but with plenty of added-on features: 'an eclectic combination of Magyar-medieval, French Renaissance, Westminsterian neo-Gothic, with a neo-Baroque ground floor plan and much polychrome inside', according to one contemporary enthusiast. It had no less than twenty-seven gates; around 40 kilos of 22-carat gold were used in its decoration. Steindl spoke little about the project while

223

work was going on, but towards the end of his life he told an interviewer about what he had been trying to achieve. 'I did not want to establish a new style with the Parliament because I could not build a monumental building of this kind, one that would be used for centuries, with ephemeral details,' he said. 'My desire was to combine this fine medieval style with national and personal features, humbly and carefully as required by art.'

For all the vast size of its Parliament, as so many people at the time pointed out, there was a pitifully small amount of Hungarian democracy. At the time the new Parliament opened only around 7 per cent of Hungary's male population had the right to vote – the nobility and townspeople who qualified within property ownership requirements. Even most of the bourgeoisie could not vote, though in Budapest the voting list was marginally higher, at around 10 per cent. Of course, other Western European countries had voting restrictions based on property ownership, too – and no women could vote until later – but the franchise was much smaller in Hungary than elsewhere with less ostentatious Parliaments. The non-Magyar population, the so called 'nationalities', the Serbs, Croats, Romanians and Slovaks who constituted almost exactly half the total population of Hungary, were drastically underrepresented. In 1907, out of 414 seats in Parliament non-Magyars had only nine, and three years later the number was fewer than that. The Hungarian elite thought that, as Catherine 'Katinka' Károlyi, born an Andrássy and brought up in the grandest of Hungarian families, explained: 'From the earliest age, we were reared to believe that democracy in Hungary was the most dangerous of evils. To let the Tóts [Slovaks] and Olahs [Romanians] have the vote would, I was always told, be the end of Hungarian supremacy, a dogma on which I was brought up to believe as others on the Holy Trinity.'

There was no secret ballot in most of the country until after the Second World War, when in any case voting didn't matter much under the Communist dictatorship – as the saying went then, 'the voting was democratic, the counting wasn't'. In around half the constituencies, even in the 1920s and 1930s, voters had to declare in public whom they were voting for – in front of gendarmes carrying notebooks. The Prime Minister in the 1920s, István Bethlen, said the secret vote was 'not compatible with the Hungarian people's open character'.[2]

*

From its earliest beginnings until the middle of the nineteenth century the Hungarian Parliament had no permanent seat but met on an ad hoc basis at different locations by royal summons. In early Habsburg times this was mostly at Pozsony/Pressburg. In the Reform Age, when nationalism grew and calls for independence increased, there was an outcry for a permanent Parliament, but not in Pressburg, which the nationalists thought was far too close to Vienna. Pest was chosen as the location – to the indignation of some worthies in Buda. The first plan for a building was designed in 1840 by Mihály Pollack, architect of the classical-styled and beautifully proportioned National Museum in the Inner City of Pest. His idea was to design a massive building by the river, but in a Florentine Renaissance style inspired by the Pitti Palace, with a bit of Palladio added on. For many years nothing came of the plan, or of several others proposed by Hungarian and foreign architects – partly because of the turmoil of the 1848 Revolution and the War of Independence.

In 1865 a parliamentary committee was set up to find a solution for a permanent Parliament; it opted for a far more modest building, decided on a location, in Bródy Sándor Street, opposite the National Museum, and commissioned Miklós Ybl, who got the job done in a hurry: it was completed in just eleven months.* But it was soon discovered how poor the construction was and a faulty design meant that things were continually going wrong in the building. The principal problem was that the acoustics were appalling – an issue that, thankfully, Ybl managed to sort out before he went on to design the Budapest Opera House.[3]

In 1880 another parliamentary committee decided to tender for a new building that would incorporate both houses and would be a 'monumental symbol representing the entirety of the Hungarian people . . . to soar above all other buildings, to express the power of the Hungarian nation on the banks of the Danube'. There was strong disagreement about the style of the new building. Gothic Revival was chosen because, the then government insisted, the Hungarian state had been at its strongest in the medieval era, the heyday of Gothic style. As the government spokesman

---

* The building is now the Italian Cultural Institute. The Upper House, the House of Peers, met there while the Lower House sat in the National Museum; the Parliament had two chambers until 1945.

Sándor Országh said: 'It is what we owe to our past, as this style was the style of its most glorious period, and its slender, dynamically vertical forms also express the present goals of the Hungarian nation.'

In the Upper House, the influential Bishop Arnold Ipolyi, an art historian as well as the second most senior churchman in Hungary, said it was vital that a grand edifice should be built as even relatively unimportant medieval towns such as Florence had become great only because they had put their energies into building cathedrals and creating art. 'Our new Parliament building should be splendid and monumental, not only to promote art and architecture, but also because the grandeur of the nation and the state demand it,' he declared.

When the plans for the new building were presented in the old House of Deputies in 1883 the otherwise penny-pinching and careful Prime Minister, Kálmán Tisza, pronounced that in this case 'there must be no place for caution, calculation and thrift. As the symbol of the constitution of Hungary, the Parliament building most be monumental and resplendent . . . to the eyes of our friends and foes alike.'[4]

As it was being built during the 1890s – a boom time when much of Budapest looked like an enormous building site – critical voices immediately grumbled that there was nothing especially Hungarian about the place, though local carpenters, stonemasons and artists were used and almost all the materials were Hungarian in origin. It was – and still is – monumental: 265 metres long, 96 metres high at the top of the dome and containing around 700 rooms.* Opinions still differ, but there is no question the building has stood the test of time. Jérôme and Jean Tharaud, in their 1920s classic book in which Budapest is a central character, *Quand Israël est roi*, loathed it, describing it as 'The Parliament . . . newly built on the banks of the Danube, by those Hungarian architects with their bizarre passion for medievalism, without reason.' But Patrick Leigh Fermor was impressed: 'Aswarm with statues, this frantic and marvellous pile was a tall, steep-roofed gothic nave escorted for a prodigious length by medieval pinnacles touched with gilding and adorned by crockets; and it was crowned, at the point where its transepts intersected, by the kind of ribbed and egg-shaped dome that might more predictably have dom-

* The 96 metres is always mentioned by tour guides as alluding to the year 896, when the Magyar tribes were supposed to have entered the Carpathian basin, and is the same height as the dome of the St Stephens Basilica, behind Andrássy Avenue.

inated the roofs of a Renaissance town in Tuscany, except that the dome itself was topped by a sharp and bristling gothic spire. Architectural dash could scarcely go further.' The novelist Kálmán Mikszáth, who in midlife tired of writing books and turned to politics, became a Member of the Hungarian Parliament and after his first session in the building judged it 'dazzling, true, but still gaudy'. The poet Endre Ady was referring more to what went on inside the building than to its appearance, but as usual phrased it pithily, calling it 'a beautiful nest of robbers'.[5]

The landed magnates ran Hungary during the Dual Monarchy in a way they were no longer doing in Austria or most other parts of the Habsburg Empire. They held over 85 per cent of the Hungarian government ministries from 1867 to the end of the First World War and an even larger proportion of the Imperial k.u.k. ministries that were granted as Hungary's share. The historic families which had once opposed the Austrians – the Batthyánys, Széchenyis, Esterházys – had long since made their peace with them and divided the Imperial spoils. Power would remain in their hands for a while yet. Serfdom may have been abolished a half-century earlier, but Hungary was still semi-feudal before the First World War.* Originally a right-wing political thinker, Oszkár Jászi, who saw the Parliament being built in Budapest, moved further to the Left in his later years and wrote on the eve of the war: 'in no other country apart from Poland before its partition in 1793–95 and

---

* Only two Prime Ministers from 1867 to 1918 came from the bourgeoisie – Sándor Wekerle was the first in 1892. Despite his position, many of the high nobles would not call on him and his family socially – they could not move in the same circles, as Catherine 'Katinka' Károlyi recalled. One afternoon her brother-in-law, Pál Esterházy, could not avoid meeting the Prime Minister and his wife at a tea party: 'Pál was so indignant about this democratization of the world, and so outraged at having to submit to the ordeal that on his way home he was literally sick. That an Esterházy should have to call on a Wekerle was enough to turn his stomach.' On the eve of war in 1914 the Prime Minister, István Tisza, whose father had been Hungarian premier for ten years a generation earlier and proudly called himself a 'liberal', said he devoutly believed it was the 'sacred mission of the nobility to lead the Hungarian nation . . . peasants are incapable of exercising political rights, unreliable from the standpoint of national unity, enlightenment and of human progress and easy targets for demagoguery.' These were the men who led the nation into the disastrous war that destroyed old Hungary and drove their people to catastrophe.

Russia did the Church and nobility so dominate economic and political life or possess such power'.

But in the late nineteenth century there was a rising new class in Hungary that would make history in future generations. A politically conscious working class was slow to appear in Hungary, but when it did – almost only in Budapest – it was bigger than anywhere else in Central and Eastern Europe, except in Germany. The first labour organization, The General Workers' Association, campaigned for universal male suffrage and for adult education. Inspired by the early socialists who led the short-lived Paris Commune of 1870, the Hungarian association was founded and chiefly organized by Mihály Táncsics after the Compromise. Briefly it had a significant following in Budapest, among the workers in the growing numbers of mills and factories, but the Industrial Revolution had been slow to arrive in Hungary. It organized a series of strikes in the textile industry in support of a ten-hour working day. When the Paris Commune was suppressed, the Hungarian government felt encouraged to break up the Association and bring treason charges against some of the strike leaders, though they were dropped for lack of evidence. Enthusiasm for strike action among its members waned.[6]

The Hungarian Social Democratic Party was formed in 1890 and led by Pál Engelmann, a good friend of Karl Marx and Friedrich Engels. A big May Day demonstration that year in Budapest attracted more than 40,000 people to a march and rally in the People's Park. The party established a trade union wing in various Budapest factories, but at the turn of the century there were still only about 20,000 union members, fewer than 3 per cent of the industrial workforce. Many industrialists refused to recognize union membership and the government clamped down hard on industrial unrest; the police and the army broke up strikes savagely at the sign of any serious dissent among workers. In the three years between 1897 and 1900, fifty-one strikers were killed and 114 badly injured. Hundreds more were jailed. That put off workers joining a union unless they were totally committed or totally desperate.

After the boom times there was an economic downturn in the early 1900s that led to mass emigration, mainly to the US, where cities like Cleveland, Ohio received a huddled mass of arrivals from Hungary. Among those who stayed, a wave of strikes between 1905 and 1906 periodically brought the iron and coal industries to a virtual standstill. This was after a failed revolution in Russia had caused chaos in St Petersburg, Moscow and other cities. Fearing the Russian troubles would spread, the Hungarian government put pressure on business owners to raise wages by around 10 per cent.

The party launched a national daily paper in 1904, *Népszava* (The People's Voice), a high-quality organ in its early days which attracted some excellent writers and reached a mass audience of people who never became socialists but were interested in decent writing and new ideas.

On 10 October 1907, more than 100,000 people turned up on a cold and rainy day to a rally calling for universal male suffrage – the largest political demonstration in Budapest there had yet been. It was named Red Thursday. Five years later, on 23 May 1912, a similar-sized rally was ruthlessly suppressed by police and the army after trams were overturned and barricades were erected in central Pest. Five people were killed, scores were injured and around 150 demonstrators were arrested.

The government responded with some improvements to working conditions, a minimal form of social insurance and accident insurance for workers, legal holidays and sick leave. By and large, however, conditions of life for Hungarian workers, in Budapest as well as the provinces, lagged way behind most of Western Europe. But in the factories, newspaper offices and coffee houses of Budapest a generation of revolutionaries was beginning to make its mark.[7]

23

MY COUNTRY RIGHT OR WRONG

History is the most dangerous product contrived by the human brain. It transports nations into a dream-world, into raptures, leads them to believe in a specious past . . . causes their sores to fester, disturbs their peace, drives them to megalomania or paranoia and embitters the nation, causing them to be full of insufferable and conceited pride . . . History justifies whatever one wants it to. It clarifies virtually nothing because there is nothing that cannot be proved by it.

Paul Valéry (1871–1945)

On 15 September 1883 an anonymous article appeared prominently in the influential conservative Vienna daily *Neues Wiener Tagblatt*. Though it was unsigned, it was obviously written by someone well in-formed about the latest political gossip in Budapest and at the court in Vienna. It concluded rousingly: 'An abyss is opening up in Hungary and much that still appears viable today can easily fall into it.' Within a few days the news seeped out that its author – in an unprecedented step for a senior member of the royal family – was the heir to the Habsburg throne, Crown Prince Rudolf. Like his mother, the empress, he was deeply sympathetic to Hungarian autonomy and was on friendly terms with many of the Liberal politicians in Budapest. But he was seriously concerned about what he would inherit as King of Hungary. 'The sad thing for Hungary is the Magyars' lack of consideration and inability to understand that nothing can be achieved by bad treatment and con-tempt . . . for the other nationalities, who are numerically superior, and of whom one has absolute need in order to preserve the same size of the Hungarian state,' he wrote. 'In many, in fact in most parts of the territories of the Crown of St Stephen only the nobility, the officials and the Jews are Hungarian – the people belong to other tribes. In their boundless blindness even in the most influential circles Hungarians forget this fact.'

The piece caused a political flurry for a few days, but prompted no changes in policy or soul-searching. Rather the opposite: successive administrations of Liberal politicians in Budapest embarked on attempts to suppress the national aspirations of Slovaks, Romanians, Serbs and Croats – 49.2 per cent of the Hungarian population, according to the first census of the new millennium. Bans were introduced on schools teaching in local languages; Magyar local government was imposed on the regions. From time to time political activists or language campaigners were jailed by the Hungarian courts – seventeen Romanians and fourteen Slovaks in 1906 – in the same way that the Austrians a century earlier had jailed Magyar nationalists.[1]

The main weakness of the Dual Monarchy – a large realm supposedly with two equally powerful political centres – had always been that it was predicated on the suppression of a voice for the Slavs. The Hungarians in their part of the Empire were allowed to dominate all their nationalities, and the German/Austrian part on their side of the River Leitha, seen as the border, would be allowed the same rights over theirs. However intricate and superficially clever the dual system seemed, this was a truth never seriously addressed. It was untenable for any length of time and was unlikely to withstand any major crisis, as some members of the court party in Vienna had warned in the 1860s. Designed to accommodate nationalism in one place, Hungary, 'dualism' was too fragile to withstand other nationalisms elsewhere. The elite in Budapest never recognized this, or even when some did they could not accept it.

The national consciousness that had driven the Hungarian revival, the 1848 Revolution and the War of Independence was growing fast among Slovaks, Croats, Serbs and Romanians in the Magyar domains. They were developing their language as the Hungarians had done earlier in the nineteenth century. The Compromise did not change these realities – it made them sharper because it solidified Hungarian rule. The Hungarians were the masters now and Vienna had barely any say, except to some extent in Croatia, where almost no Magyars lived and the local people were permitted a degree of autonomy. Otherwise the minorities who lived in Hungary had no rights of self-government at all. Increased representation in the Parliament, it was generally accepted on the 'thin end of the wedge' principle, would have meant being swamped by politicians from Slovakia, Serbia, Romania and so on.[2]

The so-called liberals were as blind as the reactionaries in this area. As for the Left, they were concerned with better conditions for workers in the factories and industrial enterprises in Budapest and a few other major towns, not nationalist dreams among Slovaks. Even the moderate and decent Kálmán Tisza, the longest-serving Prime Minister in the era of 'dualism', declared in 1875 that 'there can be only one viable nation within the frontiers of Hungary; that is the Hungarian one. Hungary cannot become an eastern Switzerland because then it would cease to exist.' He intervened in a court case in eastern Hungary to forbid the use of Romanian in local schools. He told a group of Saxons in Transylvania, an old-established and loyal community, that 'a Saxon nation does not exist'. His later successor, Dezső Bánffy, declared in 1891 that Hungary, 'a unified, national state, cannot tolerate political parties on the basis of nationality'. He forbade the use of place names in two languages, even on railway station signs in Croatia, where the Magyar population was less than 15 per cent. The teaching of the Magyar language was compulsory in every school in the kingdom, and only a few people in the regions were allowed any lessons to be taught in the local tongues. Ágoston Trefort, Minister for Religious Affairs and Education for sixteen years from 1872, declared: 'I do not wish to enforce Magyarization on anybody. However, I must assert that in Hungary the State can survive only as a Magyar one. The aspirations towards a polyglot status are politically crude and short work has to be made of them.'[3]

Ultra-nationalism in Hungary was not the main cause of the First World War or the only reason why the Dual Monarchy fell apart after the conflict. But it was certainly a major factor. In Hungary, 'chauvinism' became a positive word among many Budapest politicians and their propagandists, as opposed to the pejorative meaning it had then, and has had since, in most European languages. Jenő Rákosi, one of the most influential political commentators in Budapest around the turn of the century, demanded a total 'Hungarianness, when every man in

Hungary will feel in his innermost soul that he had become a Magyar chauvinist'. In 1899 he wrote in a long article in the *Pesti Hírlap*: 'What we need is a nation of 30 million Magyars! Then we would possess the East of Europe. That is why every Hungarian, politician or patriot . . . must tack on to his flag "30 million Magyars"; then all our problems would be solved in one stroke . . . The Hungarian nation must rise to the highest realms of a sovereign nation, and she can achieve that when she becomes, in all her members and institutions, totally Magyar.' This would mean doubling the size of the population, and quadrupling the number of ethnic Magyars.* The popular historian and political philosopher Béla Grünwald thought that the non-Magyar communities within Hungary were 'not capable of independent advancement . . . [it is] the destiny of Magyardom to assimilate them, to absorb them into a superior people . . . [fulfilling] our duty to humanity to elevate them as if we were the champions of civilization.'

Chauvinism meant something different, even in Austria, at the time. For example, Emperor Franz Jozsef in a Crown Council meeting in 1878 welcomed 'the salutary rise of patriotism within the Empire and in Hungary. But one must keep things within reason, lest such sentiments degenerate into political chauvinism.' When in 1906 R.W. Seton-Watson, the British campaigner for minority rights in Eastern Europe, asked József Kristóffy, the economist and former minister in the Hungarian government, where Magyarization would lead he said, simply, 'We shall go on until there are no Slovaks left.'[4]

The Hungarian magnates on the whole, for all their sophistication, shared the general public opinion. Although most had country estates in Transylvania, Croatia, Slovakia or the Vojvodina – the Magyar part of modern-day Serbia – they had no idea of what was happening among the nationalities. They believed they were being 'liberal' – an elastic word – in their attitudes. Oszkár Jászi, a writer who moved in aristocratic circles, was convinced 'that they firmly believed there was no suppression of any kind of the nationalist causes, but on the contrary, they thought the Magyar nation granted so many freedoms and privileges to the "inferior" ethnic groups that its liberalism was unprecedented in

---

* He possessed the zeal of the immigrant, a common phenomenon in Central and Eastern Europe. He was of German descent – his family name before he changed it was Kremsner.

history. It must have seemed outrageously ungrateful that second-class people should have responded to such magnanimity with dissatisfaction and try to incite public opinion in foreign countries against the Magyars with false accusations and slander,' he said. 'The public in Budapest was genuinely convinced of this opinion. Educated and politically interested circles . . . [in Budapest] had no contact with the intelligentsia of other nationalities and knew nothing of their opinions.'[5]

Illusions about the liberal order and the stability of the Hungarian 'constitution' abounded and occasionally reached comic levels. Count Albert Apponyi, a long-serving minister in various governments from the 1880s to 1918, caused amusement when he said at an Inter-Parliamentary Union in St Louis, Missouri that Hungary had the oldest representative government in all of Europe – nonsense to anyone who knew anything about Hungarian history or politics. He said that 'though never written down, the Hungarian constitution had grown organically and succeeded in solving the problem of strengthening the Monarchy without sacrificing freedom better than any other'. On the other hand, the old count was more clear-sighted about his national politicians. He remarked once that 'whenever three Hungarians talk politics they form a party . . . one is President, another Vice President and the third becomes General Secretary, who regards it as his duty to make "an important statement" on every occasion.'

Gyula Andrássy, son of Hungary's first post *Ausgleich* Prime Minister, in a three-volume history of Hungary written just before the outbreak of the First World War, wrote that 'Hungary's present con-stitution can be traced back in an unbroken sequence to the freedom of the nomad era . . . Of the peoples who have established states in Europe up to the ninth century, only we have succeeded . . . in maintaining the unity of the state from the first moment in an unbroken continuity by preserving . . . the hegemony of the nation until this day.' These were people unlikely to make compromises with Serbian dissidents.*

---

* These bouts of intense Magyar nationalism would recur again and again and reach absurd heights. When Johann Strauss's *Die Fledermaus* was first performed in Buda-pest in 1878 the director changed the opera's setting to ancient China in order to avoid it taking place in Vienna with German names, which, more bizarrely still, were changed to Italian ones.

Very few figures in leadership declared in public that it was time to encourage the democratic co-operation of the other people in the Danube basin. Even socialists in the opposition like Táncsics had no time for Slav nationalism. A few isolated voices stood out. In the 1900s the poet Endre Ady consistently railed against those he called 'humbug nationalists' and 'the manufacturers of new legends'. He was a literary star but even he was drowned out, though he left poems like this that had resonance later:

> When will our voices speak out loud?
> Magyar or not – it does not matter –
> We are the crushed, oppressed and cowed.
> How long must we be ruled by blackguards?
> Poor, chicken-hearted millions we?
> How long must the Hungarian people
> Like caged and captive starlings be?
> Hungary's miserable beggars.
> We've neither breath nor faith for fare;
> But all will come to us tomorrow
> If we but wish, if we but dare.[6]

Rhetoric was one thing, demonstrations of national feeling were a more reliable guide to sentiment. They could not come much bigger in Hungary than the funeral procession for Lajos Kossuth, who died aged ninety-one after three decades of Italian exile. At least a million people turned out on the streets of Budapest on 1 April 1894 for an immense show of Hungarian nationalism. Kossuth had never reconciled himself to the Compromise with Austria or Franz Jozsef as King of Hungary. He could have returned at any time since 1867 but would not. He chose to remain stateless. He was re-elected time and again to Parliament *in absentia* and dozens of Hungarian towns had made him an honorary citizen to restore the Hungarian citizenship that had been stripped from him many years earlier – on Franz Jozsef's orders.

The emperor, too, would not forgive and forget. Franz Jozsef refused to declare his funeral a state occasion. There were violent protests demanding that he change his mind – a dozen people were badly injured in the crush – but the ageing emperor would not budge.* Neither the Hungarian government, Parliament nor the Budapest city authorities were allowed to be represented officially. When Kossuth died, the city of Turin handed his body to a delegation of private citizens from Hungary who organized a special train to Budapest. There was to be no official mourning period, but the city was shrouded in black for three days and closed down almost completely. The coffin lay in the great hall of the National Museum – though a court circular and notice in the newspapers insisted that Kossuth was not 'lying in state'. Tens of thousands of people came from all over Hungary to pay their respects; the honour guard of four volunteers around the coffin changed every half-hour. Mór Jókai, his old friend and revolutionary comrade, gave the funeral oration.[7]

---

* This encouraged a new wave of anti-Austrian feeling, expressed in a way that has been common throughout the history of Budapest. Time and again over the years, statues for once-significant figures have been removed and replaced – or destroyed – when times and opinions have changed or when political correctness is redefined. The symbolic act of replacing them has itself been seen as part of history. In the early 1850s a giant statue to General Heinrich Hentzi, the Austrian defender of Buda Castle against the Hungarian national army in the War of Independence, was placed in one of the main squares of Castle Hill. It had stuck in the throats of Hungarians for forty years; there had been many demonstrations against it and numerous people had been arrested for trying to demolish it. Now another campaign to remove the loathed Hentzi was launched. The Austrians refused, but in 1899 they finally relented 'on grounds of public safety' and placed it in the park of the officer cadet school in a Budapest suburb where few ever see it.

PART THREE

THE WORLD AT WAR

24

THE BEGINNING OF THE END

When I was called up for the Austro-Hungarian army at the outbreak
of the War . . . the intoxicating joy of life was interrupted; the world
had gone mad.

Michael Curtiz (1886–1962)

Nobody in living memory had seen a tornado before in Budapest. At
around 9.30 a.m. on the morning of 23 July 1914 the sky above the city
burst open, a red flame that one witness reported 'seemed as bright as
the sun' tore through the centre of town and winds of 120 kilometres
an hour threw people, horses and a bus into buildings. A dozen people
were killed, more than seventy were rushed into hospitals, and scores of
offices and apartment blocks were demolished. Some of the statuary outside the Budapest Opera House was wrecked. The roofs of St Stephen's
Basilica in Pest and of the Matthias Church in Buda were swept away.
The Chain Bridge suffered severe damage and was closed for weeks afterwards. 'We thought the entire Danube would be sucked into the air
and the water would be deposited on to the streets,' one mother who was
walking with her daughter recalled later. 'If it was an omen, we didn't
know of what.'

Almost a month earlier, Archduke Franz Ferdinand, heir to the
Habsburg throne, and his wife Sophie had been assassinated on the
streets of Sarajevo by a Bosnian Serb teenager, sparking a chain of events
and Great Power decisions that led to catastrophic consequences for
Europe – but nowhere more so than in Hungary. War was welcomed
everywhere among almost all people, from St Petersburg to South-
ampton, with a kind of frenzied hysteria. In Budapest, on the evening
after the freak tornado, a group of journalists comprising most of the
editorial team of the city's best-selling newspaper *Az Est* (The Evening)

were seated at a long table in the New York Café. 'Never have I heard so few jokes as on that Thursday evening,' recalled Ferenc Molnár, the up-and-coming playwright and well-known reporter for a rival publication:

> The time was half past eleven. An automobile stopped in front of the café. At the journalists' table everyone rose. The café was jam-packed. There was a sudden silence, at some tables people jumped to their feet. That night remarkably few women were in the café. A gentleman comes running in, the next moment the long table is empty. More people from the café charge after them – the streets are full. Somewhere there's an automobile almost out of control; some men are standing up in it, others gripping the outside. The machine gives out a roar and rushes off with its cargo. One word lingers among the gathered crowds on the street: War. This strange, brief, thunder-like word now rises on the crowd, which rushes back inside the café with the news. Everyone is standing at a table. This one word amplifies into a howl until it reaches a terrifying crescendo, joining the thuds of many chairs put back at once – a sudden, frantic jumping to the feet, and then one great prolonged cry: War.[1]

Every morning for the next few days bells rang out from the city's churches. The newspapers competed in patriotic fervour – 'Serbia, you cur' was the splash headline in the liberal daily *Világ* (World), the day after the biggest news story for decades might have been 'Tornado tears through Budapest'. A song became a smash hit overnight and remained so for months into the war, with its refrain 'Just wait . . . just wait, Serbia you dog'.

On 28 July, the day war was declared by the Hungarian government, there was a massive spontaneous demonstration and an outpouring of joy swept through the bourgeois and substantially Jewish neighbourhood of Lipótváros in the centre of the city. Budapest-born Arthur Koestler, aged nine at the time, who would write about world politics for the next six decades, recalled it as his first political event. He was there on the streets with his governess amid the 'tremendous excitement. I tore myself away from her grip, and . . . joined the crowd as it shouted "Death to the Serbian dogs". How thrilling it was to be part of something "bigger than myself" and melting into a giant crowd ... I joined in the singing of the national song, God bless the Magyar.'

Recruiting parades with colourful uniforms and patriotic banners were held daily. At remarkable speed a large wooden National Benefaction statue of a horse was erected in the middle of Deák Square in central Budapest into which nails or small bronze plaques would be hammered to represent donations to the war effort.

The irony of the Hungarians going to war – and fervently so – after Franz Ferdinand's murder was lost on practically everybody. It was well known that the heir presumptive, nephew of the emperor, was no friend of the Magyars and had been reluctant even to set foot in Hungary. Franz Ferdinand made it known he had told Imperial officials that when he inherited the throne he would 'clip the wings of the Magyars'. In a letter to Kaiser Wilhelm II on 7 August 1909 he wrote: 'it is my repeated assertion that the so-called noble, chivalrous Magyar is the most infamous, anti-dynastic, lying and unreliable fellow and all the difficulties we have in the Monarchy have their roots exclusively in the Magyars. We must break this preponderance of the Hungarians! Otherwise, we shall indisputably become a Slav empire.'[2]

The Hungarian leadership had overwhelmingly supported the Triple Alliance with Germany and Turkey and were eager for war. Some Austrian court officials were convinced that a long war of attrition could not be won and at first Franz Jozsef, now eighty-four, agreed with them. But he was persuaded otherwise. The Prime Minister of Hungary, Count István Tisza, was a cautious man and privately had his doubts about going to war. But in public he was always as enthusiastic as were the other magnates who ran the country. When the war started he led the nation in a conflict he confidently predicted would be over in months, with the 'nationalities' being taught a lesson they would never forget. One French diplomat in Budapest described Hungary as 'the playground of four counts' who all believed that a humiliating defeat in war would halt demands for independence or autonomy on the periphery of Hungary in the Balkans and Slovakia. When the war was finally declared, Pál Esterházy, who had been in charge of several of the Habsburg offices of state over the previous twenty-five years, greeted the announcement with a loud clap of his hands and a cry of 'At last'.

The only leading public figure recognized in Budapest who spoke loudly against the clamour for war was Mihály Károlyi, one of the grandest of all the Hungarian magnates – his ancient family had the right to eleven points in their coronets instead of the usual nine allotted for a count. He alone belied his background and class. He became a convinced pacifist, would be the first President of a Hungarian Republic – and has gone down in Hungarian history as 'the scapegoat for an entire era'.

He had been a sickly child, born in 1875 with a cleft palate, a hare lip and practically blind in one eye. He was a determined and resilient character, though, as he fought a congenital speech defect. He had an operation on his palate performed in Vienna by the renowned surgeon Professor Theodor Billroth, which he never entirely overcame. But with great difficulty he worked with resolve to improve his speech and to make himself understood.

In his boyhood and youth the young Károlyi was brought up in a typical way for a Hungarian aristocrat. He spoke fluent German, French, English and understood Italian. Until he entered Parliament in 1910 he did not seem interested in politics, but appeared a dilettante. He was one of the wealthiest men in the country. He owned 17,000 hectares of farmed land and 13,000 of forests, seven hunting grounds, a mansion in the Inner City of Budapest with seventy-five rooms, a coal mine and the estate of Parád, which was turned into a spa because of its healthy mineral water. According to his own estimate his holdings were worth around 100 million gold forints.*[3]

He spent summers at his uncle's mansion on the Côte d'Azur and was known as a rake even among the group of spoilt rich kids of the era. The rest of the year he divided his time between Paris, London, Vienna and occasionally Budapest. He was a passionate card player. He lost an enormous amount of money – he estimated 12 million crowns, worth around US$60 million at 2022 values – just before he married Katinka, Catherine Andrássy. It didn't matter much; she had enough for both of

---

* His good friend Prince Esterházy was one of the wealthiest people in Europe at the turn of the century. He owned more than 300,000 hectares of land from Lake Fertő to the Great Hungarian Plain and several estates in Austria. He admitted once to Károlyi that he didn't know exactly what he owned. But others did: more than 700 villages and twenty-one palaces.

them. It was not at first a love match, but over time they became a true partnership in romance and politics. For much of his life until he was nearly forty Károlyi did not seem like a serious figure.

'When I first glimpsed him on the streets of Pest wearing his broad-brimmed, flat, arty hat – you had to be a count to get away with sporting such a hat – he still looked very much like the kind of young magnate the ordinary Budapest mortal might sight at the racetrack,' wrote Gyula Krúdy soon after the war ended:

It was not difficult to imagine him sunk into one of the easy chairs at the National Casino where it would never occur to the yawning, infinitely bored lounger to get up and stroll over to the library. One could picture him at the gaming table, losing sums that are phenome-nal in the history of Hungarian gambling – if we give credence to old neighbours in the vicinity of Károlyi Park who never saw the young count taking a walk in his garden. Likewise we may picture him at golf, tennis, yachting – in any way except in the very position that the mysterious hand of fate was to mete out to him . . . When I first saw him he was a happy-go-lucky young count who was the first to wear cream-coloured trousers with a light jacket in the summer . . . It is said that nothing happens by accident, but an examination of Mihály Károlyi's incalculable career must shatter all our beliefs in notions of calculated careers and conscious planning. Instead we are reminded of the unknown forces that create tremors deep un-derground or turbulence in the stratosphere. For it must have been from deep underground or high up in the air that the spirit emerged to guide the affairs of this bearded young man who sauntered by on the Budapest street, this impassive and nonchalant dandy, whose only worry seemed to be deciding what to do on this boring, endless summer day.

He had middle-class allies and friends in politics before the war, but by his own admission there was always a yawning gap between them. He met them, but wouldn't have brought them to dine at the Károlyi Palace in central Pest, with its extraordinary art collection and famously beautiful garden. 'Don't think it was arrogance,' he wrote in his mem-oirs later. 'In Habsburg Austro-Hungary it was simply impossible to behave otherwise. If I entered a middle-class home, I was stared at like an idol; women stood up, and those who knew how to curtsey did so as to royalty. Our world was so far apart from ordinary men, even ordinary "gentlemen".'[4]

Before the war Károlyi was much closer to the French and the English, two of the Triple Entente powers, than to Germany. He was opposed to Austria-Hungary's close alliance with Kaiser Wilhelm's military. 'I want a foreign policy in which we have a free hand and are not syco-phants of German imperialism,' he said in May 1914. 'We should draw near to England and France and Russia, thus ensuring our Balkan interests.' He made a lecture tour that spring in Europe to promote his idea of a democratic and federal Hungary with real autonomy for the nationalities.

On the eve of war in July 1914 he was on his way back from the US, where he had been holding a series of meetings on foreign policy with American, British and French policymakers. When his boat docked in France the war had already begun and he was interned for several weeks in Bordeaux before he was allowed to return to Hungary. Throughout the conflict he was the principal voice of opposition to the war. There were few in the wilderness with him anywhere in the country, to begin with. An exception was Mihály Babits, one of the most prominent authors of the first half of the twentieth century, who risked his career by protesting. 'I would rather spill gushing blood for the little finger of my sweetheart than for a hundred kings.' An entire issue of the influential magazine *Nyugat* (West) was pulped after it published his powerful anti-war poem 'Fortissimo'.*

*

---

* *Nyugat* was a high-quality literary magazine with a relatively big circulation among the intelligentsia in Budapest and at the front line of the 'culture wars' of the time. As its name suggested, its modernist writers looked towards Western Europe for influence and inspiration. They were often at odds with traditionalists – including Prime Minister Tisza, who railed against what he called the 'decadence' of the *Nyugat* group of poets and novelists. During the war, when he might have been busy elsewhere, he took up arms against the magazine: 'They want to ruin our morals, they want to disillusion us of our faith . . . A storm of protest should sweep away all those who commit such offences against the nation with their incomprehensible bombast, which is nothing more than spiritual anarchy and an emptiness of mind and heart.'

It wasn't over by Christmas. For Hungary the war became a disaster – and deeply unpopular – quickly. From the start there were defeats and little glory. Belying the dazzling uniforms of its elite regiments, the Dual Monarchy's army was poorly armed, poorly trained and poorly led. During the first month of the war Austria-Hungary lost 250,000 dead or wounded and 100,000 of its troops were taken prisoner. Hungary's losses in that time were 40 per cent of the total. Within weeks of being on the Eastern Front against the Russian army they were, humiliatingly, on the verge of being routed until German reinforcements rescued them. After less than six months the professional Habsburg army was all but wiped out and was forced to rely on conscripts and reserves. There was bloody stalemate for years of trench warfare on the Italian Front.

Károlyi continually pressed for an armistice and peace talks to start. He formed his own New Independence Party, with the support of a handful of pacifists to begin with, though its strength grew as the war of attrition dragged on. He travelled to neutral Switzerland in the spring of 1917 – just after the US entered the war – and had a long meeting with the French President, Raymond Poincaré, the details of which never became public at the time. Later it turned out that the talks ended within a couple of hours after Károlyi said that he thought the chances at that point of the Austro-Hungarians looking for a separate peace with the Western Allies were near zero. Károlyi was continually moving further to the Left, particularly after the revolutions in Russia. But in many ways he was an old-school Hungarian aristocrat in the grand manner. In early 1917 an argument with Prime Minister Tisza over an army deal, which committed Hungary to a substantial increase in defence spending, led to a duel – technically illegal in Hungary, but still often used by 'gentlemen' to settle disputes. After thirty-four bouts Károlyi was cut first, a shallow wound on the arm. Honour having been satisfied on both sides, the fight was stopped.[5]

The home front in Budapest was barely affected for the first three years of the war, though the public knew things were going badly and were war-weary. There were no serious food shortages and rationing was fairly mild. Two military hospitals had been established in the city, yet most citizens were shielded from the realities of the conflict. Krúdy captured the atmosphere and could sense the gloom: 'Often I think this

city is like a cheap hotel in a back alley where the window shades are
forever pulled down tight, never a loud word escapes into the night, the
piano player has gone to bed long ago, the desk clerk is nodding off; but
when the police raid the place they find a travelling salesman bricked
into the wall, a woman choked to death by pillows and a small child
squatting in the unused summer stove.'

There was 'an operetta-like' world of politics at the time, recalled
Ferenc Molnár, and an air of unreality. A month before the war ended in
defeat Károlyi spent several days deer-stalking with the Andrássy clan
in the Gyalu highlands in Transylvania. He told his wife and friends
back in Budapest that he'd stay hunting awhile because he didn't believe there would be any substantial change in events until the spring.
Nobody imagined that a centuries-old imperial dynasty, one of the most
powerful and influential in Europe, was about to disappear. 'Thinking
back on those days, a month or so before the fall of the Habsburg Monarchy,' Károlyi wrote years later, 'I feel better able to understand the
historical blindness of Louis XVI when he heard of the storming of the
Bastille.'

When the old emperor died in the autumn of 1916 after sixty-eight
years on the throne it seemed to nobody that the fall of the House of
Habsburg was imminent. The coronation of Franz Jozsef's great-
nephew Charles as King of Hungary on 16 December 1916 was a
splendid final curtain call by old Austria-Hungary, with its pomp, solemnity, ancient ritual – and unintentional comedy. 'The weather was
appalling, cold and wet, but it was still a magnificent occasion,' one
witness recalled:

The King-Emperor and Empress Zita were in a glass carriage, there
were men in extraordinary uniforms and headgear from another
age. The lords spiritual were in full regalia, women in their formal
dress in the middle of the day as the rain pelted down, crowds were
cheering. Cameras were not allowed into the Matthias Church for the
ceremony, but the subsequent oath-taking and the *kardvágás* – the
symbolic moment when the king ascends a mound of earth and bran-
dishes the State Sword to the four points of the compass, pledging to
protect the integrity of the nation – was a fine spectacle, though the
crown looked far too big for him. The skittish horses nearly crashed

the state carriage into some buildings at one point, but with great difficulty were secured and nobody came to harm.'[6]

When the end came it was sudden. In autumn 1918 the German army was in retreat after the failure of its summer offensive on the Western Front. Its surrender looked imminent. The Austro-Hungarian army in the Balkans was in flight and the French forces from the Salonica army, backed by Romanian forces, could have marched unhindered into Hungary. The Empire sued for peace and on 31 October the Hungarian government resigned. Military defeat led to the collapse of the state. There would be three revolutions over the next nine months – the first a spontaneous and, to begin with, euphoric celebration of a new start, a new Hungarian Republic, led by Count Károlyi. As Pál Ignotus, a student in Budapest at the time, pointed out: 'It should hardly be a surprise that when there was a so-called "Bourgeois Revolution" immediately after the war it should be led by one of the grandest of all the Hungarian aristocrats.'

Károlyi was hugely popular for a short while immediately after the fighting ended. There was genuine joy on the streets of Budapest, until the reality of defeat sank in. His was the first revolution named after a flower – the aster. On 31 October Károlyi established a National Council with headquarters in the fashionable Astoria Hotel and declared that one of his first tasks was to hold free elections with universal suffrage under new electoral lists. On the first day, soldiers with asters fixed on their lapels and in their rifle barrels – in an attempt to hide the Imperial and royal emblems – were seen dancing through the streets with civilians. Hence it was called the Aster Revolution. They had also, in a classic coup, taken over the telephone exchanges, Post Office and railway stations, but barely anyone noticed. Placards all over Budapest declaimed 'Peace', 'Democracy', 'Equal Rights'. The Archduke Joseph, cousin of the emperor and head of the branch of the ruling dynasty which had long lived in Hungary, the Habsburg-Lothringens, asked Károlyi if he should Magyarize the family name to Alcsuti, but Károlyi thought this might be overdoing it and dissuaded him. 'Beware, your Highness,

---

* A silent movie of the event is a fascinating watch, available at the Budapest Military History Museum, and well worth seeing for a glimpse of the world of yesterday.

Habsburg is still a surname one doesn't throw away.' The revolution was practically bloodless, though there was one prominent victim of violence. Prime Minister Tisza was murdered by intruders into his home in the Inner City of Pest, shot in front of his wife and great-niece.[*][7]

Emperor Charles appointed Károlyi Prime Minister at the end of October, but even before the change of power in Budapest the Romanians, Czechs, Slovaks and Croats had announced they would cede from the monarchy and the Hungarians were unable to do anything to prevent their departure. On 11 November 1918 the emperor issued a statement that amounted to an abdication – 'I withdraw from all participation in state affairs' – but technically, as it related to Hungary, it wasn't. Three days later Hungary was declared a republic for the first time and Károlyi was named President. More than 100,000 people celebrated in a demonstration in Parliament Square. He won praise from many ordinary Hungarians, though not most of his family or friends, who were appalled when he handed over one of his estates, Kálkápolna in eastern Hungary, to the peasants who worked the land.

But it was a short-lived carnival. The Great Powers – with US President Woodrow Wilson one of the key players – had already decided that Hungary would be carved up, new independent states would be created from the ethnic Slav nationalities, and that the Habsburg Empire would be assigned to the dustbin of history. Károlyi had excellent contacts among the leaders of the Allied powers, but he could make no difference to the outcome. His popularity sank – as did the value of the currency. High inflation fuelled an economic crisis. Goods that had been available in wartime Budapest no longer were, and thousands of ethnic Magyars, fearing for their future, were pouring into the city searching for refuge. They were joined by great numbers of defeated and bedraggled troops needing food and shelter. Budapest had 'recently been a thriving

---

* Sigmund Freud did not regularly comment on current affairs, but he was in regular correspondence with a close friend and fellow psychoanalyst who lived in Budapest, Sándor Ferenczi. The Aster Revolution prompted his disdain in a letter to his friend on December 3, 1918: 'I don't know what to make of this uneducated people's unruliness and immaturity. I have never been an unconditional supporter of the *ancien régime*, but I doubt that one can consider it to be a sign of political wisdom that of all those many counts, they've killed the most intelligent [István Tisza], while the most ignorant one [Mihály Károlyi] they've made Prime Minister.'

bourgeois, relatively cheerful city', as the physicist Leo Szilard said years later, after emigrating to the US. 'It changed utterly and now had a depressing atmosphere; its streets and squares were filled with ad hoc armed units representing all political factions, and mobs converging on the city centre from the outskirts.'

Perhaps nobody decent or with a conscience could have dealt with the problems facing a broke, traumatized, divided Hungary. The task was far beyond the well-intentioned but hopelessly ill-prepared Károlyi. Paul Lendvai was right in his observation that as a politician, the so-called 'Red Count' would have passed unnoticed in history as the leader of a tiny pacifist party had not circumstances pushed him accidentally to the front line of affairs in 1918.

He was unable to weather the overwhelming storms that blew him away. He was too radical for the Right and not radical enough for the Communist Left. To some he was the dangerous 'Red Count'; others called him Hungary's Kerensky.[8]

25

LENIN'S PUPIL

I know of no difference between moral and immoral acts. I know of only one standpoint: whether something is good or bad for the working class.

Béla Kun (1886–1938)

A French colonel delivered the *coup de grâce* to the Károlyi government and Hungary's first republic. On 20 March 1919 Fernand Vyx, France's envoy in Budapest, handed the President an ultimatum from the Allies ordering Hungary to withdraw to new demarcation lines in the south and east of the country which would cut off Magyar territories from Greater Hungary. If Károlyi did not comply, the note warned, Hungary could expect an invasion by a full Allied force from the East and West. When the news leaked out it caused a storm of indignation that broke the administration. 'We felt not only defeated, dejected and debauched,' Oszkár Jászi, who had briefly joined the Károlyi government, wrote in his diary, 'but far worse, psychologically swindled, betrayed and bamboozled.' Huge demonstrations against Károlyi brought Budapest to a standstill. Just six months earlier he had been hailed as the man of the moment, the modernizer who would bring Hungary back from humiliating defeat. Now he was branded the traitor who for his own personal glory was responsible for the dismemberment after 1,000 years of the Hungarian nation.

The immediate beneficiary of the crisis was the tiny Communist Party which had been formed only a few months earlier. 'Power was on the streets – and the Reds picked it up,' as the then Budapest University student Ignotus recalled, deliberately misquoting Lenin's remarks about how the Bolsheviks had seized control of Petrograd eighteen months earlier. After a day of protests and several high-profile departures from his government, Károlyi resigned the presidency and left Hungary for the South of France, via Prague, with his wife. 'I made this sacrifice, instead of accepting the cheap martyr's crown of arrest, to avoid a massacre of citizens, of useless shedding of blood on the streets of Budapest, and to save the country from the worst horrors of a civil war,' he said, leaving the government in the hands of the Communists.*[1]

The 'Red Dictatorship' presided over by Kun lasted just 133 days, but it left a deep mark on Budapest. Koestler, who lived through it, was relatively kind about the Hungarian Commune, as it was called, compared to the indictments of Communism he wrote in later years. 'I have no doubt that Communism in Hungary would in due course have degenerated into a totalitarian police state, forcibly following the example of the Russian model,' he wrote in his autobiography. 'No Communist Party in Europe has been able to hold out against the corruption imposed on it from Moscow by direct authority and indirect contamination. But this later knowledge does not invalidate the hopeful and exuberant mood of the early days of the Revolution in Hungary.'

On May Day 1919, six weeks into Kun's rule, 'the apotheosis of the short-lived Commune . . . the whole town seemed to have been turned upside down.' Public squares in Budapest were then, according to Koestler,

---

* The count never became a convinced Communist, as was often claimed – he remained a Social Democrat though he would at times be a useful tool, a fellow traveller, of the Soviets. The 'Red Countess', on the other hand, was by her own admission a committed Marxist – though not so hard-line that she didn't love and often wear her fabulous jewels. The Károlyis settled first in Paris and then in London, working and speaking for fashionable causes that were frequently Soviet fronts. He was later tried in *absentia* as a traitor and his property was confiscated by the right-wing governments that followed. After the Second World War he was briefly Hungary's Ambassador to France. He died in 1955. Katinka befriended the Communist government of János Kádár in the 1960s, which after her death allowed both their bodies to be returned and buried in Hungary. A statue of him was put up in Kossuth Square in the 1940s, but in 2012, under the Orbán government, it was moved – not just from central Pest but out of Budapest altogether, to a provincial town. Many streets named after him throughout Budapest were changed. The prominent Károlyi Mihály Street, where his palace had been, in the most fashionable part of the city was changed simply to Károlyi (Charles) Street, removing the association with him.

filled with big bronze statues of worthies, most charging the enemy on horses or orating with one arm upraised . . . On May Day, all these statues were concealed by spherical wood frames covered with red cloth on which were painted the continents and seas of the world. These gigantic globes – some over fifty feet high – had a curiously fascinating effect. They looked like balloons anchored to the public squares, ready to lift the whole town in the air. They were symbols of the new cosmopolitan spirit and of the determination of the new regime 'to lift the globe from its axis'. Even more moving and beautiful were posters which covered every wall and which converted the streets into colourful picture galleries. They had been designed by the elite of modern Hungarian painters, who later on swarmed out over Europe and America and became prominent as artists, cartoonists and magazine-cover designers . . . It is a historical curiosity, known only to experts, that the posters of the Hungarian Commune of 1919 represented one of the peaks of commercial art.*

On the other hand, the physicist Edward Teller, who was a twelve-year-old schoolboy in Budapest during the Red dictatorship, remembered being 'terrified' throughout – by the Communist marches, the giant unfurled Red flags and their enormous posters. 'On one of them,' he told an interviewer decades later, 'a stern man with his arm extended and his fingertips as large as if it were an inch from my nose said, "You, hiding in the shadows, spreading horror stories, you counter-revolutionaries, TREMBLE" . . . that finger seemed to follow me wherever I went.'

The regime had a profound effect on his family's life: 'My father could no longer practise law. In fact we became social outcasts. A lawyer was clearly a capitalist, and unlike a doctor, who provided a service, a lawyer was a thoroughly worthless person in a "good" society. Part of our apartment was requisitioned by the Communists . . . we went hungry . . . my father told me that the Communists would soon fall . . . and that anti-Semitism would follow. "Too many of the Communist

---

* Koestler was referring to a cohort of brilliant Hungarian artists who fled into exile after the Commune collapsed and emigrated to Western Europe and the US – figures such as Lajos Kassák, Sándor Bortnyik and Róbert Berény, the early creative inspirations behind twentieth-century advertising.

leaders are Jews," he explained, "and all Jews will be blamed for their excesses." How right he was."[*2]

Béla Kun had been an insurance clerk, then a little-known and politically neutral journalist on a Budapest daily when he was drafted into the Austro-Hungarian army at the end of 1914. He was soon taken prisoner by the Russians and, like many of the future Commune leadership, he was radicalized by the Bolsheviks in a prisoner-of-war camp. Helped by the Red Army, and disguised as an army surgeon, he returned to Hungary with eight comrades on 18 November 1918. Few could have foreseen that within four months he would be at the head of a socialist revolution. At no point during the Commune's hold on power did the Hungarian Communist Party have more than 5,000 members, according to one of its other founders, Mátyás Rákosi, who was its Commissar for Commerce, and later became head of the much longer-lived post-Second World War Soviet dictatorship.

The country was renamed the Hungarian Socialist Republic of Soviets – an imitation of Vladimir Lenin's Bolshevik regime in Russia, with all its expropriations, nationalizations, regimentation and terror. Short and unprepossessing, Kun had a squat face, almost no neck and a flaccid mouth. But he was a surprisingly gifted speaker and showed some remarkably practical common sense amid the ideological jargon. A torrent of decrees poured out from the Revolutionary Council, but they were patchily implemented, especially outside Budapest. Not all of them were stupid and Kun's regime, mainly of passionate young revolutionaries – Kun was one of the oldest in the leadership at the age of thirty-three – were convinced they could out-Lenin Lenin.

The Kun regime's first decree on 21 March 1919, day one of the Revolution, proclaimed martial law and imposed the death penalty for any acts of 'subversion', which meant any opposition to his committee of Soviets. The second day he replaced the existing judicial system with

---

* The 1919 Soviet regime in Budapest left a mark on him for the rest of his life. He became a vitriolic Cold Warrior after the Second World War, during which he had worked on the Manhattan Project. He then went on to develop the H-bomb and built bigger and better weapons he called 'Super bombs'. He was an enthusiastic participant in the McCarthyite 'anti-American activities' hearings in the late 1940s and 1950s and was later dubbed 'the real Dr Strangelove'.

'Revolutionary tribunals' along the lines of those that had operated in the French Revolution.

He was honest and clear – up to a point. He stated that his system was 'a dictatorship of an active minority on behalf of the, by and large, passive proletariat . . . which has to act in strong and merciless fashion at least until such time as the Revolution has spread to other European countries'. Kun, said one of his initial supporters, but later an opponent, 'believed in world revolution as passionately as did Lenin – but then he believed everything Lenin had taught him, without the Bolshevik leader's brain power'. Again parroting Lenin, Kun declared: 'I know of no difference between moral and immoral acts. I know of only one standpoint: whether something is good or bad for the proletariat.'

The Commune nationalized all the banks and froze bank deposits; all businesses that employed more than ten people were taken over by the state – and all private housing, limiting each adult to living in one room and billeting zealous proletarians in the homes of bourgeois families. The Budapest racecourse was closed and ploughed up in readiness for planting vegetables. Racing was considered the sport of aristocrats. Religious schools were banned and the most important new school rule stated that 'all utterances and actions in school or outside it directed against Society as a whole . . . or revealing a lack of faith, lack of will-power, or a deficient sense of socialist self-discipline or solidarity . . . will be punished'.[3]

The state confiscated any landholdings above 75 *hold* (around 45 hectares), not to distribute among the peasantry, as the Communists had once promised, but to turn them into collective farms. The Kun government introduced a rigorous system of food rationing. Nobody could buy food without ration cards – but the cards were issued only to members of trade unions, which forced people who worked in the professions either to join a union or starve. On the other hand, Kun introduced an eight-hour working day, gave women equality of pay with men and extended the basic system of unemployment benefit that had been introduced by the Károlyi regime.

The Academy of Science, denounced as 'a reactionary institution', was closed down, thirty-seven professors at the universities were fired, a new electoral law enfranchised all men and women over the age of eighteen – but disenfranchised 'exploiters', defined as anyone who employed labour, including the better-off peasants who hired a seasonal farmhand. The Social Democrats were initially in coalition with the Communists but then became subsumed by Kun's party. Their leader, Sándor Garbai, announced that 'within three months, the greater part of the existing institutions have been destroyed'.

Red Terror began from the Commune's first day, presided over by Tibor Szamuely, a sinister figure who modelled himself on Felix Dzerzhinsky, the head of the Russian Soviets' secret service, the Cheka. He introduced Red death squads – the most feared, active in many parts of Budapest, were the red-scarved and leather-jacketed Lenin Boys led by a sadistic twenty-three-year-old thug, József Czerny. It is estimated that at least 1,000 people were murdered in Budapest and the surrounding area in 133 days.

Some of Kun's rhetoric went down well – for example when he blamed the Entente Allies in the war, the French and the English, for their 'vindictive' treatment of Hungary. He said: 'the imperialism of the Entente, whose intention is and was to rob Hungary of its food supply, its industry and raw materials, and all the necessities of existence, now plans to dismember our nation', which had more than a kernel of truth.

When some members of the Congress of Revolutionary Councils, the Soviet-style parliament, began to complain about the commissars' corruption, Kun – as Lenin had done a few weeks after the Russian Revolution – closed it down at gunpoint and replaced it with a Central Executive Committee with himself as its head.[4]

The Russian Bolsheviks gave the Hungarian Soviet plenty of vocal support and a modest sum of financial backing, but when it faced the prospect of losing power did nothing to intervene on behalf of world revolution or the cause of Communism close-ish to home – Hungary has a border with Ukraine, then still part of the Russian Empire. Romanian and Czech troops invaded Hungary in the summer of 1919 in their battle for independence and nationhood. Between them they controlled nearly half the country by the time the Kun regime collapsed and its leadership fled – most of them to Russia. The Romanians occupied Budapest from 4 August. Three nightmare months 'of horror and misery as bad as the Soviet Commune followed ... it was one of the darkest periods,' one survivor of the invasion recalled. 'The Romanians

embarked on a systematic programme of looting, expropriation, deportations and terror.'

Children were taken from homes and sent into servitude in Romanian villages and towns. More than 500 Hungarians were murdered by
Romanian troops and estimates suggest that 1,000 women were raped.
Valuable art treasures, large amounts of agricultural produce and industrial plant were loaded on trains and sent east to Romania. They stole,
among other things, 4,000 telephones from private homes they had
ransacked. Bands of soldier-looters took railway locomotives and carriages, industrial machinery, and thousands of horses and cattle worth
nearly 3 million gold crowns, more than twelve times in value than all
the loans Hungary received four years later to get the country back on
its feet. The Romanians took treasures from the National Museum,
but were prevented from taking more by Brigadier General Harry Hill
Bandholtz, the American member of the Allied Control Commission,
which was supposed to supervise the Romanian army's disengagement
from Hungary.*

Kun escaped in November 1919 and found refuge in Russia. As he
left, without a hint of irony, he told a comrade: 'the Hungarian proletariat betrayed us' – by 'us' he meant the Communists. For a while he
was treated as a hero in Soviet Russia, as one of the leading martyrs of
the cause of world revolution. He was relatively successful in a series of
roles in the Comintern in the 1920s and early 1930s. But Stalin loathed
him. He disappeared into the great maw of the Gulag and was shot
during the Great Purge in 1938.

---

* There's a rather ugly statue to Bandholtz next to the bigger one of Ronald Reagan
outside the US Embassy in Budapest. Once the chief of the Philippines Constabulary
at the time of violent anti-American rebellions in Manila, he had also led the expeditionary forces against Pancho Villa in Mexico. He is remembered in Hungary because
one night in October 1919, as the rotating president of the Commission and armed only
with a riding whip, he allegedly prevented Romanian soldiers from removing Transylvanian treasures from the National Museum. His statue was damaged during the
Allied bombing of Budapest in 1944. It was removed for repair but the Communists
never bothered to put it back. It lay in storage until it was hastily replaced in July 1989,
when the Communist regime had collapsed, just a day before the visit of President
George H.W. Bush. Every 18 December, the general's birthday, the military attaché of
the US Embassy lays a wreath by the statue.

Embarrassing stories about Kun emerged as late as 1979. Once, as a young Social Democrat activist in Hungary, he claimed 110 crowns in travel expenses – quite a lot of money in those days – on a trip he never took. He had to repay the money when the Party found out. Much more seriously, later, as a Comintern agent, he left his briefcase in a taxi during a mission to Vienna. It contained, among other things, the names and contact details of a list of Hungarian Party members – then an illegal organization – and other secret documents about its organization. The taxi driver passed them to the Hungarian Legation in Austria, who photographed the list before returning the briefcase to Kun. It was a disaster for the Communist Party in Budapest – scores of members were rounded up and jailed as a result.[5]

26

THE ADMIRAL WITHOUT A NAVY

We will punish Budapest, the sinful city, which has denied its
thousand-year history . . . flung its crown, its national colours, into
the mud, and wrapped itself in red flags.

Miklós Horthy de Nagybánya (1868–1957)

While Romanian troops, supplied and financed by the French, were
despoiling Budapest and a Czech army occupied much of northern
Hungary, the former head of the Habsburg navy was conspiring with
foreign armies and enemy nations to seize power for himself. When
Admiral Miklós Horthy, who would rule Hungary for nearly a quarter
of a century, is invariably referred to in Hungary even by his opponents
as a patriot, the circumstances under which his regime was born are
often forgotten.

Amid the chaos after the war and the fall of the Habsburg Empire,
more than 400,000 ethnic Magyars fled or left the 'separated territories'
no longer controlled by Hungary. They were mainly Hungarian civil
servants, army officers and members of the professional middle class.
Tens of thousands were forced to find shelter for months in railway
wagons in Budapest and its surroundings, in improvised barracks or
homeless shelters. These politically conscious people, demoted almost
overnight from the 'ruling class' to beggars, became a vast reservoir of
support for demagogues, populist rabble-rousers and ultra-nationalist
gangs.[1]

Horthy, joined by a group of generals and established right-wing
politicians, formed a National Army, based in the south of Hungary,
to topple the Béla Kun regime. They pledged to 'bring order from this
ruinous chaos . . . and restore traditional Christian values to Hungary',
according to one of its military commanders. Horthy was immensely

popular and would remain so for most of the next twenty-five years – except on the far Left and extreme Right. At the end of October 1919 he began to march on Budapest from the provincial town of Szeged. Horthy was cheered by crowds wherever he went. But his soldiers and the thuggish gangs of hoodlums that followed in their wake left a trail of blood in areas which showed any degree of support for the Kun regime. Often, though by no means always, the victims were Jews, who were often assumed to be Communists – or at least sympathizers. In Siófok, around 100 kilometres south of Budapest, 200 civilians were murdered in cold blood, a substantial number of them Jews. In nearby Kecskemét a similar number were burned or flayed alive. In Diszel dozens of children were thrown down a well, a horrendous act which also polluted the local water supply for months. Pogroms returned under Horthy's National Army.

On 16 November, a freezing-cold day, and in torrential rain Horthy rode into Budapest at the head of his army on a white horse, wearing full-dress admiral's uniform. His speech to cheering crowds was not exactly emollient. He clearly stated the 'Christian nationalist' line his regime would take. He called Budapest 'the sinful' or 'the guilty' city – he used the Hungarian word *bűnös*, which has a double meaning. '[Budapest] has denied its thousand-year history . . . flung its crown, its national colours, into the mud, and wrapped itself in red rags,' he declared. Deliberately the admiral 'sharpened the contest, long brewing, between the country, supposedly healthy and unselfconsciously natural, and the big city, always looking abroad, depraved, and, of course, with a substantial Jewish presence', as one of his listeners that wet morning recorded. 'In most countries this urban/rural contest exists but in Hungary it took a vicious turn.'[2]

Most of the political parties that still existed after the Soviet experiment wanted Hungary to remain a monarchy, but to break with the Habsburgs. However, the British had insisted on an end to the Austro-Hungarian Empire under the old dynasty, and the other Allies agreed. 'The restoration of a dynasty personifying, in the eyes of their subjects, a system of oppression of other races, in alliance with Germany, would not be compatible with the principles for which they fought, nor with the results the war had allowed them to achieve,' stated a memorandum from the British Prime Minister, David Lloyd George, to the Allied

Control Commission which supervised the armistice and ceasefire arrangements.

So a strange compromise was agreed: the throne would remain vacant for the time being and a regency would be established.* The Allies' idea was to allow the regent to possess the authority of a constitutional monarch. Horthy was the obvious choice; he held the power in Budapest, was highly popular among the Hungarian people and had the support of the army. But some figures on the legitimist wing among the Conservative nobility hoped the role might be taken by Count Albert Apponyi, even though he was already seventy-four, known to suffer from ill health, and was too committed to the Habsburg dynasty for the Allied taste, especially the British. Horthy was 'elected' regent on 1 March 1920 unopposed, though the admiral was taking no chances with the parliamentary vote. Army officers formed a guard of honour for the admiral at the entrance to Parliament – fully armed, with hand grenades visible in their belts. A corps of crack troops were in the chamber during the counting of the votes. Horthy was given nearly all the prerogatives of a Habsburg ruler. 'This made him more than a constitutional monarch in the West European meaning of the term, but rather less than the dictator he was often labelled,' as his biographer István Deák put it. 'There were some restraints on his power.'[3]

Horthy said in his memoirs that when he was confronted with a problem he always asked himself what the Emperor Franz Jozsef would have done – he invariably 'searched for the noble, the chivalrous and humane'. Yet he was responsible for a regime of domestic terrorism that murdered thousands of his own people; he introduced the first of Europe's anti-Jewish laws between the two world wars, more than a decade before the Nazis took power in Germany. In the 1930s he enthusiastically entered into an alliance with Hitler and in the spring of 1944 washed his hands of the deportations to Auschwitz of around half a million of his loyal and patriotic Jewish citizens. It is highly unlikely that the old Habsburg emperor would have done any of these things. Ultimately Horthy was

* A precedent found twice in Hungarian history. First, in the fifteenth century after János Hunyadi's death, and then following Kossuth's break with Austria after the Revolution of 1848. This time the settlement spawned the saying, between the wars, that Hungary was a kingdom without a king, run by an admiral without a navy.

a disastrous failure for Hungary – the leader who couldn't protect his people from German or Soviet imperialism – and that is how he should be judged. Horthy no doubt sincerely believed that he devoted his life to the fatherland – he titled his memoirs *A Life for Hungary*. But he left the country he served in ruins and chaos under totalitarian foreign powers.

His responsibility for the various disasters that befell Hungary have been hotly debated since the last war. Under the Communist regime, he was blamed for everything and labelled a fascist. In 1993, when according to his original wishes he was reburied in his native village of Kenderes, in central Hungary, there were big demonstrations in Budapest against all that he had represented between the wars. He has been rehabilitated to some extent since by right-wing governments, and statues that disappeared in the Communist years have in some places re-appeared in his memory. No doubt, in time these too will be torn down and replaced, as is usual in Hungarian history.[4]

He was born in 1868 into a family long known for its service to the Imperial state – untypical, as the Horthys were Calvinists, histori-cally an ultra-nationalist, anti-Habsburg section of the Hungarian population. He was admitted to the naval academy – one of forty-two candidates chosen from 612 applications. He had been so mediocre at school that his parents sent him to a private 'crammer' that catered for the less gifted boys from good families. After the *Ausgleich*, which es-tablished the Dual Monarchy, there was a move to get more Hungarian officers into the armed services, and the young Horthy benefited from a Habsburg-style policy of affirmative action. Yet the Imperial armed services were tough, and whatever advantages he had enjoyed to get into the navy as an officer, he later prospered by his own merits.

He was a gifted linguist. He had perfect German, as all Austrian-Hungarian officers were required to possess, and he had fluent French, Italian, Czech and Croatian – with a smattering of Spanish too. His Eng-lish was excellent; he had once had James Joyce as his English teacher in Trieste. Some critics have wondered whether Horthy may have been the source for the Hungarian obscenities and scatological references in *Ulysses* and *Finnegan's Wake*.

As a naval commander he was an ardent Anglophile in his early life. He often repeated his conviction that the British would always win any war because of the power of their navy, which made it all the more strange that he would serve in two world wars opposed to Britain, on the losing side in both.

Before the First World War he served for four years as Franz Jozsef's devoted aide-de-camp, a period which he described as 'the best years by far of my life'. Even his loyal supporters accepted that he was intellectually mediocre. Through his impeccable manners, charm when he chose to exercise it and an air of rectitude, he rose to become Austria-Hungary's only successful naval commander in the First World War. In May 1917 he led a few ships against greatly superior forces to break an enemy blockade in the Adriatic. Despite receiving a serious wound, he continued in command and won the Battle of the Strait of Otranto. He was promoted to full admiral of the fleet in February 1918 and became a household name in the Habsburg Empire – and well known to the Habsburg heir, Archduke, later Emperor, Charles. He was acceptable to the court. He was good-looking, diligent and rode a horse well. He was personally honest and lived modestly. 'Culture, for him, meant very occasional visits to the opera; love meant marriage to a devoted and modest woman from a well-connected Catholic gentry family; ideals meant an absolute loyalty to Franz Jozsef and the Hungarian "race"; entertainment meant shooting, riding, bridge and tennis; politics consisted mainly of the detestation of Slavs and socialists,' as Deák described him.[5]

After just a few months as the Imperial navy chief, following defeat in the war he had the ignominious task of surrendering the fleet at Pula – and saw the ships handed over to the newly established state of Yugoslavia. When Horthy had an audience with the king-emperor on the eve of the abdication in November 1918 he almost broke down in tears and said: 'I vow that I shall not rest until I have restored your Majesty to his thrones in Vienna and Budapest.' He professed unwavering fealty to the House of Habsburg. Yet when the king returned to Hungary to reclaim his throne, Horthy twice refused to surrender his position as regent.

The deposed King Charles appeared unexpectedly on Easter Sunday 1921 and announced he was demanding a restoration. He told Horthy that the population wanted his return, members of 'my government have urged this upon me – and it is our will'. Horthy welcomed the ex-emperor politely, but during a two-hour conversation he said that the Great Powers had threatened military action if the Habsburgs were returned, 'and there is no alternative but to continue with the present arrangement until circumstances change'. Charles went back to Switzerland, but did not give up his efforts.

Naïvely, the ex-emperor still believed Horthy's protestations of loyalty and returned barely half a year later, on 20 October. This time he had some military backing. Soldiers under the regional commander in western Hungary, Colonel Anton Lehár (brother of the *Merry Widow* composer Franz), swore loyalty to Charles, who had announced the formation of a new government. Charles's march on Budapest 'resembled more an operetta in the Lehár style than a serious military operation', as Pál Ignotus recorded. It took ten hours for the former monarch's train to get from Sopron on the Hungary-Austria border to Győr, around 75 kilometres away. At every small village en route the train would stop as people wanted a glimpse of the one-time king. Meanwhile Horthy mobilized troops and diplomatic protests from the Great Powers. There was a skirmish just outside Budapest with a few casualties on both sides, but Horthy's troops prevailed easily. The so-called ardent royalist Horthy had Charles arrested and handed over to the representatives of the Entente. On 6 November the Hungarian Parliament deposed the House of Habsburg, but reconfirmed Horthy as regent in a country with no monarch.[*6]

The white terror that followed the coup by Horthy far exceeded the crimes of Béla Kun – mainly because it continued for so much longer. No exact numbers exist, but the most recent research based on archives opened after the collapse of Communism in 1989 show that at least 6,000 people were killed in the first three months and around 70,000 suspected 'socialist' collaborators or sympathizers were imprisoned or interned in camps from 1920 to 1926.

Horthy and his closest supporters always denied that the admiral played any personal role in the 'early excesses' of his rule (his words). But on the other hand, in his memoirs he excused the atrocities by

---

[*] The British had the last Habsburg ruler exiled to Madeira, where he died aged only thirty-four on 1 April 1922 of pneumonia, though it is believed that in fact he was a late victim of a third wave of the post-world-war influenza pandemic.

arguing that 'soft hearts' had no place in such an extreme situation. The main victims were trade unionists, members of the revolutionary committees and workers' councils, and poor peasants who had the temerity to rise up against landlords. The recollections of his erstwhile friend Anton Lehár and the commander of one of the most vicious of the Radical Right Death Squads, Pál Prónay, implicate him in the terror before and after he seized power. The kindest interpretation is that his was a sin of omission. He knew that innocent people were being beaten up, tortured to death or hanged, but he did nothing to halt the atrocities – and sometimes protected the guilty perpetrators against the innocent victims. Just two days before he was confirmed as regent, two editors of the Social Democrats' newspaper *Népszava* (The People's Voice), Béla Somogyi and Béla Bacsó, were murdered by a death squad led by Prónay and their mutilated bodies were thrown into the Danube. To Horthy's certain knowledge, the killers were among the guard of honour outside the Parliament building when he was 'elected' regent.

As Arthur Koestler, who lived through this period, said: 'the early Horthy era with its organized pogroms, its torture chambers and manhunts . . . gave a nasty taste of things to come'. Armed gangs with motley uniforms roamed the streets. Georg Solti, the celebrated conductor who was born and grew up in Budapest and began his musical career with the Hungarian State Opera, but left Hungary before the Second World War, recalled years later in London exile: 'Since then I was never able to rid myself of the fear of anyone wearing a military or police uniform, or even a customs officer uniform, because in Hungary uniforms always meant persecution in one form or another.' Budapest had once been the most bourgeois city in Central Europe but was now noted for its depression, its impoverished districts and its beggars. 'Pest is like a courtly mistress fallen to disrepute, abandoned by her benefactor,' as Gyula Krúdy, one of the city's shrewdest chroniclers, put it.[7]

The counter-revolutionary regime advocated a militant Christian ideology, opposed liberalism of any kind, democracy, atheism, secularism, Jewish influences, Marxism, Bolshevism, freemasonry, cosmopolitanism, modernity, homosexuality, divorce, avant-garde art and modernist music. Yet many of these 'sinful' activities and ideas flourished in Horthy's Hungary. Despite the government's incessant anti-urban propaganda, Budapest remained a highly sophisticated place – if much poorer – within a much less developed country. After a few years' absence, tourists began to return to Budapest; it became a fashionable place to visit once again. The Prince of Wales, later Edward VIII, was a frequent visitor on his own and 'gave the town's nightclubs and gaming tables new glamour – just like his grandfather used to do', according to the *Pesti Hírlap* newspaper. Later he would return frequently with Wallis Simpson, who often said how much she enjoyed visits to Budapest. The American journalist H.L. Mencken regularly mentioned Budapest in his syndicated columns. In a letter to his wife on his first visit in the late 1920s he wrote: 'this town is really outstanding. It is by far the most beautiful that I have ever seen. I came expecting to see a somewhat dingy Vienna, but it makes Vienna look like a village. There is something thoroughly *Royal* about it.'

The press was not entirely free, but it was freer in Horthy's Hungary than in the Soviet Union, in Nazi Germany or fascist Italy; the judiciary, although certainly friendly to the regime's ideology, often ruled in defiance of government interests. The elite was split between those who cultivated old-fashioned conservative values and those with fascistic inclinations. Sometimes the two interests aligned; occasionally they clashed. 'In place of an intellect Horthy had acquired a small collection of idées fixes, which predetermined his approach to any given issue,' according to Thomas Hohler, the British ambassador in Budapest, who had known Horthy well before the war and was a friend. Hohler said after he left his posting in Budapest that Horthy 'was a man of sterling honesty if not of great cleverness; he has no suppleness of mind and when he gets hold of an idea, it crystallises within him into a principle'. He was blinded by a nationalism highly blinkered even by Hungarian standards. He had always loathed Communism but – understandable to anyone who had witnessed the crazed three months of the Kun regime – his hatred festered to the extent that it poisoned his view of anyone with liberal sentiments of any kind. He hated trade unions or even modern social democracy. In 1926, during the General Strike in Britain, he told the military attaché at the British Embassy that the world 'would have been eternally grateful to his government for an unsurpassable service' if they had shot the miners' union leader, A.J. Cook. At all times Bolshevism was for him the ultimate enemy. 'He was often stupid, occasionally wicked, invariably blind,' the writer György Faludy, an opponent of his regime in the 1930s, wrote later. 'He was a true conservative, an author-itarian, but not the fascist he is often made out to be.'

Horthy's anti-intellectual 'Christian nationalism' prompted a flight from Hungary of talented writers, artists, photographers, scientists and musicians, by no means all of them Jewish. This is a familiar pattern in Hungarian history that happened many times before and would in the future: there were thousands of exiles from Communism after the Second World War, a wave of emigration after 1989 and again in the 2000s after accession to the European Union. Those who left were per-haps wiser than those who chose to remain.* Many who stayed – from the composers Zoltán Kodály and Béla Bartók to the authors Zsigmond Móricz, Antal Szerb, Mihály Babits and Endre Ady before his death from natural causes – suffered harassment and worse. In 1920 the reac-tionary Catholic Bishop Ottokár Prohászka, who helped form a militia group, Awakening Magyars, said that most of the writers of 'sinful' Budapest had been 'inoculated with Jewish blood'.[8]

Literature flourished for a while, as it often does, briefly, under authoritarianism. But then a baleful, dull conformity of officially sanc-tioned art set in – as it did at the same time and for the same reasons in the Soviet Union, Nazi Germany and in Italy under Mussolini. Many Budapest theatres closed down in the inter-war years. Opera survived relatively unscathed, but operetta, the most popular 'performance' art in the city by far – often seen as slightly subversive and decadent – was forced to close or move underground.

The once-thriving cinema industry, which started earlier in Budapest than in most European cities and grew faster, underwent a crisis that lasted decades.

The first film shot in Hungary was made by the theatrical impresario Arnold Sziklai of the Emperor Franz Jozsef at the millennium celebra-tion in 1896, just a few months after the Lumière brothers showed their

---

* Some of the most brilliant scientists of their generation born in Budapest, including four Nobel Laureates, left in the 1920s. Several worked on developing the Atom Bomb: Leo Szilard, Eugene Wigner, John von Neumann and Edward Teller. One famous biochemist stayed behind: Albert Szent-Györgyi, who won the Nobel Prize for discov-ering the component parts of Vitamin C. He stayed in Budapest and with extraordinary courage led an underground group against the Nazis there during the war.

first moving picture in a café in the Boulevard des Capucines in Paris. By 1914, 108 of Budapest's coffee houses, cabarets and theatres doubled as cinemas – the first purpose-built movie house in Budapest opened in Erzsébetváros in November 1899.*

Films had been the most popular form of entertainment before 1914. Even during the war more than a dozen silent movies a year had been produced. There were two major studios in Budapest at the end of the war – the Star on Pasaréti Street in Buda, which specialized in adaptations of Hungarian and foreign literary works; and the Corvin Studios on Gyarmat Street in Pest's Zugló district, founded by Sándor Korda, which made high-quality historical epics. Defeat in the war, the revolutions, the White Terror and the ideology of Horthy's Hungary dispersed much of this talent. Hollywood was the winner.

Two of the biggest names in movie history, figures who had created Budapest as a boom town for film, became exiles after 1919. Michael Curtiz had been drafted into the Austro-Hungarian army in 1914, had seen some of the fighting and was filled with rage at the incompetence of the generals and politicians in the conflict. He was conscripted again, reluctantly, by Kun's Soviet Republic in 1919, though he had little interest in politics of either Left or Right. Though the Commune was short-lived, Curtiz managed to make a film during that time, *My Brother is Coming* – 'a rousing if heavy-handed tale of a returned POW from the war who becomes a Communist', as he described it himself. It is his earliest film to have survived, all the others having decomposed through time or been destroyed during studio clear-outs. As soon as he could after Horthy seized power, Curtiz, thirty-five, left Hungary for Los Angeles.

Alexander Korda, who was already a well-known producer and owner of a movie studio, had a harder time amid the political ructions of the period and barely escaped Hungary with his life. Before the war and during the conflict Korda had made patriotic pro-Habsburg films – like his first feature film, *The Officer's Swordknot*. During the brief Károlyi government he made a pro-Republic film, and in Kun's even shorter Soviet regime he had been given a seat on the State Directory of Film

* The abbreviated word for movie comes from the Hungarian word *mozi* (meaning moving picture) which appeared for the first time in a 1905 cabaret lyric by the Hungarian writer Jenő Heltai, 'Song About the Cinema'.

and Arts – though he was never a Communist sympathizer and barely did a stroke of work for the organization. He dealt – or tried to deal – with whatever regime was in power and allowed him to make movies.

But Korda was everything that Horthy and his acolytes loathed: Jewish, intellectual, urban-dwelling, an habitué of cafés – all that Horthy blamed for the Communist experiment and the moral decline of Hungary. Korda was too well known to ignore. He was arrested at his suite in the Royal Hotel, and one of the thugs who handcuffed him was overheard by an acquaintance boasting that 'tonight I'm going to beat the shit out of that Communist Jew Korda'. But he was well connected. His brother, the film screenwriter Zoltán and Korda's new bride, the actor María Farkas, called the former Mayor of Budapest, Jenő Heltai, who knew Horthy and said he would make Korda's arrest an international issue with the British and French unless he was released. Horthy let him go and he made a career in Hollywood, and then in London, where Sándor Kellner, as he once had been, was knighted as Sir Alexander Korda.[9]

All day throughout Hungary on Friday, 4 June 1920 church bells tolled a dirge, black flags flew over public buildings, traffic came to a standstill in the centre of Budapest for long periods, newspapers appeared with black borders and funeral services were held in churches. It was the day the Treaty of Trianon was signed – still regarded 100 years later 'as the most devastating tragedy in the nation's history . . . a live issue now from which Hungary has not recovered', according to the philosopher Miklós Haraszti, who under the post-Second World War Communist regime was a dissident leader and in the 1970s the last political prisoner in the country. Trianon 'was the vivisection of the nation . . . the death certificate of the 1,000-year realm of King Stephen'.*

Hungary was the biggest loser from the First World War – around a third of its territory was handed over to successor states to form new nations, Czechoslovakia and Yugoslavia. Large slices of Hungary were given over by the Great Powers to existing states: the whole of

---

* The treaty was negotiated just after the Versailles peace talks, which had been held in the palace a kilometre away. Trianon was the smallest of the various palaces in the royal grounds at Versailles – originally built as the home of Mme de Montespan, the *maîtresse-en-titre* of Louis XIV.

Transylvania, part of historic Hungary for hundreds of years, was given to Romania. Half of the population was lost and millions of Hungarians became 'foreigners' in new countries overnight. Towns and cities with deep Hungarian roots were renamed: Kassa became Košice in Slovakia, Kolozsvár in Transylvania became Cluj: Temesvár in Romania was now Timişoara; Pozsony became the Slovak capital, Bratislava. As Horthy remarked on the day the treaty was signed: 'They dismembered the Germans, the Bulgarians and the Turks too. But from them they only took only one or two fingers. From the Hungarians they took his hands and feet.'

The peacemakers of the new world order – particularly the French, who pushed hardest in the Trianon talks – believed they were acting in the interests of self-determination for peoples who had been long held subject. The Hungarians thought they were victims of an ahistorical act of vindictive punishment. The Hungarian army was limited to no more than 35,000 troops and was allowed no heavy artillery, tanks or an air force. Hungary – like Germany – was forced to pay enormous reparations. The French President, Georges Clemenceau, declared that Hungary would be 'permanently deprived of the means of making war'.[*][10]

For long afterwards in kindergartens and schools, during church services and in the press, the notion that the lost territories could be restored was kept alive. The slogan taught to children – and often used as a greeting when people met socially – was: 'No, No Never' – meaning 'No, it can never happen'. The saying modulated daily life in Hungary between the wars. The legacy of Trianon defined life in Horthy's Hungary.

Classes in all schools began and ended with a recitation of what came to be called the Hungarian Credo, blessed by the Catholic Church. The

---

* The independent, post-Habsburg Kingdom of Hungary was left with 210,000 of its previous 620,000 square kilometres. As well as losing 5.8 million inhabitants from Transylvania, at least half of whom were ethnic Hungarians, Hungary would no longer possess the eastern Banat, now part of northern Serbia, which had been part of Hungary for 650 years. So too the Vojvodina, where hundreds of thousands of ethnic Hungarians lived, and Croatia. Many communities along the borders of the new states changed hands. Hungary lost a coastline, forests, mines, mountains and a market for manufactured goods, as well as the means of manufacturing them.

'resurrection' of Old Hungary was instilled into a generation of children as God's eternal truth.

Pupils from age five to eighteen would intone:

> I believe in God,
> I believe in a Fatherland
> I believe in eternal divine justice
> I believe in Hungary's resurrection. Amen.

Rump Hungary became a homogeneous state in a way it had never been in 1,000 years. Only 10 per cent of the population were not ethnic Magyars or did not use Hungarian as their native tongue. Trianon, as Paul Lendvai, the best historian of 1920s and 1930s Hungary, noted, 'was the breeding ground for the transformation of nationalism from an ideology of liberation to one of distraction'. A hundred years later, in the 2020s, the best-selling items of tat in cheap market stalls are pre-Trianon fridge magnets and plastic flags with Greater Hungary maps.[*11]

The post-Trianon shock determined the Horthy regime's revisionist policies. It drove public opinion to an ever more extreme nationalism and further isolated the country from its neighbours. After the peace treaty, 'Hungary became the quintessential have-not state, ready to ally itself with the Devil himself to undo the injustices perpetrated at Trianon.' All politics was seen through the prism of the infamous treaty. Horthy moved Hungarian foreign policy closer to the Nazis in the 1930s because Hitler promised to return the lost lands. In reality,

---

* In the Communist years after the Second World War, keeping one of these pre-Trianon maps was a criminal offence – even in the 1980s they were printed off only as samizdat and were kept hidden. All mention of Trianon was taboo, along with any talk of the hardships faced by Hungarians living beyond the borders; to bring up these issues was labelled 'bourgeois nationalism'. But of course the 'injustices' of Trianon were regularly discussed within families and among friends. The governments immediately after the collapse of Communism hoped that gradually the nationalist nostalgia would disappear, placing hopes on European integration as a solution to the 'nationalities' questions. But not so. They remain very much alive and flare up at election times in particular. The FIDESZ government of Viktor Orbán, for example, dealt with one of the emotional issues after his 2010 victory by giving ethnic Hungarians and their communities in parts of Slovakia, Transylvania and Serbia the right to vote in Hungarian elections.

Hungary drew some unacknowledged benefits from its dismemberment because its industrial base remained in and around Budapest, and it was now largely free of the ethnic problems that had bedevilled the country in the past – and would do so again, most obviously and violently in Yugoslavia. But no rational arguments were ever allowed to disturb the dream that one day a Greater Hungary would be restored.

Who was to blame for the disaster? The Soviet Republic, as the ruling regime and most of the population firmly believed. And who were they? The Jews were made the scapegoats. It was Jewish agents of world Bolshevism, as Horthy's propagandists and a population desperate to blame someone agreed; Jewish intellectuals who subverted national and Christian values were to blame; Jewish black-market millionaires who were profiting from the nation's miseries.[12]

27

MARCHING IN STEP WITH HITLER

It is hate rather than love that unites people.

G.K. Chesterton (1874–1936)

Not all victims were Jews, but all Jews were victims.

Elie Wiesel (1928–2016)

Horthy introduced anti-Jewish laws in Hungary while Hitler was still speaking to tiny groups of disaffected Germans in Munich beer halls. The first legislation specifically to target Hungarian Jews for discrimination was passed on 22 September 1920, barely six months after the admiral was elected regent. It was the *Numerus Clausus* Act, which restricted the number of Jews admitted to universities to 7 per cent of the total population, effectively ending the legal equality for Hungarian Jews that had been established under the *Ausgleich* in 1867. This had a profound effect in Budapest, where more than a quarter of the inhabitants at the end of the First World War were Jews – and on the universities. Many young people who could afford to leave went to study abroad, never to return. So did some of the ablest professors – a drain of talent that was never replaced. Horthy was not interested when a few academics, even among his own supporters, objected. 'Concerning the Jewish question, for all my life, I have been an anti-Semite,' he wrote to a friend, the future Prime Minister Pál Teleki. 'I have never made any contact with Jews. I have found it intolerable that here, in Hungary, every single factory, bank, asset, shop, theatre, newspaper, trade, etc., is in Jewish hands.'*

---

* In 1928 the *Numerus Clausus* measures were softened slightly but were never revoked. By 1935 Jews held only 7.2 per cent of the university places in Budapest, compared to 36 per cent in 1919.

The passage of the law was accompanied by a wave of pogroms throughout Hungary. In Budapest a dozen Jews were killed and more than 150 injured during a vicious riot by the far-Right *Turul* organization, led by the highly ambitious ultra-nationalist politician Gyula Gömbös, who a decade later would become Prime Minister.[1]

In 1925 the League of Nations threatened to impose sanctions and other retaliatory measures against Hungary unless it removed anti-Semitic legislation. Budapest's Jews begged them not to. The National Jewish Congress of Hungary asked the League not to interfere, for fear of a further backlash against Jews: 'We want to settle this matter here at home with our own government . . . we did not apply, and did not appeal to any foreign actor to intervene and ask for no help. Such help, even if it stems from good intentions, we reject.' A leading member of Budapest's Jewish community, the long-serving MP and former Hungarian Justice Minister Vilmos Vázsonyi, spoke at the Congress's annual meeting – just a few days earlier he had suffered a heart attack after he was beaten up in a street by an anti-Semitic thug: 'We are a part of the Hungarian constitution, the Hungarian nation. We are not Hungarian Jews, but Jewish Hungarians. We adhere to our ancestral religion, but this fatherland is also ours . . . We do not give away our Magyardom.' A few days later he died after another coronary.

But anti-Semitism became the 'alpha and omega of political life' in Hungary, as the novelist György Konrád, who survived a childhood of anti-Jewish violence against his family, said. Every Prime Minister Horthy appointed from 1928 onwards was an avowed anti-Semite and would support closer ties with the Nazis in Germany. Kálmán Darányi, premier for two years from 1936, expressed the official government view – Horthy's view – clearly: 'I see the essence of the question in that the Jews living within the borders of this country, due to their specific disposition and situation, but partly also to their indifference to the Hungarian race, play a disproportionately great role in certain branches of economic life . . . and [should be] reduced to a proper scale.'[2]

The regent believed as an article of faith all the rhetoric his propagandists dredged up about a 'Jewish Bolshevik conspiracy' against the Hungarian nation. He thought that Hungary was the Christian bulwark against Bolshevism and atheism – as it had been against the Turks and Islam centuries earlier. Though he had charm, Horthy was unsophisticated and had barely travelled outside the Habsburg lands, apart from on board ships in his naval days. Some foreigners were shocked when he uttered the kind of anti-Semitic sentiments he routinely shared within his like-minded entourage at home. In 1922 he enthusiastically greeted the visiting general secretary of the American YMCA with the comment: 'I am delighted the head of such an important anti-Semitic organization has come to us in Hungary.' When the Hungarian currency fell that same year Horthy told the Austrian ambassador that it was all the fault of the 'Elders of Zion . . . because they had not succeeded in establishing Bolshevism, they are now trying to undermine the Hungarian economy.'

Anti-Semitism became far more open on the Budapest streets, on buses and on trams. Horthy himself may not have been a fascist, and he personally found the armed militia groups marching through cities and causing mayhem vulgar. But he did little to stop them – the gendarmerie and city police forces throughout Hungary were full of members of various Nazi-type gangs. One night a few months after the *Numerus Clausus* Act became law, thugs from the anti-Semitic group the Association of Awakening Magyars burst into the Club Café, next to the Comedy Theatre – a popular meeting place for after-show drinks. They killed two of the regular clients they knew to be Jews and beat up three more. They were given jail sentences, but at the height of the White Terror, with Horthy's blessing, they were released after just a few months. It didn't matter that the vast majority of Budapest Jews had wanted nothing to do with the Bolshevik regime – or that many of the wealthy bourgeois that the Kun regime had terrorized and whose property had been expropriated were themselves Jews. 'Yes it is true that several of the Commune's leadership were Jews,' Koestler noted. 'But very few Jews were Communists.'

Nor did it matter that around 12,500 Hungarian Jews were killed in the war and tens of thousands had been wounded, a high proportion considering the numbers who served. They were still responsible for the humiliation of Trianon, the stab in the back. 'The most gruesome paradox in the history of Central European Jewry is reflected in the medals and photographs left behind by Jewish veterans of the First World War on the walls of their Aryanised Budapest apartments when they were forced out of their homes,' wrote Horthy's biographer, István Deák.

The psychoanalyst Sándor Ferenczi knew what was happening and understood where it could easily lead, but like the vast majority of Central Europe's Jews he stayed where he was. He wrote to his friend Sigmund Freud from Budapest at the end of 1920: 'We are now facing a period of brutal persecution *as Jews*. They will, I think, have cured us in a very short time of the illusion with which we were brought up, namely that we are "Hungarians of Jewish faith". I picture Hungarian anti-Semitism – commensurate with the national character – to be more brutal than the petty type of the Austrians . . . One will have to take this trauma as an occasion to abandon prejudices brought long from the nursery and to come to terms with the bitter truth of being, as a Jew, really without a country.' Freud begged him continually over the next few years to leave Hungary, but he refused.

Jews had begun to feel differently about their homeland. 'We Jews, together with the gypsies, became unwelcome guests in a Hungary reduced to one-third of its territory,' Konrád pointed out:

We were emphatically reminded that we were an alien element. Previously we appeared too forgetful of our status as 'guests'. We had forgotten our true status. We were then to learn that the law was not all. It was quite possible to wipe us from the face of the earth legally, by meticulously drafted regulations. When more and more non-Jewish intellectuals were of the opinion that there was a 'Jewish Question', or even that it was the most important issue of all, crying out for a 'solution', then it was only a matter of time and logical consistency to get from there to the gas chambers.[3]

After Horthy met Hitler for the first time in 1934 at Berchtesgaden in Bavaria he told the British minister in Budapest that he 'admired' the Führer, who seemed to him 'a moderate and wise statesman . . . well mannered and reasonable'. Three years later, at a meeting with a successor British ambassador at his Budapest office, Horthy described Hitler as 'a madman determined to cause trouble, and if he provoked a war we would fight them to the last ditch'. The duplicity seems naïve and clumsy, but for Horthy any deceit was considered justified if it furthered the higher revisionist cause of regaining the territories lost at Trianon. That was the principal – the only – foreign-policy goal between the wars.

In the 1920s the Hungarians had tried to gain the sympathy of the Entente powers and the US, Britain especially. Many in the landowning and business class close to the regent who still ran Hungary were Anglophiles, and Horthy always said he admired the British way of life. They were mystified that the British – and indeed the French – did not see Central and Eastern Europe as remotely important or politically significant. But after Hitler came to power, it became obvious that German and Hungarian aims were closely aligned and everything changed. Horthy could see an opportunity. Fascism began to appeal to a broad swathe of public opinion in Hungary, a range of ultra-extreme nationalist groups similar to the Nazis gained increased support, and Horthy's type of authoritarian conservatism began to look weak and moderate. Despite his deep and abiding anti-Semitism, the regent retained a core of Jews, bankers and rich industrialists he regarded as 'honorary Magyars', with whom he was prepared to socialize and who had helped his family financially. He played bridge every week with the vastly rich iron and steel magnate Ferenc Chorin.

It was clear, too, that Horthy was getting nowhere with the British and the French towards realizing Hungary's irredentist hopes. Horthy and his entourage thought the Nazis went too far and were uncouth. But the regime needed them and an alliance with Hitler. From 1938 Hungary became ever closer to Germany. The Hungarian Parliament began passing a series of increasingly stringent anti-Jewish laws – and Horthy approved them. Yet despite all the anti-Semitic rhetoric in Hungarian public life and in the press, for many in Budapest not much had changed in practical terms. A substantial part of banking and industry was still owned by Jews and nearly half of Budapest's doctors were Jewish. György Konrád is clear that 'members of my family thought of themselves as good Hungarians and good Jews. The two did not come to be viewed as separate until the Second World War.'[4]

In 1931 Jews had been forced to register their ethnicity. Many writers and artists objected. Bartók and Kodály, who were not Jewish, stated on the legally binding questionnaire that they were acting 'out of solidarity with our brothers and sisters'. They put their names to a string of public protests in the international press throughout the 1930s, as Hungary moved increasingly into the orbit of Nazi Germany. Bartók loathed any idea of racial superiority: 'I believe the brotherhood of peoples, brotherhood in spite of all wars and conflicts. I try, to the best of my ability, to serve this ideal in my music. Therefore, I don't reject any influence on my music . . . only that the source must be clean, fresh and healthy.' After a while he could no longer bear the stifling atmosphere and left. 'So much for Hungary, where, unfortunately, nearly all of our "educated" Christians are adherents of the Nazi regime. I feel quite ashamed of coming from this class,' he wrote in 1938.* Kodály chose to stay. His home was a villa on the Körönd (Circus) two-thirds of the way along Andrássy Avenue that was renamed Hitler Circus in 1938, despite his protest.

The First Jewish Law was passed in 1938, immediately after the 1938 *Anschluss* in Austria. Jews were barred from jobs in the civil service, the judiciary and local government. There was a new quota: Jews were limited to no more than 20 per cent in any business enterprise. So doctors and lawyers, journalists, musicians, cinemas and theatres had to establish, in effect, closed shops to regulate how many Jews could remain in work. All the Christian Churches supported the law. A few politicians on the Right stood out, including, courageously, the Prime Minister for the first decade of the Horthy years, István Bethlen, who wrote to the regent, once a close friend, arguing that the law 'will open wounds without thinking of a cure . . . and will transform the nearly one million intelligent Jews who live in our country into desperate internal enemies of the Hungarian nation'. A few months later, under the First Vienna Award, Hitler gave Hungary a slice of Slovakia which it had lost under the Treaty of Trianon. Horthy wrote effusively to the Führer: 'I shall never forget this proof of friendship and Your Excellency can at all times rely steadfastly on my gratitude.' Around the same time, Imre Kertész, who in 1919 had stayed in Budapest when his brother, the great photographer André Kertész, left for Paris and later New York, wrote to him: 'It is difficult to live here, when the earth shakes under one's feet. What the immediate future brings we don't know but there is no promise of anything good. Human lives are reduced to zero . . . Jews here are now an isolated new subspecies.'[5]

A Second Jewish Law in 1939 tightened the quotas, effectively banned Jewish lawyers from the legal profession and prevented Jews

---

* He thought of emigration then, but couldn't bear to leave his mother behind. After her death, though, he packed his bags and, after giving one final concert in Budapest on 8 October 1940, he left for the US, where he spent the last five years of his life.

from owning property, including a wide range of businesses. The laws expropriated Jewish property, which was then handed over to those whom the regime labelled 'real Magyars'. The Jewish Laws, according to the political theorist István Bibó, who had survived arrest and incarceration by the Horthy administration,

> marked the moral decline of Hungarian society . . . they gave a large section of the middle and petty bourgeoisie the chance to make a profit without any effort, thanks to the State and at the expense of others. Large sections of Hungarian society got to like the idea that one could make a living not only by work and enterprise, but also by seeking out someone else's position, researching his ancestry, denouncing him, having him dismissed and claiming his business . . . by the total usurpation of that person's existence. There was alarming greed, unscrupulous mendacity, and at best, calculated pushiness by a considerable section of this society. This was an unforgettable blow not only for the Jews affected by it but also for all decent Hungarians.[6]

Horthy was privately furious about the Nazi-Soviet pact in 1939 – an accommodation with the Soviet Union was anathema to him. But by then Hungary was so close to Germany, its fortunes and economy so interlinked, its military so dependent, that it was hard to pull away from the alliance. After the pact was signed Horthy sent Hitler a basket of Hungarian fruit, with handwritten instructions about how best to store and prepare them. The accompanying letter warned him not to trust Stalin or any Bolshevik, and went on: 'We are a grateful and absolutely reliable people and we realize what we owe to you and the German nation. We want the German people to feel that even though it wishes to fight its great battles alone, it need not face its cares alone. Whatever we can spare is at your disposal.' He signed the letter 'Your Excellency's devoted friend'. Soon afterwards, under the Second Vienna Award, Hungary was given back most of Transylvania and Horthy was being hailed by Hungarian public opinion as a diplomatic genius. But not everyone was so enthusiastic. Privately the Prime Minister, Count Teleki, was deeply worried where the mood would lead. 'Our people have gone quite mad,' he confided to his diary. 'Let's get it all back! By whatever means, with whoever's help, at whatever cost! The Germans know this well, and are making the most of it. People have lost their better judgement, listening to all the terrible revisionist propaganda: the soldiers want to fight alongside the Germans, and have the Regent's ear; today, the revisionists and the army are one, they're the ones who'll get us into trouble . . . Revisionism will be the death of us; it's revisionism that will embroil us in the war, which we will lose.'[7]

The Third Jewish Law of August 1941 was introduced a few weeks after Hungary declared war on the Soviet Union. Among other things, it banned sexual relations between Jews and non-Jews and defined who was and who wasn't a Jew. As Elie Wiesel, the Auschwitz survivor whose birthplace in Transylvania had been part of Hungary until Trianon, explained, the regulations in Hungary went even further than the Nuremberg Laws in Germany in racial ideology. Everyone who had at least two Jewish grandparents was categorized as Jewish; under Hitler's law a half-Jew who could show he or she was a Christian and was married to a quarter-Jew was not classified as Jewish – and was therefore safe. This was the world of the mad in terms of legal classification, but the practical effect was that overnight 65,000 more people were designated Jews and around half of them would soon perish in the Holocaust. The erstwhile Hungarian National Bank chairman and 1930s Finance Minister Béla Imrédy justified the laws on the grounds that 'a single drop of Jewish blood . . . is enough to spoil the character and patriotism of a person'.*

The writer Sándor Márai recalled a family dinner in which one of his relatives announced he had become a Nazi and attempted to explain why he and thousands of Hungarians had been converted to fascist ideology:

When I took issue with him he gave a surprising reply. 'I am a National Socialist,' he shouted. 'You . . . can't understand this because you are talented. But I am not and that is why I need National Socialism.' The passionate words died away after my hot-blooded relative

---

* Imrédy was briefly Prime Minister in 1938–9. When an investigative reporter discovered that his great-grandfather had been a Jew, the fact was news to him. He was summoned to Horthy's presence, broke down and wept, and resigned on the spot.

had declared the truth of his life . . . Several others in the party began to laugh; but the laughter was bitter . . . When we caught the drift of what he said, I answered that I don't put much faith in 'my talent' – it is of the kind that must be proven newly every day – but I would not follow the ideals of National Socialism even if I had no talent of any kind . . . My relative shook his head. 'You can't possibly understand . . . Now it's about us.' He struck his chest out and declared 'Our time has come.'[8]

28

MADNESS VISIBLE

Hungary took up arms . . . with the aim of recovering part of its lost territories, and it was willing to send half a million Jews to German camps in exchange. It was a bad bargain because in the end they lost not only the Jews, but the territory as well, and were left with the shame of it all. True, not everyone feels this way; there are those who feel that while many Hungarian Jews were killed the number was too small.

György Konrád, A Guest in My Own Country, 2008

Hungary entered the war in June 1941, immediately after Hitler's invasion of the USSR, not because Germany demanded it but in order to win favours from Hitler, which it did. For these gains it became an enthusiastic member of the Axis alliance, until it became clear that the Germans were losing the war, when it tried – far too late – to make a separate peace. Geography made it difficult for Hungary to be neutral or ally itself with the West, but the Horthy regime's revisionist policies and relentless pro-Nazi propaganda in the 1930s made it impossible. The regent was naïve enough to believe that Hungary could be involved in a war against Soviet Russia without significant loss in Hungarian lives, and could regain almost all that had been ceded under the Treaty of Trianon. He thought he could avoid Hungary becoming a German satellite, and that, if the Germans lost, the British and Americans would somehow overlook Hungary's alliance with the Nazis. He believed almost to the end that Britain and America would break their alliance with the Soviets for the sake of Hungary.

For most of the war, the home front in Budapest was hardly affected – for most Hungarians. Modest numbers of Hungarian troops had fought in the invasion of Yugoslavia in 1941, which gave Hungary control once again of the northern part of Serbia, the Vojvodina, where around half a million ethnic Hungarians lived. But after Stalingrad and the Battle of Kursk, when Hungarian losses began to mount in Ukraine, it was becoming obvious the Germans were losing the war; it was only a matter of time. Horthy had since 1943 put out tentative feelers with the Allies to make a separate peace deal, but no agreement was ever reached. The terms of 'total surrender' were unacceptable to the Hungarians. At the start of 1944 the regent tried again and despatched Prime Minister Miklós Kállay to begin secret talks with the Allies. This time Horthy was even prepared to reach a settlement with the Soviets. But Hitler knew all along about Kállay's peace talks – 'Hungary's treachery', he called it – and implemented Operation Margarethe to ensure that unreliable Hungary did not defect from the Axis alliance.

On 15 March 1944 he summoned Horthy to an immediate meeting at Klessheim Palace, near Salzburg, to get him away from Budapest. Four days later the *Wehrmacht* occupied Hungary in an entirely peaceful operation. Horthy objected but eventually agreed, and the two leaders issued a joint statement: 'On the basis of mutual agreement, German troops have arrived in Hungary in order to help Hungary to fight more effectively in the common war against the common enemy, especially in our efforts of defeating Bolshevism. The two allied governments agree that in the spirit of traditional friendship and military co-operation, the arrival of the troops would contribute to the final victory of our joint cause.'[1]

There was no military or civil resistance. Only two shots were fired, both by one man, the sixty-year-old MP Endre Bajcsy-Zsilinszky, when three Gestapo goons arrived to arrest him at his apartment in Attila Boulevard in downtown Pest on the first day of the occupation. He missed his target and was shot in the arm. As he was dragged into the back of a car, he shouted 'Long live independent Hungary' and was taken to a German prison.*

---

* Bajcsy-Zsilinszky was a rare hero. As a young man he was on the far Right and joined the Race Protection Party of virulent anti-Semites. But he moved further towards a moderate liberal position, and opposed Horthy (whom he knew well) and the drift towards Hungary's Nazification. He began to speak out openly against anti-Semitism and did what he could to help Jews who had been sent on labour service to the front, as around 30,000 had from 1941. Six months after his arrest by the Gestapo he was

Andy Grove, born András Gróf in Budapest – who decades later as a refugee to the US founded the giant tech firm Intel – was an eight-year-old boy when the Germans occupied the city. 'My mother and I stood on the sidewalk of the Ring Boulevard, watching as the cars and troop carriers filled with soldiers passed by in March 1944,' he wrote later. 'The German soldiers were neat and wore shiny boots and had a self-confident air about them. The sidewalk was lined with passers-by, all watching the procession of soldiers, all looking very serious . . . There was no sound except for the engine and tyre noise from the cars . . . they set up headquarters just a few blocks from our house . . . our lives changed in a major way. From then on things were happening to us one after the other.'

At a time when it might have been clear to all that Germany had lost the war, that the Red Army would soon occupy Hungary and that it would wipe out the Hungarian ruling elite, the government and the administration spent most of its time and energy on devising edicts for the confiscation of Jewish telephones, radios, horses, cars, motorcycles, bicycles, jewellery, stamp collections, bank accounts and furs, as well as licences to practise any trade or profession. Jews were given reduced-rate ration cards; they were excluded from all clubs, cinemas, theatres, swimming pools and most restaurants, and were allowed into public baths only when 'true Magyar' were not there. But even that privilege was of little value, because in many cities either the mayor's office or the directorate of the public baths decided that at no time should Jews be allowed to bathe.

The Germans installed as Prime Minister the prominent Nazi sympathizer Döme Sztojáy, who they knew would be loyal to Hitler. Horthy retired to his apartment in the Royal Castle in Buda, announced he wanted 'no prior notice of the decrees of a government appointed by a foreign power' and refused to countersign them as head of state. But he did nothing to prevent the Germans from doing what they wanted in Hungary. The Hungarian army became fully mobilized, essentially

---

released, but immediately he helped to form an underground opposition group, the National Committee of Liberation. Within a fortnight he was rearrested – this time by the home-grown Hungarian fascists, the Arrow Cross, who executed him on 24 December 1944. There is a wide boulevard named after him on the Pest side of the river and a major metro hub.

under the *Wehrmacht*'s strategic orders. Increasing numbers of Hungarian troops were sent to the Ukrainian Front in an attempt to prevent the Red Army breaking through the Carpathian mountains. It was at this point in March 1944 – long after other European cities had experienced air raids – that British and American planes began bombing targets in Hungary, mainly industrial areas of Budapest. Around 20,000 Hungarians were killed in Allied air raids before the late autumn of 1944.[2]

Immediately after the German occupation, a special German SS unit of 'experts', the *Sonderkommando* led by Adolf Eichmann, then thirty-eight, arrived in Budapest to plan, co-ordinate and eventually carry out the deportation of the Jews. Nowhere else in Central and Eastern Europe had so many Jews – more than 820,000 – been able to live so long in relative safety as in Hungary. But nowhere else were they sent to their death so quickly. All the Hungarian Jews outside Budapest were herded into ghettoes in the first part of the 'final solution' in Hungary.* Andor Jaross, the Finance Minister, was open about the new government's plans concerning Jewish wealth: 'Let me emphasize that all the assets and valuables that Jewish greed was able to amass during the liberal period no longer belongs to them. It is now the property of the Hungarian nation . . . It must be used to enrich the whole of the nation. It must be incorporated into the circulation of the national economy, so that every decent, hard-working Hungarian can share in it.'

Eichmann had a staff of just sixty, based at the Majestic Hotel on Buda's fashionable but quiet Sváb Hill. He was in charge of the process – a grim, logistical success story. But Hungarian gendarmes, fascist volunteers, 40,000 civil servants and around 200,000 civilians carried out the work and rounded the victims into cattle trucks for their final journey. They reported proudly to their German masters that between 15 May and 7 July – less than two months – they had deported 437,402 Jews, all but 15,000 of them to Auschwitz, in 147 trains. Eichmann was delighted by what he experienced after his arrival. 'It seems the

---

* The first mass killings of Hungarian Jews were in August 1941, when more than 20,000 Jews deported by the Hungarian government to Ukraine, under German occupation, were murdered there by the SS. But technically they were Ukrainian citizens by then. Around 20,000 Jews were killed in the part of Yugoslavia which Hungary had retaken in 1941, but they were not technically Hungarian Jews either.

Hungarians are indeed the descendants of the Huns; we would never have managed so well without them,' remarked one of his deputies to a member of the Hungarian Jewish Council. Rudolf Höss, the commander of Auschwitz, begged the Hungarian authorities not to send more than one transport every second day, as the camp crematoria did not have the capacity to cope with the sheer number of bodies arriving from the gas chambers. The Hungarians wanted to send six transports a day, and as a sensible compromise Eichmann suggested two trainloads every other day. In the end, three, sometimes four trains, each with about 3,000 deportees, left the stations every day for fifty-six days. The camp authorities in Auschwitz dug open pits to burn the corpses. The Italian writer Primo Levi, a survivor, said later that at one point in the summer of 1944 he heard no other language spoken at Auschwitz except Hungarian.[3]

The mass deportations from provincial Hungary were extraordinarily efficient. Following a rigid timetable, which had been jointly set by Eichmann, the two Hungarian deputy ministers in charge of deportations and a Hungarian army lieutenant-colonel, the country's ten gendarmerie districts proceeded to assemble the Jews in hastily created ghettoes. They then moved them from brick factories, lumber yards and other assembly points outside the larger towns to railway stations, where they were crammed seventy to eighty in a wagon.

The conditions in the ghettoes had often been far worse than governmental decrees had prescribed: too little water; too little food. Yet even those were better than conditions in the brickyards, where the sheds had no walls, latrines had to be dug and health care was non-existent. Torture and robbery by the authorities were routine. In nearly every ghetto, brickyard and railway station the gendarmes operated a so-called 'mint' at which wealthier Jews were thrashed until they gave up their hidden gold.

Almost unimaginably, hundreds of qualified doctors, licensed nurses and midwives assisted the gendarmes in performing vaginal and anal searches on Jewish women for hidden jewels. They were paid reasonable sums of money for the job and not a single doctor refused to perform the task. History does not record one instance of a Hungarian police officer, soldier or public servant openly refusing to co-operate with the deportation of the Jews outside Budapest.[4]

*

In Budapest, Jews were safe from deportation for the moment, though they did not know it. Within a few days of the occupation, the Orthodox Synagogue on Kazinczy Street in the heart of Pest was turned into a stable; the Rabbinical Seminary at nearby Rökk Szilárd Street became the most dreaded prison in the city, operated by the Gestapo. Jews had to wear the yellow Star of David; they were allowed to ride only on the last car of the trams. Jews were barred from theatres, the cinema, concert halls, swimming pools. 'We had to move out of our apartment and into special buildings designated as houses for Jews,' recalled Andy Grove. 'A big Star of David was painted in yellow above the entrance . . . Things were happening to us one after the other. I was eight at the time but I remember . . . We were forbidden to step outside the Jewish house without wearing a star, just one more of those things to accept numbly and silently.'

The novelist György Konrád was aged eleven: 'There were around eighty of us living in a three-room apartment on the fourth floor. At night we would stack up any furniture that could be slept on. Not everyone got a bed or a mattress but all of us had at least a rug.' In a diary entry for a sweltering-hot 24 June 1944 the writer Miksa Fenyő recalled that Jews 'were allowed out of the Yellow Star House only between two and five o'clock in the afternoon and even then only to go to the doctor, to wash or go shopping. We are crammed inside four or five to a room, with one kitchen or WC between fifteen or twenty people. Reduced to a state of complete torpor, we suffer horribly from the heat, unable to leave our rooms or even to go for a walk, receive visitors or to set foot in non-Jewish homes.'

Thousands of Jews were sent on forced marches west as slave labour to camps on the Hungarian–Austrian border in appalling conditions. This was the fate of Antal Szerb, author of the exquisite novel *Journey by Moonlight.** Szerb was born Jewish in 1901, but his family converted to Catholicism when Szerb was an infant. He was educated in a rigorously Catholic school. His godfather was the rabidly anti-Semitic Bishop Ottokár Prohászka, whose sermons about the danger to Hungarian so-

---

* As well as a hilarious but subtly written must-read book for any visitor to the city called *A Martian's Guide to Budapest.*

ciety of Jewish influence were highly popular between the wars. Szerb's masterly *History of Hungarian Literature* had at one point been taught to all pupils in secondary schools, but was banned and publicly burned in 1941. Three years later he was marched to a labour camp, where less than a month before the end of the war he was beaten to death by the prison guards. The poet Miklós Radnóti was sent on a different forced labour march, west towards Austria. Unable to walk any further, he was shot by guards and left on the side of the road. Some of his haunting last poems were found with his body in a notebook after he died. The final one concluded:

> Shot through the nape. I whispered to myself,
> That's how you too will end. No more now, peace.
> Patience will flower in death. And I could hear
> A voice above me say: *der springt noch auf*
> Earth and dried blood mingling in my ear.[5]

The Churches had supported all the anti-Jewish laws. But having seen the horror of the deportations, many finally began to speak out. In early summer the Reformed and Evangelical Churches submitted a joint Protestant Memorandum to the Sztójay government demanding a halt to the deportations, and finally, on 29 June 1944, the Catholic Church, silent throughout the years Hungary had Nazified, spoke. Cardinal Jusztinián Serédi, Primate of Hungary, wrote a circular condemning the persecutions. The government responded by banning the publication of the memorandum and the reading in church of the circular. But the pressure on Horthy mounted. A week later, after protests by the Vatican, the neutral states, direct personal appeals from Britain's King George VI, Sweden's King Gustav V and President Roosevelt, Horthy ordered the deportations of Jews to cease. The order saved most of the Jews in Budapest.

In his memoirs Horthy said that he had been powerless to stop the deportations and claimed that he had no idea what the real goal of them was. He may have been right that he was powerless. But he was lying about the rest. He had been informed about the 'final solution' and how it was implemented even before he met Hitler in April 1943, when, according to German minutes of the encounter, Hitler reprimanded him for being too lenient on the Hungarian Jews. Horthy asked: 'What shall I do with them after having almost completely deprived them of their livelihoods? We can't beat them to death, after all.' The German Minister for Foreign Affairs, Joachim von Ribbentrop, who was also present, answered: 'The Jews must be exterminated or taken to concentration camps.' Hitler raised the situation in Poland as an example to follow: 'If the Jews do not want to work there, they have to perish. They have to be treated like the bacillus of tuberculosis that can infect the healthy body.'*

Better late than never, Horthy deserves some credit for saving the lives of most of Budapest's Jews. But as one of his biographers, Thomas Sakmyster, noted, 'skeptics might suggest that this merely demonstrated the truth of the cliché that even a stopped clock is accurate twice a day'. He took military measures to oppose the gendarmes who wanted to continue with the deportations, which under the circumstances showed some courage. World condemnation and the appeals of some of Horthy's friends counted too. In the end, about 40 per cent of Hungary's Jews – and 90 per cent of Budapest's, around 365,000 people – survived the war, a higher number than anywhere else within Hitler's Europe.[6]

Horthy – finally – was prevailed on by his family and some in his court to break with Hitler. By mid October, in another round of secret talks using neutral diplomats as intermediaries, he had negotiated a ceasefire with the Soviets. It was by then far too late to salvage Hungary from the fate it would soon endure or his own, much-vaunted honour. The keenest in his entourage to argue for doing a deal with the Allies

---

* Horthy's staff prepared a draft letter to Hitler a few weeks later about the meeting. One sentence reads: 'Your Excellency further reproached me because the [Hungarian] government did not implement the extermination of the Jews as thoroughly as it happened in Germany and as it is desirable in other countries as well.' Horthy eventually deleted the sentence, but the original document clearly shows that he understood precisely what Hitler and Ribbentrop told him. If anyone in the higher circles of Hungarian government had any doubt about the fate of Jews, eyewitness accounts of prisoners who escaped from Auschwitz (the so-called Auschwitz Protocols) provided proof that the rumours of murder were true. The documents reached prominent Hungarian cultural figures and politicians in May–June 1944. There can be no doubt that the regent was well aware of Nazi extermination policies long before the German occupation of Hungary.

was his son, Miklós Jnr, an Anglophile who believed there was still time for his father to rehabilitate himself in the eyes of the British and the Americans, who might moderate the harsh occupation the Red Army would most likely begin when they entered Hungary.

On the morning of 15 October, 'Miki' Horthy was on the way to his office in the Castle district of Buda when his car encountered a road block just a few hundred metres from the castle. He was suddenly surrounded by hooded men in trench coats bearing the yellow Star of David. He drew his pistol, but before he could take aim he was overpowered, knocked unconscious and thrown into the back of a lorry parked on the side of the road. His bodyguards lay bleeding.

The well-planned kidnapping was the work of one of Hitler's favourites, an SS officer named Otto Skorzeny, who had come to the Führer's attention the previous year when he had organized the daring rescue of Mussolini from the mountain-top fortress of Gran Sasso. Now Skorzeny and his cohorts had disguised themselves as Jews, so eyewitnesses could blame the abduction on them. Within minutes of being told the younger Horthy was a prisoner, Hitler's representative in Budapest, Edmund Veesenmayer, stood before the regent and told him: 'We have your son. Call off this armistice and you can see him again.' The regent did as he was told – 'How could I have done otherwise,' he told anyone who would listen. 'I am a father . . .' In fact Miki was immediately bundled away, wrapped in a Turkish rug and packed off to Germany; they did not meet again for months.[7]

But Hungarians knew about the armistice. Regent Horthy had already made a pre-recorded radio broadcast that was beamed across much of the country, including Budapest. Army trucks with loudspeakers had been circulating the city: 'Citizens. This is Admiral Horthy. Please go to your radios.' Then they heard the regent announcing: 'We shall not become the scene of the Reich's rearguard combat zone. We have agreed to abandon further participation in the fight against the Soviet Union.'

Thousands of people in Budapest began a party to celebrate. 'It was a bright autumn Sunday morning,' György Konrád, being hidden on false diplomatic papers issued by Swiss diplomats, recalled. 'People flowed out on to the street. We were giddy with the news. Everyone in our building . . . was Jewish. The old men climbed a ladder to take down the yellow paper star on the plank over the entrance. Some ripped off the yellow stars on their coats, right there in the street. We waited for confirmation of the news.'

But that afternoon, amid the celebrations, four German divisions moved on the capital and tanks surrounded the Royal Castle. Hungary's troops laid down their arms, led by the officer corps, who were overwhelmingly pro-Nazi. Budapest was recaptured and the Germans appointed as Prime Minister of Hungary Ferenc Szálasi, head of the Arrow Cross, the fascist group Horthy had once banned for being too extreme and whom he called gangsters and thugs. 'Power fell into the hands of the dregs of society,' as the historian Miklós Molnár, a student at Budapest University at the time, put it.

Horthy gave away his kingdom but didn't get back his son. Miki was taken to Dachau concentration camp, Admiral Horthy to a castle in Bavaria 'in accordance with his rank', as Hitler said. He was freed by the Americans in the spring of 1945, but then rearrested and sent to various internment camps in which, as he complained in his memoirs, he had to learn to make his bed and scrub his mess-tin. The Yugoslavs tried to extradite him for war crimes the Hungarians had allegedly committed in Serbia, but President Harry Truman blocked their efforts. The Soviets were not interested in pursuing him and – lucky to evade prosecution – he was exiled to Estoril in Portugal, where he lived quietly until his death in 1957, reunited with his son. The ageing anti-Semite lived comfortably, thanks mainly to charity from the Jewish Chorin family – an irony he never once acknowledged. But he was not allowed to return, alive, to Hungary.*

Hungary has never come to terms with the enormous part – for good or ill – that the 'admiral on a white horse' played in the country's history. He has been used as a political football. Vilified in the Communist years and by the pro-democracy liberals who succeeded them after 1989, in the twenty-first century revisionist historians have tried to rehabilitate him; monuments have been erected in his honour in several provincial towns. The Prime Minister from 2010, Viktor Orbán, at one point

---

* After the collapse of Communism and the Soviet army had left Hungary his remains were returned. He had a large ceremonial reburial in September 1993 – the Hungarians do burials well, reburials even better.

called him an 'exceptional statesman, who safeguarded the existence of Hungary'. But on the other hand he later backtracked on that and has been highly critical of Horthy's role. Each successive government has rewritten a version of the admiral's story in its own image.[8]

29

THE SIEGE OF BUDAPEST

I will never forget those frightened faces . . . their life depended on my words. This was the last sign of their hope before they lost their will to live . . . this having to make snap choices of whom to save – it's insanity. Where is God?

> Carl Lutz, vice consul of the Swiss Legation in Budapest,
> November 1944

The battle for Budapest was the longest and bloodiest siege of any capital city in the Second World War. In summer 1944 the Germans had surrendered Rome and Paris to the Allies, partly in order to avoid bloody revenge by resistance movements. Warsaw had been practically destroyed during the war, but at the end the Germans retreated and the Soviets walked in virtually unopposed. The SS put up a bitter struggle for six days in Vienna. Berlin was a bloodbath, but the final assault by the Russians took around two weeks.

The Soviet siege of Budapest was a titanic struggle for three months, 102 days altogether, and ended only after a failed attempt by the Germans and Hungarian defenders to break out of what Hitler had called 'Fortress Budapest'. Around a million inhabitants, including an enormous number of refugees, Hungarian army deserters and more than 100,000 Jews (one of the biggest surviving Jewish communities in Hitler's Europe), hid in the city's basements. Nearly 40,000 civilians died, mostly from sniper fire in streets or shellfire in people's bedrooms, bathrooms and kitchens.

'No one but those who were there can fail to recall the experience,' the historian István Deák, who was an eighteen-year-old student at the time of the siege, wrote later in a brilliant essay, 'Improvising the Holocaust':

They will remember the naked bodies floating down the Danube . . . the crazed Arrow Cross hoodlums beating old Jewish women in the rain and snow. Or the deaf-mute squad of militiamen who ordered all passing men into a courtyard there to drop their pants and submit to a quick 'racial test'. Or people standing in line for water while Soviet planes – which we all called *Ratas* – flew overhead so close that we could see the pilots' faces. I learned that a city with a million inhabitants is a vast place. While towards the end those in Buda, the western half of the city, were still under siege, in Pest, east of the Danube, a movie house was already showing films.

There had been fourteen sieges, mostly of Buda and of varying intensity, over the centuries, but the devastation caused in the Second World War was worse than anything before. The struggle was so ferocious that even at the time it was being compared to Stalingrad, though at that monumental battle most of the hand-to-hand fighting had happened outside the city and the majority of the civilian population had been evacuated. Some Red Army soldiers who had fought in both thought the battle for Budapest was more vicious and difficult. Around 40,000 German and Hungarian soldiers were killed, and at least 80,000 Soviets, on top of the civilian casualties.

By the time Admiral Horthy was deposed the Russians had reconquered Ukraine and were massing troops on the Soviet border with Hungary to march west. At the beginning of November, two Soviet armies commanded by Marshal Rodion Malinovsky had encircled Budapest and the defeat of Hungary was anticipated as an imminent prospect celebrated by the Allies. The Cold War was in the future, Hungary had not yet attained plucky victim status around the world and it was lost on nobody that the country had been on the 'wrong side' in two world wars. That winter the views of Harold Nicolson, a man usually of liberal opinions, were shared by many people:

When I learned that the Russian armies were within cannon range of Budapest, I was conscious of delight, which I felt to be neither virtuous nor sane. My reason tells me that the Hungarians found themselves in a difficult position, and that it would have been hard indeed for them to maintain a stubborn neutrality. They were forced into the war by geographical necessity and by a burning resentment against the Treaty of Trianon. The fact is that since the day, more than a thousand years ago, when Árpád first entered Hungary, the Magyars have done much harm and little good to Europe ... My satisfaction may be due to the quite rational feeling that this time the Hungarians will not again be able to disturb the peace.[1]

With the noose tightening around Budapest, neither the Germans nor the new Hungarian Arrow Cross government took any decisions about the fate of Budapest's population. The Hungarians would in any case have been unable to carry out a major evacuation and the Germans were not interested in helping them. Both commanders simply told civilians it was up to them if they wanted to leave the city. Posters telling them so appeared on some street corners on 7 November. Szálasi and his top henchmen had planned to leave for Sopron, on the border with Austria, a few days after that. But he changed his mind when Edmund Veesenmayer, the German envoy to Hungary, told him on 8 November that the German Embassy would stay in Budapest even if the government departed. The Führer, the ambassador told him, had ordered that Budapest must be defended 'to the last man'.

The German commander, General Karl Pfeffer-Wildenbruch, had an impossible task. He had at his disposal 100,000 troops, nearly a half of them Hungarian. He was short of ammunition and food and was up against a formidable, battled-hardened and well-supplied Red Army under experienced leadership. It didn't help that he detested his Hungarian allies, even the army officers who had generally been pro-German and had betrayed Horthy with their mutiny against the admiral's final order to lay down their weapons and surrender to the Soviets. The siege of Budapest was a hopeless battle that simply delayed the inevitable at great cost. Stalin was infuriated and saw the Hungarians as Hitler's last allies.

In the following month, while it was still just about feasible, 75,000 civilians managed to leave the city, including many thousands of child evacuees. The rest stayed, knowing the Soviets would arrive soon. They realised at around 2 p.m. on Saturday, 4 November what the siege would be like – that the war's end was really in sight – when Margaret Bridge blew up. People had got used to US and British air raids – in the suburbs, on industrial targets. But this explosion in the heart of the city stunned Budapest's residents.

Miklós Kovalovszky, who kept a diary of the siege, recalled:

When we arrived in front of the Comedy Theatre we were shaken by a tremendous explosion. I ran back to the Danube embankment (around 250 metres away) where a huge crowd of people had gathered. On the Pest side two arches of the bridge had collapsed. Trams, cars and hundreds of people had fallen into the river. Two shattered carriages of the Number 6 tram jutted out of the water and the moans of the injured could be heard. Bodies were hanging from the railings and in the swirling water there were dead and wounded. Ships, boats and police craft were trying to save whoever they could.

Around 600 people died – nobody knows the exact number. It was at this point that the inhabitants of Budapest realized the Germans were planning to blow up all the bridges over the Danube, though this blast had been premature, an accident. Explosive charges were being primed and the fuse had been ignited by a spark from a passing tram. The dead included forty German sappers. Relentless heavy bombardment from Soviet guns east and north of the city began three days later.[2]

Nobody in Budapest could say as an excuse later that they did not know what was happening to the city's Jews. People could see with their own eyes every day. Unlike anywhere else in Europe, the slaughter was taking place openly on streets in the centre of the city with practically no effort made to hide what was being done. 'None of this was happening anywhere else in Nazi-occupied Western Europe,' wrote Randolph Braham, the Budapest-born but US-based historian of the Holocaust. The favoured place for the murders – though not the only place – was the Danube embankment, and they continued throughout the day and night. A senior police officer told the Swiss diplomat Carl Lutz that there were no more than 4,000 armed Arrow Cross militiamen in Budapest in the autumn of 1944 – yet they terrorized a million people while the gendarmerie, the general civilian population and Hungarian soldiers stood by and watched. 'In normal circumstances 4,000 could not terrorize a million,' Lutz said. But nothing was normal any longer in Budapest.

The Arrow Cross was a Nazi-inspired movement, but with a specific Hungarian element. Originally when it was formed in the 1920s members wore brown shirts, used the swastika symbol and the Hitler salute. After Regent Horthy banned the organization in 1933 for inciting violence – it organized murder squads throughout Hungary, but especially in Budapest to assassinate well-known Jewish business leaders and 'celebrities' – it switched to green shirts and acquired the notorious arrow cross, which had been the symbol of St László, an eleventh-century Magyar king whose emblem was two flying arrows shaped as crosses. The party salute became *Kitartás* (Endurance). Their membership comprised not just the lumpenproletariat and urban workers, but also officials threatened by becoming *déclassé*, frustrated, radicalized intellectuals, badly paid former soldiers and bored students. Vast swathes of the Hungarian poor blamed their condition on foreigners who had seized Magyar territory. The Arrow Cross promised them, according to one party leaflet, 'deliverance from Jewish capitalists and the great aristocratic landlords'. It formed a protest movement against the power cartel of the feudal elite, high finance and the 'old bureaucracy that had controlled Hungary for generations'. It was the classic populist brew of Europe between the wars.

They demanded racial purity and 'proof of Magyarness' for people in public life. But when the Germans gave them power in October 1944, only one in five of the Arrow Cross ministers could furnish their proof. Even their leader, the former army major Ferenc Szálasi, then aged forty-seven who called himself 'leader of the nation', was born with the surname Salosjan in Kassa in what is now eastern Slovakia. According to Horthy's security agents, who had his family tree investigated, his forebears were Armenian, Slovak and German. He was 'at most one-quarter Hungarian' according to the regent – and it wasn't entirely clear whether he was in fact a Hungarian citizen at all.[3]

For Szálasi and his gang, making Hungary Jew free seemed more important than anything, even than winning the war or saving themselves from the Red Army. There can be no other plausible explanation for their irrational behaviour. Occasionally some in their leadership looked inward and questioned themselves – but usually in private or in their diaries. An exception was the Arrow Cross Foreign Minister, Gábor Kemény, who asked in a Cabinet meeting whether 'we are rich enough' to lose millions of working days. He was shouted down. It led to an even crazier policy. Szálasi complained to the German authorities for allowing Jewish forced labourers to work on Hungarian soil, demanding their immediate removal.

From the moment the Arrow Cross government was installed the hoodlums, some as young as sixteen, began to implement the 'final solution' – in their own way. For the Jews of Budapest, this period 'waiting for the Russians to arrive was the worst, most frightening time. We knew that if we could survive we would probably be alright . . . Only if . . .' recalled one survivor, Judit Fargás, a young mother of two small children at the time. Another who lived through that winter witnessed the Arrow Cross's methods:

> They preferred the cover of darkness for their work, but towards the end of the siege they were no longer very particular. They would march their victims to an open area on the bank of the Danube. In the freezing cold of December and January their captives were usually stripped of their clothing . . . The favoured number was three at a time, with their wrists wired together, facing the river. A rifleman would then fire into the back of the person standing in the middle. He would slump forward, dragging the other two into the Danube. This saved bullets and was just as effective as shooting all three. The freezing river and the weight of the corpse dragging them down would finish the job.[4]

The Arrow Cross was helped by a familiar face. Adolf Eichmann, organizer and godfather of the final solution, had left Budapest at the end of June, shortly before the deportation of Jews from outside Budapest ceased. But he reappeared on 18 October for a short period to advise the new government. He and the small team of Gestapo officers set up headquarters in the Royal Hotel on the Ring Boulevard. Occasionally the vicious crudity of the Arrow Cross militias – nearly all of whom had been civilians before October 1944 – revolted even the Germans. The army commander, Pfeffer-Wildenbruch, was no faint heart but he forbade his soldiers from taking part in the Arrow Cross pogroms. The German civilian command was less scrupulous. Ambassador Veesenmayer received instructions from Berlin pointing out that it was convenient that somebody else was solving the 'Jewish question' even more brutally than they were. He was told to 'assist the Arrow Cross in every way . . . it is in our interests that the Hungarians should now proceed against the Jews in the harshest possible manner.' About 105,000 Jews were murdered in Budapest that autumn and winter.

Many brave Hungarians did what they could to save Jews by giving them protection in homes and empty apartments – my own family was being sheltered and kept alive by the extraordinary gentleness and courage of my sister's nurse, Agnés Zsindely. But the majority of people were concerned about saving their own lives in the siege and almost nobody intervened on the streets. One gendarme told the student Miklós Molnár what he had just witnessed – a group of Jews had been stripped, shot and thrown into the river. 'Oh hell, how ghastly,' came the reply. 'Well the trouble is not that this was done. It's that some were left alive . . . because so long as they aren't completely exterminated they will turn into vindictive swine.'

After a few weeks the official policy changed and Szálasi was concerned about how his government was seen by neutral diplomats. He ordered his gangs to operate with more discretion. As Károlyi Maróthy, one of their parliamentary deputies, put it: 'We must not allow individual cases to create compassion for them . . . something must be done to stop the death rattle going on in the ditches all day and night . . . the population must not be able to see them dying.' Hungarian National Police Commissioner Pál Hódosy was clear: 'The problem is not that the Jews are being murdered . . . the trouble is the method. The bodies must be made to disappear, not put out on the streets.'

But the official exhortations were often ignored and eyewitnesses recorded many scenes of brutality. A young Hungarian officer, Lieutenant Iván Hermándy, saw an execution on the embankment. 'I popped round the corner of the Vigadó Concert Hall [just set back a few metres from the river] and saw the victims standing on the track of the Number 2 tram line in a long row,' he told an interviewer later. 'They were completely resigned to their fate. Those close to the Danube were already naked, the others were slowly walking along and undressing. It all happened in total silence, with only the occasional sound of a gunshot or machine-gun salvo. Later in the afternoon, when there was nobody left, we took another look. The dead were lying in their blood on the ice slabs, or floating in the Danube. Among them were women, children, old men.' A police officer recalled: 'They were herding Jews along the Great Boulevard. Four or five Arrow Cross boys, aged maybe fourteen to sixteen, were escorting them towards Erzsébet Bridge. An old woman collapsed . . . she couldn't cope with the march. One of the boys began to beat her with his rifle butt. I went up to him in my uniform. "Haven't you got a mother? How can you do this?" He replied, "Why do you mind? She's only a Jew, Uncle."'[5]

The boundaries of the 'general' Jewish ghetto just outside the Inner City were declared on 18 November and all Jews were told to move in by 2 December. On 10 December the area was closed off with wooden boards, leaving just four exit gates. At one point around 60,000 people were packed into 4,513 apartments, sometimes fourteen to a room. Conditions were appalling, as one survivor recalled in his diary:

> In narrow Kazinczy Street enfeebled men . . . were pushing a wheel-barrow. On the rattling contraption naked human bodies as yellow as wax were jolted along and a stiff arm with black patches was dangling and knocking against the spokes of the wheel. They stopped in front of the Kazinczy baths and . . . turned into the latticed gate. In the court-yard of the baths behind the weather-beaten façade bodies were piled up, frozen stiff like pieces of wood. I crossed into Klauzál Square. In the middle people were squatting or kneeling around a dead horse, hacking the meat off with knives. The animal's head was lying just a few metres away. The yellow and blue intestines, jelly-like and with cold sheen, were bursting out of the opened and mutilated body.

Between 14 November and 18 January 1945 the average number of daily deaths inside the ghetto (not including the murders committee against Jews outside) was eighty.

Suicide was common. In one week during November 1944 the number of Jews who killed themselves in Budapest was greater than the entire total of Jewish suicides throughout Hungary in 1943, the year before the deportations began. 'Old men, young girls, pregnant women killed themselves. Some mothers knocked their reluctant daughters uncon-scious with rolling pins and laid them under gas pipes.' On 3 January 1945 Inspector General István Lőcsei, the Arrow Cross Commissioner for the Concentration of Jews, ordered the formation of twelve Jewish labour regiments. The order could not be carried out because by then the starving inmates of the ghetto were barely able to walk.

A separate International Ghetto of seventy-two buildings near St Stephen's Square, in central Pest, where Jews were relatively safe was placed under Swiss protection as part of an arrangement made between the Arrow Cross government and Carl Lutz, the vice consul of the Swiss Legation. It was intended to concentrate together all the Jews with foreign passports. Originally it was supposed to hold 3,969 people, according to official figures the Swiss Legation gave the Hungarian government and the Germans. But right from the start it contained 15,600 people, and by the end of the siege nearly 40,000 crammed inside the buildings and their basements. The International Ghetto was dangerous, too, as it was closer to the Danube embankment; fascist militias regularly raided the buildings and seized Jews, whether 'protected' or not.

Cardinal Serédi met the Arrow Cross leader early in November 1944 and pleaded with him to halt the massacre of people on the streets of Budapest. Szálasi tried to mollify him and assured the prelate that the murders were the work of 'hotheads' and he in the leadership would try to stop their excesses. Not all churchmen agreed with the cardinal, though. One of the most notorious of the Arrow Cross commanders was the Franciscan friar András Kun, who personally directed several bloodbaths. Along with a silver crucifix, he wore a holster belt and revolver around his black habit. After Jews had been rounded up and taken to the Danube embankment his order was: 'In the name of Christ, Fire!'*[6]

The winter was one of the coldest on record. By early December the Danube had frozen over solid, the first time for many years. Many people

---

* Kun admitted after the war that he had committed 500 murders, although in an interview just before his trial and execution on 19 September 1945 he denied any involvement with atrocities. One of the most vicious of the Arrow Cross thugs turned out to be a fifteen-year-old boy, who after the war became an officer in the Hungarian air force. He and other members of his gang were arrested in 1966 after an investigation into Arrow Cross atrocities during the war – the only inquiry there has ever been since 1945. He and his companions carried out continuous murders, preceded by torture, and killed between 1,000 and 1,200 people. One gang member said he 'couldn't remember exactly how many'. On Christmas Day 1944 alone they shot more than fifty Jews.

were seen trying to cross, which would become a great danger later in the siege when the Russians were nearer to the centre of the city. But food supplies had reached a critical level before that. The sight of people hacking away at horse carcasses was common from early November. Szálasi wrote to the German army commander: 'food supplies are catastrophic. In Budapest the number of deaths by starvation is alarmingly high, particularly among children. We must expect some hunger riots.' But people were too exhausted and hungry to riot. On Christmas Eve Endre Rajk, the Arrow Cross Secretary of State, told the German high command that food stocks would last a maximum of ten days even after rationing had halved to 150 grams of bread a day, and, as a special treat for Christmas, 150 grams of meat. Nevertheless, when the International Red Cross offered 50 million pengős'(the unit of currency later replaced by the forint) worth of aid – enough to feed the city for a couple of weeks – the government refused because a condition was attached that part of it must be delivered to the ghetto.*

Public transport stopped running after Christmas, the water supply was all but exhausted and organized food supplies ceased almost entirely. An official cull of horses began from New Year's Day, and soon only horse meat and carrots were available – no grain or other vegetables had entered Budapest for weeks. The biggest problem was distribution of the scarce food supply that there was. 'Some people were feasting while others had almost nothing to eat,' said Reinhard Noll, a sergeant from one of the German units in Pest. 'Our life was full of contradictions. There was barely enough water for a soup a day, but in some former hotel supply warehouses, the best spirits were available in huge quantities. We got only one slice of army bread a day, but were fully supplied with lard, jam ... the most expensive Hungarian cigars and wines we had never even heard of surrounded us in our cellars, by the case.'

When the water supply ran out people melted snow. But this could be fatal because soldiers from both sides would open fire indiscriminately on any civilians who ventured out of doors. The gas supply broke down

---

* Rajk and his brother – from a well-to-do family – were an intriguing pair. Endre's brother László was a leading Communist and leader of the Budapest underground opposition. When he was arrested, his fascist brother saved his life. After the war, when Endre was captured and about to be executed, László, by then a senior official in the Communist regime, intervened to rescue his brother.

entirely on 28 December; all the telephones were dead in Pest on 30 November, but in a few areas of Buda they were still working until the end of January. Electricity supplies finally failed throughout the city on 30 December. Gas pipes were often blown up in the Soviet bombardment and caused fires; when the main gas supply for the Buda Hills was destroyed flames rose into the sky for days.

On 26 December Lieutenant-General Iván Hindy, commander of Hungarian forces in Budapest, made an uplifting speech on the radio promising that the city would be relieved by the Germans and other Hungarian forces soon. But he didn't mean it. In a dispatch to the Hungarian Ministry of Defence four days later he was more realistic. 'Food supplies to the army and civilian population will be catastrophic . . . The population of the capital, according to the information I am receiving, regards the position as desperate. The wildest rumours are spreading . . . A few days ago it was said that I and my staff, as well as the German General Staff, were supposed to have left Budapest by air – an impossibility, but many people believed it. The masses . . . are resigned to a Soviet occupation.'

The Hungarian and German officers were barely on speaking terms; the Germans had long since ceased to consult the Hungarians on anything significant. They showed total indifference to the plight of Hungarian civilians. Hindy's anger grew. In mid January he wrote to his Ministry of Defence:

In many places the city centre now is a pile of burning ruins . . . In the southern parts of the Pest bridgehead only the strongpoints are still holding on. With enemy pressure increasing, Buda can soon expect a similar fate . . . the streets are blocked by huge heaps of rubble, there is no hope of clearing them. The water supply is exhausted. At the few wells, the queues are enormous. An infestation of lice is spreading rapidly. Many German soldiers have acquired civilian uniforms . . . The combat value of the troops is deteriorating hour by hour, most notably among the German troops.

On 30 January 1945, when Soviet troops were already in control of half of Pest, Hindy saw little point in retaining diplomatic tact:

Civilians, bombed out of their homes and shelter, stripped of their possessions, and tormented by hunger, lack of water and suffering both friendly and enemy fire, are increasingly expressing their hatred of the Germans and the Arrow Cross . . . because they regard their suffering and the destruction of the capital as pointless. They hate the appearance of our own soldiers at the shelters, where Russians have distributed cigarettes and brought water to civilians on some occasions. The Russians are awaited as liberators by many. The Russians respond to every military movement by shelling, but they clearly do not deliberately fire on civilians . . . even the best officers' nerves can no longer bear the siege. None of us, officers or men, expect to be relieved.*

On 3 February Angelo Rotta, the papal nuncio and head of the diplomatic corps in Budapest – or what remained of it – tried to persuade the German high command to agree to a ceasefire and end the city's suffering. He and his secretary, Archbishop Gennaro Verolino, called on Pfeffer-Wildenbruch. 'Wherever we went, wounded were lying in every room and in every corridor,' Verolino wrote later. 'Doctors were performing operations on ordinary tables. We heard moaning and whimpering everywhere. It was hell. Eventually we reached the German general somewhere in the depths of his bunker and he said "if anyone wants to defect to the Russians he can. The Danube is frozen, one can walk across the ice."' Pfeffer-Wildenbruch told the nuncio he would ask the Supreme Command in Berlin about a ceasefire – or a German breakout of Budapest to end the siege. He knew it was only a matter of days before the Russians stormed through. The following day he told Rotta that Hitler's orders remained the same as earlier in November. Budapest had to be defended to the bitter end.

For weeks the cellars of the big apartment blocks in Pest sheltered hundreds of thousands of people. But the shelters had been designed

---

* There was a small Russian community in downtown Pest that survived and continued to function throughout the siege, though most of them, émigré White Russians who had escaped the 1917 Revolution, faced potentially grave danger. It included some celebrities: Count Kutuzov Tolstoy, a descendant of the Russian general who defeated Napoleon's invasion of Russia; General Shulgin, adjutant to Tsar Nicholas II; and Count Pushkin, a great-great-nephew of the poet, who was a pastor at the Pravoslav parish church. These three lived on and escaped to the West later.

for use in short air raids, not for large crowds staying day and night for weeks. After the water supply broke down the lavatories stopped working. For a while people continued to use them regardless and the drains soon discharged a ghastly stench throughout the city. Since November people had simply taken rubbish out and dumped it in streets and parks. It was not until the summer of 1945 that the mountains of rubbish began to be cleared away. Eichmann could no longer be of use. Mass murder on the streets did not require his specialized skills. He and his staff left Budapest on 23 December.[7]

Apartment blocks in Pest became the 'front line' in the first week of a freezing February. György Konrád had been forced out of his hiding place on 4 February. A shell burst through the apartment block where he was staying:

We trudged out in the snow, clutched quilts, and pulled the rest of our meagre belongings on a sled behind us. The wind was kicking up snow dust. It was well below freezing and as we had no gloves our fingers were purplish-red. We passed burning buildings in the darkening evening. Through blackened windows we saw dying flames painting the ceilings a rusty red. They were like a cross-section revealing the building's naked innards after a bomb had torn its façade off; a bathtub dangling, but the sink still in place; a heavy mahogany cupboard on the wall, but the dining table three flights down. It was the shameless, twisted humour of destruction . . . Exhausted people were carting their belongings from place to place, going home, going in search of their loved ones, going just to go . . . People trudged through the streets weighed down with their goods and chattels, while soldiers sat around on tanks.

A fifteen-year-old boy, László Deseő, who lived just off the Ring Boulevard, kept a diary of the last fortnight of the siege. 'They are installing machine guns in the upper floors of the building,' he recorded on 7 February:

In my room they wanted to set up an automatic cannon. I was talking to one of the Germans in the hall when a mine exploded in front of the door and the German collapsed. A splinter had nearly shaved his fingers off down to the roots. The poor devil is screaming. They are collecting firewood from the garden to build barricades in the windows. They are also putting furniture in the windows.

8 January. The wounded are uncountable. In the house opposite there are Russian snipers. If anyone appears at the window he is shot at.

10 February. A quarter to ten. One of the soldiers looked out of the lounge window . . . bang, shot in the head. When I was trying to crawl through the room underneath that window (I didn't fancy showing myself) I accidentally put my hand in the bloody brain matter that had spilled on the floor. At lunch I remembered I hadn't washed my hands but went on eating calmly. Washing hands is a luxury.

11 February. The Russians have reached the Preisingers' house, the third down the street. At 5 the Germans leave because they have heard that the buildings are encircled and the Russians are attacking from a nearby hill . . . 8.30 the Germans come back. At 9 they have gone again.

12 February. At a quarter to three in the morning the first two Russians arrive. They look smart. They have machine guns. They are jolly. I go up into the apartment. One could howl as one walks through the apartment . . . There are eight dead horses there . . . everything is full of muck and debris.

That night the shellfire ceased and the city finally fell to the Red Army.[8]

One of the most moving memorials of the Holocaust anywhere in the world is a simple display on the Pest side of the Danube embankment, near the statue of the poet Attila József. Sixty sculpted pairs of shoes are arranged at apparent random, but all point towards the river, to remember the thousands of Jews who were murdered by the Arrow Cross between October 1944 and February 1945. There are assorted men's shoes, women's shoes and children's shoes, made of iron and set into the concrete of the riverbank. It's in a relatively busy part of town, close to the Parliament building, but somehow, despite the nearby bustle, it is always a quiet and contemplative spot. Soon after the sculpture was made in 2005 the public began a tradition of leaving flowers and candles inside the rusting shoes and filling them with small pebbles as an act of remembrance. The work was the idea of the film-maker and actor Can Togay, child of Hungarian parents but based in Berlin, and the sculptor was Gyula Pauer, a Budapest artist who died in 2012.

It is an extraordinary work of stillness and depth – designed not only in memory of the murdered victims but also those who tried, often at great risk to themselves, to save them. A section of wall on the embankment nearby names some of them. The best known outside Hungary is Raoul Wallenberg, the Swedish diplomat who was the first to establish safe houses for Jews in Budapest, organized food supplies and issued thousands of passports and exit visas after the Germans occupied the country.* Wallenberg disappeared at the end of the war, arrested by the Russian secret police and taken to the USSR, where he was murdered in a prison camp. After Soviet archives were released following the collapse of the Soviet Union his full story could finally be told – and has been several times, in some excellent books and films. But Wallenberg was by no means the only one, or necessarily the most effective.

Carl Lutz was vice consul at the Swiss Legation in Budapest from 1942, when he was aged forty-seven, a middle-ranking diplomat. When the Nazis began transporting Jews to the death camps he set up safe houses under Swiss protection. There were more than seventy of them in various parts of Budapest, but the most famous was the Glass House – once the shop and showroom of a plate-glass manufacturer in central Pest. At one point more than 3,000 people were crammed into the building; they all survived the war. He negotiated with the Nazis and the Arrow Cross to issue 8,000 safe conduct passes for Jews to leave the country. Altogether Lutz is credited with saving more than 60,000 Budapest Jews, probably more than any other individual.

One night in October 1944, right in front of an Arrow Cross militia group who had been murdering a group of Jews, Lutz dived into the Danube from the bank of the river that now bears his name to save a bleeding woman. He rescued her and, drenched from head to foot, demanded to speak to the officer in charge of the firing squad. He declared that the wounded woman was a foreign citizen protected by the Swiss

---

* My family had one a decade before I was born, though with great good fortune it never had to be used – many of them were known to be forged.

government under international law. Calmly, he carried the woman to his car and drove her away to seek medical attention. 'Fearing to shoot at this tall man who appeared to be so important and spoke so eloquently, nobody stopped him,' one Jewish survivor in Budapest who witnessed the scene wrote.

Lutz was such a thorn in the side of the Germans that Veesenmayer wired Berlin asking permission to have him killed. He received no reply. Before his posting in Hungary, Lutz was vice consul at the Swiss Consulate in Jaffa, Palestine, which made him especially sensitive to the tragedy of European Jews: through his contacts there he managed to help as many as 10,000 Hungarian children immigrate to Palestine on diplomatic passports. When Hungary declared war on the US and America cut diplomatic ties, Lutz became the representative of Britain, the US and a dozen other countries in Hungary and moved to the US Embassy building, where he hid dozens of Jews.

Like many of Wallenberg's, Lutz's passports were often forged, which after a time endangered the whole rescue operation. One night, the Germans insisted that Lutz personally authenticate a batch of passports. He was taken to an abandoned brick factory on the outskirts of Budapest, where in the last months of the war, when there was no longer train transport, Jews were forced to march on foot towards death in the Austrian labour camps. There, as Lutz recorded in his diary, he was confronted with 5,000 people. He had to inspect their papers, decide, and tell the Germans which ones were genuine and which were forgeries. Together with his wife, he stood there 'in the snow and freezing wind, while the five thousand, standing in military lines, freezing, dressed in rags, were handing their papers to me. I will never forget those frightened faces; the police had to intervene, as the people were begging me desperately to state that the paper was genuine; their life depended on my words. This was the last sign of their hope before they lost their will to live . . . this having to make snap choices of whom to save – it's insanity. Where is God?'[*9]

Diplomats were protected, up to a point. Hungarian citizens were a different matter. They had no safety net. In 1920 Margit Slachta, a

---

* Lutz lived on and returned to Switzerland after the war. He divorced his wife, who also risked her life helping Jews in Budapest, and married a Hungarian woman, Magda Csányi, whom he had rescued and given an exit visa.

deeply religious human rights activist, was the first woman to be elected to Parliament in Hungary, for a constituency in Budapest. She was the founder of the Sisters of Social Service – never officially an order of nuns, but a religious foundation that operated a dozen convents around Hungary, including in Budapest. She was one of the very few MPs who opposed all the anti-Jewish laws when they were introduced. The independent newspaper she opened was closed down, but she managed to produce it by samizdat means. When the deportations of Jews began she met Horthy's wife, Magdolna, a devout Catholic, to persuade her to intercede against them with her husband. She told the women in her convents to save Jews – 'at the risk of your own lives if needs must'. At least 6,000 were protected in her religious houses. Her close confidante Sára Salkaházi, who ran one of her convents, was murdered by an Arrow Cross militia gang in December 1944. As the war ended Slachta was lying wounded in the basement of a Budapest apartment block recovering from serious injuries after she was beaten up by anti-Semitic thugs.[*10]

---

* She remained in Parliament for a short period after the war, but was no friend of the Communists, who closed down the party she had formed, the Hungarian Christian Women's League.

30

LIBERATION

We have had three great tragedies in our country: the Tatar invasion
in the thirteenth century, the Turkish occupation lasting 150 years –
and the Soviet liberation.

György Faludy (1910–2006)

On the morning of 12 February 1945 an eerie silence descended on
the city. Machine-gun fire could be heard in the Buda Hills, where
skirmishes were continuing and the population was still hiding in apartments and basements. But in Pest the streets were empty apart from
a few stray animals and some sad, starving German and Hungarian
soldiers.

At around 9 a.m., after six weeks hiding in his cellar, Ferenc Nagy,
shortly to become Hungarian Prime Minister in a coalition government, carefully stepped outside. His beloved Budapest lay in ruins.
'Man-high rubble covered the streets. High blockades of concrete, steel
girders, lumber, bricks and glass from the collapsed buildings jammed
the thoroughfares. The wrecks of planes, tanks, armoured cars were
everywhere . . . Merciful snow covered the uncounted dead. Animal
carcasses littered the streets. Shop windows were full of the dead, while
the wraith-like living ransacked the abandoned stores. Twisted tram
rails jutted skywards like the fingers of an imploring hand.'

The following day, on the other side of the Danube, fighting seemed
to have come to a halt in Buda. The writer Sándor Márai clambered from
his basement to a scene of devastation.* The streets of the Castle district
could hardly be found:

---

* As did my immediate family from a Buda basement after around half a year in
hiding.

What I see is at first horrifying but after every hundred metres becomes more and more grotesque and improbable . . . It is as if I wandered not through city districts but excavations. Some streets must be guessed at: this was the corner house with the Flórián café, this is the street where I once lived – no trace of the building – this pile of rubble at the corner of Statisztika Street and Margit Boulevard was a five-storey block with many flats and a coffee house until a few days ago. Here is a wall of a building where friends used to live, there the remnants of a street, over there in Széll Kálmán Square the wrecks of trams and then the devastation of Vérmező Meadow . . . and the castle.

The most famous of all war photographers, Robert Capa, born Endre Friedmann in Budapest, left home aged nineteen in 1931 after having been beaten up by an anti-Semitic gang amid the White Terror following Horthy's takeover. He made a new life for himself in Paris and later in New York, with a worldwide reputation. He returned to Budapest for a short work trip within weeks of the war's end. Budapest, he said, 'appeared like a beautiful woman with her teeth knocked out'.

At first warily and then rapturously, the Red Army troops were welcomed as saviours. But that lasted just a few days; there was no time to celebrate 'liberation'. The front-line Soviet regiments moved on for the final assault on Germany, leaving behind soldiers who soon made the Hungarians understand what it meant to be a conquered enemy. The Red Army occupation caused despair even among those who initially welcomed it as a defeat of fascism. Quickly, hatred of the Soviets became stronger than before the war, when the population had been fed on a constant diet of anti-Bolshevik propaganda. The first Russian phrase most Hungarians learned was *Davai tchassey* (Give me your watch). Just a few days after the siege ended, when a few cinemas were opened in Budapest, a newsreel showed some news footage of the recently concluded Yalta Conference. When at one point in the film US President Franklin Roosevelt, seated next to Stalin, raised his hand and the audience could see the President's wristwatch the cry went around as one: 'Hey Mr President . . . mind your watch.'[1]

Looting was rampant, from officially sanctioned 'trophy brigades', which sought valuables that were sent back to Moscow straight away, to soldiers emptying the stores of anything that remained. For many

Hungarians 'official looting', as they referred to reparations agreed after the post-war peace settlement, seemed as bad as the indiscriminate pillaging by Soviet troops. 'We have had three great tragedies in our country: the Tatar invasion in the thirteenth century, the Turkish occupation lasting 150 years – and the Soviet liberation', went a well-rehearsed quip originally made by the poet György Faludy. The Russians phrased things with straightforward simplicity. 'The victorious country demands us to assert its rights for the reason that the vanquished country started the war against it,' Vladimir Dekanozov, the Soviet Union's Deputy Commissar for Foreign Affairs, said on an early post-war visit to Budapest.

The 'trophy brigades' – officially sanctioned by Moscow – began work in late January even before the siege was over, when the Red Army had control of part of Pest but fighting was still raging in Buda. 'A small but very meticulous group of officers plundered the strongboxes – particularly the American and British – in every bank and took away all the cash,' a Swiss Legation report sent to the Foreign Office in London and the State Department in Washington recorded. The manager of the Hungarian General Credit Bank (in 2022 the Hungarian Finance Ministry) wrote later that a group of Soviet officers entered the building early one morning: 'they opened every safe and strongbox, at times by force. They took away 113 million pengős in cash as well as about 800 suitcases and other containers deposited by clients, and emptied 1,400 safe-deposit boxes. It is impossible to estimate the value of the objects taken but it is certain that it was a very large amount. They also took securities . . . which belonged partly to clients and partly to the bank.' A third of all Hungarian gold and silver reserves were seized by the Russians in a few weeks.[2]

Even diplomats were not exempt from looting. Carl Lutz, the Swiss chargé d'affaires who had so courageously helped Jews survive the war, recalled that the day after the Soviet army had seized Pest, 'the Russian military descended on us in the ruins of the British Embassy. An officer demanded our cars, some of which were no longer functioning, and gave me five minutes to get the "missing spare part". Then he drew his pistol . . . and shot towards me several times. I barely managed to escape through an emergency exit in the air-raid shelter. Subsequently we were harassed and looted for ten days and nights by drunken soldiers.'

A separate report from the Swiss Legation to the British Foreign Office said that 'soon after the arrival of the Russians the head of the Swiss Legation, Harald Feller and his chief clerk Herr Hans Mayer were arrested by the NKVD. They have not been heard of since.* The premises were thoroughly looted. During one of the raids a Russian put a noose around the neck of an Embassy employee, Herr Ember, in an attempt to force him to hand over the safe key. When he refused, the noose was drawn so tight that he lost consciousness. The Russians took the key from his pocket and cleared out the safe.'

After victory, General Malinovsky permitted his troops 'free looting' for three days – officers were permitted to send home to Russia crates weighing 20 kilos. All the furniture and equipment from the hotels on Margaret Island were taken, as well as art works from the public galleries, though most of those had been removed at the start of the siege for safekeeping. In Budafök, a southern suburb of the city noted for its wine cellars, the district commander of the Russian forces and all their political officers were replaced twice within the first week because their exploits under the influence of looted alcohol became known not only to their direct superior officers in Budapest but also to the high command in Moscow.[3]

Jews were saved from the death camps and the Arrow Cross murderers. Whatever else the Soviet war victory would mean, it was life for the 90,000 or so Jews who had survived. But even the little that was left of their property was looted. Most of the extraordinary works of art the Soviets stole over the next few weeks – selected by experts sent from Moscow – were from famous collections owned by Jewish bankers and industrialists like Móric Kornfeld, Bertalan Demény and Sándor Harsányi. But the greatest prize was the finest private art collection in Hungary, owned by the Hatvany family, stolen from the secure vault at the Bank for Commerce (in 2022 the Interior Ministry, close to the Parliament building), which included scores of works by Tintoretto, El Greco, both Cranachs, Delacroix, Manet, Corot, Rodin, Constable, Pissarro and Renoir, among others. The Germans had pillaged most of the collection in the spring of 1944 and transferred it to the bank. But

---

* They were later found, traumatized and terrified but not physically harmed.

they had not managed to transport the pictures back to Berlin. Now the Soviets seized them.*

Márai had his belongings stripped, as did many of his friends:

The Russian who dropped by in the morning conversed amicably with the family, showed pictures of his wife and children back home, sentimentally patted the heads of the children and gave them candy, departed and then returned later that afternoon or that night and robbed the same family he had made friends with in the morning . . . the looting was not aimed at 'the fascist enemy' but caused simply by abject poverty. These Communist Russians were so impoverished, so miserably destitute, so completely stripped of everything . . . that now, set loose after 30 years of privation and drudgery, they threw themselves hungrily on everything that fell into their hands.[4]

That included women. For more than forty years, until Soviet troops left Hungary in 1990, almost nobody mentioned the taboo subject of the rapes committed by Russian troops in 1945. Many victims would not talk about it even among their families and friends, let alone in public. It is still not known exactly how many Hungarian women were raped, but a report from the Swiss Legation that appeared a few years later estimated the number at around 150,000 (of a female population of 4.5 million). 'The worst suffering of the Hungarian population is due to the rape of women,' the report said. 'Rapes – affecting all age groups from ten to seventy – are so common that very few women in Hungary or in Budapest have been spared. They are sometimes accompanied by incredible brutalities. Many women prefer suicide to these horrors . . . The misery is made worse by the fact that many Russian soldiers are diseased and there are absolutely no medicines in Hungary.'

Women were attacked from day one of the liberation, as Christine Arnothy, a fifteen-year-old girl emerging with her sister Ilas from a Budapest cellar, recalled:

---

* Two years later, though, the Hatvanys, who had managed to escape the Holocaust, bought some of the pieces back from the Russians and in dramatic fashion smuggled them to the West.

The Russians were advancing and . . . at each house a group of soldiers left the main body . . . One detachment entered our house. The officer who commanded it yelled at us to know if there were any Germans in the house. Several of us nodded in the direction of the staircase. The German was killed on the spot and Ilas, whom they had found close to the wounded man, was raped beside the still-warm corpse. From the first instant we understood that what was happening was very different from what we had hoped.

Alaine Polcz was in her early twenties in February 1945. Even before the siege of Buda had ended, Soviet troops held her with a group of other women in a church presbytery. She could hear constant gunfire close by. Years later she remembered her ordeal: 'Earlier in the war I had seen those posters in Budapest showing a Russian soldier tearing a crucifix off a young woman's neck and I'd read pamphlets saying that Russians did this and that, I didn't believe any of it. Propaganda, I thought.' Soon she was to learn better. On the second evening of her captivity she saw a young girl whose head was bleeding – a lock of her hair had been torn out. '"The Russians rode her," her mother said. I didn't understand. "With a bicycle?" I asked. The woman became angry. "You fool. Don't you know what they do to women?"'

The next day, Polcz was in a room with her mother-in-law:

In came three Russians and told me to go with them. Now I knew exactly what they wanted. I put on my boots and tied my headscarf, then I untied it and tied it again, in order to save time. As I stood there I heard something knocking against the door. It was the heels of my boots I was trembling so much. We stepped out into an L-shaped corridor. I started to attack them wildly . . . kicked and hit them with all my strength, but the next moment I was on the ground. Nobody made a sound. We fought in silence. They took me to the kitchen at the back of the building . . . they flung me down and I hit my head against the corner of the rubbish bin. It was made of hard wood.

I came round in the priest's room. The window panes were broken and the windows had been boarded up. There was nothing on the bed except the bare boards on which I was lying. A Russian was on top of me . . . the feeling in my body hadn't returned with my consciousness;

it was as if I was numb or had gone cold . . . In that windowless room I was naked from the waist down. I didn't know how many Russians used me after that, or how many there had been before. As dawn was breaking they left. I got up. I could move only with great difficulty. My head and my whole body ached. I was bleeding profusely. Over the next few days new troops arrived and I was pestered a lot.

She was infected with syphilis from the repeated rapes.

It is not often we are told what Russian soldiers thought about the women concerned, but later some Red Army soldiers' letters – unsent – were found in a Budapest cellar: 'There are enough women and they don't speak a word of Russian. So much the better. We don't have to try to persuade them – we just point the pistol at them and tell them to lie down; that settles the matter and we move on.'

Stalin made light of the rapes and looting. When some members of the Yugoslav Communist leadership mentioned them to him as a reason the Soviets would be loathed by their 'liberators' he dismissed their protests. The Yugoslav politician Milovan Djilas, on a visit to Moscow, noted in his diary. 'He [Stalin] told us . . . Don't you understand that a soldier who has marched thousands of kilometres through pools of blood and through fire will want to have a little fun with a wench or steal a trifle.'[5]

If women were scared of rape, the fear among men was to be picked up off the streets and used as slave labour by the Soviets for public works like clearing rubble, shoring up buildings and repairing the city's bridges. General Malinovsky reported back to Moscow that 110,000 men had been taken as 'prisoners' in this way. According to one well-informed journalist, 'Count Géza Teleki [who would later himself become briefly Minister for Public Works] and a former Mayor of Budapest were seized without any warning and found two days later when an officer to whom they could talk finally released them. Prince Pál Esterházy was discovered in a cemetery burying dead horses.'

Around half of these detainees were returned home within weeks of the end of the siege. But the rest, including men from all walks of life and essential workers like firefighters, ambulance drivers, train and bus drivers – people who would be needed to rebuild Hungary – were transported east to the Soviet Union for forced labour on building projects in the Urals and Siberia. Some returned to Hungary decades later, but most never did – one of the Soviet war crimes rarely mentioned amid all the other horrors of the Second World War.

Forty thousand of these men – abducted from their homes and from the streets – were corralled into a concentration camp near Gödöllő, 30 kilometres north-east of Budapest, in appalling conditions before being taken to the USSR. Imre Kovács found himself on the edge of the camp, in the grounds of a three storey-building that before the war had been one of the best high schools in Hungary. It was

> surrounded by a double barbed-wire fence . . . guards were doing the rounds, constantly yelling and shooting . . . We really had the impression that the whole of Budapest was crammed together before us. Fur-coated gentlemen, distinguished in their bearing but shabby and worn out, were marking time in the courtyard next to tram conductors, street sweepers, postmen and policemen . . . for some reason the camp command was continually taking stock of the people. Names were being called out and flying through the air.

Budapest in the spring of 1945 'was nothing short of hell on earth', said the high-ranking prelate Bishop József Grősz at the end of the year. 'Thousands of women from girls of twelve to women in the ninth month of pregnancy raped; men deported for slave labour. Almost every home looted; the city and its churches in ruins; the restaurants and stores empty, dead horses in the streets along with unburied bodies; in the cellars people half-demented with hunger, cutting pieces of flesh from animals dead for days . . . This is how things may have been in Jerusalem when the prophet Jeremiah uttered his laments.'[6]

Under the terms of the ceasefire agreements, Russia was entitled to all German-owned property in Hungary. This was designed to compensate the USSR for some of the losses incurred at the hands of the Nazis. About a third of Hungarian industry had been German-controlled – worth around US$1 billion in 1945 (about US$14 billion in 2022). This was how the Soviets got their hands on the Manfréd Weiss works on Csepel Island in the suburbs of Budapest – Hungary's single biggest industrial plant, which manufactured everything from kettles to munitions.*Around 200 other complete factories, and most of the machinery from 300 more, were dismantled and sent to the Soviet Union. Russia took over entire Hungarian industries and later established joint Russian-Hungarian companies, which enabled the USSR to profit from steel plants, uranium mines, oilfields and coal mines. István Ries, Hungary's first post-war Minister for Justice (a socialist), joked to a friend about the terms of the joint Hungarian-Soviet Shipping Company set up in 1945: 'You know, the agreement came about on the basis of perfect equality. The Russians have the right to ship up and down the Danube. We have the right to ship across.' This turned out to be an expensive joke. When, some time later, he was arrested, tortured and tried, this saying was brought up as evidence of his 'bourgeois anti-Communist behaviour'.

The Hungarian national budget over the next eighteen months set aside as reparations five times more than was allotted for post-war reconstruction for Budapest. UN officials estimated three years after the war that total losses, calculating reparations, occupation costs and looting, amounted to 40 per cent of national income.

The currency collapsed – as it did in many places immediately after the war. Yet Hungary beat all records in terms of inflation. In July 1945 one US dollar was worth 1,320 pengős; by 1 November that year the exchange rate was one US dollar to 296,000. By spring 1946 hyper-inflation took the rate to 4.6 quadrillion to the dollar (that is an almost unimaginable 15 noughts, 158,000 per cent a day). Most people in Budapest refused to be paid in money. As buildings were being repaired throughout the city, the walls in many rooms were decorated with large banknotes in fantastical denominations. In his marvellous book *My Happy Days in Hell*, György Faludy described the effect this had on daily life. A year after the war ended his publisher brought out a new edition of one of his books. He was paid 300 million pengős (which before the war would have been worth something like US$60 billion). When he collected his money, in cash, knowing it would have devalued

* The Weiss family had handed over all its shares to the SS in the summer of 1944 on being allowed to escape to Switzerland.

by the time he had walked through Budapest, he ran to the central market a few blocks away. He spent the entire amount, he said, 'on one chicken, a litre of olive oil and a handful of vegetables'. On 5 July a 100-quintillion-pengő note was issued – that's twenty noughts; when an elderly gentleman in Budapest received one as wages he used it as part of the lining of his hat.

The currency was stabilized, largely with the help of the Americans. In April 1944, a fortnight after the German occupation, the Nazis had taken US$40 million ($570 million at 2022 values) in gold from various Hungarian banks. It fell into US hands at the end of the war and the Americans returned it a year later. Had the gold remained in Hungary at the moment of liberation, it is certain it would have been looted by the Red Army.

Amid the wreckage and ruin and cruelty, there were nonetheless many examples of human kindness shown by the soldiers of the Red Army. There are numerous records of Soviet troops taking whole families under their protection and establishing mobile kitchens to entire quarters of Budapest. One of Géza Benefi's earliest memories as a four-year-old was receiving great kindness from a Russian infantry captain which he never forgot. He was found in a shelter with his grandfather, hungry and freezing. '"Daddy," I said, because his stubble made me think he was my father home from the front. The captain asked what I had said. Somebody answered in Serbo-Croat and he burst into tears. He hugged me, saying that he was a teacher with a child at home the same age, and showed us a picture. Later he kept bringing us food . . . He posted a guard in front of our house to protect us – and at times of looting made sure we didn't go out on to the streets.'

The writer Ephraim Kishon, who left Hungary for Palestine soon after the war, recalled the story of one of his neighbours, who told him: 'My sister Ági decided to thank the liberators personally. One evening, soon after the retreat of the Germans . . . she dolled herself up in a dress with a low neckline and set out for the nearby Soviet command post. We waited for her for half the night, worried out of our minds. She came back in the small hours in high spirits, telling us how politely the Russians had treated her. They fed her and gave her a food parcel to take home.'

Above all, they managed relatively quickly to get food supplies to the people of Budapest – the single biggest achievement of the Soviet conquerors in their new imperium in Eastern Europe, at a time when millions were starving in the West or suffering hardship in refugee camps. And the bridges of Budapest were being rebuilt.

Within five days of the end of the siege another vital sign of the survival of Budapest was visible. The Belvárosi Kávéház (Inner City Coffee House) on Ferenciek Square reopened amid the ruins on 18 February. The once-famous Belvárosi opened at the turn of the century and was subsequently owned by three generations of the Rónai family. It reopened its doors under an enormous sign announcing 'We Are Open'. The walls were blackened by fire, there were no windows, no electricity or hot water, but – incredibly to the customers – it was there. Coffee was practically unavailable. But hot soup was made on a temporary stove.*

---

* The sign was written by a young boy, Egon, who later escaped to the UK, changed the spelling of his name to Ronay and became a noted food expert. The whole area around the café was redeveloped in the 1960s, but it had been closed down three years after the war ended by the Communist regime, which didn't see the point of people idling away their time over coffee while they should be building socialism. But in reality they feared that groups of people trying to enjoy some social time together were potentially dangerous and could lead to counter-revolutionary plots.

31

THE IRON CURTAIN DESCENDS

Our demands were always modest at first – and then were increased
. . . It was precision measures, salami tactics, slice by slice, that we got
what we wanted . . . that enabled us to defeat the reactionaries.

Mátyás Rákosi (1892–1971)

Not only was one not free to speak, one was not even free to remain
silent.

Sándor Márai (1900–89)

Right behind the Red Army there came to Budapest a group of around
300 Hungarian-born Communists, known as 'Muscovites' because
they had lived for years as exiles in the Soviet Union. Hand-picked by
Joseph Stalin, their purpose was to act as proconsuls in the Hungarian
province of the Soviet leader's new European imperium. They were
chosen for unwavering loyalty to the USSR – and to him. Most of them
were Soviet citizens and had spent between fifteen and twenty years in
Russia, building their lives and families there. They had lost contact
with the land of their birth. The Soviet Union had given them shelter, a
cause to believe in and a job. Most were professional Communist agita-
tors or espionage agents and had never worked at anything else. Almost
all of them had at one time earned their credentials by spending time in
Horthy's jails. When they returned to Hungary after the war they were
going 'home' only in a limited sense. Hungary had ceased to be 'home'
a long time ago. They returned as representatives of a foreign power, to
serve the interests of the USSR.

Life as an *émigré* in the Soviet Union had been a dangerous existence.
Surviving in Stalin's Russia in the 1930s was hard enough for a native.
A foreigner who might be working as a Comintern agent, regularly in
touch with other dubious foreigners, was always a mistrusted figure.

Several prominent Hungarian Communists had perished in the purges between 1937 and 1939 – Béla Kun, for example, despite his minor-celebrity status among many Communists for his leadership in the 1919 Hungarian Soviet Republic.

Stalin had no precise idea of what to do with his domains conquered in battle, though he knew the war had left him with the opportunity to Sovietize them all. Over time that is what he did. 'Whoever occupies a territory also imposes on it his social system,' he told the Yugoslav politician Milovan Djilas at the end of the war. 'Everyone imposes his system as far as his army can reach. It cannot be otherwise.' But it did not happen overnight or at the same speed everywhere in Eastern Europe. Almost uniquely in his new empire, Stalin allowed genuinely free elections in Hungary. The vote on 4 November 1945 was the first honest and fair election in Hungarian history, based on universal suffrage, with a secret ballot – and would be the last for another forty-five years. Stalin had, of course, intended to take total power in Hungary and he thought he was entitled to do so under the Yalta Agreement and under the terms of a deal he had made with Winston Churchill in Moscow in October 1944 which divided Central Europe and the Balkans into spheres of influence. But he restrained himself from immediately installing a puppet regime in Budapest, as he had done in Poland, Romania, Bulgaria and most of his newly acquired fiefdoms. He was prepared to be patient for a while – and, for now, he wanted to keep the Western Allies on his side.[1]

When the results came in that evening they were a profound shock to the Communists. They won only around 17 per cent of the vote. The Centre-Left Social Democrats got around the same. The Centre-Right Smallholders' Party, traditional representatives of the urban bourgeoisie and landed gentry, won a plurality. The results were even worse than the Budapest municipal election results that had been held six weeks earlier when the Communists had won 18.5 per cent of the vote and Stalin's plenipotentiary in Budapest, Kliment Voroshilov, had struck some Hungarian Communist officials in his fury. The Soviets had been led to believe by the 'Muscovite' contingent that had been despatched to Budapest that they would perform much better.

Some local Communists who had survived in Hungary during the 1930s and the war were much more realistic and knew that twenty-five years of anti-Soviet propaganda and a general hatred of the Russians made Hungary less than fertile ground for socialism – despite the cata-strophic state in which the country found itself because of its ties with fascism. The underground Communist Party leader in Budapest during the last part of the war, the barely known thirty-two-year-old one-time typewriter mechanic János Kádár, estimated there were at the most 200 Party members in the whole of the country, a score of whom he knew personally. With such limited support it would not be an easy task. But there were 75,000 Soviet troops in Hungary ready to lend a hand – and if the Communists had little expertise as democratic politicians they had plenty of experience in the arts of intrigue, bribery, intimidation and terrorism.

Voroshilov had already declared before the election that, whatever the results, the coalition government that had been in place since the end of the war would remain. The Deputy Prime Minister was a Communist and the Party had a share in power. Most importantly, as would happen elsewhere behind the Iron Curtain, they held the Interior Ministry. This was the most important force in Hungarians' everyday lives, which gave the Communists control of the police and security apparatus, the appointment of judges, the issuance of identity papers, passports and exit visas, and granted licences to print newspapers and run radio stations.

Ultimately, though, it was Soviet troops on the ground that made sure the Communists got what they wanted. One of the Communist ministers, the sinister but formidably clever Muscovite József Révai, who would later boss Hungarian literature and art as a kind of Culture Tsar, put it in simple terms: 'We were a minority in Parliament and in the government but at the same time we represented the leading force. We had decisive control of the police . . . our force was multiplied by the fact that the Soviet army was always there to support us with their assistance.'[2]

Stalin's viceroy in Budapest was Mátyás Rákosi. His crimes are little known outside Hungary. Had he acted on a bigger stage he would now be recognized as one of the greatest monsters of the twentieth century, despite competition from so many challengers. Over less than a decade in power he murdered and jailed as many Hungarians, proportionately, as his patron managed in the Soviet Union after thirty years.

Rákosi was born on 9 March 1892 in the small town of Ada, in the Vojvodina. His father, József Rosenfeld, was a well-off grocer who Magyarized his name in 1904. At seventeen, the precocious Rákosi was awarded a place to study Classics at the prestigious Oriental Academy. But he wanted commercial experience, so he went abroad in 1912 and worked for a while in Hamburg and then for a year in London at Lloyd's underwriters.

He returned to Hungary at the start of the First World War and immediately volunteered for the army. He was quickly promoted to sergeant in an infantry battalion but was soon taken prisoner by the Russians. He had been apolitical as a youth, but became a passionate Communist convert as a prisoner of war. He said often that one of the proudest moments in his life was when he briefly met Lenin in Petrograd in 1918. But Rákosi was a supreme liar and it is unlikely this meeting ever happened. No record of it exists.

He was one of the founding members of the Hungarian Communist Party and deputy Commissar (for Commerce) in Béla Kun's Commune. He escaped to Austria when Horthy came to power and then to Russia, where the Soviets recognized his abilities. Rákosi was a brilliant linguist, an invaluable asset in his chosen career of making world revolution. He spoke ten languages fluently, including Turkish, which he picked up as a prisoner of war at the same time as he was learning Russian. As Secretary of the Comintern he travelled on six forged passports helping to set up Communist Parties in Czechoslovakia, Italy and Austria.

In 1925 he was ordered back to Hungary, where the Communist Party was banned, on a dangerous mission and was arrested almost immediately on arrival. He was sentenced to eight years in jail on sedition charges. He became a well-known figure of international standing on the Left when his jail term ended in 1935. Instead of releasing him, the regent's regime tried him again – this time for his activities in 1919. Protests were made to the Hungarian government from all over the world but Horthy rejected them.

Rákosi conducted his own defence and, when sentenced to life imprisonment with little hope of seeing daylight again, he confronted his fate with the bravery expected in Moscow of a revolutionary. He declared to the Budapest court: 'My personal fate is indifferent to me but I know the cause I live for will triumph.' He became a cause célèbre on

the Left everywhere. The Hungarian battalion of the International Brigade in the Spanish Civil War was named after him. In 1940, after the
Hitler-Stalin pact, he was allowed to go free and leave for the USSR. He
was exchanged for two banners of the Hungarian revolutionary army
captured by the Tsarist army during the War of Independence in 1849.[3]

He received a hero's welcome in Moscow. Stalin gave him pride of
place with himself on the dais at the Red Square celebrations on 7 November 1940 to celebrate the twenty-third anniversary of the Russian
Revolution. Rákosi, though, had anything but heroic looks. Short, fat
and bald, he was later invariably called behind his back 'Arsehead'.
The playwright Gyula Háy, who knew him well from exile in Russia,
described him: 'A short, squat body, as if the creator had been unable to
finish his work for abhorrence; the head disproportionately large, topped
by an enormous bald dome and fronted by a pallid, bloated face with a
sweet-and-sour smile frozen on to it. Virtually no neck between the high
shoulders, so that it was left more or less to the observer whether he
called him a hunchback or not. Clumsy in movement, with a tendency
to flat footedness; short, stubby fingers.'

His biographers agree that he had no passions apart from the exercise
of power. He did not drink, or philander. In sexual matters he was a
pillar of Bolshevik rectitude. Two years after his release from jail he
met and married a lawyer from Yakutsk in Siberia. Fenya Feodorovna
Kornilova was eleven years younger than him and they lived happily
together until he died in 1971. His cynicism was overwhelming. Some
years after the war he tried to ban the word 'rape' in Hungarian literature
after one writer, Tibor Déry, had written a story that dared to mention
that a woman had been violated by a Russian soldier following the siege
of Budapest. Rákosi was furious at the author: 'Can't you leave this
idiocy alone?' he told Déry. 'What is there to write about? In Hungary
there are, say, 3,000 villages. Supposing the Russians had their way with
three from each village, that makes 9,000 in all. Is that so many? You
writers have no idea of the law of large numbers.'*

But he had his admirers and some redeeming qualities. He could be
highly impressive and he fooled many people who met him with his

---

* Rákosi wasn't so good with numbers either. He vastly underestimated how many
Hungarian women were raped.

genuine talents and eloquence. He had a phenomenal memory. He had wit when he chose to exercise it. He spoke in straightforward language and seldom used Marxist-Leninist jargon.

Stalin did not like him and frequently humiliated him in front of the Soviet magnates during Rákosi's visits to the USSR. For a start, Rákosi was of Jewish origin and Stalin was a vociferous anti-Semite who became even more of a Jew-hater the older he got. Stalin also knew the Hungarian was no real hero. When Rákosi was arrested in 1925, under interrogation by Horthy's counter-intelligence service he had given away some secrets about the Comintern that found their way to the espionage agencies in Britain and France. Many faithful Party workers, however long they had suffered in fascist prisons, perished for lesser offences. But all Rákosi received was a reprimand. Stalin, in an untypical forgiving moment, said that Rákosi had 'atoned in jail'. He judged Rákosi to be useful, named him leader of the Hungarian Communists and despatched him to Budapest to turn Hungary into a model Soviet colony.[4]

The orders he was given were to be cautious at first and not to overreach. 'You must move towards socialism not directly but in zigzags and in roundabout ways,' Stalin told East European apparatchiks. 'Avoid the temptation to adopt a premature path towards a people's democracy.' He wrote directly to Rákosi with advice, telling him to move step by step: 'Don't be grudging with words. Don't scare anyone. But once you have gained ground then move ahead. You must utilize as many people as possible who may be of use to us.' Later Rákosi would be brutally frank, boastful even, about how the Communists organized this slow-motion putsch. Speaking to Party workers, he explained: 'Our demands were always modest at first – and then were increased. For example, at first we demanded "government control" of the banks; only later did we call for outright nationalization of the biggest three banks. It was precision measures, salami tactics, slice by slice, that we got what we wanted . . . that enabled us to defeat the reactionaries.'

The first targets of the coalition were relatively uncontroversial: scores had to be settled after the war and a quarter century of Horthy's regime. A total of 279 war criminals, including four former Prime Ministers, prominent Arrow Cross officials, Hungarian volunteers with the SS and well-known fascists, were hanged. This was popular justice – and similar in scale to what was happening at the same time in Western Europe. A year after 'liberation' angry mobs stormed the gate of the Central Prison yard in Budapest when they heard that admission tickets would be required to witness the execution of war criminals. Ultra-cautious at the start, Rákosi banned the phrase 'dictatorship of the proletariat' from Communist Party literature in case it scared Hungarians.

Meanwhile, some people with good anti-fascist records – but no supporters of the Communists – disappeared into the Soviet Gulag. Many thousands were arrested and deported to the Soviet Union, never to be heard of in Hungary again. This was the fate of István Bethlen, Prime Minister for ten years under Horthy, who had urged a separate peace with the Soviets as early as 1942. In the Cabinet he countered the objection that the Red Army would rape and loot with the answer: 'Perhaps so, but they will do so less if they come as friends.' No records exist, but it is presumed he died somewhere in Siberia.[5]

Then the Communists began to move against their main coalition 'partners', the Smallholders' Party. Rákosi claimed he had uncovered a plot by a secret right-wing organization to restore the pre-war regime and the Habsburg regency. It was nonsense, but he named twenty-seven Smallholders MPs who were forced to resign. The ablest of them, Béla Kovács, was seen as the biggest threat. He was implicated in the so-called plot but refused to resign and claimed an MP's privilege, which was supposed to give him immunity from arrest. On 27 February 1947 Russian troops entered Parliament, marched him out of the building and flew him to the Soviet Union. He did not return to Hungary for nine years.

In the spring of 1947 Rákosi targeted the coalition Prime Minister, Ferenc Nagy. When Nagy was at an international conference Rákosi called him and made him an offer he couldn't refuse to remain abroad and never return: he would be unmasked as a traitor in another plot if he came back to Hungary. On the other hand, if he stayed in the West, his baby son would be sent to him in safety. Nagy accepted the deal and lived the rest of his life in exile in the US.

Despite all the signals of the way Rákosi was moving, and the knowledge that the Red Army would be occupying Hungary for some time to come, voters still rejected the Communists. The election in August

1947 was far less honest than the poll two years earlier, particularly in Budapest, where the majority of Party workers lived. Hundreds of thousands of voters had mysteriously been disenfranchised in what was popularly known as the 'blue chit' election, because many absentee voters gave their proxies on blue paper to Communist activists, some of whom voted early and often with them. Even so, the Communists won just 22.5 per cent of the vote.

Next the Social Democrats were sliced. The Communist Party had been banned in the Horthy years, but one wing of the Social Democrats was tolerated – just. Now the SDs voted themselves out of existence when they held a rigged internal referendum on merging with the Communists. As all those who had declared themselves against the merger were barred from voting, the result was a foregone conclusion. In June 1948 the two parties were united. Rákosi said it would take three years, the timeframe Stalin had in mind. Essentially, Hungary was now a one-party state.[6]

On 21 May, in the small town of Kunmadaras about 85 kilometres east of Budapest, a protest in the market square against food price increases turned into a pogrom. A mob attacked the only people in the town identified as Jews and four people were beaten to death; three others were badly injured. Worse attacks against Jews were occurring at the same time in Poland and Czechoslovakia immediately after details of the Holocaust were known, which from a distance of years may seem inconceivable. But as the wise philosopher Stanisław Ossowski pointed out after one of the most murderous of the post-war pogroms, 'compassion is not the only imaginable response to a misfortune suffered by others'. Many people in Eastern Europe who had been living in houses previously owned by Jews were boiling with new resentment when after the war the few surviving Jews returned to reclaim their property seized under the Nazis' anti-Jewish laws. Under new legislation introduced by the Communists, the property was swiftly returned, but it was not always made easy.*

---

* As so often, Jews found the best way of dealing with the renewed misery was with black humour. A joke went round Budapest quickly after the war finished. A Jew returns home and bumps into a Christian acquaintance. 'How are things?' he is asked. 'Oh, don't ask,' the Jew replies. 'I've come home from the camps and now I have nothing except the clothes you're wearing.'

It did not help social harmony in Hungary that some of the most prominent Communist magnates in Budapest were Jews, including Rákosi and his top three lieutenants, who ran the economy, the security network and the Party bureaucracy. Not to be outflanked, grotesquely and cynically, for public consumption Rákosi became one of the keenest anti-Semites in the country. 'You would think the Catholic Church was the largest centre of anti-State [as in anti-Communist] intelligence,' he wrote to a fellow Communist not long after the Kunmadaras riot. 'But in reality, because Jews are everywhere, Zionism is the real centre of espionage.' A supreme cynic even by the standards of post-war Soviet hatchet men, Rákosi was keen to recruit former fascists to the Communist cause, even those whom he knew had murdered Jews under the old regime. He was happy to employ former Arrow Cross thugs, if they could be useful to him. Rákosi differentiated between the bourgeois fascists and the 'working-class fascists, the little fish', whom he welcomed into the fold. 'These little fascists aren't bad fellows really,' he told a group of workers. 'They were forced into fascism, see. All they have to do is pledge loyalty to us and we'll happily take them in.'[7]

By the end of 1948 the Communists possessed untrammelled power, which they would hold for the next forty years. The red star began appearing on public buildings, the biggest of them shining with lights twenty-four hours a day at the top of the dome of the Parliament building until 1989. Rákosi's ugly features were on posters throughout Budapest in which he was hailed as 'Stalin's best pupil'. The Party began to take direct control of people's daily lives in the city. Most of the coffee houses were closed down – the Communists did not approve of people socializing without supervision. The Party controlled the newspapers, radio, eventually TV and every form of art. The stifling straitjacket of socialist realism became the only permitted form of expression in literature, painting and music. The Churches were suppressed. Hundreds of priests and monks were jailed – including the Catholic Prince Primate, Cardinal József Mindszenty, arrested on the day after Christmas 1948, tried on trumped-up charges of embezzling money, imprisoned and not seen again in public for seven and a half years. Church schools were banned.

In almost every walk of life Soviet 'advisers' were invited to show how things should be done. Rákosi himself hardly moved a step without referring to his advisers on the spot in Budapest, or directly to Moscow – about matters from the education system to army uniforms to the creation of collective farms. The national flag was changed to please the USSR: the tricolour remained, but the emblem designed by Kossuth in 1848 became a Soviet-style hammer and sickle. Public holidays conformed to those in Russia. The twentieth of August, the traditional Feast of St Stephen honouring the patron saint, was changed to Constitution Day. The first clause in the new post-war constitution itself, which named Hungary as a 'People's Republic' and came into effect, with gross insensitivity to any national feelings, on 20 August 1949, declared thanks 'to the glorious Soviet Union for its historic role in liberating Hungary'.

The Russification of the country became a profound national griev-ance. 'That hurt the most,' Sándor Zsindely, a chemistry student at the time who became a distinguished Hungarian scientist, recalled. 'Having Communism thrust down our throats unwillingly was bad enough ... But having so many alien ways imposed on us, and being told they were superior, was a constant insult. Every day the Russians seemed to grind our noses in the fact that they were the masters.'

For a while after the war the economy grew at a rapid rate, albeit from a low base. The government rebuilt most of the bridges over the Danube relatively speedily – Rákosi's number two, the vulpine Ernő Gerő, was credited with getting the work done and earned headlines as 'the bridge builder'. Budapest was never hungry until the early 1950s. Food production rose – until the Communists broke their pledge about giving 'land to the people' and collectivized farms, giving land, effectively, to the Party. From then on queues formed. Shortage was one thing there was plenty of, as the economist János Kornai – a rig-orous Marxist until he saw how 'actually existing socialism' operated in practice – said: 'Nine million Hungarians queued – both physically and metaphorically – in front of the shops; the factories in front of their suppliers; state enterprises in front of the coffers of the self-same state.' All the banks were nationalized from 1948; every enterprise that em-ployed more than ten people was taken over by the state. 'A handful of cobblers survived to repair shoes, as long as there was no shortage of soles,' quipped Miklós Molnár, who had become a history lecturer at Budapest University.[8]

Without any legal process more than 13,000 class enemies (aristocrats, high gentry, officials from the old regime, judges) were evicted from their Budapest homes and sent to work, under close supervision, in appalling conditions on the land. This included twenty-one Horthy ministers, twenty-five secretaries of state, 190 generals, 1,012 other professional army officers, 274 police officers, eighty-eight gendarmerie officers, 810 high-to-medium-ranking civil servants, 172 factory owners, 157 bankers, 391 wholesale traders, 252 large landowners, nine princes, 163 counts and 121 barons. The list does not include scores of restaurateurs and café owners. They were given twenty-four hours' notice to vacate their premises and then declared 'non persons'. The official reason, as the Party newspaper *Szabad Nép* (A Free People) put it, was that this was 'inevitable at a time of imperialist incitement and sharpening of the class struggle'. But the real reason was to satisfy the demand for decent housing among the new boss class of Party apparatchiks. Their villas on Rózsadomb and handsome apartments in downtown Pest were handed over to Communist Party hacks.

'I was beginning to sense that what went on around me was not mere organized terror but an enemy more dangerous than anything, against whom there was no defence – stupidity,' said Sándor Márai before he emigrated in 1948 for the US. 'Everything they plan and execute here is not just avaricious and brutal but deeply and hopelessly redundant and stupid.' He was joined, until the borders were sealed tight and the Iron Curtain descended, by thousands of young and creative people; a constant theme in Hungarian history has been a drain of talent during political turmoil.

The Communists found a powerful and hideous way to make their power clear in Budapest. At the end of 1951, one of the city's most elegant and graceful churches, the Regnum Marianum on one side of Heroes' Square, was pulled down – overnight, with almost no prior warning. It was replaced by an eight-metre-high bronze statue of Stalin, standing on a red-limestone plinth, which dominated a central position in Budapest. When it was officially unveiled by the Party's chief of ideology, József Révai, onlookers – including some hard-line Communists – could barely suppress their disgust by his observation that 'this is a statue which springs from the soul of our nation . . . It is a *Hungarian* statue.'[9]

32

THE HOUSE OF TERROR

We may not use force to compel other nations to ally themselves to
Russia. Only a really voluntary, free agreement may be used and this
is impossible if there is no freedom to repeal the agreement.

Vladimir Lenin (1870–1924)

Number 60 Andrássy Avenue – or Stalin Avenue as it was after the
war – was one of the smartest addresses in Budapest. It formed an entire
city block 300 metres or so from the Opera House and at first glance
it seemed like any of the other elegant, turn-of-the-century buildings
nearby. But look more closely 'and it was a scary, chilling place', recalled György Konrád, who passed it every day en route to school. 'Red
geraniums bloomed in a flowerbox outside every window but guards
carrying machine guns stood in every doorway and on every corner.'
The building was busy all day and all night. Official cars – always
black-curtained Soviet-made Pobedas – turned into a narrow side road,
Csengery Street, through a gate into a courtyard that looked ordinary.
But on one side of the yard there was a six-metre wall with a tower where
a machine-gunner was placed around the clock. This was the headquarters of the feared AVO, which established itself as the 'engine room of
the most brutal police state in Central and Eastern Europe', as a former
Communist Party Politburo member described it.*

The building had been the base of the Arrow Cross in the last months
of the war. The fascists had called it 'Loyalty House' and the Communists kept the name. They kept many of the fixtures and fittings, too,
including its dungeons. Inside this world were dank cells and torture

---

* The AVO, *Államvédelmi Osztály* (State Security Department), became the AVH,
Államvédelmi Hátoság, in 1948 but everyone continued to call it the AVO (pronounced
Ah-voe).

rooms with equipment ranging from whips, truncheons and nail presses to electrodes. The basement housed the *lefolyo*, an acid bath where victims' remains were sent into the city's main drainage system.[1]

The AVO was modelled on the Soviet Union's political police during the height of Stalin's great purge of the 1930s. As Rákosi made plain: 'There was one position in which our Party staked a claim from the first minute – and we permitted no coalitionist compromise. This was the state security service . . . We took a tight grip on this organization from the first day it was set up.' The AVO was the Communist Party's 'sword and shield', charged with eliminating any form of opposition, and for its first few years it was ruthlessly efficient. A Hungarian word widely used in Budapest during the late 1940s and early 1950s held grim echoes for millions of people in later years: *csengőfrász*, which translates as 'bell fright'. It meant the terror of the ring at the door in the middle of the night. 'Like most secret police the AVO preferred to work in the dark, in the small hours,' one prisoner who survived arrest and two weeks at 60 Stalin Avenue recalled. AVO officers could be recognized by their blue uniforms with green epaulettes and their swagger.

After Rákosi, the head of the AVO, Gábor Péter, was the most hated man in Budapest. He was born Benö Auspitz (though he had another 'alias' name, Benjamin Eisenberger) in 1906 and worked as a tailor's assistant before realizing his vocation in espionage. He had been arrested in 1931 for Communist agitation but managed to escape to the Soviet Union and immediately began to work for the NKVD, as an enforcer throughout Europe tasked with keeping local Communist parties loyal to Moscow.* When he returned to Budapest in 1945 with the other Muscovites he set to work building the AVO. The writer Pál Ignotus was interrogated by him at 60 Stalin Avenue while his torturers looked on: 'Péter had a huge wood-panelled study, with a huge chandelier. Everything connected with him was on a big scale except himself. He was a short man with rodent eyes and a Hitler moustache . . . His taste for good tailoring had never left him. He was in an impeccable grey suit with a perfect silk tie, which he fingered all the time.'

---

* Péter was the Comintern agent who helped to 'turn' Kim Philby, one of Britain's Cambridge Five traitors, to the Communist cause. In the 1930s Péter had an affair with Litzi Friedmann, Philby's first wife, and recruited her to work for Soviet intelligence.

He drank heavily and everyone, including his beautiful but terrifying wife Jolán Simon, knew he kept a string of mistresses. They had an unconventional (for the staid 1950s) 'open' relationship and lived in luxury surrounded by servants in a huge villa on Rózsadomb, with a sweeping view of the Danube below. Even by the standards of Communist hatchet men in Eastern Europe he was staggeringly cynical. When he interrogated the poet György Faludy, who had fled from the Horthy regime in the 1930s and voluntarily returned to Hungary in 1947 from the safety and comfort of the US, Péter taunted him: 'We don't need such idiots as you . . . You silly fool, returning from America to live in this filth.'[2]

The chief torturer at 60 Stalin Avenue was Gyula Prinz, a coalman and former Arrow Cross member who had worked in the same building, doing the same job for the fascist dictatorship. Rákosi recruited many Arrow Cross thugs for work with the AVO as they had experience in certain specialized skills. He argued that their experience would be useful and they could be relied on to be loyal out of self-interest because they could easily be blackmailed later. If they proved to be difficult they could be eliminated when they were no longer needed.

Prinz was a 'huge, pot-bellied, immensely strong man – bald on the top of his head but hirsute everywhere else', according to one of his victims. He estimated that he had personally tortured around 25,000 people in his lifetime. He took great pride in his work. His task was to extract confessions and he insisted it had to be done 'correctly'. During his interrogation by Prinz, Ignotus was ordered to stand by the wall holding a pencil between his nose and his mouth. 'Of course eventually the pencil fell,' Ignotus wrote. 'He beat me until my whole body was swollen with purple bruises and a couple of teeth were kicked out. He said to me, "Why don't you use a writer's imagination and write a confession?" The object was not to write absurd things but to tell credible lies only.'

Most of the AVO heavies were not exactly subtle or sophisticated. Faludy tried to fool them and partially succeeded, as he explained in his frightening and funny memoir *My Happy Days in Hell*:

They extracted a detailed confession from me in which I admitted that I had gone to France to join a Trotskyite group to engage in anti-Soviet activity ... I was handed over to an 'American expert' [in the AVO] who made me describe how I had engaged in subversive activity and, while in America, had joined the OSS, America's [pre-CIA] espionage agency ... I concluded they were preparing a ... spy trial at which I would be one of the principal accused. I therefore did my best to invent details of a kind to make foreign journalists guess what was going on. I told my interrogator that I had been recruited to the OSS by two American agents: Captain Edgar Allan Poe and Major Walt Whitman, describing the two men in great detail. In case one of the investigators or the judge might discover my purpose, I invented a third American agent, the club-footed Z.E. Bubbel – an anagram of Beelzebub – whom I intended to unmask only at the trial. I talked about the wild orgies at the New York offices of the OSS ... When the interrogator asked me for the New York address, I was unable to give it because I had never been there, so I suggested he look it up in the NYC phone book; upon which he gave me a beating and made me stand for two days with my nose pressed against the wall. By then he had put an address into my 'confession'.[3]

The AVO became a vast bureaucracy of terror that treated its own well. The elite were those who operated in Budapest. They were handsomely rewarded. About a tenth of the AVO's force of 48,000 (in 1950) were assigned to mundane duties like border patrols. They received average salaries. But senior officers involved in the more grisly end of the work were paid around twenty times the national average, the same as a judge's salary. In Budapest, according to one estimate, 100,000 people were regular informers for the AVO, 7 per cent of the population, which at first sight seems far-fetched. But a top-secret state security review for the Budapest branch of the AVO shows the thoroughness and breadth that went into looking for informers: 'Insurance agents, rent collectors, gas meter readers are excellent ... chimney sweeps are very useful. They can move about freely in people's homes ... and often they can engage in friendly conversation and no one suspects them.' Anyone could be an AVO snoop – and everyone knew it.

The AVO did not admit to mistakes. Gyula Fazekas was a vet, arrested with alleged friends – whom in fact he didn't know – for involvement in 'subversion'. He denied all the charges but interrogators beat and tortured him for three weeks. One night an AVO colonel came to his cell and told him that, unfortunately, it was another Gyula Fazekas they were looking for, but in the state he was in it was impossible to release him. He languished in a labour camp for years.[*4]

The Communists had got rid of their real opposition or cowed them into submission. Now, in the classic Bolshevik manner, they turned on each other. 'It was the execution of László Rajk in October 1949 that marked the moment when the Revolution began devouring its own children in an orgy of bloodletting,' wrote one Party official who would play a prominent role in the collapse of the Soviet system decades later. Relations between the East and West had reached freezing point soon after the war's end – accelerated by Winston Churchill's 'Iron Curtain' speech in Fulton, Missouri in 1946. Then, in the winter of 1948–9, a separate cold war broke out *within* the socialist bloc. A Communist leader in one of the 'liberated territories' dared to challenge Moscow. Josip Broz Tito, the partisan leader against the Nazis in Yugoslavia, established a Marxist dictatorship after the war, with Soviet support and materiél. But he began to resist the descent into colonial status Stalin demanded of the other 'satellite' states in Eastern Europe and the Balkans. Tito said there were various paths to socialism, called himself a 'national Communist' and declared that Yugoslavia would be 'non-aligned'. This was all heresy in the eyes of Stalin, who boasted: 'I could crack Tito with a snap of my fingers.' It was not so easy. Stalin believed he could afford to show no split in Communist unity in case it was exploited by the West; Tito's defiance could not go without punishment. Anyone in the Soviets' new European empire who showed sympathy with the Yugoslavs had to be crushed. Moscow organized a purge of 'Titoist, Trotskyite spies'

---

* The House of Terror has been a museum commemorating the victims of fascist and Communist terror since the early 2000s. Sadly, Right and Left have used it as a political football, but is it still a fascinating place. Both sides complain of a lack of balance when the other is in charge. The usually excellent historian István Rév condemned the display as 'a total propaganda space, where death and victims are used as rhetorical devices' because it commemorates more victims of Communist violence. But he is way off the mark. It is simply a fact that it was the Communists who were torturing people there for a lot longer than the Arrow Cross did – around seven years rather than seven months or so.

throughout the satellite states which convulsed the Communist world for the next three years.

As Stalin's best pupil, Rákosi was predictably zealous to prove his reliability and the purges hit Hungary the hardest of all the Central European states. He volunteered several battalions for a war against Tito, but Stalin vetoed that kind of conflict. Rákosi had to content himself with organizing the most spectacular of the show trials, implicating thousands of loyal Communists in the Rajk Affair. Who was or was not a traitor did not matter: the argument was semantic. Stalin believed in constant purges as the most effective way of retaining power – it worked for him for a quarter of a century – and when things were not going so well he required a regular and willing supply of scapegoats. The system as created by him could not be in error; *someone* had to be responsible for its failures.

László Rajk was one of the chief architects of Hungary's police state. As Interior Minister he had been in charge of the regime's suppression of the Churches and the trial of Cardinal Mindszenty. He was a hard-line Stalinist – more orthodox in his Marxism than Rákosi – and unforgiving of opposition. 'Every man needs a compass and mine is the Soviet Union,' he often said. But he understood public relations and, unlike so many of the dull, grey men in the regime, he had flair. He was tall, slim, arrestingly good-looking and married to one of the great beauties of Communist Budapest, Júlia Földi. They were the glamour couple of the day. Rákosi hated him for his looks and celebrity status – and distrusted those Communists who had stayed in Hungary during the Horthy years and the Nazi occupation, as Rajk had done. He saw him, rightly, as a potential leadership rival. So when the purge was launched, he chose Rajk as the principal target.

László Rajk was born in 1909 into a well-off trader's family from Transylvania. They moved to Budapest after the Treaty of Trianon. He became radicalized at university and organized an illegal Communist Party cell at Eötvös József College, the elite training ground for lawyers, civil servants and academics. A fellow student informed on him and Rajk was thrown out of the college and briefly jailed. Banned from returning to university, he became a building worker, but was jailed again and deported after organizing a construction workers' strike. He fought in the Spanish Civil War as a volunteer in the Rákosi Battalion of the International Brigade. Back from Spain, he returned to Hungary and became the acknowledged leader of the illegal Communist underground until he was arrested in 1944 soon after the Germans occupied Budapest.

Rajk might have had an intimation of his fate when he was dropped as Interior Minister early in 1949. But he retained a post as Foreign Minister. On 10 May 1949 he and his wife were invited to lunch by Rákosi at his villa. Júlia Rajk had just given birth and Rákosi told her he wanted to wet the baby's head. All was good cheer – even though the Party boss had already signed the Rajks' arrest warrants.[5] The next day Rajk was arrested by the AVO at his apartment. He knew what would await him. Initially he refused to confess to a string of espionage and treason charges – as had the thirteen other leading Communist officials charged with him. But Rákosi and the Soviets were leaving nothing to chance. Stalin had sent to Budapest a thirty-strong team of interrogators led by Fyodor Bielkin, the KGB official in charge of the satellite states, who had experience in orchestrating show trials. After repeatedly torturing him for several weeks they broke Rajk and all his co-defendants. As was expected of them, they played the parts allotted them in the grim farce of Soviet-style justice, as though it was theatre described in the pages of Arthur Koestler's anti-Stalin novel *Darkness at Noon*.*

The trial in October 1949 did not take place in a court, but in a big trade union hall that could accommodate a larger audience, all hand-picked by the Party, of course. The charges were absurd. Rajk, the most loyal of Communists, was alleged to have conspired with a long list of foreign powers, primarily Yugoslavia but also the US, France and Franco's Spain. When the expected death sentences were passed, court officials and the entire audience showed their approval by collective rhythmic applause. Júlia Rajk, who had been arrested shortly after her husband, was jailed for six years. Her baby son, also László, was sent to a state orphanage under a different name.

The Terror following the Rajk case lasted more than three years. The numbers, in a small country of fewer than 10 million people, were

---

* By this time Arthur Koestler, having been a Communist for some years, had become a resolute opponent of the USSR. Stalin's purges and show trials had changed him. He was living in London at this time – and though now he wrote books in German and in English, he 'always dreamed in Hungarian'.

staggering. Between 1950 and 1953, more than 1.3 million people were prosecuted (and half of them jailed). Around 50,000 more were arrested but never faced a charge or appeared in court. More than 2,400 were summarily executed – but many times that number rotted to death in police cells or in the three concentration camps that formed the Magyar gulag, where 40,000 people were interned. Of 850,000 members of the Communist Party in 1950, almost half were either dead, in prison or in labour camps three years later. Often the roles changed between victim and executioner with dramatic speed. In summer 1950 General Kálmán Révay, Commandant of the Military Academy, was shot in the courtyard of the Budapest Military Police headquarters on trumped-up charges of treason. Barely six months earlier he had commanded the firing squad which in the same place had killed his good friend and comrade in arms György Pálffy, the well-known underground resistance fighter against the Nazis and the post-war chief of military counter-intelligence.

Within the Party, almost anyone could be suspect. If you had left the country during the Horthy years you might have been a spy for the West. If you had stayed in Hungary, underground, you were a police informer. As Pál Ignotus, himself jailed for six years after he was tortured, explained:

> Innocence or guilt were irrelevant in a constant purge . . . To gauge the proportion of victims who had simply had bad luck, as against those who had genuinely had a spark of patriotism or human feeling, would be difficult. In general, those who had survived the purges unharmed were probably more sycophantic and barbarous than others who were murdered or imprisoned . . . But some of the executed were chiefly sorry for not being the executioners. The selection of criminals was based quite openly on assumptions of political deviation, rather than upon anything they had actually said or done.

One of the most dangerous jobs to hold was Interior Minister. Rajk's predecessor had ended up on the scaffold, and his three successors were all shot. Perhaps the most tragic was Sándor Zöld, a distinguished Budapest doctor and medical researcher, who had worked courageously in the underground in the city during the last months of the war. On 15 April 1951 he was criticized at a Cabinet meeting by Rákosi and fired from the government. He was convinced he would be imminently arrested, tortured and tried. Terrified of his fate, he broke down. He drove home to his apartment in Pest, murdered his wife and two children, and then shot himself dead. The family was found the next morning. The news spread like wildfire throughout the city and was a profound shock. 'If these tragedies can happen to the top people no one could be safe,' the postgraduate research student Sándor Zsindely wrote. 'The message was clear to us all. In the new Hungary, anyone could disappear from one day to the next.' A grim joke was regularly told throughout Budapest in the early 1950s: 'There are still three classes in this country: those who have been in jail; those who are in jail; and those who will be in jail.'[6]

33

REVOLUTION – AGAIN

Experience teaches us that the most dangerous time for a bad government is when it begins to reform.

Alexis de Tocqueville (1805–59)

At the beginning of 1953 the gloom in Budapest was at its deepest. 'That was the worst time for many people,' recalled Éva Walko, a sophisticated, worldly woman, a mother of three, who had survived fascism, hiding in a basement to avoid deportation to a concentration camp and the depredations of the Red Army. 'There was nothing to eat, and little to hope for.' The intra-Communist Party purges were running out of steam – there were few left to arrest by that time – but Stalin was preparing a murderous new wave of terror. The ageing tyrant, now seventy-four, was convinced that doctors – 'men in white coats', most of them Jews – were conspiring to murder Communist officials in the Eastern bloc and identified them as his latest target. In Budapest, Rákosi did what he normally did to survive and slavishly followed his master in the Kremlin – 'he tried to show that he could be as anti-Semitic as the next Stalinist'. The AVO drew up a list of doctors and prominent intellectuals to be arrested. But then, suddenly, on 5 March, Stalin died of a massive stroke at his dacha outside Moscow – and everything changed.*

Immediately after Stalin's death a collective leadership of bitter rivals emerged in the Soviet Union. They disagreed on a lot, but collectively could recognize that a crisis was brewing in Hungary and they

---

* In Budapest, the first victim of the so-called Doctors' Plot and Stalin's last big purge wasn't a medic but the AVO boss Gábor Péter, who was arrested at Rákosi's villa after lunch and along with his wife transferred to the dungeons at 60 Andrássy Avenue, where he was placed under the tender mercy of his erstwhile torturer-in-chief Gyula Prinz.

were determined to prevent one. Two and a half months after Stalin's funeral, the top leadership from Budapest were summoned to Moscow and told to change their ways. For years Rákosi – unusually under the Soviet system – had held the two positions of General Secretary of the Party and Prime Minister, head of the government. Now in Moscow he was ordered to give up the premiership. Stalin's long-time secret police chief, Lavrenty Beria, told him: 'Listen, Comrade Rákosi, we know that Hungary has had Habsburg emperors, Tatar khans, Polish princes and Turkish sultans. But as far as we know it has never had a Jewish king and that is what you are trying to become. You can be sure we will not allow it.' He then began to list the Hungarian's 'many errors', beginning with complaints about the AVO, 'which you have allowed to become a law unto itself'. If anyone around the table saw any irony about these points coming from a mass murderer of Beria's accomplishments nobody dared to mention it.

Rákosi was replaced as head of the government in Budapest by a man who was low down in the pecking order in the Hungarian leadership, a figure who had a chequered history within the Party and a comrade whom he despised.[1]

Imre Nagy did not look like one of the great tragic heroes of Hungarian history. He had the appearance of a second-tier civil servant or village schoolmaster: plump, balding, moustachioed, avuncular, cheerful, invariably with half a smile on his face. He was never a firebrand revolutionary, though he led the most significant rebellion there would be against Soviet totalitarianism. For much of his life he had himself served tyranny, but towards the end, when the moment came, he became a martyr for the cause of freedom. He died better than he lived – a decent, honourable man, but a hopeless politician.

He was born in the millennium year, 1896, in Kaposvár, a small, sleepy town in southern Hungary between Lake Balaton and the Serbian border. His parents had grown up in appalling poverty, but had bettered themselves. They were in service to the local sheriff. They were devout and brought up their only son and three daughters as strict Calvinists. Nagy was awarded a place at the local *gimnázium*, rare for a young boy from such humble stock, but he showed no particular academic abilities. His formal education ended when he was twelve. He was briefly apprenticed to a small agricultural machinery manufacturer near his own town, but as a teenager moved to Budapest. He found work in the Hungarian railways' machine foundry amid the urban squalor of the city's biggest industrial area, Angyalföld.

At the start of the First World War he was conscripted into an infantry regiment and sent to the Italian Front, where he was wounded. After release he was immediately sent to the Eastern Front, where he was taken prisoner by the Russians. By the time of the Bolshevik Revolution he was in a Siberian prisoner-of-war camp. He had never shown much interest in politics, even when he worked in dismal factory conditions in Budapest. But the war radicalized him. At the age of twenty-two he became a Communist and found a faith he never lost.

Instead of returning to Hungary after his release, Nagy volunteered for the Red Army in the Russian Civil War. He was taken prisoner by White guards but managed to escape and rejoined his unit with the Bolshevik troops. In 1921 he was sent back to Budapest by the Comintern to recruit members in the Communist Party, by then illegal, and to infiltrate the legal leftist organization, the Social Democrats. He married Mária Egetö, daughter of one of the most prominent SDP leaders in the country.[2]

Like almost all of the Communists who would take power after 1945, Nagy had spent time in Admiral Horthy's prisons. He was arrested in 1927, jailed for two years and on his release expelled from Hungary, leaving behind his wife and two-year-old daughter, Erzsébet, born while he was in jail, who joined him on his release.

He and his family lived in exile in Moscow for the next fifteen years. His daughter could hardly speak a word of Hungarian when they all returned after the Second World War. This period is the hardest to assess in Nagy's biography and still gives rise to spirited disagreement. He lived quietly throughout the purges of the 1930s, when half the intelligentsia of Moscow and many Hungarian *émigrés* were killed. Some documents from KGB archives that emerged after the Berlin Wall fell in 1989 seem to show that he was a trusted informer for the Soviet secret police – but there has long been doubt about the authenticity of these documents and besides, they don't prove anything. One way or another, almost every foreigner at the time, working for a Soviet organ of state, was an agent of some kind. There is no evidence he actually did anything significant for the secret police. But he survived in Moscow, prospered and made some important contacts among the top officials in the Soviet Communist Party, among them the head of Soviet intelligence, Lavrenty Beria.

Nagy wanted to join the army to fight the fascists. But the Soviets gave him a job on the Hungarian-language Kossuth Rádió, established under the playwright Gyula Háy, to beam anti-Nazi propaganda into Hungary. He turned out to be a success on radio: he had a clear voice and could speak in straightforward language free of Marxist-Leninist jargon. The philosopher György Lukács, who knew him well in Russian exile, said that at the time, 'I thought highly of his personal integrity and intelligence . . . But I did not regard him as a real politician.'

Nevertheless, when the Muscovites returned to Hungary, Nagy, who had made himself an expert on farming, became Minister for Agriculture – to fulfil the Communists' promise of giving 'land to the people'. Nagy took the pledge seriously, unlike Rákosi, which is why he lasted just a few months in the job. He thought collectivizing farms was a mistake in Hungarian conditions, an honest and shrewd analysis for an otherwise orthodox Marxist. He was different in other ways too. He put on few grandiose airs. He was cheerful, fond of laughter and told jokes – often a dangerous practice in those days. He walked around Budapest chatting to strangers. Most Sundays he could be found watching a football game.

His daughter's marriage in 1946 caused him political problems. Erzsébet's husband was a Protestant pastor (though he did join the Soviet army and the Communist Party). The wedding was celebrated at the main Calvinist church in Budapest. Nagy had to get special permission from the Party to attend the church service, which later would be held against him by Party diehards.

When after 1948 Communists had won total control Nagy was brought back in the fold, but given a decorative, if powerless, post as President of Parliament. Again it didn't last long. When the Party leadership began to speed up collectivization of farms, Nagy bombarded them with warnings that the process was being done dangerously fast and would lead to disaster. He was fired and, in the time-honoured Leninist manner, made to perform 'self-criticism'. He made a humiliating speech confessing 'my rightist deviation . . . oppositionism became apparent in my style of work.'

Many were surprised that Nagy was not purged at this point, along with Rajk and thousands of others. Instead he was allowed to return to academic life, teaching at Karl Marx University in Budapest. He had supporters in the Soviet Union, and very few of the original Muscovites were jailed. A year later he was back again – as Deputy Prime Minister. Within a few weeks of his appointment Stalin died and he had the job of making the official eulogy speech in the Hungarian Parliament. 'My heart is heavy as I mount the speaker's platform to face our deeply mourning people,' he said. 'To express their deep love for our greatest friend and liberator and teacher, the Hungarian people are rallying around the Party, the government and our beloved Comrade Rákosi and they are devoting all their energies towards carrying Stalin's great cause to triumph in our country.' Within three months he was catapulted into his role as Prime Minister.[3]

Nagy immediately introduced a series of modest reforms which he called, portentously, 'the new course'. Thousands of political prisoners were released, some independent traders were allowed to run small businesses and he slowed down – though did not halt – collectivization. In Budapest life felt more relaxed. The problem for Nagy was that Rákosi was still General Secretary of the Party and supposedly held equal power, but was much more ruthless about using it. He, too, had friends in the Kremlin and plotted ceaselessly against Nagy. After just eighteen months the Soviet magnates summoned the Hungarian Party leadership to the Kremlin for another dressing down and removed Nagy from the premiership. He was sent into retirement and, refusing to endure again the usual ritual of 'self-criticism', was thrown out of the Party.

After Stalin's death the collective leadership in the USSR could not settle on a policy of how to deal with their colonies in Eastern Europe. They changed direction repeatedly, depending on their internal feuds, until mid 1956, when Nikita Khrushchev emerged as winner of the power struggle in the Kremlin. But the zigzags in policy had a profound impact behind the Iron Curtain – especially in Hungary. Rákosi regained his leading position but couldn't operate in the old way. He had to restrain his more brutal urges – and in the summer of 1956 he was removed again, this time for good, and went into exile to the USSR. By then the regime in Budapest had 'relaxed its grip significantly enough for rage and loathing to replace fear as the motivating factor for people – a dangerous time for a dictatorship', as one acute Party official who would soon leave Hungary said. Writers became a little more free to voice criticism about the system, many Communist officials were more open at meetings about the mistakes that had been made since the war, former political prisoners told their stories about the treatment under which they had suffered during the purges. 'The whole mood in Budapest had changed . . . everyone could feel it,' Mátyás Sárközi, then a journalism student, recalled.

On a miserably wet and cold Saturday, 6 October 1956, more than 100,000 people were in the streets of the city to witness the most bizarre event in the two decades so far in the story of Communist Hungary: the reburial of László Rajk and the four men who had been hanged along with him seven years earlier. While he lived, Rajk had been loathed by most Hungarians as the diehard Stalinist who had helped to install the rotten system. Then he became the most prominent victim of the Terror and he had been transformed into a true patriot deserving of a state funeral at Kerepesi Cemetery, where a long list of Hungarian heroes have been buried. 'Having had a show trial, he now had a show burial.' The date held significance. It was the anniversary of the day in 1849 when Lajos Batthyány, the Prime Minister of revolutionary Hungary, and thirteen generals from the army of the War of Independence were executed by the Austrians.

The new leadership of the Party, led now by Rákosi's former number two and an equally rigid Stalinist, Ernő Gerő, was persuaded that the reburial would show how the Party had made a fresh start. It was a mistake and only fuelled public anger. Rajk's widow was chief mourner, clutching her seven-year-old son at her side, with whom she had recently been reunited. Next to them was Imre Nagy, looking sombre, who wasn't allowed to speak publicly but was heard to tell those close by him that 'soon it will be Stalinism that is buried'. The entire show was macabre.

It was followed that evening by the first political demonstration in Budapest since the Communists took power. Around 500 students marched to the Batthyány monument by the river on the Buda side of the city, where they displayed anti-Party placards and bemused a few onlookers by shouting anti-government slogans. The police broke up the rally peacefully and quietly, but 'it was a warning sign that the Communist elite did not understand'.[4]

Even in the 2020s, with Budapest a bustling, vibrant capital in the EU, there are a few public buildings and apartment blocks pockmarked by bullet holes, left as a deliberate reminder of the stirring, tragic Uprising that began a fortnight later. The 1956 Revolution was the defining moment of the Cold War and of modern Hungary. The pictures, usually in grainy black and white, of Soviet tanks firing shells indiscriminately in the centre of Budapest, and of Russian troops shooting at children, aroused sympathy for Hungary throughout the world. It is a story of heroic failure in a doomed cause, of extraordinary courage – and of brutal cruelty. The determination of the Hungarians to claim their independence astonished outsiders, gave hope to all those who were fighting tyranny and to some extent wiped away the country's recent history as a willing ally of Hitler. The fate of Hungary fired the imagination of people across the Western world. For a week or so it seemed as though a small, impoverished nation, its people armed with little more than a few rifles and petrol bombs, might prevail over one of the world's superpowers. But the euphoria was premature and reality bit back.

The Soviets withdrew temporarily, but returned with overwhelming numbers and firepower. They crushed the Hungarian Uprising, destroyed much of the capital, killed thousands of people and occupied the country for a further thirty years. Decades later, images of Soviet savagery in suppressing the Revolution still have the power to shock. More than 200,000 Hungarians – around two-thirds of them from Budapest – fled the country within a few weeks;* Hungarian refugees from 1956 can be found in substantial numbers from Alaska to South Australia. It is a trauma that has left scars, physical and psychological, from which the country – and particularly Budapest, where most of the events happened – has not healed more than sixty years later.

At the beginning, much of the script deliberately echoed March 1848, though this time there was no poet to orchestrate it or write ballads about it. The opening move on 22 October was haphazard and spontaneous. Instead of in a coffee house, students from the two biggest Budapest

---

* Including my own immediate family – my mother, father, sister and brother.

universities – the Technological University, where most of the country's top scientists and engineers had been trained, and the Humanities department of the main University of Budapest – held meetings at their main campus halls. Echoing the Twelve Points of 1848, they produced a manifesto of Sixteen Points that became the core demands 'of the people': the removal of Soviet troops, free and fair elections, a free press, Imre Nagy to be returned as Prime Minister, freedom for all political prisoners, and a host of demands about changes to the lives of Budapest students. They agreed they would hold two separate marches the next afternoon, one from Pest and one from Buda, which would meet at the statue of the Polish General József Bem, who had fought with the Hungarians in the War of Independence, on the embankment at the Buda side of the river. Nobody expected that the marches would begin a dramatic chain of events that would bring down the regime and prompt the biggest Soviet military operation since the end of the Second World War.[5]

Tuesday, 23 October was a bright and sunny autumn day. Throughout the morning the regime leadership had repeatedly changed its mind about the demonstration – first permitting it, then later in the morning banning it, and later still allowing it to proceed. The vacillation was clear proof, if any was needed, that it had no idea about the mood in Budapest. The demonstrations set off punctually at 3 p.m. At the bigger of the two, which started at the Petőfi statue on the Pest side of the river embankment, there were about 12,000 people, most but not all of them students. They marched along the Danube promenade and then, ten abreast, crossed Margaret Bridge. No demonstration on this scale had been seen in Budapest for decades. Károly Makk, then at film school but later one of the most successful movie directors in Hungary, was working with a news crew that kept their cameras running for the next few days: 'The first few moments of the marches were maybe the most extraordinary. The pent-up emotions, the feeling that at last after years people could show what they felt was so liberating. Nobody thought that in a few hours there would be a revolution and this was the start of it. But people felt – I felt – a huge weight being lifted from our shoulders. All kinds of people were joining the march the whole time. Older people you could see were crying tears of joy that at last they could find a way to speak.' It took around one and a half hours for the protestors to make the two kilometres to the Bem statue.

There were about 8,000 people at the start of the other demonstration, which started from the Technological University. Their route was around two and a half kilometres along the Buda embankment, past offices and apartment blocks. They were cheered from thousands of windows. This is where the most powerful and visible symbol of the Revolution was born. Someone had cut out the hammer and sickle emblem from the national tricolour. The new flag, with a hole at its heart, was passed to the marchers at the front of the procession. Soon, this was almost the only flag seen around the city. By 4.30 p.m. there were more than 25,000 people crammed into Bem Square and thousands more in adjoining streets, standing around idly. There had been nothing planned, apart from the rally – until hundreds of voices cried: 'To Parliament'. The route was two kilometres across the Danube, into the heart of Pest, through Budapest's main commercial district. But now the composition of the protest changed. Workers who had finished their shifts went to see if what they had heard on the grapevine was true – the radio was not mentioning a huge, unprecedented demonstration in the city. People left their offices to swell the numbers, and the mood was getting angrier. The main cry heard now from the crowd was *'Ruszkik haza!'* – 'Russians Go Home'. By the time the march reached Parliament Square there were more than 175,000 people massed there.[6]

Nagy had been reluctant to support the protestors. He was a loyal, deeply conservative Party man who did not agree with most of the student demands and – rightly, as it turned out – thought the demonstration could lead to violence in Budapest that was hard to control. But the crowd was calling for him to appear and he was persuaded by his friends and advisers to turn up to address them. When he spoke at 8.45, at first he fell flat. 'Comrades,' he began. There were boos and catcalls throughout the square. 'We are not comrades,' thousands of people roared back in protest. Nagy was staggered and froze for a few seconds. He could not immediately grasp what was happening or why the term he had used routinely most of his life should be rejected. He tried again: 'Citizens . . .' But then he talked about 'democratic socialism' and how the 'Communist Party will come to the right decisions . . . everything must be done in the bosom of the Party.' He concluded: 'You have proved patriotism . . . now go home.' He was booed again and heckled. 'We will stay. YOU go home.' Thousands whistled and said: 'We do not whistle at you, but at your words.' This identified the main problem Nagy had for the first few days of the Revolution: he was invariably behind the mass of the people's demands and was trying to catch up.

Throughout the evening, groups of protestors broke off from the main demonstration and spread out to other points in the city. By 7 p.m. around 4,000 people had crammed themselves into a narrow, cobbled street near the National Museum, Sándor Bródy Street, where the national radio station was based – Hungary's main source of news for most people. The majority of the crowd were students and they were determined that the Sixteen Points be broadcast on air. There was an uneasy stand-off for two hours while crowds outside demanded 'a microphone on the street' and a student delegation negotiated inside the building with the radio's director, a stern Stalinist named Valéria Benke, who was under strict orders not to allow the students' demands to be heard. Meanwhile the government had reinforced the building with heavily armed AVO guards.

Benke had been a Minister for Education under Rákosi and, despite her supreme sycophancy, was known to be a clever woman, but she tried a desperate trick in an attempt to fool the crowd and solve her dilemma. She agreed to send a microphone outside with an announcer to read the Sixteen Points live. But at the same time she had halted live broadcasts. Instead of listening to the protestors' manifesto, people were hearing recorded music by Franz Liszt. When the demonstrators realized they had been tricked they began using a vehicle parked in the street as a ram to batter down the doors as they laid siege to the building. The entirely peaceful protest turned ugly.

A trigger-happy AVO guard began to fire on the students – and this is when death came to Budapest again and violent revolution erupted. Two students were killed instantly and three were seriously wounded, but the crowd refused to disperse. Army units arrived with orders to use all necessary force against the demonstrators. But they mutinied and joined the protestors, handing them weapons – 'anyone who asked was handed a gun' said General Béla Király, who would shortly assume command of Hungarian armed forces. 'Soldiers anywhere with a universal draft are nothing but young people in uniforms,' he said. 'That night on 23 October the young men under arms refused to fire on their compatriots. The People's Army proved its prime loyalty was to the People . . . not to the Party.' It soon turned out that the commander of Budapest's police, the thirty-four-year-old former lathe operator Sándor Kopácsi, decided he too would go over to the Revolution and opened up police weapons stores.

The news of the shooting at the radio station swept through Budapest. One of the city's main ammunition depots, in a Budapest suburb, was raided by a group of young people who had seen the first students die. At the United Lamp Factory on Csepel Island, well known as a cover for an arms manufacturer, workers removed 1,000 rifles and sent them on lorries to the radio station and elsewhere in the city. At Budapest's two military academies, the Zrínyi and the Petöfi, cadets sent weapons – against the express orders of their commanders. 'A protest had turned into an armed insurrection within a matter of a few hours,' said Miklós Vásárhelyi, one of Imre Nagy's closest confidants.[7]

As the name suggests, Heroes' Square, the main entrance to the City Park, had been designed to be a memorial for great Hungarians. To the resentment of almost everyone in Budapest, for the last seven years it had been dominated by a giant bronze statue of Stalin. Worse, the murderous subject was depicted with a benevolent smile on his face. Throughout the day of protests some Soviet targets had been attacked: Horizont, the Russian bookshop on the main Ring Boulevard, was partially burned down and crowds set fire to volumes by Marx, Lenin and others. The Hungarian-Soviet Friendship Society was set on fire and it was a miracle nobody inside was injured. Red stars on public buildings were torn down and smashed. As dusk fell a huge crowd congregated around the Stalin statue. 'This was the ultimate symbol of our slavery and we were determined to bring it down,' as one of the students there that night said. But, given its size and weight, it was not an easy task. Some young people had tried climbing up the tyrant's torso and placed a noose around his neck connected to a lorry. But the rope snapped straight away. More industrial methods were needed. The police chief, Kopácsi, sent a detachment of men under the command of an eager young Communist named Lieutenant Kiss to ensure peace – and safety for the late despot's memorial. Immediately he arrived on the scene Kiss called his commander:

> Kiss: Comrade Colonel, people are pulling down the statue. Please send orders immediately.
> Kopácsi: OK, Comrade Lieutenant, tell me about this pulling down.
> Kiss: There are at least 100,000 people around the statue.
> Kopácsi: Are you sure there are as many as that?
> Kiss: All of Heroes' Square, the edge of the woods is thick with people. What should I do?
> Kopácsi: OK, how many men have you got?
> Kiss: Well, twenty-five, Comrade Colonel.
> Kopácsi: OK, you are willing to sacrifice yourself for the Party, but for a statue? It is useless to try anything. Leave the crowd to get on with it.

There were three more futile attempts with ropes and then a group of workers arrived with some heavy machinery. Engineers used metal-burning equipment and the statue was attached to three cranes commandeered from the city's tram system. Even then it took forty minutes before the statue began to totter. At 9.37 p.m. Stalin fell. The writer Stephen Vizinczey, a student at the time, remembered the moment: 'It was such an eerie sound; several thousand people sighing with joy. I think we all had the sense of making history. We thought the whole world was looking at us and the whole world was happy. Then another sound could be heard.' Hundreds of people were hammering away with stones at the bronze trying to take a piece of Stalin. The head was dragged along busy streets for hours and then dumped outside the National Theatre. All that was left of the statue was the Great Dictator's jackboots and for days everyone in Budapest called it Boot Square.

The Communist leadership holed up in Party HQ were 'gripped by panic and paralysed as if by a stroke', admitted András Hegedüs, the Prime Minster, years later. That night he was replaced as premier by the return of Imre Nagy. 'As things were falling apart somebody would propose a measure, it was unanimously adopted. Minutes later they convened again and adopted a totally different measure.' Within a few hours the army, the police, even some pampered senior officers of the AVO abandoned them. 'Ten years of the most thorough indoctrination could not buy them four hours' precious time.'* One thing they could agree on was to beg for help from the Soviet Union, and with hardly a debate the top leadership in the Kremlin approved the request. Soviet troops based in Hungary went to Budapest to 'restore order'. They had no idea what was about to confront them.[8]

---

* Hegedüs had been a Rákosi aide, a devout Stalinist from an early age and parachuted to the premiership at just thirty-two. Soon after the Revolution he renounced hard-line Communism, taught sociology at a university and became one of the best-known dissidents in Hungary.

34

BETRAYAL IN MOSCOW

This is the time for decisive action to catch all the scoundrels. To disarm them.

Marshal Georgy Zhukov (1896–1974)

The first Soviet troops and tanks were spotted in central Budapest around 3 a.m. on 24 October. The Kremlin was expecting no significant resistance. The intervention was supposed to be a police operation to punish and arrest rioting students, a simple task that even semi-trained units of the Red Army had performed before behind the Iron Curtain. But this time Soviet soldiers immediately found themselves in an urban guerrilla war against a surprisingly determined and inventive enemy in the most widespread rebellion there had been to Soviet rule in Eastern Europe. The Russians had a massive reserve of firepower: 1,100 tanks, 159 planes and 185 heavy guns based in Hungary if they were needed. But all this weaponry was useless in the first act of the Hungarian Revolution in Budapest. The Russians did not know what had hit them. The moment their soldiers were spotted, 'We were greeted by a hail of gunfire and bullets from an ill-organized band of rebels, many of them in their teens, armed with a few rifles and some hastily prepared Molotov cocktails,' Lieutenant-General Yevgeny Malashenko, second in command of the Soviet army in Hungary, wired back to Moscow.

The character of the fighting was set on the first morning. The rebels relied on local knowledge to harry the Soviets with hit-and-run tactics they found hard to beat. Tanks are frighteningly powerful weapons. But in a crowded city centre their usefulness had limits – unless the Soviets were prepared to demolish everything in their way, which, at this stage in Budapest, they were not prepared to do. It was easy for the Soviets to hold the main bridges and main traffic intersections. But tanks could

not follow freedom fighters down narrow streets and alleyways or ma-
noeuvre into the courtyards of apartment blocks, where most people in
Budapest lived. The Russians were not prepared to face the potentially
heavy losses involved in sending infantry troops for hand-to-hand
combat in areas they didn't know and their opponents did.

'It was the least organized revolution in history,' as the leader of one
of the fighting bands declared. There were no generals or planners.
Groups of young men and women – sometimes children as young as
twelve and thirteen – 'spontaneously formed in places that offered a
vantage point to strike a swift blow and then hide. Sometimes a group
of a dozen or so would come together for one firefight; when that was
over they would split up and never see each other again,' recalled one
young student 'fighter'. Guns would be blazing along one street, while
round the corner the grocery store would be open and people would
be queuing for bread. They used unconventional methods, which
worked for a while against the lumbering old-style T-34 Soviet tanks
with caterpillar tracks that the Red Army in Hungary possessed then.
'Ordinary saucepans or frying pans were filled with water, balanced
on cables and stretched across the road,' one street fighter explained.
'When we heard the Soviets coming along we lowered the pans slowly
until they were about a metre above the ground. At first the Russian
soldiers would hesitate. That would give fighters in place in offices or
apartments above time to throw Molotov cocktails or grenades from
the windows.' Another trick was to place bricks across the road covered
by wooden paving. At a distance these looked as though they could be
landmines, and when the tanks halted to check they were open to attack
from above. The rebels realized that once a tank was disabled it made a
good barricade for the next skirmish so that each Soviet loss benefited
the revolutionaries twice over.

'Even those who weren't actively taking part, doing any fighting,
fed off each other's enthusiasm,' said the writer Ágnes Gergely, who
was a student teacher at the time. 'The real success of the rebels was
not so much to capture a building and to keep it for a few hours, but to
raise people's hopes by holding out for a while against such a superior
force.'[1] Often children built the roadblocks and threw the Molotov
cocktails. In many parts of Budapest the Revolution was a schoolkids'
war and – extraordinarily – few older people seemed to have qualms

about allowing children to kill and die for a cause they could not have understood with enough depth or clarity. Gergely Pongrátz, one of the leaders of the Corvin Group, a rebel gang based in what had been a giant cinema complex, became a well-known figure. 'The average age didn't reach eighteen. We had children at the Corvin as young as twelve,' he said years later in Western exile. 'They didn't want to leave. At first I think it was excitement; they were there because they had a gun, it was a thrill. But things changed when a few of them were killed. The ones who stayed did so from true patriotism and ideals . . . it was impossible to send them home.'

Within four and a half days nearly 500 Soviet troops had been killed and dozens of tanks had been disabled. The soldiers were hungry and exhausted and cold. The Soviets sued for peace – or pretended to.

At first, Khrushchev and the other Kremlin leaders vacillated and could not make up their minds about what to do in Hungary. They were shocked by the losses in what the Hungarian leadership and their own military assured them would be a simple operation. They despatched two senior magnates to Budapest: Anastas Mikoyan, the Armenian economics expert who had a reputation as a 'liberal', and the hard-line chief of socialist ideology, Mikhail Suslov. Both wanted to negotiate a deal with Imre Nagy, whom the Soviets had insisted should be 'brought back into the fold' as he was thought to be a reliable ally of the Kremlin. They tried to work out a deal that would grant the Hungarians some concessions about increased autonomy and the relaxation of harsh secret police violations, but changed little of substance. They fired Gerő and replaced him with a more emollient figure, János Kádár.

The problem was that events in Budapest had spun out of Nagy's control. Each day the revolutionaries grew stronger and were well armed with the rifles and small arms they had obtained from weapons stores. Much – though not all – of the army was on the rebels' side. The insurgents' demands grew. They wanted Russian troops to leave Hungary, the Soviet Union to have less political control – essentially neutrality and independence from the socialist bloc. Nagy knew this would never be accepted by the Kremlin, but lacked the ability to persuade the radicals to moderate their demands. The revolutionaries had also convinced themselves that the West would come to their aid against the nuclear-armed USSR – which was never going to happen. Nagy took five days to make up his mind whose side he was on, and then came down for the Revolution. He was genuine in his belief: he wanted 'socialism with a human face'. But he knew he could be swept away by the speed and force of events. This is when he became the true leader of the rebellion, when it was too late for the Uprising to succeed. He declared there would be free elections under a multi-party system – something he never believed in before, arguing they were 'bourgeois democracy'. He stopped censorship of the press and radio: people in Budapest woke on 30 October to a radio announcement that a new day was dawning in broadcasting: 'For many years our radio has been an instrument of lies. It carried out orders. It lied by night and by day; it lied on all wavelengths . . . from now, as the old saying has it, we shall tell the truth, the whole truth and nothing but the truth.' Nagy said talks would begin with the USSR about Hungary leaving the Warsaw Pact of Soviet satellite states in Central/Eastern Europe.[2]

On 29 October the Russians had declared that their troops would leave Hungary by the end of the month. It looked as though the rebels had won and celebrations began. There were parties throughout Budapest. But it was an illusion – as Nagy, his chief advisers and so-phisticated opinion in Hungary knew. Russian soldiers and their tanks and guns began marching out of the country. But the Soviet withdrawal was an elaborate feint. Fresh new troops arrived in massive force from 3 November with orders this time to crush the Uprising with ruthless savagery. Operation Whirlwind, as the Soviets called it, led by a full marshal, with 150,000 professional troops, 2,100 tanks, massive artillery and air support. Heavy guns blasted into the centre of Budapest from dawn on Sunday, 4 November. 'I felt the ground shake, and I saw the horizon light up. I heard explosion after explosion,' said Éva Walko, who hid in her basement in Buda. 'So much for victory.'

This time modern tanks did not wait for insurgents to get close enough to throw petrol bombs. They simply demolished whole apartment blocks if they thought one rebel was inside. Entire areas of the city were strafed by fighter jets if they spotted rebels on the street. Much of central Pest lay in ruins – again. There were appeals for help from foreign capitals – by Nagy, by neutral diplomats, by Church leaders. No help arrived. The CIA-funded Radio Free Europe had encouraged

Hungarians to rise up in revolt against their Soviet masters and suggested the US would assist them. The American cavalry never came. Some rebel groups and workers councils fought on for a few days, but were crushed. The Soviets left a window open for four days in which families could leave the country with relative ease via Austria. After that it became exceedingly difficult to exit. Imre Nagy and his immediate entourage were offered refuge in the Yugoslav Embassy on the first day of the invasion. Cardinal Mindszenty had been freed by an army unit from close house arrest at his bishop's palace outside Budapest and moved back to the capital. On the afternoon of the Soviet invasion he sought asylum in the US Embassy, where he was to remain for fifteen years.

Around 2,400 Hungarians were killed in the struggle, about 2,100 of them in Budapest. The other thing to die was hope: 1956 was the point in the Cold War when everything became clear. The Soviets would keep their possessions behind the Iron Curtain in Eastern Europe and the West, despite its rhetoric about 'freeing captive peoples', would do little to prevent them. Budapest was the victim.[3]

35

THE MERRIEST BARRACKS IN THE CAMP

*If my life is needed to prove that not all Communists are enemies
of the people, I gladly make the sacrifice. I know that one day there
will be another Nagy trial, which will rehabilitate me. I also know I
will have another reburial. I fear only that the funeral oration will be
delivered by those who betrayed me.*

Imre Nagy, 16 June 1958

At 6 a.m. on 4 November, on a Soviet-controlled radio station, residents
of Budapest heard the voice of the Hungarian Communist Party chief,
János Kádár, who a few days ago had told a broadcast interview how
proud he was to be a part 'of the great and glorious Revolution of the
Hungarian people' and what an 'inspirational figure' he saw in Imre
Nagy. Now, claiming to speak from the small town of Szolnok, in eastern
Hungary, he declared the formation 'of a new Hungarian Revolutionary
Worker-Peasant government . . . Acting in the interests of our people,
our working class and our country, we requested the Soviet army command to help to smash the dark reactionary forces and restore order and
calm in the country.' Three days earlier, on the evening of 1 November,
Kádár had slipped his security detail, was picked up by a curtained ZIS
limousine on the corner of a side road and the Ring Boulevard and –
with the utmost secrecy – ushered into the Soviet Embassy, where he
was immediately whisked away to the Soviet military air base and then
to Moscow.

Khrushchev and the other Kremlin chieftains persuaded him to
turn coat and made him an offer he wouldn't refuse. The Soviets, he
was told, were determined to crush Hungarian resistance by whatever
means necessary. 'Nagy and the rest are done for,' the Soviet ambassador to Hungary, Yuri Andropov, told him bluntly. 'You can either

join them and suffer their fate – or rejoin us and lead Hungary to get back on its feet and rebuild socialism.' The Russians understood their man. Kádár was a circumspect, ascetic and highly complex figure. He was no coward, but he did not believe in pointless heroics either. He had betrayed people before with a smiling face – and would do so again. He always afterwards denied he was a traitor and claimed he acted for the cause of Communism. But he was a practical man and later said that if the Russians had not chosen him 'they would have picked someone else, probably far worse'. He was almost certainly right.

At around 10 a.m. on 7 November, two Soviet tanks negotiated the debris in central Budapest and halted outside one of the entrances to the Parliament building. The square was empty apart from a corps of Russian troops, who had cleared the area a few hours earlier. There were still some armed skirmishes continuing in isolated parts of Budapest, on both sides of the river, but the Soviets had destroyed the main rebel strongholds and were mopping up the few pockets of remaining armed resistance. After ensuring the square was safe, the turret of one of the tanks was lifted and Kádár clambered out of the vehicle as the Kremlin's appointed boss in Budapest. He would remain in charge for the next three decades.[1]

János Czermanik was born, illegitimate, in the port of Fiume (now Rijeka in Croatia), the son of a Slovak servant girl. His soldier father abandoned them both when he was born and he was brought up in abject poverty. At fourteen he was apprenticed to a toolmaker and was trained in repairing typewriters. He became a Communist at nineteen, when under the Horthy regime it was a banned organization. He was arrested in 1937 and spent three years in jail. During the war, under the codename Kádár (meaning 'cooper' or 'barrel maker'), he ran the underground Communist Party and the pseudonym stuck. He narrowly avoided death when he was arrested again in 1944 and sent to Mauthausen concentration camp, but managed to escape and return to Budapest. A tall, handsome, brown-haired man, he affected a cheerful disposition and an easy manner but was famously reserved. 'Nobody ever knew what he was thinking,' a long-time comrade said many years later. He was formally uneducated – he admitted once that he had 'never

359

read Marx's *Das Kapital* and not much of Lenin'. But he had a naturally intuitive intelligence, was deeply perceptive about people and an extremely fast learner. He rose through the ranks as an apparatchik under Rákosi and succeeded Rajk, his great friend, as Interior Minister. It was his behaviour after Rajk was arrested that earned him a reputation for untrustworthiness and cynicism.

Godfather to Rajk's baby son, Kádár betrayed his friend in a chilling manner, visiting him in a police cell to extract a false confession out of him. He knew Rajk was innocent yet made many speeches accusing him of a series of crimes. He was forced to watch Rajk's execution, which left a deep impression on him. He told people that he felt sick at the sight and had to vomit – but he also noted, impressed, that the last words Rajk spoke were in praise of Stalin. Inevitably, it was soon his turn to be a victim of the purges. Arrested on bogus charges of treason, he was tortured until he 'confessed' and spent three years in jail; he was released during Nagy's premiership when thousands of prisoners were freed. Soon afterwards he met Nagy and thanked him for his help in getting him released. 'I hope that when my turn comes you would do the same for me,' Nagy replied.[2]

Kádár was no Stalinist and at the start of the Revolution he appeared enthusiastic about Nagy and his reforms. He voted within the leadership to press the Russians to withdraw their troops and for Hungary to leave the Warsaw Pact. But when the time came he could withstand neither the temptations nor the threats from Moscow. When he returned at the head of the new government he was loathed as a Judas. He could not leave the Parliament building in safety, so he would not have seen the placards which immediately went up around Budapest abusing him. A famous one that the Soviets destroyed several times but was immediately replaced somewhere else in the city declared: 'Lost: the confidence of the People. Honest finder is asked to return to János Kádár, at 10,000 tanks Street'. He was so hated that when Khrushchev visited Budapest five months after the Uprising was crushed, even the Soviet leader seemed less unpopular than 'the collaborator in chief', as he was called for many years in Budapest. The Soviets did not entirely trust him either. Kádár was under probation by them for some time. Two KGB officers followed him wherever he went, ostensibly for his security, but also to keep an eye on him.

The immediate reprisals against the revolutionaries were brutal. Three hundred and thirty people charged with involvement in fighting during the Uprising were executed, including several in their teens; 22,000 were jailed for various periods.* Hundreds were imprisoned merely for taking part in the brief general strike that was called on the day the Soviets began pounding Budapest with gunfire. Scores more were jailed for attending a march by women a month after the Soviet invasion.

In his treatment of Imre Nagy, Kádár revealed how ruthlessly he could deceive. The Yugoslav Embassy gave the ousted Prime Minister and thirty of his friends and aides refuge on 4 November, but that would never be a permanent solution. Tito in any case had decided that in order to keep stable relations with the USSR it was better to ditch the defeated, failed Nagy than risk souring relations with Moscow that had taken years to mend. After a series of negotiations over the next two weeks, through intermediaries Kádár gave clear assurances in writing that Nagy and his entourage were free to return to their homes. Nagy believed the deal was genuine and never expected the Yugoslavs to betray him. At 6.30 p.m. on 22 November he rang his home in Buda and told his wife that he would be home for dinner. The Interior Department, he said, had sent a bus to collect him and his friends. 'We had hardly gone 200 metres when the bus stopped and we were physically pulled from the bus,' one of the party recalled. The Yugoslavs were involved in the plan and aware of what was happening. Some were set free. Nagy and his closest associates were bundled into a Soviet car and taken to the Red Army's barracks on the outskirts of Budapest under arrest by the KGB. Four days later Nagy and his closest associates were flown to Romania, imprisoned at a villa in Snagov, close to Bucharest. For more than eighteen months ordinary Hungarians had no idea whether they

---

* The saddest story was the case of Péter Mansfeld, barely fifteen at the time of the Revolution, who did no fighting himself but smuggled weapons to various bands of guerrillas. He was active with the insurgents for a few days but then drifted away. After the Revolution he got into trouble with the police for a few petty crimes – stealing food and drinking alcohol. Then he was recognized as a freedom fighter and arrested for his relatively minor role. Originally he was given a ten-year jail sentence. Then, eleven days after his eighteenth birthday, he was hanged.

were alive or dead, while the Hungarians and the Soviets debated what to do with them.[3]

For thirty years it was assumed it was the Russians who decided that Nagy should be tried and executed as an example to others of what their fate would be if they crossed a line of opposition to the USSR. But the evidence that appeared after the collapse of Communism after 1990 prove that in fact it was Kádár who was the most determined to hang him; Khrushchev was 'disheartened' by the prospect and thought it was unnecessary. But Kádár believed that he would never entirely establish himself as the legitimate leader in Hungary if Nagy remained alive, even in jail or in permanent exile. Khrushchev eventually approved the execution. After a six-day secret trial Nagy and two of his closest associates were hanged at dawn on 16 June 1958. In his last recorded words before his death he said: 'If my life is needed to prove that not all Communists are enemies of the people, I gladly make the sacrifice. I know that one day there will be another Nagy trial, which will rehabilitate me. I also know I will have another reburial. I fear only that the funeral oration will be delivered by those who betrayed me.'

The three were buried in the courtyard at Fő Street police headquarters in Budapest, face down, their bodies wrapped in tar paper. Four years later they were secretly buried in an out-of-the-way spot at Rákoskeresztúr Cemetery in an eastern suburb of Budapest.

Kádár was the only East European Communist leader who merited an 'ism' after his name. After the agony of defeat, the immediate crackdown and brutal reprisals in Budapest, he began a partial thaw. Soviet troops returned to barracks and were no longer visible in the city streets. Within two years their numbers were halved. With the help of loans from Moscow, wages went up by 15 to 20 per cent by the middle of 1957, but times were hard for most people. 'In Budapest it took three years before the city stopped looking like a war zone – again,' said Zsindely, who was then working as a research chemist and trying to support two children. 'The appearance of the city altered: it looked dowdier, greyer.' The centre of Pest retained its Habsburg-era charm and beauty, even if it was grimier and dirtier, more tawdry. But the suburbs and the outskirts of the city were transformed over the next fifteen years. A series of housing estates to the south and east temporarily lifted the pressures of homelessness but changed the cityscape. Soon inhabitants saw one major drawback in the Soviet-era buildings, commercial and residential: the 'five-year-plan windows' which continually kept falling out of the blocks or broke their seals, adding to the inefficiency and ugliness. This was a common problem in large parts of the Soviet bloc and the story of these windows and the tower blocks is a microcosm of the craziness and rigidity of the economic system behind the Iron Curtain. Nationalized glass companies were set a production schedule as part of the larger 'five-year plan'. The requirement was invariably the number of panes produced. When they were behind the quota – which was often – workers simply reduced the width and size of the glass to make up the numbers to save time. Hence, when the windows were installed they didn't fit properly. Windows became a huge issue in Budapest living spaces throughout the 1960s and 1970s. Broken windows were frequently a metaphor in Budapest literature at the time for much of what was wrong with life in Communist Hungary.[4]

Over time and in stages the mood thawed and Kádár relaxed his iron grip. From 1959 there was a series of amnesties for many of the rebels from the Uprising, though at the same time a few others were still being executed. The AVO never returned with its brutal old ways, though there was a security force and secret police kept an eye on potential 'troublemakers'. Kádár tried to show some independence, that he was no mere Soviet puppet. He was a clever political tactician. His most significant step in November 1962, six years after the Uprising, was his widely publicized statement, carefully crafted by his intelligent propagandists, that 'those who are not against us are with us'. It was a smart move, performed with deft timing – and, above everything, not at all Hungarian: as this story has shown, and history has proved since, Hungary is a nation of political extremes where differences are not always settled with calm moderation and common sense. Kádárism depended on a social contract. People would appear to forget the trauma of 1956, and Kádár's own less than heroic role in it; they paid lip service to socialism, even if they clearly did not believe in it, and they had to accept the presence of 75,000 Russian troops on Hungarian soil. In return Kádár would provide peace, stability, material benefits and as little interference from the Russians as he could negotiate from Moscow. 'A collective amnesia of the willing took over in Budapest from that moment on,' said the psychologist Ferenc Mérei, who had been jailed after the Revolution but was released in the first amnesty of 1959. The Party's smartest and most sophisticated apologist, György Aczél, put it another way: 'This, once again, was victory in defeat.' The contract depended on the Revolution never being mentioned; Nagy's name was absolutely taboo almost until the collapse of Communism.[5]

Budapest became 'the merriest barracks in the camp'. Kádár got rid of the most creaking elements of central planning and introduced something his propagandists called 'gulyas Communism' that allowed a few private business to operate in Budapest and some private farms in the countryside. On the surface, Budapest flourished from the 1970s – at least compared with Bucharest, Warsaw, Prague or other cities behind the Iron Curtain. A Hilton hotel opened – the first capital in a Communist country to see one – typically a concrete eyesore, but built over the remnants of a medieval monastery in Buda with a magnificent view over the Danube.

By East European standards Budapest was flashy. Elizabeth Taylor celebrated her fortieth birthday at a big party in February 1972 in one of the new hotels that had just opened on the Corso. Richard Burton was filming *Bluebeard* in Budapest – and the couple happened to be there together during one of their marriages. Around 200 guests flew in from all over the world, including Princess Grace of Monaco, Ringo Starr and Raquel Welch – 'Little Mickey Caine had flown in from LA,' wrote Burton in his diary.* A dozen years later, in a coup for the Hungarian Party boss, the British Prime Minister Margaret Thatcher visited Budapest; she was filmed shopping at the central market and was allowed to extol the virtues of laissez-faire capitalism on state-controlled Hungarian TV. People were relatively free to travel to the West – unlike anywhere else in the Eastern bloc.

Dissidents were allowed to operate, within limits. Intellectuals in Budapest were free to hold discreet meetings among themselves and to produce samizdat publications – unheard-of activities in East Berlin, Bucharest or Bratislava. They were monitored, of course, by the secret police but for the most part left alone. The philosopher Miklós Haraszti,

---

* A few nights later, when Burton was filming the movie, the star got wildly drunk at a British Embassy party, insulted two ambassadors and their wives, swore at his host – and then stumbled out. It was gossiped about in Budapest for years afterwards.

editor of the best-known of the underground Budapest magazines, *Beszélő* (Speaker), estimated that by the mid 1980s there were no more than 1,000 regular opposition activists in the whole of the country, 90 per cent of them in Budapest. Every Monday night throughout the 1980s a 'samizdat boutique' was held in the beautiful Andrássy Avenue apartment of the architect László Rajk, son of the most prominent victim of the Stalinist purges, who became an outspoken dissident. Various underground magazines would be on display on a long trestle table; people would select the item they wanted to read and during the week Rajk's team of 'copiers' would produce the texts in time for them to be collected the following Monday night.

Occasionally a writer or activist would be picked up and grilled by the police for a few hours and then released. But on the whole dissidents were allowed to operate unmolested as long as they stayed in Budapest and talked among themselves or within the Communist Party, where various reform groups were growing in size and influence. They were stopped only when they tried to stir up trouble among workers in the factories or labourers on the land. The last political prisoner under the Communists was Haraszti, who took a job in a provincial factory for six months in 1973. His book *Worker in a Worker's State* revealed the appalling inefficiency and dreadful working conditions in Hungarian industry. He was jailed for eight months after it appeared in samizdat. On the whole, the contract between the regime and the people worked – for a while. Kádár became a popular and highly respected figure inside Hungary, more admired by his people than any of the other East European leaders. But over time the unwritten deal was beginning to fall apart.[6]

The main problem with what Kádár called 'the new economic mechanism', but his talented spin doctors called gulyas Communism, was simple. It didn't work. It freed up a few enterprises – small business in Budapest and a few private farms. In Budapest people were encouraged to set up trades for themselves – 'and the predictable thing happened', as one economist from a Budapest research institute, also a part-time small business founder, said. 'The black economy outside the state multiplied and of course was much more efficient than the official state one. Within a few years around 80,000 artisans and part-time traders were

meeting nearly two-thirds of demand, from plumbing to lap dancing.'
The reforms looked good. Economists in the West hailed them as major
steps towards progress in the right direction. When Mikhail Gorbachev
took power in the Soviet Union, his reform agenda of *Perestroika* (re-
structuring) and *Glasnost* (openness) were heavily influenced by the
Hungarian experiment.

But it was a mirage. Gulyas Communism revealed itself after a relatively short time as the worst of both worlds: it retained the constraints
of Communism – bureaucracy and central planning – without the
free-market benefits of capitalism. By the mid 1980s Hungary had to
borrow from the West on a huge scale simply to feed itself – and then
had to borrow increasingly more in order to find the money to repay
the debts. By 1985 Hungary owed foreign banks and some governments
US$18.5 billion (worth around $50 billion in 2022 – more than $200 for
each Hungarian, not far short of an average person's annual income at
that time). Hungary had the highest per capita debt in Europe. It had to
exist on the international equivalent of payday loans. As much as any
other factor, it was debt that brought down the Communist system in
Eastern Europe. Miklós Németh, the economist at the Finance Ministry
who in 1988 became the last Prime Minister in Soviet-era Communist
Hungary, explained the position when he arrived in office. During the
first week he became premier, Hungary received a billion-Deutschmark
credit (worth around US$800 million now). All of it went immediately
towards paying the interest on existing loans: 'In a nutshell everything
had gone wrong with Communism. We were close to an abyss at this
point. Total crisis. The killing of the socialist bloc, of the Communist
system, began the moment the Western banks and financial institutions
gave loans to countries like Hungary. At that point we were on a hook.'[7]

One of the things Hungarians liked about Kádár was that he always led
a simple life and was personally incorruptible – unlike so many of the
other Communist magnates within the socialist bloc, or the leaders of
various persuasions who succeeded him. He lived modestly with his wife
Mária in a medium-sized apartment in the Rózsadomb district of Buda.
He never had a foreign bank account, a villa in the country packed with
servants or wore Savile Row suits. His one obvious pleasure was playing
chess. He had never allowed a personality cult to build up around him.

No pictures of him were on prominent display in Budapest – it was even hard to find archive photos of him in the Party newspaper *Népszabadság* (A Free People). By the 1980s he still held a grip on power, but opposition was growing, mainly from younger men jockeying for their own position within the Party, some of whom could see that the Communist system was falling apart and the Soviets were in no position to shore up their authority. The USSR had lost the will and the ability to cling on to its empire in Eastern Europe.

By 1988 Kádár was visibly ageing and at seventy-six 'he was a shadow of himself. He had always been so sharp. Now he was forgetful, repeating himself at meetings and losing his thread of argument in long rambling monologues,' wrote one of his chief aides. He could barely sleep – some said wracked by guilt about his role in the crackdown after 1956, others simply that insomnia was a common symptom in old age. Many among those who worked for him were sad and embarrassed for him and hoped he would see what was happening and retire gracefully. But he refused to go. In former days the Soviets would simply have replaced him with a younger Comrade. But the new-style Soviet leadership under Gorbachev did not wish to intervene, or at least be seen to. Eventually the ambitious younger Party hacks, discreetly supported by the Kremlin, gave him the rope to hang himself.

That spring the deputy KGB chief, Vladimir Kryuchkov, passed through Budapest and tried to negotiate a dignified exit for the old man. But even then he was reluctant to budge. The grey younger underlings – 'like sharks circling for the kill', as Haraszti described them – organized a Party meeting for 20 May 1988 at Budapest's central Trade Union Hall, close to the Parliament building. It was a humiliating night. Kádár made a long, rambling, semi-incoherent speech justifying his actions over the thirty-two years he had been General Secretary. Towards the end he dried up and froze. He was heard in total silence by an embarrassed audience. At the end Kádár – an ebullient, chatty man in his prime – remained in the hall, alone, talking to nobody, waiting for his wife to collect him and drive him home. It was a pathetic finale to an extraordinary career. He was replaced that night by a dull apparatchik, fifty-seven-year-old Károly Grósz, a Party man through and through, who would be the gravedigger of Communism in Hungary.[8]

36

THE LAST RITES

How to bury people. That is something the Hungarians know very well.

> János Lukács, Budapest, 1900

Stagehands and building contractors had been working for almost a week to turn Heroes' Square into a monumental theatrical set. The twelve giant columns were draped in black cloth. The grand façades of the buildings and the entrance to the People's Park were covered with enormous green, red and white tricolour flags, but with a hole in the middle to remember the revolutionaries of 1956. On one side of the square, high on pedestals and flanked by flares, lay six coffins. By 9 a.m. on Friday, 16 June 1989 around 200,000 people were already packed into the square – an hour before the ceremony they had come to see was due to begin. At least 100,000 more had crowded into the park and the bottom of Andrássy Avenue, then still called Avenue of the People. For the past thirty years Imre Nagy had been an unspoken name. He had been buried in secret after he was hanged exactly thirty-one years earlier; even his family were not allowed to know where he had been laid to rest. Now his funeral was a state occasion, broadcast live on government-controlled television, attended by the most powerful Communists in the land. His prediction at the hour of his death that he would receive an honourable reburial was about to be proved right.

For most people in Europe the most powerful symbol of the collapse of the Soviet Empire in that dizzying year of revolutions was the fall of the Berlin Wall. In Budapest it was the emotional reburial of Nagy – the funeral of an entire era of Hungarian history. 'It was then that we knew for sure the system would change and things would be different,' said teacher Mária Kovács, who along with a majority of mourners that day was not even born when the Uprising had begun. 'Before that we couldn't be certain.'[1]

Four others had been buried with Nagy in unmarked graves. His Defence Minister, Pál Maléter, his secretary, József Szilágyi, his chief political aide, Géza Losonczy, and one of the principal intellectual voices of the 1956 Revolution, the journalist Miklós Gimes.* The regime in 1958 kept the burial a state secret because it did not want the cemetery to become a place of pilgrimage and Nagy to become a martyr. The story of how and where they were buried – plot 301 at Rákoskeresztúr Cemetery – was unlocked in the 1980s by one of the father figures of the dissident movement, Miklós Vásárhelyi, who had been jailed for his brief role as Nagy's press secretary. He was still a well-known journalist who had excellent contacts with the Western press, and the burial place was revealed to him by a friendly prison guard. He could do nothing with the information while Kádár was still in power – rehabilitating Nagy would have condemned the three decades of Kádár's rule, still a dangerous place to go at that time for him and his family of daughters. But when the old man was ousted he and the Nagy family established a Committee for Historical Justice to clear the name of Nagy and the 329 others who were executed for their role in the Uprising.

At the beginning of 1989 the Communist Party in Budapest faced a split about how to deal with the findings about the Nagy era. Was it a revolution or a counter-revolution? It might seem like an abstruse point with the passage of time, but entire careers and livelihoods depended on the outcome of this final struggle of Hungarian Communism – and so did the future of the Party in a new age when the Soviet Empire was falling apart. The reformers broadly won the argument: they accepted Nagy as a martyr and tragic hero. They tried to make deals with an opposition that was now recognized and was growing exponentially. They still believed they might preserve the Party in government. In March they allowed the buried bodies to be exhumed for the reburial and began informal talks with the dissident opposition. On 13 June – three days before the funeral – they announced that a series of 'Round Table Talks' would begin in a few weeks of the kind that had brought Communism

---

* The sixth coffin during the reburial was empty and represented 'the unknown insurgent'.

to a negotiated end in Poland. The Communists believed they could hijack the funeral, and the leaders insisted on being there and speaking – again, as Nagy had predicted the funeral oration at his reburial would be made by those who had betrayed and murdered him – or at least their children.'[2]

The ceremony began at 10 a.m. and from the first moment emotions were raw. The celebrated actor Imre Sinkovits, who as a young man on the first day of the 1956 Revolution had recited Petőfi's National Song at the start of one of the marches, read a letter to the crowd from Imre Nagy's daughter. For two hours mourners filed past the caskets while the names of every Hungarian who died in the Revolution, and the reprisals that followed, were read out.

The most often recalled part of the extraordinary occasion was a fiery and brilliant speech by a twenty-six-year-old bearded figure wearing jeans: Viktor Orbán, head of a newly formed political party of young liberals, FIDESZ. When he approached the platform to speak, most people in the crowd had never heard of him. By the time he finished less than ten minutes later he was a major name in Hungarian public life. 'Young people fail to understand a lot of things about the older generation,' he began:

> We do not understand that the same Party and government leaders who told us to learn from books falsifying the history of the Revolution now vie with each other to touch these coffins, as if they were lucky charms. We do not think there is any reason for us to be grateful for being allowed to bury our martyred dead. We do not owe thanks to anyone for the fact that our political organizations can work today . . . If we can trust our strength . . . we can put an end to the Communist dictatorship; if we are determined enough we can force the Party to submit itself to free elections; and if we don't lose sight of the ideals of 1956, then we will be able to elect a government that will start immediate negotiations for the swift withdrawal of Russian troops.

Huge applause and cheers rang around Heroes' Square for at least five minutes, accompanied by the roar 'Ruszkik haza!' – Russians Go Home. Even at this stage it was daring at a public event to call for Russian troops to leave Hungary. Orbán caused a sensation. It was little surprise that nine years later he became Prime Minister for the first time.

A month later, thousands of mourners attended another funeral in Budapest which laid a major part of Hungary's past to rest. János Kádár lived long enough to see his rival's reburial, though according to one of his friends he was so senile and ill by then that, watching on television, he could not tell what was happening. He died on 6 July and the news was met with genuine grief. Many Hungarians couldn't remember a time without him as leader, and even if they came to despise what had become of the country they nevertheless respected the man. His funeral on 14 July was a major political event. More than 100,000 people turned up at Kerepesi Cemetery, many of whom had been at Nagy's ceremony the previous month. Three million watched on television. He was buried in the same section of the cemetery as many other leading Communists, called 'The Pantheon of the Working Class'. The inscription on his marble gravestone was typical of the man – a personal credo that also spoke for countless numbers of other Communists who had fought for their cause during the twentieth century: 'I was where I had to be. I did what I had to do.'[3]

That summer parts of central Budapest had turned into a refugee camp and there were fights on the streets between rival groups of East Germans. For many years Hungary had been a major summer holiday destination for East Germans. Many stayed in Budapest, which had restaurants and other forms of entertainment that did not exist in dull and staid Dresden, Leipzig or, at that time, Berlin. Many others would head for nearby Lake Balaton, where the beaches were sandy. Hungary was where German families could be reunited, at least briefly, as many West Germans took their holidays there too. In the past the East Germans had returned home after a week or two when the holidays were over. But this summer Hungarian immigration officials began to notice a phenomenon they had not seen before. Many of the East Germans were staying, in the hope that as change seemed possible in Hungary and a new regime close to the West could conceivably be near, they could find a route to West Germany – around the Curtain, not through it. The East German government under the diehard Stalinist leader Erich Honecker insisted the Hungarians send its citizens back, but Budapest was refusing. From mid June new numbers were joining the so-called Trail of the Trabants (after the tinny, box-like, pollution-spewing but charming East German cars) driving through Czechoslovakia and into Hungary, with no intention of returning home. It was causing a crisis in East Germany that would later, in the summer and early autumn, fuel huge demonstrations against the regime there, and prompted a major argument between the two governments.

In Budapest the sheer numbers were causing a humanitarian crisis that was graphically driven home to Prime Minister Németh: 'I was visiting a friend of mine who happened to live near the West German Consul General's house,' he recalled later. 'I had to step over bodies lying along the pavement waiting for the Consulate to open in the morning . . . to get West German passports. I could see the problem with my own eyes. We had to get a solution.'[4]

Budapest had to balance the humanitarian dilemma with the fact that it had a binding agreement with Berlin – made decades ago as part of a Warsaw Pact settlement – not to permit East Germans to cross freely into the West. The East Germans wanted to send planes and trains to take their citizens back. 'We refused and told them they couldn't hunt down people on our streets and take them,' said Németh. Groups of East German secret police spooks – the Stasi – went to Budapest to keep a watch on the refugees. They were attacked by both Hungarians and East Germans, who threw stones at them. The Stasi placed a van outside one of the refugee relief centres from which officials were taking photos of East German families. One night the van was vandalized and the next day it was withdrawn.

Hungarian families were being generous with food and accommodation for the refugees, but in high summer there were more than 15,000 of them in Budapest, along with many more in the provinces, 'and this cannot continue', said Party boss Károly Grósz. There was the prospect of serious violence on Budapest streets and 'some East Germans are already clashing with our border guards'.

The government agonized about what to do. Hungarian people and the West were demanding that the borders be opened for the East Germans. But old Communist Party functionaries were worried about a split with East Germany and what that would mean for the future of the socialist bloc. The final arbiter was the Soviet Union; after all, it was their empire, created by the USSR for the USSR. To the fury of Berlin the Russians said they would not interfere and the decision was up to the Hungarians, even if it meant, as it would, a mass of people leaving East Germany. On 10 September 1989 the Hungarians brought down the Iron Curtian: the (still Communist) government decided to allow any East German who wanted to do so to leave for Austria – a decision that led directly, two months later, to the fall of the Berlin Wall. The Hungarians were not just freeing themselves from a despotic regime, but making history by helping millions of others to seek freedom.[5]

CONCLUSION

Hungarians are the only people in Europe without racial and linguistic relatives. The peculiar intensity of their existence can perhaps be explained by their exceptional loneliness . . . To be a Hungarian is a collective neurosis.

Arthur Koestler, *Arrow in the Blue* (1952)

One of the principal landmarks of Budapest is the Liberty Statue at the high point of the city at the top of Gellért Hill. It has fabulous views across the Danube to Pest, and is also one of the few places in Buda where one can look upwards to the highest reaches of the hills. The monument is eerily beautiful in its way: a female nude Victory figure bearing a palm branch. At 14 metres high on a base of 26 meters, the statue is of epic proportions and can be seen clearly from scores of vantage points throughout the city. Modern guidebooks will say that the figure is an echo of the Statue of Liberty in New York, and represents a similar ideal. But it was not intended as such when the artist Kisfaludi Strobl originally started to make it. Strobl had an eye for the grandiose and the work was personally commissioned by Admiral Horthy in 1942 to be a permanent monument for his younger son István, who was killed in a plane crash on the Eastern Front fighting the Russians during the Second World War.

Strobl hadn't completed the piece by the time the siege of Budapest ended, when some Red Army officers found the work in the sculptor's studio. Somehow Stalin's emissary in charge of Hungary after the war, Kliment Voroshilov, heard about the statue and was told about Strobl's high reputation as a designer of monumental figures. The artist was told to rework it as a memorial to the USSR's heroic Liberation of Hungary from the fascists.

Strobl was just as happy to work for the Communists as for the Horthy regime – he would, after all, get paid twice. But some tweaks were required. Originally the main figure was a man and the palm had been intended as a baby boy. When the work was unveiled in 1947 there was also another figure on the plinth that was definitely not in the original design – a Red Army soldier kneeling by the symbol of 'freedom'. The dedication at the base of the statue was a grateful thanks from Hungary to the USSR. The monument was at that time called the Liberation Statue.

After the first free elections following the collapse of Communism, when a democratic government was installed, the message of the statue was again transformed entirely. The Soviet soldier was removed, along with the original dedication. A plaque has since read: 'In memory of all who gave their lives for the independence, freedom and prosperity of Hungary'.[*1]

The year 1989 was not the end of history. The triumphalists for liberal democracy got that wrong. In Budapest, perhaps more than any other city in Europe, the battle over interpreting the past goes on daily. No ideology, political party or noisy demagogue has possessed the nation's history for long, not even in the ghastly twentieth century during which Hungary and Budapest suffered so much.

The coming and going of statues and memorials in Budapest has itself been the process of history. When Stalin's statue was finally brought down on the first night of the Revolution in 1956 the symbolic act resonated throughout the world – and has since. Was it a token gesture or a piece of vandalism? Was it a skirmish in a wider culture war? I prefer to think of it, rather, as history being made. Similarly, in 2019 the statue of Imre Nagy that had been standing by Parliament Square for a quarter of a century was removed and transferred to a new home in a rarely visited, out-of-the-way spot a kilometre and half from the centre of town. That too made history.

Between 1990 and 2020 more than 450 street names were changed in Budapest, more than 5 per cent of the total – occasionally it was quite confusing as GPS and Google Maps sometimes took a while to catch up. Most, but by no means all, were names of old socialists or writers, artists and musicians with leftist leanings.

---

* Other memorials to the Red Army were removed too, though, surprisingly, it was a few years before it was the turn of a rather moving one to go which had stood for three decades, opposite the US Embassy, with no irony intended, in Freedom Square.

The old regime of Communists did the same. Mussolini Circus, the intersection between the Ring Boulevard and Andrássy Avenue, was re-named Oktogon, as it was before. The elegant Italian Pillar, by the main steps to the Hungarian National Museum in a prime position in central Pest, is an original column from the Forum in Rome. It was given to Hungary in 1929 as an act of friendship – the Italian dictator professed himself a supporter of Hungary's claims to revise the Treaty of Trianon. Up to 1945 a plinth declared that the column was 'A gift to Hungary from Mussolini'. After the war the column remained but the dedica-tion changed; it would not do highlight that it had been presented by a fascist dictator. So the wording became 'A gift from the city of Rome'. Then after 1989 the wording changed again to 'A gift from the Italian nation'.[*2]

After 1989 Budapest became much cleaner and, despite increased traffic, far less polluted. For the most part, decent architects were com-missioned to build some shiny new buildings like the National Theatre, and old ones have been preserved with sensitivity. The heart of Pest is a nineteenth-century creation beloved by film-makers – when Holly-wood wants to reproduce Paris, as often as not they go to Budapest to film it, where production costs and pay rates are far lower. Budapest is – or before the travel restrictions imposed by the Covid-19 pandemic, was – the most often-visited capital in Europe after London, Rome and Paris.[†]

Much has changed over the last three decades of great political, social and economic upheaval. The major fault lines in Budapest's history are as clear now as ever. During the Communist years and immediately afterwards the great popular demand was for Hungary to return to the 'heart of Europe', where Western-oriented figures have identified the

---

* Budapest has devised an interesting and creative way to solve the dilemma of what to do with unwanted statues that are no longer politically correct or have turned into inconvenient parts of history. Instead of being sent to the knackers' yard, a number of giant socialist realist sculptures are on display in an outdoor museum in a southern suburb of the city. It's a fascinating place – not just for those nostalgic for the dead and buried former regime. In the culture wars debate it also strikes me as an intelligent way of acknowledging the past without celebrating it.
† The pandemic obviously played havoc with tourism and no meaningful figures are available about visitor numbers since then.

country's place. Hungary joined NATO in 1999 and, after more than two-thirds of the electorate voted Yes in a referendum, became a member of the European Union in 2004. Yet for many the charm of Europe is wearing thin and the calls of nationalism are growing loud and strong, as they have so often before. Ties with Russia and China were growing stronger – or at least they were before the war in Ukraine broke out in 2022. Hungary is in Europe – and voluntarily apart, between East and West. The role of Jews in Budapest has been a theme woven throughout this narrative. Like everywhere in Europe, it is easy to find examples of anti-Semitism in Hungary. Yet there are around 90,000 Jews living in Budapest who have no wish to leave, feel at home, and form stable communities with lively cultural and social institutions. For most Budapest Jews life is easier and more comfortable in the 2020s – they are more free and equal – than at any time since 1920. The same cannot be said in many other parts of Central and Eastern Europe which endured fascism and Communism.

Another familiar theme in Hungarian history is mass emigration, and this has returned as a significant issue, though it is rarely talked about within the country. Since Hungary joined the EU the population has fallen by at least 9 per cent, mostly because people have left – again, as so often before, the younger and better-educated, more able to begin lives elsewhere.[3]

Revolutionary and sudden transformation – political, social, economic – have been constant features of life in Budapest. But in so many ways the city has stayed the same. I started writing the first few pages of this book in one of my favourite coffee houses in downtown Pest – at exactly the same location where many other authors have worked, or sat, or loafed over many generations. At the next table an animated group of young people were gossiping about life and love. A small band of musicians were playing in the square opposite, as performers have done most days at that early evening hour for more than a century. Despite turmoil, there are things in Budapest that never change.

NOTES

INTRODUCTION

[1] János Lukács, *Budapest 1900: A Historical Portrait of a City and its Culture* (New York, 1988), p. 35

PROLOGUE

[1] Lukács, p. 41
[2] Useful sources for the millennium celebration come from Lukács, Bob Dent, *Budapest: A Cultural and Literary History* (Oxford, 2007) and László Kontler, *A History of Hungary: Millennium in Central Europe* (Basingstoke, 2002)
[3] Judit Frigyesi, *Béla Bartók and Turn-of-the-Century Budapest* (Berkeley, CA, 2000), p. 67
[4] Ibid., p. 85
[5] Gyula Krúdy, ed. and trans. John Bátki, *Krúdy's Chronicles: Turn-of-the-Century Hungary in Gyula Krúdy's Journalism* (Budapest, 2000), p. 67
[6] Lukács, p. 88
[7] Kati Marton, *The Great Escape: Nine Jews Who Fled Hitler and Changed the World* (New York, 2008), p. 97.
[8] Krúdy, p. 92

CHAPTER ONE: AQUINCUM

[1] Annabel Barber, *Blue Guide: Budapest* (London, 2018), p. 103
[2] *New Hungarian Quarterly*, vol. 2 (Spring 1991), special issue on Aquincum and Roman Buda, p. 97
[3] Sir Bryan Cartledge, *The Will to Survive: A History of Hungary* (London, 2009), p. 72
[4] C. A. MacArtney, *The Magyars in the Ninth Century* (Cambridge, 1930), p. 238
[5] *New Hungarian Quarterly*, vol. 2 (Spring 1991), p. 133
[6] Arminius Vámbéry, *Hungary in Ancient, Medieval and Modern Times* (London, 1986), p. 178

CHAPTER TWO: THE MAGYARS

[1] Quoted in Paul Lendvai, trans. Ann Major, *The Hungarians* (London, 1990), p. 74
[2] Denis Sinor, *History of Hungary* (New York, 1959), p. 103
[3] Kontler, p. 46
[4] Géza Buzinkay, *An Illustrated History of Budapest* (Budapest, 1998), p. 23
[5] Lendvai, p. 84
[6] Vámbéry, p. 59
[7] Buzinkay, p. 46

8 Lendvai, p. 81
9 Cartledge, pp. 86–9
10 Kálmán Benda and Erik Fügedi, *A Magyar korona regénye* (Budapest, 1988), p. 135
11 Miklós Molnár, *A Concise History of Hungary* (Cambridge, 2001), pp. 78–88
12 Sinor, p. 88
13 Vámbéry, p. 87

CHAPTER THREE: THE KHANS INVADE

1 Kontler, p. 90; his account of the Mongol invasion is excellent and lively. Other useful sources are Lendvai and Molnár. I have drawn from all of them for this chapter.
2 Molnár, p. 101
3 György Györffy, *Az Árpád-kori Magyarország történeti földrajza* (Budapest, 1986), p. 47

CHAPTER FOUR: THE RAVEN KING

1 Lendvai, p. 103
2 Cartledge, p. 137
3 Kontler, p. 88
4 János Arany, Klára Zách, trans. Watson Kirkconnell, *The Hungarian Reader* (Budapest, 1991), p. 137
5 Molnár, p. 102
6 Brendan Simms, *Europe: The Struggle for Ascendancy, 1453 to the Present* (London, 2013), p. 75
7 Molnár, p. 107
8 Lendvai, p. 119
9 Marcus Tanner, *The Raven King: Matthias Corvinus and the Fate of His Lost Library* (New Haven, CT, and London, 2008), p. 95. This is a wonderful book on the reign of Matthias and Renaissance Hungary. It is a major source for this chapter, along with Lendvai and Kontler.

CHAPTER FIVE: THE EMPIRE STRIKES BACK

1 Györffy, p. 102
2 Cartledge, p. 138
3 Lendvai, p. 157
4 Simms, p. 176
5 Quoted in Molnár, p. 116
6 Tanner, p. 235
7 Ibid., p. 242

CHAPTER SIX: BUDUN – A TURKISH TOWN

1 András Török, *Budapest: A Critical Guide* (Budapest, 2006), p. 125
2 Tanner, p. 267
3 Lendvai, p. 195
4 Vámbéry, p. 162
5 Quoted in Kontler, p. 156
6 Klára Hegyi, *Egy világbirodalom végvidékén* (Budapest, 1976), pp. 46–9. Part of the short book series *Magyar História*. This is excellent on Ottoman Buda.
7 Ibid., p. 78

CHAPTER SEVEN: DIVISION OF THE SPOILS

1 Gábor Vermes, *Hungarian Culture and Politics in the Habsburg Monarchy, 1711–1848* (Budapest, 2014), p. 134
2 Andrew Wheatcroft, *The Enemy at the Gate: Habsburgs, Ottomans and the Battle for Europe* (London, 2009), p. 137
3 Jenő Szűcs, trans. Warren Turner, *The Three Regions of Historical Hungary* (Budapest, 1983), p. 47
4 Ibid., p. 98
5 Lady Mary Wortley Montagu, *Letters and Works* (London, 1962), p. 149

CHAPTER EIGHT: BUDA REGAINED

1 Jacob Richards, *A Journal of the Siege of Buda* (London, 1701), p. 65
2 Lendvai, p. 246
3 Wheatcroft, p. 298
4 Richards, p. 71
5 Hegyi, p. 67
6 Quoted in Buzinkay, p. 134
7 Quoted in Lendvai, p. 197
8 Quoted in Buzinkay, p. 202

CHAPTER NINE: THE BAROQUE – GLOOM AND GLORY

1 Henrik Marczali, *Hungary in the Eighteenth Century* (Budapest, 2019), p. 67
2 Vermes, p. 179
3 Lendvai, p. 214
4 Ferenc Rákóczi, *Confessions of a Sinner* (Paris, 1778), p. 157
5 Marczali, p. 71
6 Gyula Szekfű, *A Samuzott Rákóczi* (Budapest, 1940), p. 90
7 Domokos Kosáry, *Culture and Society in Eighteenth-Century Hungary* (Budapest, 1987), pp. 178–80
8 Szűcs, p. 105
9 Julia Pardoe, *The City of the Magyar* (London, 1840), p. 77, and John Paget, *Hungary and Transylvania* (London, 1839), p. 98
10 Sinor, p. 263
11 Kosáry, p. 110
12 Robert Townson, *Travels in Hungary, With a Short Account of Vienna in the Year 1793* (London, 1797), p. 135

CHAPTER TEN: LANGUAGE, TRUTH AND LOGIC

1 Lendvai, pp. 275–7
2 Martyn Rady, *The Habsburgs: The Rise and Fall of a World Power* (London, 2020), pp. 146–8
3 For the Hungarian Jacobins see Kosáry, pp. 266–71, Lendvai, pp. 280–3, and Rady, pp. 149–52
4 I am indebted to the brilliant George Szirtes, an exile from Budapest who has managed the feat of writing great poetry in Hungarian and English, for tips on the Hungarian language – and to the late Norman Stone, an incomparably gifted linguist, for advice about the neologs and their work in transforming the Hungarian language.
5 Cartledge, pp. 279–83

[6] Norman Stone, *Hungary: A Short History* (London, 2019), p. 48
[7] Dent, pp. 123–5
[8] Paget, p. 83
[9] Lendvai, p. 296

CHAPTER ELEVEN: THE BRIDGE BUILDER

[1] Kosáry, p. 287; quote from Széchenyi, Barber, p. 157
[2] George Barany, *Stephen Széchenyi and the Awakening of Hungarian Nationalism, 1791–1841* (Princeton, NJ, 1991), p. 114
[3] Lendvai, p. 313
[4] Molnár, p. 217
[5] Barany, p. 126
[6] Ibid., pp. 136–9, and Lendvai, pp. 316–18
[7] Kosáry, pp. 291–3
[8] Barany, pp. 132–5
[9] Lendvai, p. 315
[10] Ibid., p. 317

CHAPTER TWELVE: THE GREAT FLOOD

[1] Kontler, pp. 265–6
[2] Wesselényi quotes in Dent, p. 186, and Pardoe, p. 136
[3] Péter Hanák, *The Garden and the Workshop* (Princeton, NJ, 1998), p. 113
[4] Alan Walker, *Reflections on Liszt* (Ithaca, NY, 2011), pp. 109–11
[5] Pardoe, p. 146
[6] Oliver Hilmes, trans. Stewart Spencer, *Franz Liszt: Musician, Celebrity, Superstar* (New Haven, CT, and London, 2017), pp. 49–53
[7] Molnár, pp. 266–8, and Cartledge, pp. 291–4
[8] Quoted in Lendvai, p. 329

CHAPTER THIRTEEN: THE IDES OF MARCH

[1] Rady, pp. 289–91
[2] Lendvai, p. 298
[3] István Deák, *The Lawful Revolution: Louis Kossuth and the Hungarians, 1848–1849* (New York, 1979), p. 35
[4] Ibid., pp. 42–9
[5] Molnár, pp. 219–26
[6] Deák, pp. 55–7
[7] Alexander Herzen, trans. Constance Garnett, *My Past and Thoughts: Memoirs* (London, 1968), p. 67; background on Kossuth, Lendvai, pp. 299–302, and Cartledge, pp. 368–71
[8] Deák, pp. 67–70
[9] Louis Kossuth, trans. Ferencz Jausz, *Memories of My Exile* (London and New York, 1880), pp. 19–25
[10] Deák, pp. 80–6
[11] Ibid., pp. 91–6, and Lendvai, pp. 312–16

CHAPTER FOURTEEN: THE REVOLUTIONARY WAR

[1] Molnár, pp. 234–6, and Deák, pp. 138–40
[2] Lendvai, pp. 320–4, and Mary Gluck, *The Invisible Jewish Budapest: Metropolitan Culture at the Fin de Siècle* (Madison, WI, 2019), pp. 39–41
[3] Cartledge, pp. 370–2
[4] Deák, pp. 178–81
[5] Lendvai, pp. 341–3, and Kontler, pp. 291–3
[6] Kossuth, pp. 49–51
[7] Deák, pp. 259–62, and Paul Ignotus, *Hungary* (London, 1972), p. 77
[8] Deák, pp. 291–6, and Lendvai, pp. 370–3

CHAPTER FIFTEEN: A REVENGE TRAGEDY

[1] Cartledge, p. 383
[2] Deák, pp. 301–5, and Kontler, pp. 218–20
[3] Lendvai, pp. 391–4
[4] Deák, pp. 309–10
[5] Ibid., pp. 337–9

CHAPTER SIXTEEN: JUDAPEST

[1] Kinga Frojimovics et al., *Jewish Budapest: Monuments, Rites, History* (Budapest, 1998, 2 vols), vol. 1, p. 19
[2] Lukács, p. 67
[3] Gluck, pp. 98–101
[4] George Konrád, trans. Jim Tucker, *A Guest in My Own Country: A Hungarian Life* (London, 2008), p. 17, and Lendvai, p. 386
[5] Frojimovics et al., vol. 1, pp. 210–13
[6] Raphael Patai, *The Jews of Hungary: History, Culture, Psychology* (Detroit, MI, 1996), pp. 56–7
[7] Endre Ady, trans. G.F. Cushing, *The Explosive Country: A Selection of Articles and Studies 1898–1916* (Budapest, 1977), pp. 45–6

CHAPTER SEVENTEEN: EMPRESS SISI

[1] Éva Somogyi, *Absulotizmus és kiegyezés 1849–1867* (Budapest, 1981)
[2] Lendvai, pp. 296–8
[3] Cartledge, p. 393
[4] Brigitte Hamann, trans. Ruth Hein, *The Reluctant Empress: A Biography of Empress Elisabeth of Austria* (New York, 1986), p. 157
[5] Rady, pp. 229–31, and Hamann, pp. 168–71
[6] Kontler, pp. 293–5
[7] Quoted in Dent, p. 175
[8] András Gerő (ed.), *Hungarian Liberals* (Budapest, 1999), p. 117
[9] Lendvai, p. 338

CHAPTER EIGHTEEN: THE DUAL MONARCHY – VICTORY IN DEFEAT

[1] Rady, pp. 271–4
[2] Somogyi, pp. 86–9

3 Hamann, pp. 195–7
4 Lendvai, p. 339
5 Hamann, pp. 205–8
6 Rady, pp. 276–8
7 Lendvai, pp. 349–53, and Hamann, pp. 204–15, are both excellent on these negotiations.
8 Molnár, pp. 276–81
9 Hamann, pp. 310–13. For sources on dualism read Robert Musil, *The Man Without Qualities* (London, 1999), and Rady, pp. 289–92

CHAPTER NINETEEN: BUDAPEST IS BORN

1 Quoted in Cartledge, p. 315
2 Antal Szerb, trans. Len Rix, *A Martian's Guide to Budapest* (Budapest, 2015), p. 12
3 Sándor Márai, *Memoir of Hungary, 1944–1948* (Budapest, 2002), p. 166, and Frojimovics et al., vol. 2, p. 128
4 Lukács, pp. 45–8
5 Krúdy, p. 58
6 Norman Lebrecht, *Why Mahler?* (London, 2010), p. 87
7 Ignotus, pp. 209–12
8 Walker, p. 109, and Ignotus, p. 214
9 Hilmes, p. 276

CHAPTER TWENTY: CAFÉ CULTURE

1 Dezső Kosztolányi, trans. Richard Aczel, *Skylark* (Budapest, 2001), p. 88
2 Lukács, p. 114
3 Krúdy, p. 136
4 Marton, pp. 146–9, and Mátyás Sárközi, *The Play's the Thing: The Life of Ferenc Molnár* (London, 2004), p. 93
5 Gluck, p. 189
6 Quoted in Gluck, p. 198; Barber, p. 176

CHAPTER TWENTY-ONE: THE HUNGARIAN POGROMS

1 Patai, pp. 93–5
2 Lendvai, p. 387
3 Frojimovics et al., vol. 2, pp. 98–9
4 István Deák, 'The Holocaust in Hungary', *New Hungarian Quarterly*, vol. 3 (Autumn 1997), p. 87
5 Gluck, p. 88
6 Patai, pp. 67–8
7 Randolph Braham, *The Politics of Genocide: The Holocaust in Hungary* (New York, 1994, 2 vols), vol. 1, pp. 74–5
8 Kontler, p. 277

CHAPTER TWENTY-TWO: ILLIBERAL DEMOCRACY

1 Gyula Illyés, trans. G.F. Cushing, *People of the Puszta* (Budapest, 1969), p. 101
2 Péter Hanák, *Hungary in the Austro-Hungarian Monarchy* (Vienna, 1967), p. 46
3 Kosáry, p. 288
4 Lukács, p. 89

[5] Dent, p. 176
[6] Andrew Janos, *The Politics of Backwardness in Hungary, 1825–1945* (Princeton, NJ, 1982), p. 167
[7] Oszkár Jászi, *Revolution and Counter-Revolution in Hungary* (London, 1924), p. 79

CHAPTER TWENTY-THREE: MY COUNTRY RIGHT OR WRONG

[1] Lendvai, p. 401
[2] Eric Hobsbawm, *Nations and Nationalism since 1780: Programme, Myth, Reality* (Cambridge, 1990), pp. 148–9
[3] Gerő, p. 98
[4] Quoted in Cartledge, p. 418
[5] Jászi, p. 101
[6] Endre Ady, *New Poems* (Budapest, 1910) p. 32
[7] Deák, p. 313

CHAPTER TWENTY-FOUR: THE BEGINNING OF THE END

[1] Sárközi, p. 139
[2] Arthur Koestler, *Arrow in the Blue* (London, 1952), p. 79
[3] Mihály Károlyi, *Memoirs of Michael Karolyi: Faith Without Illusion* (London, 1956), pp. 156–7
[4] Krúdy, p. 157, and Mihály Károlyi, pp. 146–7
[5] Lendvai, p. 418
[6] Mihály Károlyi, pp. 267–8
[7] Norman Stone, *The Eastern Front, 1914–1917* (London, 1998), p. 89
[8] Marton, p. 176, for Szilard quote, and Catherine Károlyi, *A Life Together: Memoirs* (London, 1966), p. 135

CHAPTER TWENTY-FIVE: LENIN'S PUPIL

[1] Mihály Károlyi, pp. 312–14
[2] Koestler, pp. 89–90; Szilard quoted in Marton, p. 109
[3] Zsunna Nagy, 'The Hungarian Republic of Councils', *New Hungarian Quarterly*, vol. 3 (1969), p. 76
[4] Rudolf Tőkés, *Béla Kun and the Hungarian Soviet Republic* (New York, 1967), p. 87
[5] Lendvai, p. 412

CHAPTER TWENTY-SIX: THE ADMIRAL WITHOUT A NAVY

[1] Thomas Sakmyster, *Hungary's Admiral on Horseback: Miklós Horthy, 1918–1944* (Boulder, CO, 1994), pp. 56–7
[2] Jászi, p. 243
[3] Deák, 'The Holocaust in Hungary', p. 14
[4] Lendvai, p. 415
[5] Deák, 'The Holocaust in Hungary', p. 25
[6] Sakmyster, pp. 118–20
[7] Koestler, p. 230
[8] Kontler, pp. 415–16
[9] Marton, pp. 216–18
[10] Molnár, pp. 298–9
[11] Lendvai, p. 417

[12] Raul Hilberg, *The Destruction of the European Jews* (New Haven, CT, and London, 2003), p. 98

CHAPTER TWENTY-SEVEN: MARCHING IN STEP WITH HITLER

[1] Sakmyster, p. 267
[2] Konrád, p. 158
[3] Konrád, p. 54
[4] Sakmyster, pp. 219–21, and Konrád, p. 115
[5] Marton, p. 227
[6] Quoted in Victor Sebestyen, *Twelve Days: The Story of the 1956 Hungarian Revolution* (London, 2006), p. 197
[7] Lendvai, pp. 420–2
[8] Márai, p. 204

CHAPTER TWENTY-EIGHT: MADNESS VISIBLE

[1] Deák, 'The Holocaust in Hungary', p. 49
[2] Andy Grove quoted in Marton, p. 219; German invasion of Hungary, Sakmyster, pp. 289–92
[3] Braham, vol. 1, pp. 298–300
[4] Deák, 'The Holocaust in Hungary', p. 56
[5] Hilberg, pp. 289–91; Miklós Radnóti poem in Adam Makkai, *In Quest of the 'Miracle Stag': The Poetry of Hungary* (Chicago, 1996), p. 88; and Feyno quote, Barber, p. 202
[6] Braham, vol. 1, pp. 215–16
[7] Sakmyster, p. 290
[8] For public attitudes and media coverage of Horthy legacy the website https://hungarianspectrum.org is very useful

CHAPTER TWENTY-NINE: THE SIEGE OF BUDAPEST

[1] Harold Nicolson, ed. Nigel Nicolson, *Diaries*, vol. 2 (London, 2009), p. 146
[2] Deák, 'The Holocaust in Hungary', p. 37
[3] Krisztián Ungváry, *The Siege of Budapest: One Hundred Days in World War II* (New Haven, CT, and London, 2006), p. 105
[4] Ibid., p. 129
[5] Braham, vol. 2, pp. 315–18
[6] Hilberg, pp. 297–300, and Deák, 'The Holocaust in Hungary', pp. 37–8
[7] Ungváry, pp. 201–32
[8] Ibid., pp. 289–91
[9] Hilberg, pp. 365–7, and Patai, pp. 387–90
[10] Deák, 'The Holocaust in Hungary', pp. 38–9

CHAPTER THIRTY: LIBERATION

[1] Ferenc Nagy, trans. Stephen K. Swift, *The Struggle Behind the Iron Curtain* (New York, 1948), and Márai, p. 198
[2] George Paloczi-Horvath, *The Undefeated* (London, 1993), p. 89
[3] Charles Gati, *Hungary and the Soviet Bloc* (Durham, NC, 1986), p. 146
[4] Márai, p. 187
[5] Sebestyen, p. 48

6 Tibor Méray, trans. Charles Lam Markmann, *That Day in Budapest* (New York, 1969), p. 89

CHAPTER THIRTY-ONE: THE IRON CURTAIN DESCENDS

1 Sebestyen, pp. 51–3
2 Ignotus, pp. 218–19
3 Sebestyen, pp. 67–70
4 György Litván (ed.), trans. János M. Bak and Lyman H. Legters, *The Hungarian Revolution of 1956: Reform, Revolt, and Repression, 1953–1963* (London, 1996), p. 265
5 George Faludy, trans. Kathleen Szasz, *My Happy Days in Hell* (London, 1987), p. 156
6 Béla Király et al. (eds.), *The First War Between Socialist States: The Hungarian Revolution of 1956 and Its Impact* (New York, 1984), p. 192
7 Sebestyen, p. 71
8 Molnár, p. 328
9 Charles Gati, *Failed Illusions: Moscow, Washington, Budapest and the 1956 Hungarian Revolt* (Stanford, CA, 2006), p. 178

CHAPTER THIRTY-TWO: THE HOUSE OF TERROR

1 Konrád, p. 198
2 Sebestyen, p. 162
3 Faludy, pp. 279–80
4 Litván, p. 114
5 Ignotus, pp. 289–91
6 Sebestyen, pp. 178–82

CHAPTER THIRTY-THREE: REVOLUTION – AGAIN

1 Sebestyen, pp. 93–5
2 Litván, p. 104
3 For the best background on Imre Nagy and his opinions see János Rainer, *Imre Nagy: A Biography* (London, 2009), and Tamás Aczél and Tibor Méray, *The Revolt of the Mind: A Case History of Intellectual Resistance Behind the Iron Curtain* (London, 2015)
4 Rainer, pp. 196–200
5 Sebestyen, pp. 135–7
6 Ignotus, p. 298
7 Molnár, p. 301
8 Sándor Kopácsi, *In the Name of the Working Class: The Inside Story of the Hungarian Revolution* (New York, 1987), pp. 120–3

CHAPTER THIRTY-FOUR: BETRAYAL IN MOSCOW

1 Sebestyen, pp. 201–4
2 Aczél and Méray, pp. 186–9
3 Litván, pp. 208–10

CHAPTER THIRTY-FIVE: THE MERRIEST BARRACKS IN THE CAMP

1 Rainer, pp. 189–91

2 Sebestyen, pp. 205–8, and Roger Gough, *A Good Comrade: János Kádár, Communism and Hungary* (London, 2006), p. 146

3 Rainer, p. 301

4 Lendvai, pp. 413–14

5 From conversation with Miklós Haraszti, 15 June 2002

6 Victor Sebestyen, *Revolution 1989: The Fall of the Soviet Empire* (London, 2009), pp. 89–91

7 Mária Schmidt and László Tóth (eds.), *From Totalitarian to Democratic Hungary: Evolution and Transformation, 1990–2000* (Boulder, CO, 2000), pp. 134–5

8 Sebestyen, *Revolution 1989*, p. 167

CHAPTER THIRTY-SIX: THE LAST RITES

1 The most brilliant account of the events of 1989 remains Timothy Garton Ash, *The Magic Lantern: The Revolution of '89 Witnessed in Warsaw, Budapest, Berlin and Prague* (London, 1990)

2 Sebestyen, *Revolution 1989*, pp. 209–11

3 Garton Ash, pp. 127–8

4 Nigel Swain, *Hungary: The Rise and Fall of Feasible Socialism* (London, 1992), pp. 189–91

5 Sebestyen, *Revolution 1989*, pp. 218–20

CONCLUSION

1 Bob Dent, *Budapest: A Cultural and Literary History* (Oxford, 2007) contains an amusing and interesting guide to the various name changes in Budapest streets over the last decades and of the fate of various politically charged statues.

2 Stone, *Hungary*, p. 198

3 Ivan Krastev and Stephen Holmes, *The Light that Failed: A Reckoning* (London, 2019), p. 129

BIBLIOGRAPHY

Ady, Endre, trans. G.F. Cushing, *The Explosive Country: A Selection of Articles and Studies 1898–1916* (Budapest, 1977)

Ady, Endre, trans. George Szirtes, *Lyrics* (Budapest, 1986)

Barany, George, *Stephen Széchenyi and the Awakening of Hungarian Nationalism, 1791–1841* (Princeton, NJ, 1991)

Barber, Annabel, *Blue Guide: Budapest* (London, 2018)

Bede, Béla, *225 Highlights of Hungarian Art Nouveau Architecture* (Budapest, 2012)

Braham, Randolph, *The Nazis' Last Victims: The Holocaust in Hungary* (New York, 2002)

Buzinkay, Géza, *An Illustrated History of Budapest* (Budapest, 1998)

Carlberg, Ingrid, *Raoul Wallenberg* (London, 2017)

Cartledge, Sir Bryan, *The Will to Survive: A History of Hungary* (London, 2009)

Deák, István, *The Lawful Revolution: Louis Kossuth and the Hungarians, 1848–1849* (New York, 1979)

Dent, Bob, *Budapest: A Cultural and Literary History* (Oxford, 2007)

Faludy, George, trans. Kathleen Szasz, *My Happy Days in Hell* (London, 1987)

Frigyesi, Judit, *Béla Bartók and Turn-of-the-Century Budapest* (Berkeley, CA, 2000)

Garton Ash, Timothy, *The Magic Lantern: The Revolution of '89 Witnessed in Warsaw, Budapest, Berlin and Prague* (London, 1990)

Gati, Charles, *Failed Illusions: Moscow, Washington, Budapest and the 1956 Hungarian Revolt* (Stanford, CA, 2006)

Gerő, András, *The Hungarian Parliament 1867–1918: A Mirage of Power* (Boulder, CO, 1997)

Gluck, Mary, *George Lukács and His Generation 1900–1918* (Cambridge, MA, 1991)

Gluck, Mary, *The Invisible Jewish Budapest: Metropolitan Culture at the Fin de Siècle* (Madison, WI, 2019)

Györffy, György, *Az Árpád-kori Magyarország történeti földrajza* (Budapest, 1986)

Gyurgyák, János, *A Zsidókérdés Magyarországon* (Budapest, 2001)

Hajdu, Joe, *Budapest: A History of Grandeur and Catastrophe* (London, 2015)

Hamann, Brigitte, trans. Ruth Hein, *The Reluctant Empress: A Biography of Empress Elisabeth of Austria* (New York, 1986)

Hegyi, Klára, *Egy világbirodalom végvidékén* (Budapest, 1976)

Hilberg, Raul, *The Destruction of the European Jews* (New Haven, CT, and London, 2003)

Hilmes, Oliver, trans. Stewart Spencer, *Franz Liszt: Musician, Celebrity, Superstar* (New Haven, CT, and London, 2017)

Horthy, Miklós, *A Life for Hungary: Memoirs* (New York, 1957)

Ignotus, Paul, *Hungary* (London, 1972)

Károlyi, Catherine, *A Life Together: Memoirs* (London, 1966)

Károlyi, Mihály, *Memoirs: Faith Without Illusion* (London, 1956)

Koestler, Arthur, *Arrow in the Blue* (London, 1952)

Koestler, Arthur, *The Invisible Writing* (London, 2005)

Konrád, George, trans. Jim Tucker, *A Guest in My Own Country: A Hungarian Life* (London, 2008)

Kontler, László, *A History of Hungary: Millennium in Central Europe* (Basingstoke, 2002)

Kosáry, Domokos, *Culture and Society in Eighteenth-Century Hungary* (Budapest, 1987)

Kovrig, Bennett, *The Myth of Liberation: East-Central Europe in U.S. Diplomacy and Politics Since 1941* (Baltimore, MD, and London, 1973)

Krasznahorkai, László, trans. George Szirtes, *The Melancholy of Resistance* (London, 1998)

Krúdy, Gyula, trans. George Szirtes, *The Adventures of Sindbad* (Budapest, 1997)

Krúdy, Gyula, ed. and trans. John Bátki, *Krúdy's Chronicles: Turn-of-the-Century Hungary in Gyula Krúdy's Journalism* (Budapest, 2000)

Lebrecht, Norman, *Why Mahler?* (London, 2010)

Lendvai, Paul, trans. Ann Major, *The Hungarians* (London, 1990)

Litván, György (ed.), trans. János M. Bak and Lyman H. Legters, *The Hungarian Revolution of 1956: Reform, Revolt and Repression 1953–1963* (London, 1996)

Lukács, János, *Budapest 1900: A Historical Portrait of a City and its Culture* (New York, 1988)

MacArtney, C. A., *The Magyars in the Ninth Century* (Cambridge, 1930)

MacArtney, C. A., *October Fifteenth: A History of Modern Hungary 1929–1945* (Edinburgh, 1963)

Márai, Sándor, *Memoir of Hungary, 1944–1948* (Budapest, 2002)

Marczali, Henrik, *Hungary in the Eighteenth Century* (Budapest, 2019)

Marton, Kati, *Wallenberg: Missing Hero* (New York, 1982)

Marton, Kati, *The Great Escape: Nine Jews Who Fled Hitler and Changed the World* (New York, 2008)

Mindszenty, Cardinal József, trans. Richard and Clara Winston, *Memoirs* (London, 1974)

Molnár, Miklós, *A Concise History of Hungary* (Cambridge, 2001)

Nagy, Ferenc, trans. Stephen K. Swift, *The Struggle Behind the Iron Curtain* (New York, 1948)

Paget, John, *Hungary and Transylvania* (London, 1839)

Paloczi-Horvath, George, *The Undefeated* (London, 1993)

Pardoe, Julia, *The City of the Magyar* (London, 1840)

Patai, Raphael, *The Jews of Hungary: History, Culture, Psychology* (Detroit, MI, 1996)

Rady, Martyn, *The Habsburgs: The Rise and Fall of a World Power* (London, 2020)

Rainer, János et al. (eds.), *The 1956 Hungarian Revolution: A History in Documents* (Budapest, 2002)

Rainer, János, trans. Lyman H. Legters, *Imre Nagy: A Biography* (London, 2009)

Ripp, Zoltán, *Rendszerváltás Magyarországon 1987–1990* (Budapest, 2006)

Romcsis, Ignác, *Magyaorsszág története a XX században* (Budapest, 2000)

Rupnik, Jacques, *The Other Europe* (London, 1988)

Sárközi, Mátyás, *The Play's the Thing: The Life of Ferenc Molnár* (London, 2004)

Schmidt, Maria, *Diktatúrák ördögszekéren* (Budapest, 1998)

Sebestyen, Victor, *Twelve Days: The Story of the 1956 Hungarian Revolution* (London, 2006)

Sebestyen, Victor, *Revolution 1989: The Fall of the Soviet Empire* (London, 2009)

Simms, Brendan, *Europe: The Struggle for Ascendancy, 1453 to the Present* (London, 2013)

Sinor, Denis, *A History of Hungary* (New York, 1959)

Somogyi, Éva, *Absulotizmus és kiegyezés 1849–1867* (Budapest, 1981)

Stone, Norman, *Hungary: A Short History* (London, 2019)

Szerb, Antal, *A Magyar irodalom története* (Budapest, 1936)

Szerb, Antal, trans. Len Rix, *Love in a Bottle* (London, 2010)

Szerb, Antal, trans. Len Rix, *A Martian's Guide to Budapest* (Budapest, 2015)

Szirtes, George, *The Budapest File* (London, 2000)

Tanner, Marcus, *The Raven King: Matthias Corvinus and the Fate of His Lost Library* (New Haven, CT, and London, 2008)

Taylor, A.J.P., *The Habsburg Monarchy 1809–1918* (London, 1948)

Thorpe, Nick, *The Danube: A Journey Upriver from the Black Sea to the Black Forest* (New Haven, CT, and London, 2013)

Török, András, *Budapest: A Critical Guide* (Budapest, 2006)

Ungváry, Krisztián, *The Siege of Budapest: One Hundred Days in World War II* (New Haven, CT, and London, 2006)

Vámbéry, Arminius, *Hungary in Ancient, Medieval and Modern Times* (London, 1986)

Vermes, Gábor, *Hungarian Culture and Politics in the Habsburg Monarchy, 1711–1848* (Budapest, 2014)

Walker, Alan, *Reflections on Liszt* (Ithaca, NY, 2011)

Wheatcroft, Andrew, *The Enemy at the Gate: Habsburgs, Ottomans and the Battle for Europe* (London, 2009)

ACKNOWLEDGEMENTS

I have been returning to Budapest since the mid 1970s and this book has been a journey into my background, which I have loved researching and writing. The work moved me and occasionally disturbed me. It has been the result over the decades of probably 150 visits, some of months (for example during research on my book about the Hungarian Revolution) and some of just a few days.

Two superb books have been an inspiration and have offered a wealth of ideas and insights: My friend Paul Lendvai's magnificent work *The Hungarians*, and the late János Lukács's *Budapest 1900*, which portrayed the personality of the city like no others. I am indebted to both.

Innumerable people have helped me with advice, tours of their favourite places of the city, restaurant tips, political explications, sharing their artistic sensibilities. They have all coloured the work in various ways. In particular I wish to thank for the time they have so generously given to me: Anne Applebaum, Dominic Arbuthnott, Annabel Barber, Csaba Békés, Katalin Bogyay, Gábor Demszky, István Dénes, Jayne Diggory, Paul Diggory, Géza Doromby, László Eörsi, Wendy Franks, Júlia Gábor, the late William de Gelsey, Ágnes Gergely, Miklós Haraszti, Victoria Hislop, Katalin Jánosi, Andrea Kalman, Klára Keleméri, Barbara Kiss, János Kiss, György Konrád, Ferenc Köszeg, Tony Láng, Adam LeBor, Károly Makk, Simon Sebag Montefiore, Mark Odescalchi, the late Norman Stone, László Rajk, István Rév, Sándor Révész, Andrew Roberts, Mátyás Sárközi, Amanda Sebestyen, András Simor, Csilla Strbik, Mihály Szilágyi, George Szirtes, Nick Thorpe, Sándor Vas, Mária Vásárhelyi, Zsolt Walko, Adrian Wilsdon and Sándor Zsindely. Having no direct childhood memories of Budapest of my own, a big thanks to my sister Judy Maynard and my brother John Walko for sharing with me their recollections of life in the city as children and adolescents.

The staff at the Hungarian National Archive, the Budapest City Archive, the Hungarian National Museum, the Hungarian Academy of

Sciences, the Institute for the History of the 1956 Revolution, the Hungarian University of Fine Arts, the Hungarian Mindszenty Archive, the Hungarian Royal Palace Museum and the Eötvös Loránd University Library all went out of their way to be of assistance whenever I needed it; the staff at the London Library, the British Library and the Bodleian Library in Oxford were immensely helpful.

This book was the idea of Alan Samson, who commissioned it for Weidenfeld and Nicolson, my publisher now for many years – always a calm and reassuring figure. But he departed for pastures new just as I completed the manuscript. It has been superbly and enthusiastically edited by Maddy Price, who has been a delight to work with. Lucinda McNeile has done a fabulous job as assistant editor and I feel so lucky to have had the exceptional, utterly meticulous Linden Lawson as copy editor.

I cannot praise my agent and good friend Georgina Capel highly enough. She has been a tower of support, ever tactful and extraordinarily generous through the last two trying years.

I would not have started writing books or continued doing so without the loving encouragement of Jessica Pulay. Her enthusiasm for central Europe, clear-sighted mind and imaginative view of the world have been invaluable during this project, as ever. I owe her a huge debt of gratitude.

LIST OF ILLUSTRATIONS

1 (above) Roman 'Budapest' (Alamy Stock Photo/David Bagnall)

1 (below) Budapest statue to István, first King of Hungary (Alamy Stock Photo/Michael Wald)

2 (above left) Matthias Corvinus, the Raven King (Alamy Stock Photo/Maidun Collection)

2 (above right) Suleiman the Magnificent (Alamy Stock Photo/Niday Picture Library)

2 (below) Ferenc Rákóczi II (PAINTING)

3 (above) Lajos Kossuth (Alamy Stock Photo/INTERFOTO)

3 (below left) Empress Elisabeth ('Sisi') (Alamy Stock Photo/EDR Archives)

3 (below right) Franz Jozsef (Alamy/IanDagnall Computing)

4 (above) Charles IV, the last Habsburg Emperor (Getty Images/ullstein bild Dtl)

4 (centre left) Mihály Károlyi (Alamy Stock Photo/Alpha Stock)

4 (centre right) Katinka Károlyi (Alamy Stock Photo/UtCon Collection)

4 (below) Miklós Horthy (Alamy Stock Photo/World History Archive)

5 (above) Béla Kun (Alamy Stock Photo/Shim Harno)

5 (below left) Adolf Eichmann (Alamy Stock Photo/GL Archive)

5 (below right) Sculpted shoes by the artist Gyula Pauer (Alamy Stock Photo/wanderluster)

6 Siege of Budapest (Alamy Stock Photo/Sueddeutsche Zeitung Photo)

7 (above) Mátyás Rákosi (Getty Images/Keystone-France)

7 (centre) Imre Nagy (Getty Images/Bettmann)

7 (below) Fallen statue of Stalin (Getty Images/Hulton Archive)

8 (above) Reburial of Imre Nagy (Getty Images/Thierry Orban)

8 (below) View of Budapest (Alamy Stock/PhotoZGPhotography)

INDEX

Abaza Sivayuş, Grand Vizier, 79
Abbey of St Gallen, 23–4
Abdurrahman, Pasha Abdi, 70n,
    80–1, 83
Academy of Sciences, 7, 122, 254
Act 1870:10, 199
Aczél, György, 364
Adler, Erzsébet, 166
Ady, Endre, 106n, 165, 173, 206,
    227, 235, 266
Aelia Sabina, 20–1
Aelius Triccianus, 21
Ágai, Adolf, 199
'age of adventures', 29
Agrarian Revolution, 95
Ahmet III, Sultan, 94
Alexander I, Tsar, 121
Alexander Leopold, Archduke,
    107
Allnoch, Lieutenant-Colonel
    Alois, 155
Almanach de Gotha, 76n
Álmos, Prince, 27n
Alpár, Ignác, 7
Amerighi, Paolo, 83
Andersen, Hans Christian, 2,
    223
Andrássy, Gyula, 175, 181,
    184–92, 194–9, 217
Andrássy, Gyula (son), 234

Andrássy, Károly, 185
Andrew I, King, 35
Andrew II, King, 36–7
Andrew III, King, 43
Andropov, Yuri, 358
animal fights, 103
Anna of Antioch, 192n
anti-Semitism, see Jews
Antonine Plague, 19–20
Apponyi, Count Albert, 203, 234,
    260
April Laws, 148, 152
Aquincum, 18–22, 25, 28–9, 36n
Arany, János, 45, 138
Arnold, Matthew, 141
Arnothy, Christine and Ilas,
    313–14
Arnulf of Bavaria, 23
Árpád, Prince, 6, 8n, 27n, 28–31,
    75, 294
Árpád dynasty, 30–2, 35–6, 42–3,
    132, 177, 192n
Arrow Cross, 283n, 290, 293–
    301, 303, 305–6, 308, 312,
    325, 328, 331, 333, 335n
Aster Revolution, 247–8
astrology, 52n
Augsburger Allgemeine Zeitung,
    144
Augustus, Emperor, 18

Auschwitz, 169, 260, 279, 284–5, 288n
Ausgleich agreement, 178, 191–2, 194, 198, 234, 261, 272
Austrian Anschluss, 277
Austrian Empire, 46n, 80, 96, 101, 152–3, 190
Austrian–Prussian War, 189, 194
Avars, 25, 29
AVO, 331–5, 337, 340, 349, 352, 363
Awakening Magyars, 221, 266, 274
Az Est, 239

Babits, Mihály, 64, 244, 266
Bach, Alexander von, 184
Bacsó, Béla, 264
Bajcsy-Zsilinszky, Endre, 282
Bakócz, Támas, Archbishop of Esztergom, 59–60
Bandholtz, Brigadier-General Harry Hill, 256
Bánffy, Count Dezső, 9, 232
banking and finance, 13, 150, 172, 217, 222, 325, 329, 366
Bartók, Béla, 4, 205, 266, 276–7
Báthory, Erzsébet, 76n
Báthory, Gábor, 76n
Báthory, Prince István, 76
Báthory, Zsigmond, 76n
Batsányi, János, 106, 111
Batthyány, Count Lajos, 140, 147–9, 153, 159–60, 345
Batthyány, László and Elemér, 176
Batu, 38–40
Beatrice, Queen, 52–3, 57, 63

Bektashi monks, 64
Béla I, King, 35
Béla III, King, 36, 192n
Béla IV, King, 38–42, 142
Belgrade, Battle of, 48–9, 62
Belvárosi Kávéház, 319
Bem, General József, 154, 156, 347–8
Benda, Kálmán, 34
bene possessionati, 96
Benefi, Géza, 319
Beniczky, Ferenc von, 203
Benke, Valéria, 349
Bentham, Jeremy, 121
Berengar I, King of Lombardy, 23, 29
Berény, Róbert, 252n
Beria, Lavrenty, 342–3
Berlin Wall, fall of, 342, 368, 373
Berzeviczy, Gergely, 98
Bessenyei, György, 111
Beszélö, 365
Bethlen, István, 224, 277, 326
Bevilaqua-Borsody, Béla, 207
Bibó, István, 278
Bielkin, Fyodor, 337
Billroth, Professor Theodor, 242
Bismarck, Otto von, 163
Black Death, 46
Blowitz, Henri de, 6
'blue chit election', 327
Bonfini, Antonio, 50–3, 55
Bornemisza, Péter, 72
Borsszem Jankó, 199
Bortnyik, Sándor, 252n
botanical gardens, 102
Botticelli, Sandro, 54

Brace, Charles Loring, 162
Braham, Randolph, 295
Brahms, Johannes, 202–3
Braudle, Ferdinand, 25
Braun, Lípot, 215
bridges, 1n, 6, 195n, 294–5, 329,
    353
  Chain Bridge (Széchenyi
    Bridge), 116–19, 139, 155,
    175–6, 180, 239
  Erzsébet Bridge, 299
  Liberty Bridge, 164n
  Margaret Bridge, 200, 294–5,
    347
  Petőfi Bridge, 200
  pontoon bridge, 70, 91, 102,
    104, 116–17, 121, 139
Bronze Age civilization, 17
Bruno of Querfurt, 31
Buda, sieges of, 2–3, 78–85, 91,
    102–3, 293
Budapest, siege of, 292–308
Budapest Bridge Association,
    117
Budapest Military History
    Museum, 247n
Budapest Opera House, 7, 201–4,
    206, 225, 239, 331
Budapest racecourse, 254
Budapest Stock Exchange, 218
Budapest University, 133, 347
Bulcsú, 30
Bulgars, 29
Burton, Richard, 364
Bush, George H. W., 256n
Buxbaum, Ábraham, 215
Büyük Cami (Great Mosque), 65

Byron, Lord, 136, 156
Byzantine Empire, 47–8

Café Pilvax, 136–8, 140, 150, 161
Caine, Michael, 364
Caius Septimius Castinus, 21
Calvinists and Calvinism, 68, 73,
    76, 90, 92, 101, 167, 261,
    341, 343
Camicia, Chimenti, 54
Capa, Robert, 304
Caraffa, General Antonio, 90
Casimir, King of Poland, 45
Cassius Dio, 21
Castle Garden (Várket Bazár),
    201n
Castle Hill tunnel, 118
Cavour, Count, 163
Caxton, William, 52
Çelebi, Evliya, 62, 65, 70
censorship, 109, 112, 135, 137,
    143–4, 161, 182, 184, 356
Chanson de Roland, 23
Charlemagne, Emperor, 25
Charles of Lorraine, Duke, 79,
    81–2, 84
Charles, Emperor, 219, 246, 248,
    262–3
Charles V, Holy Roman Emperor,
    58, 60, 73–4, 110n
Charles VI, Holy Roman
    Emperor, 94, 99
Charles I, King, 43–5
Charles VII, King of France, 47
Charlotte, Princess, 120
Chateaubriand, François-René
    de, 121

Chaucer, Geoffrey, 110
'chauvinism', 232–3
cholera, 142
Chorin, Ferenc, 218, 276
Chownitz, Julian, 149
Christian I, King of Denmark and Norway, 47
Christianity, conversion to, 27n, 30–2
Church of St Mary Magdalene, 44, 67
church schools, ban on, 328
Churchill, Winston, 321, 335
cinema industry, 266–7
City Park (Városliget), 7
civil service grades, 194
Clark, Adam, 118, 155n
Clark, William Tierney, 118
'class enemies', eviction of, 330
Clemenceau, Georges, 269
Clement II, Pope, 24
Club Café murders, 274
coffee houses, 104, 125, 135, 206–14, 267, 319, 328, 377
collectivization, 329, 343
Coloman, King, 36
Comintern, 256–7, 320, 323, 325, 332n, 342
Committe for Historical Justice, 369
Committee of National Defence, 153
Committee of Public Safety, 139
'Compromise', the, 13, 190–4, 197, 217, 228, 231, 235
Congress of Vienna, 1, 120–1
Constantinople, fall of, 47–8, 51

Constitution Day, 329
Cook, A. J., 265
Corvin Group, 355
Corvinus library, 52, 62–3
Counter-Reformation, 74, 89
Crankshaw, Edward, 163
Crown of St Stephen, 10, 33–4, 153, 174, 230
Csekonics, Baron, 126
Csele River, 61
csengőfrász ('bell fright'), 332
Csepel Island, 13, 28–9, 217, 350
Cumans, 43, 176
currency, 149, 152, 274, 301, 317–18
Curtiz, Michael, 211n, 239, 267
Czech Wars, 48
Czerny, József, 255
Cziráky, Chief Justice, 119

d'Agoult, Countess Marie, 129
Darányi, Kálmán, 273
d'Asti, Lieutenant-colonel Michele, 82
de Cröy, Marshal Eugène, 83
de Jonghe, Countess, 176
Deák, Ferenc, 181, 182n, 184, 190–2, 194, 197
Deák, István, 134, 260, 274, 292
death squads, 255, 264, 296
Degré, Alajos, 139
Dekanozov, Vladimir, 311
Demény, Bertalan, 312
democracy, 109, 224, 247, 264–5, 290, 325, 356, 375
see also universal suffrage

Dért, Tibor, 324
Deseő, László, 304
Dietz, Johann, 78, 83–4
Diósy, Marton, 114
dissidents, Soviet-era, 364–5
Diszel, massacre in, 259
Djilas, Milovan, 315, 321
Dohány Street Synagogue, 214,
    219–20
Domitian, Emperor, 18
Doukas, 48
Dózsa, György, 59–60
Dual Monarchy, 13, 217
    coffee houses under, 206–14
    collapse of, 231–2, 247–8
    establishment of, 13, 178,
        191–3, 199, 261
    Jews under, 215–22
duelling, 203, 245
Duknovic, 56
Dzerzhinsky, Felix, 255

Edelpők, Barbara, 57
Edward I, King of England, 46
Egetö, Mária, 342
Eichmann, Adolf, 284–5, 297,
    304
Ekkehard the Younger, 24
Elisabeth ('Sisi'), Empress, 8–10,
    94n, 166, 174–85, 187–91,
    194–5
Elisabeth, Queen, 45
Ember, Herr, 312
Emese, Princess, 27n
emigration, 228, 266–7, 346, 357,
    377
Engelmann, Pál, 228

Engels, Friedrich, 123, 141, 148,
    228
Enlightenment, 109, 111, 120
Eötvös, Baron József, 191
Eötvös, Károly, 216
Eötvös József College, 336
Eperjes, executions in, 90
Eravisci, 17–18
Esterházy, Count Miklós, 75
Esterházy, Count Pál, 90, 113
Esterházy, Prince Pál, 227n, 241,
    242n, 315
Esztergom Round Tower, 80, 82
Etelköz, 27
European Union, 346, 377
Evidenzbureau, 143, 184
Erzsébet, Princess, 192

Falk, Max ('Miksa'), 182,
    182–3n
Falk, Peter, 183n
Faludy, György, 265, 309, 311,
    317, 333–4
Fargás, Judit, 297
Farkas, María, 268
Fáy, András, 132
Fazekas, Gyula, 334–5
Feller, Harald, 312
Fenyő, Miksa, 286
Ferdinand I 'the Benign',
    Emperor, 61n, 128, 135, 140,
    148, 152–3
Ferenc Rákóczi II of
    Transylvania, Prince, 89,
    92–4
Ferenczi, Sándor, 111n, 248n, 275
Ferenczy, Ida, 181, 187, 189

Festetics, Marie, 178
Festival of Jewish-Magyar
    Brotherhood, 168
Feszl, Frigyes, 168
feudalism, 32, 36–7, 95, 101, 172,
    197
    see also serfs and serfdom
Field of Blood (Vérmező), 11,
    106, 109, 177
fires, 67, 70
First Hungarian Commercial
    Bank, 13
First World War
    collapse of Dual Monarchy,
    232, 239–49
    naval surrender, 262
    territorial losses, 268–71,
    277–8, 281–2
Fisher, Samuel, 170
fishing rights, 37
FitzJames, James, Duke of
    Berwick, 79
floods, 72, 125–30
flour mills, 12–13
Földi, Júlia, 336
Folliot de Crenneville, General
    Count Franz, 188
Förster, Lajos, 167–8
Fort Knox, 34
Fox, William, 211n
Francis I, Emperor, 108, 121–2
Franciscan Church, 127
Franco, General Francisco,
    337
Frankish Empire, 25, 28
Franz Ferdinand, Archduke,
    assassination of, 239, 241

Franz Jozsef, Emperor, 8–10, 153,
    155–9, 233, 241, 246, 266
    coronation, 174–7, 191–2
    and Dual Monarchy, 185,
    187–92
    and Empress Elisabeth,
    178–82, 194
    Horthy and, 260, 262
    and Jews, 166, 168–9, 173, 218,
    220
    and Kossuth's funeral, 235–6
Frederick II, Holy Roman
    Emperor, 38
Frederick III, Holy Roman
    Empire, 50
Freemasons, 108, 264
French Revolution, 106–7, 158,
    254
Freud, Sigmund, 111n, 248n, 275
Friedman, Mór, 220
Friedmann, Litzi, 332n
Frindt's Tavern, 20n
Friss building, 70
Fritsch, Colonel, 82
Fügedi, Erik, 34
Fürstenberg, Lieutenant-Colonel,
    82

Gagarin, Yuri, 2
Gallery of Applied Art, 7
gambling, 11, 93, 94n, 117, 120,
    209, 243
Garbai, Sándor, 255
Gazette Musicale, 129
Gellért Hill, 17, 66n, 374
General Workers' Association,
    228

Genghis Khan, 38

George VI, King of great Britain, 287

Gepids, 25

Gerbeaud pastry shop, 200

Gergely, Ágnes, 354

German language, decline in use of, 197–8

German Theatre, 125

Gerő, András, 180

Gerő, Ernő, 329, 345, 355

Gesta Hungarorum, 28

Géza, Chief Prince, 30

Géza I, King, 33

Gimes, Miklós, 369

Gisela, Queen, 30–1

Glass House, 306

Glembay, Károlyi, 153

Glorious Fifteenth, 139

Gödöllő concentration camp, 316

Goethe, Johann Wolfgang von, 109

gold deposits, 36, 44

Goldberger and Sons, 165–7

Golden Bull, 36–7

Golden Horde, 38

Gorbachev, Mikhail, 366–7

Gore, Catherine, 118n

Görgey, General Artúr, 154–5, 158

Goths, 25

Gotthardi, Ferenc, 107

Grace of Monaco, Princess, 364

Grand Boulevard (Nagykörút), 6, 200, 209, 299

Grassalkovich, Count, 194

Great Hungarian Plain, 9, 59, 242n

Great Migrations, 19n, 25

Great Suleiman Mosque (Istanbul), 69

Great Synagogue, 167–70

Greater Hungary, 14, 43, 150, 172, 250, 270–1

Greek Orthodox Church, 117n, 167

Greek traders, 103

Grillparzer, Franz, 148

Grősz, Bishop József, 316

Grósz, Károly, 367, 372

Grove, Andy, 283, 286

Grünwald, Béla, 197, 233

Gül Baba, 64–5

'gulyas Communism', 364–5

Gundel restaurant, 200

gunpowder, 39

Gustavus III, King of Sweden, 161

Gustav V, King of Sweden, 287

Guyon, Captain Richard, 154n

Guzmics, Izidor, 110n

Györffy, György, 40

habeas corpus, 97

Hadrian, Emperor, 18

Hagia Sophia (Constantinople), 62

Hajnóczy, József, 105

Hamann, Brigitte, 188, 383, 384, 390

Haraszti, Miklós, 268, 364–5, 367

Harsányi, Sándor, 312

Hatvany art collection, 312–13

Haussmann, George-Eugène, 199
Hauszmann, Alajos, 210
Háy, Gyula, 324, 343
Haynau, Baron Ludwig von, 159–62, 163n, 165, 184
Hazai és Külföldi Tudósítások (Reports from Home and Abroad), 112
Hegedüs, András, 351, 352n
Heine, Heinrich, 128, 131n, 141, 158, 179, 218
Heltai, Ferenc, 219
Heltai, Jenő, 267n, 268
Henry II, Holy Roman Emperor, 30
Henry III, Holy Roman Emperor, 33, 35
Henry III, King of England, 38
Hentzi, General Heinrich, 154–5, 236n
Herder, Johann Gottfried, 111
'hereditary princes', 74
Heribald, 24
Hermándy, Lieutenant Iván, 298
Hermann of Niederaltaich, Abbot, 38
Herules, 25
Herzen, Alexander, 141
Herzl, Theodor, 215, 219, 221n
Hess, András, 52
Hevesi, Lajos, 171
Hindy, Lieutenant-General Iván, 302
Hirschler, Dr Ignác, 169
Hitler, Adolf, 64, 163, 200, 260, 270, 272, 275–7, 279, 282–3, 287–90, 292, 294, 303, 346

Hódosy, Pál, 298
Hohler, Thomas, 265
Holocaust memorial, 305–6
Holy Roman Empire, 47, 74
Homoky, Father, 181
Honecker, Erich, 371
Honvédség (national army), 150, 152–4, 156, 160–1, 165, 185
Horizont bookshop, 350
Horthy, Magdolna, 308
Horthy, Admiral Miklós, 164n, 258–79, 281–3, 287–91, 293–4, 296, 310, 320, 323, 325–7, 330, 336, 338, 342, 359, 374
Horthy, Miklós ('Miki'), 289–90
Horvát, István, 133
Höss, Rudolf, 285
House of Anjou, 43
House of Terror museum, 335n
Hübner, Count Joseph, 186
Humboldt, Wilhelm von, 121
Hunfalvy, Pál, 161
Hungarian Academy of Music, 130, 204
Hungarian Christian Women's League, 308n
Hungarian Commercial Bank of Pest, 172
Hungarian Commune, 106n, 251–5, 267, 274, 323
    see also Hungarian Soviet Republic
Hungarian constitution, 113, 121–2, 135, 140, 145–6, 176, 192, 226, 234, 273, 329

Hungarian Credit Bank, 13

Hungarian credo, 269–70

Hungarian General Credit Bank, 311

Hungarian Jewish Council, 285

Hungarian language, 2, 29, 104, 109–15, 122–3, 130–1, 133, 198, 202

   Empress Elisabeth and, 181–2, 187–8, 191

   Jews and, 114, 166, 169–70, 172

   note on, 113n

   spoken in Auschwitz, 285

Hungarian national anthem, 206–7

Hungarian National Bank, 279

Hungarian national flag, 329, 348

Hungarian National Gallery, 94

Hungarian Renaissance, 52–6

Hungarian Republic, declaration of, 247–8

Hungarian Soviet Republic, 106n, 267, 271, 321

   see also Hungarian Commune

Hungarian Uprising, see Revolution of 1956

Hungarian-Soviet Friendship Society, 350

Hungarian-Soviet Shipping Company, 317

Hunor, 75

Huns, 22, 25

Hunyadi, Elisabeth, 49

Hunyadi, János, 48–50, 55, 60, 62, 260n

Hunyadi, János, King of Bosnia, 57

Hunyadi, László, 49, 55

Hunyadi, Matthias, see Matthias I Corvinus, King

Iazyges, 19n

Ibrahim, Vizier, 63

Ignotus, Pál, 105, 135, 156, 247, 250, 263, 332–3, 338

Illésházy, István, 73

Illyés, Gyula, 223

Imre, Prince, 32

Imrédy, Béla, 279

Industrial Revolution, 12, 121, 228

informers, Soviet-era, 334

Innocent XI, Pope, 79

Ipolyi, Bishop Arnold, 226

Irinyi, János, 136, 138

iron stirrup, introduction of, 25, 28

Isabella of Anjou, Princess, 42–3

Istóczy, Győző, 214, 220–1

Jacobins, 106–9, 111

Jagiełło, Ladislaus, 57

James II, King of England, 79

Janissaries, 48, 62, 64–5, 69, 75

Jaross, Andor, 284

Jászi, Oszkár, 227, 250, 233

Jazyges, 176

Jelačić, Josip, 151–3

Jesuits, 108

Jewish Laws, 277–9

Jews, 4, 36–7, 46–7, 51–2, 53n, 101, 182, 198, 208, 213n, 230, 377

Jews – *contd*
and Dual Monarchy, 215–22
and Horthy regime, 259–60,
264, 266, 268, 271–9
and Hungarian Commune,
252–3
and Hungarian language, 114,
166, 169–70, 172, 198
'Jew Judges', 46–7, 51
and 'Judapest', 165–73
and music, 203, 204n
Neolog Jews, 169, 219–20
and Ottoman occupation, 65,
68–9
and Revolution of 1848,
149–50, 154, 161, 165
and Second World War, 282n,
283–90, 292–3, 295–300,
305–7
and siege of Buda, 80, 83–4
and Soviet liberation, 312–13
and Soviet occupation, 325,
327–8, 340–1
taxation of, 37, 46, 51, 68, 101,
161, 165
and Zionism, 219, 221n, 328
John, King of Bohemia, 44–5
John III Sobieski, King of Poland,
78
Jókai, Mór, 6, 134, 136, 137n,
138–9, 150, 177, 180, 184,
192, 195, 236
jokes, circulation of, 208
Jonquil, Jean-Baptiste, 162
Joseph II, Emperor, 100n, 112–15
Joseph, Archduke (palatine
1843), 145–6

Joseph, Archduke (palatine
1918), 247
Joyce, James, 261
József, Attila, 1, 42, 305

Kádár, János, 251n, 355, 358–67,
369, 371
Kálkolna estate, 248
Kállay, Miklós, 282
Kánya, Emilia, 162
Karács, Teréz, 132
kardvágás, 246
Karinthy, Frigyes, 208
Karl Marx University, 344
Károlyi, Catherine ('Katinka'),
224, 227n, 242, 251n
Károlyi, Count István, 201n
Károlyi, Count Julius, 222
Károlyi, Mihály, 242–51, 267
Karton, Kati, 12
Kassák, Lajos, 252n
Kazinczy, Ferenc, 105,
109–12
Kecskemét, massacre in, 259
Kellner, Zoltán, 268
Kemalpaşazâde, Ahmed, 61
Kemény, Gabor, 296
Kemény, Zsigmond, 141
Kemnitzer, Johann, 104
Kempf, Franz Xavier, 167–8
Kendeffy, Countess Katinka,
186
Kerepesi Cemetery, 106n, 118,
345, 371
Kertbeny, Karl-Maria, 123
Kertész, André, 277
Kertész, Imre, 277

KGB, 337, 342, 360–1, 367
   see also NKVD
Khrushchev, Nikita, 344, 355,
   358, 360, 263
Király, General Béla, 349–50
Királydomb (King's Hill), 19n
Kishon, Ephraim, 318
Kiss, General Ernő, 161
Kiss, József, 170
Kiss, Lieutenant, 350–1
Klemperer, Otto, 204n
Kóbor, Tamás, 214
Kodály, Zoltan, 4, 21, 200n, 205,
   266, 276–7
Koestler, Arthur, 12, 29, 164n,
   240, 251, 264, 274, 337,
   374
Kohlmayer, Samuel, 112
Kohn, Baron Samu, 218–19
Kohn, Chief Rabbi Samuel,
   220
Kölcsey, Ferenc, 207
Kollonitsch, Cardinal Leopold
   Karl von, 90–1, 94
Kolozsvár, 73, 269
Königsegg, Countess Pauline
   von, 182
Konrád, György, 169, 273, 275–6,
   281, 286, 304, 331
Kopácsi, Sándor, 350–1
Koppány, Prince, 31
Korda, Sir Alexander, 211, 267–8
Kornai, János, 329
Kornfeld, Móric, 312
Kornfeld, Zsigmond, 218
Kornilova, Fenya Feodorovna,
   324

Kossuth, Lajos, 116, 140–58,
   160–5, 184–5, 192, 196–7,
   260n, 329
   his funeral, 235–6
Kossuth Rádió, 343
Kosztolányi, Dezső, 212
Kovács, Béla, 326
Kovács, Imre, 316
Kovács, Mária, 368
Kovalovszky, Miklós, 295
Kristóffy, József, 233
Krúdy, Gyula, 11, 13, 119, 200,
   209, 243, 264
Kryuchkov, Vladimir, 367
Kubinyi, Ágoston, 139
Kultsár, István, 112
Kun, András, 300
Kun, Béla, 250–1, 253–9, 263,
   265, 267, 274, 321, 323
Kunmadaras pogrom, 327–8
Kursk, Battle of, 282
Kurszán, 29
Kurtág, György, 205

Laczovics, János, 105
Ladislaus IV King, 42–3
Ladislaus V, King, 49
Ladislaus VI, King, 49
Lafayette, Marquis de, 163
Lamartine, Alphonse de, 121
Lambeck, Peter, 65
Lamberg, General Ferenc, 152, 154
Lánczy, Leó, 172, 218
land tenure, by entail, 95, 123
Landerer, Lajos, 138, 143, 146
Landor, Walter Savage, 140
Latin, 32, 100, 110, 112–14, 122

League of Nations, 273
Lechfeld, Battle of, 30
Lechner Ödön, 213
Lechner, Lajos, 199
lefolyo (acid bath), 332
Legio II Adiutrix, 18
Lehár, Colonel Anton, 263–4
Lehár, Franz, 263
Leigh Fermor, Patrick, 226
Leiningen-Westerburg, General
    Count Karl, 154n
Leipzig, Battle of, 120
Lél, Prince, 30
Lendvai, Paul, 50, 249, 270
Lenin, Vladimir, 253–5, 323, 331,
    350, 360
Lenin Boys, 255
Leo X, Pope, 59
Leonardo da Vinci, 54
Leopold I, Holy Roman
    Emperor, 78–9, 81, 90, 92
Leopold II, Holy Roman
    Emperor, 107–8
Levi, Primo, 285
Liberty Statue, 374–5
Ligeti, György, 205
Lincoln, Abraham, 1, 140
Lippi, Filippo, 54
Liszt, Cosima, 175
Liszt, Ferenc, 125, 128–31, 168
Liszt, Franz, 21, 175, 204–5, 349
Liszt Concert Hall, 206
Lloyd George, David, 259
Lőcsei, Inspector General István,
    299
Losonczy, Géza, 369
Louis I the Great, King, 45–7

Louis II, King, 59, 60–3
Louis IX, King of France, 39
Louis XIV, King of France, 93–4,
    268n
Louis XVI, King of France, 246
Louis-Philippe, King of France,
    134
Löw, Aabbi, 161
Löw, Aare, 219
Löw, Lipót, 162
Lucheni, Luigi, 195n
Ludovika of Bavaria, Princess,
    184
Lueger, Karl, 217
Lukács, György, 343
Lukács, János, 7, 91, 111n, 200,
    368
Lutherans, 67, 73, 77, 90, 101,
    142, 167
Lutz, Carl, 292, 295, 300, 306–7,
    311

Macrinus, Emperor, 21
Magna Carta, 36–7
Magnates Table, 96
Magyar rebellions, 91–4
Magyar tribes, 17, 23–32, 39, 75,
    176, 226n
Mahler, Gustav, 7, 201–4
Majláth, Count János, 153, 181
Makk, Károly, 347
malaria, 73
Malashenko, Lieutenant-General
    Yevgeny, 353
Maléter, Pál, 369
Malinovsky, Marshal Rodion,
    293, 312, 315

Manhattan Project, 13, 209, 253n
Mann, Golo, 163
Mansfeld, Péter, 361
Mantegna, Andrea, 54
Mányoki, Ádám, 94
Márai, Sándor, 198, 279, 309, 313, 320, 330
March Youth, 135–6
Marcomanni, 19n
Marcus Aurelius, Emperor, 17, 19
Marczius Tizenötödike (March Fifteenth), 149
Margaret, Princess, 46n
Maria, Queen, 60–1, 63
Maria Theresa, Empress, 43n, 99–102, 112
Marie Antoinette, Queen of France, 106
Marie Valerie, Princess, 188
Maróthy, Károlyi, 298
Martinovics, Ignác, 105–8
Marx, Karl, 141, 148, 228, 350, 360
Mary of Naples, 43
Matthias Church, 44, 65, 102, 174, 239, 246
Matthias I Corvinus, King, 43–4, 49–57, 62–3, 65, 74, 81
Maximilian, King of Mexico, 181
Mayer, Hans, 312
Mayer, Louis B., 211n
Mayerhofer, Andreas, 171
Mehmed II, Sultan, 47
Mehmed IV 'the Hunter', Sultan, 78, 84n
Mencken, H. L., 265

Mendel, Jakob, 51, 53n
Mérei, Ferenc, 364
Mészáros, Lőrinc, 59–60
Metropolitan Board of Public Works, 199
Metternich, Klemens von, 1, 106, 110, 116, 120–3, 134, 143, 144n, 146
MFTR, 13
Michael VII, Emperor, 33
Middleton, Bay, 179
Mihailovich, Ödön, 205
Mikoyan, Anastas, 355
Mikszáth, Kálmán, 194, 227
military academies, and Revolution of 1956, 350
Mill, John Stuart, 121
Millennium Exhibition, 8–9, 48n
Mimar Sinan, 69
Mindszenty, Cardinal József, 328, 336, 357
Mohács, Battle of, 60–1, 63, 65, 68, 73
Molière, 109
Molnár, Ferenc, 212, 240, 246
Molnár, Miklós, 290, 298, 329
Mongol invasion, 38–41, 157, 309, 311
Montagu, Lady Mary Wortley, 77
Montecuccoli, Raimondo, 74
Montespan, Mme de, 268n
Móricz, Zsigmond, 266
Muhammad, Prophet, 47
'Muscovites', 320–2, 343
Musil, Robert, 193
Mussolini, Benito, 2, 163, 171n, 200n, 266, 376

Mustapha Jami, 69

Nagy, Erzsébet, 342–3
Nagy, Ferenc, 309, 326
Nagy, Imre, 341–5, 347–50,
    355–8, 360–2, 364, 375
  reburial of, 368–71
Naima, Mustafa, 80
names, Hungarian, 131–2, 218
Napoleon Bonaparte, 108n, 117,
    303n
Napoleon III, Emperor of France,
    163, 186
natio Hungarica, 97
National Army, 258–9
National Association of
    Manufacturers, 218
National Benefaction statue, 241
National Casino, 208, 221, 243
National Committee of
    Liberation, 283n
National Guard, 139, 149, 150n
National Jewish Congress of
    Hungary, 273
National Library, 120
National Museum, 34, 120, 138,
    160, 167, 225, 236, 256, 349,
    376
National Song, 137, 138, 370
National Theatre, 125, 130–1,
    202n, 351, 376
NATO, 377
Nazis, 64, 260, 270, 276–7,
    279–80
Nazi-Soviet pact, 278, 324
Németh, László, 109
Németh, Miklós, 366

Népszabadság (A Free People),
    367
Népszava (The People's Voice),
    229, 264
Neues Wiener Tagblatt, 230
Neumann, John von, 266n
New Independence Party, 245
New York Café, 210–13, 240
Nicholas I, Tsar, 155, 159
Nicholas II, Tsar, 303n
Nicolson, Harold, 293
NKVD, 312, 332
  see also KGB
nobility, 95–9
  and Buda (vs. Pest), 197
  ceremonial dress (Attila), 187
  exemption from detention, 143
  exemption from taxation, 90,
    95, 98–9, 119, 123, 145, 149
  and Hungarian language,
    113–14, 122–3
  Jewish, 173
  and reform, 122–3
  'sandalled nobility', 97, 123,
    142
Noll, Reinhard, 301
Nordau, Max, 219
Numerus Clausus Act, 272, 274
Nuremberg Laws, 279
Nyugat (West), 244

Óbuda, 18, 19n, 29, 37, 46, 155,
    170, 173n
Oettingen, Colonel, 82
Ögedei Khan, 38, 40
Oláh, Miklós, Archbishop of
    Esztergom, 56, 63

Operation Margarethe, 282
Operation Whirlwind, 356
operetta, 266
Oppenheimer, Samuel, 84
Orbán, Viktor, 2, 34, 41, 251n,
    270n, 370–1
    and Admiral Horthy, 290–1
Orczy, Baroness Emma, 171n
Orczy House, 171–2
Örs, 75
Országgyűlési Tudósítások
    (Municipal Reports), 142
Országh, Sándor, 225
Orthodox Synagogue, 286
Ossowski, Stanisław, 327
Otto the Great, Holy Roman
    Emperor, 29
Ottomans, 47–8, 50–1, 56–63,
    132, 148, 157, 185, 207, 273,
    309, 311
    compared with Habsburgs,
    89–91
    occupation of Buda, 64–71
    occupation of Hungary, 64–77
    and siege of Buda, 78–85

pagan rebellions, 35–6
Paleolithic footprints, 17
Pálffy, Albert, 149
Pálffy, Colonel Ferenc, 82
Pálffy, György, 338
Pálffy, Count János, 91
Pálffy, Count Miklós, 222
Palmerston, Lord, 120, 157–8,
    163
Pannonia, 18–22, 25
Pannons, 17

Pardoe, Julia, 98, 121, 127, 129
Paris Commune, 228
Párkány, 79
Parliament building, 7, 10, 34,
    164, 182n, 223–7, 264, 305,
    328, 359–60, 367
Pashazde, 62
Paskevich, Prince Ivan, 156,
    158
Patai, Raphael, 216
Pauer, Gyula, 306
Pavarotti, Luciano, 2
Pázmány, Péter, 74
Peace of Szatmár, 94
peasants' revolt, 59–60
Pechenegs, 24, 27, 30
Peel, Robert, 120
People's Park, 228, 368
Pest Youth, 132
Pester Lloyd, 166, 174, 182n,
    191
Pesti Hírlap (Pest Journal), 143,
    145–6, 149, 233, 265
Pesti Napló (Pest Daily), 9n,
    182
Pesti Vigadó (House of
    Merriment), 130
Péter, Gabor, 332–3, 340n
Péter, Provost, 28
Peter Orseolo, King, 32, 35
Petőfi, Sándor, 2–3, 41, 54n,
    135–41, 156, 168, 177, 370
Petrőczy, István, 74
Pfeffer-Wildenbruch, General
    Karl, 294, 297, 303
Philby, Kim, 332n
Philip of Felső, 43

411

Pilisy, Róza, 211n
Pilvax, Károlyi, 138n
Pius II, Pope, 47
plague, 49, 72, 94
  see also Antonine Plague; Black
  Death
Poincaré, Raymond, 245
Polcz, Alaine, 314
Polgár, Alfred, 206
Pollack, Mihály, 225
Pongrátz, Gergely, 355
population, 11–12, 26, 29, 41,
  44, 68, 72, 91, 101, 198,
  377
  female, 313
  Jewish, 166, 272
  post-First World War, 269n,
  272
  and post-war Terror, 337–8
Pozsony/Pressburg, 91, 95, 100,
  122, 134, 149, 225
Pragmatic Sanction, 43n, 99
Prince of Wales (Edward VII),
  210, 211n, 222
Prince of Wales (Edward VIII),
  265
Prinz, Gyula, 333, 340n
Privorsky, Ferenc, 138n
Prohászka, Bishop Ottokár, 221,
  266, 286
Prónay, Albert, 127
Prónay, Pál, 264
Przibram, Ludwig von, 175
public executions, 105–6, 109
public holidays, 329
public works, 199–201
Pushkin, Count, 303n

Quadi, 19n

Rabbinical Seminary, 169, 286
Race Protection Party, 282n
Radetzky, Field Marshal Jozsef,
  160
Radio Free Europe, 356
Radnóti, Miklós, 287
Rajk, Endre, 301
Rajk, Júlia, 337, 345
Rajk, László, 301n, 335–7,
  344–5, 360
Rajk, László (son), 365
Rajnay, Gábor, 211
Rákosi, Jenő, 209, 232
Rákosi, Mátyás, 253, 320,
  322–9, 332, 336–8,
  340–1, 343–5, 352n,
  360
Rákoskeresztúr Cemetery, 362,
  369
Reagan, Ronald, 160, 256n
Red Thursday, 229
Reform Movement, 122, 130,
  156, 190
Reformation, 67, 73
refugees, East German, 371–3
Regino, Abbot of Prüm, 24
Regnum Marianum, demolition
  of, 330
religious tolerance, 52n, 67–8,
  76–7, 101, 145, 149
  Habsburg intolerance, 90
Rév, István, 335n
Révai, József, 322, 330
Révai, Miklós, 112
Révay, General Kálmán, 338

Revival Movement, 109–15

Revolution of 1848 and War
  of Independence, 131n,
    134–58, 206, 225, 231, 236n,
    260n, 324, 347
  aftermath and reprisals,
    159–62, 177, 180, 184–6,
    196–8
  and Revolution of 1956,
    345–7

Ribbentrop, Joachim von, 288

Richards, Jacob, 79–83

Riedkirchen, Captain Ramming
  von, 157

Ries, István, 317

robot (labour dues), 74

Rogerius, Master, 40

Romanian invasion, 255–6, 258

Ronay, Egon, 319n

Roosevelt, Franklin D., 2870

Roosevelt, Theodore, 2

Roth, Joseph, 193

Rothschild, Nathan, 120

Rothschild, Solomon, 118

Rotta, Cardinal Angelo, 303

Rousseau, Jean-Jacques, 107–8

Royal Castle, 6, 10, 12, 27n, 54–5,
    70, 100n, 149, 162, 188,
    201n, 210, 283, 290

Royal Hungary, 68, 72–6

Rózsadomb, 64, 66, 330, 333, 366

Rudas bath houses, 67n

Rudolf, Crown Prince, 8, 219–20,
    230

Rudolf, Prince, 189

Russian revolutions, 228, 245,
    324, 342

Sadowa (Königgratz), Battle of,
    189

St John Nepomuk, 102

St László, 296

St Rókus Church, 128

Saint-Saëns, Camille, 168

Saint-Simon, Duc de, 93

St Stephen, King of Hungary, 10,
    30–5, 37, 44, 268
  Exhortations, 34–5
  Feast of St Stephen, 329

St Stephen's Cathedral, 9, 201n,
    226n, 239

St Wiborada, 23–4

Sakmyster, Thomas, 288

Salic law, 43n, 99

Salkházi, Sára, 308

samizdat publications, 108,
    364–5

Sámuel Aba, King, 35

Sand, George, 140

Sárközi, Mátyás, 212n, 345

Sarmatians, 18, 25

Sayn-Wittgenstein, Countess
  Carolyne zu, 129

Schiller, Friedrich, 109

Schulhof, Izsák, 83

Schwarcz, Salamon, 215

Schwartz, Peter, 51

Schwarzenberg, Prince Felix, 153,
    159, 160, 161

Schwechat, Battle of, 185

Schweitzer, Eduard von, 218

Scitovszky, Cardinal János,
    168

Scythians, 17, 47

Sebestyén, Mátyás, 218n

Second World War, 281–91
  siege of Budapest, 292–308
  Soviet liberation, 309–19
Sedlnitzky, Count Josef, 134
Segesvár, Battle of, 156
Seidler, Tobias, 75
Seilern, Countess Crescence,
  121–2
Septimius Severus, Emperor,
  20–1
Serédi, Cardinal Jusztinián, 287,
  300
serfs and serfdom, 60, 73–4, 95,
  97, 101, 105, 123, 145, 149
  see also feudalism
Seton-Watson, R. W., 233
Sevso Treasure, 21–2
Seward, William H., 1
Shakespeare, William, 38, 109,
  143, 163
shamans, 30
Sharf, Móricz, 216
shop signs, 132, 161, 170
Shulgin, General, 303n
Sighani, 63
Sigismund, King, 48–9, 70
Sigray, Count Jakab, 105
Simon, Jolán, 333
Simor, Cardinal János, 175
Simpson, Wallis, 2
Sina, Baron Georg von, 180
Sina, György, 118
Sinkovits, Imre, 350
Siófok, massacre in, 259
Sisters of Social Service, 308
Sixteen Points of 1956, 347, 349
Sixtus IV, Pope, 54

Skorzeny, Otto, 289
Slachta, Margit, 307–8
Smallholders' Party, 321, 326
smallpox, 72
Smith, Adam, 121
socialist realism, 328, 376n
Society of Equality and Liberty,
  108
Society of Reformers, 108
Society of Ten, 135–6
Sokollu Mustafa, Pasha, 70n
Solti, Georg, 264
Solymosi, Eszter, 215
Somogyi, Béla, 264
Sophie, Archduchess, 156,
  179–80, 185
Sophie, Archduchess,
  assassination of, 239
Soviet Union
  collapse of communism, 4–5,
    367, 369, 372–3
  and death of Stalin, 340–1, 344
  Gulags, 256, 326, 338
  Hungrian émigrés, 320–1, 342
  liberation of Hungary, 309–19
  occupation of Hungary, 3, 71,
    320–73
  and Uprising of 1956, 352–62
Spanish Civil War, 324, 336–7
'Springtime of Nations', 134, 140,
  158
Stalin, Josef, 64, 256, 278, 294,
  310, 315, 320–2, 324–5,
  327–8, 335–7, 360, 374
  death of, 340–1, 344
  his statue, 330, 350–1, 375
Stalingrad, Battle of, 282, 293

Starr, Ringo, 364
Stasi, 372
Steindl, Imre, 223–4
Stéphanie, Archduchess, 8
Stephen, Archduke, 152
Stephen I, King, *see* St Stephen, King of Hungary
Stephen V, King, 42
Stobl, Kisfaludi, 374
Strait of Otranto, Battle of, 262
Stratimirović, Đorđe, 151
Strauss, Johann, 234n
street names, 132, 148, 161, 164, 182–3n, 200, 251n, 277, 375–6
strikes, 134, 203, 228, 265, 336, 361
Suebi, 25
suicides, 164n, 299
Suleiman I the Magnificent, Sultan, 57, 60–5, 75–6, 78
Suleiman II, Sultan, 84n
Suslov, Mikhail, 355
Swift, Jonathan, 208n
Swinburne, Algernon Charles, 140
Sylvester II, Pope, 32
Szabad Nép, 330
Szálasi, Ferenc, 290, 294, 296–8, 300–1
Szamuely, Tibor, 255
Szapáry, Countess Etelka, 186
Szapáry, Count Gyula, 204
Széchenyi, Ferenc, 120
Széchenyi, Count István, 116–25, 131–2, 139–41, 143, 145–7, 150–1, 153, 196

Széchenyi, Julianna, 123
Szekfű, Gyula, 89, 217
Szeklers, 46
Szemere, Bertalan, 157
Szendrey, Júlia, 135, 139
Szent-Györgyi, Albert, 266n
Szentkirályi, Mór, 198
Szentmarjay, Ferenc, 105
Szép, Ernő, 213
Szerb, Antal, 197, 266, 286–7
Sziklai, Arnold, 266
Szilágyi, József, 369
Szilágyi, Mihály, 49–50
Szilard, Leo, 13, 249, 266n
Szilard, Tekla, 13
Szirtes, George, 2, 113n
'Szózat' (Vörösmarty's Call), 168
Sztojáy, Döme, 283, 287
Szűcs, Jenő, 57, 98

Talleyrand, Charles Maurice de, 121
Táncsics, Mihály, 139, 151, 196, 198, 228, 235
Tarjan, Willy, 212n
taxation, 44, 53, 60, 74, 94
  exemption for nobility, 90, 95, 98–9, 119, 123, 145, 149
  of Jews, 37, 46, 51, 68, 101, 161, 165
  and Ottoman occupation, 68–9
  and siege of Buda, 89–90
Taylor, Elizabeth, 364
Technological University, 347–8
Teleki, Count Géza, 315
Teleki, Count Pál, 272, 278
Telepy, Karl, 176

Teller, Edward, 252, 253n, 266n
Temesvár, Battle of, 156
Temesvár, siege of, 59
Tennyson, Alfred, 45
territorial expansion, under
    Árpad dynasty, 35–6
Testetics, Count Leó, 129
Tharaud, Jean, 226
Tharaud, Jérôme, 226
Thatcher, Margaret, 364
Thomas II, Archbishop of
    Esztergom, 43
Thomas, Archdeacon of Spalato,
    39, 40n
Thononzoba, 30
Times, The, 10, 163n
Tisza, István, 227n
Tisza, Kálmán, 194, 204, 217, 223,
    226, 232, 241, 244n, 245, 248
Tiszaeszlár Affair, 215–16, 220
Tito, Josip Broz, 335–6, 361
Titus Aelius Justus, 21
Tocqueville, Alexis de, 134, 340
Togay, Can, 306
Tolstoy, Count Kutuzov, 303n
tornados, 239
torture, 90, 108
Törvényhatósági Tudósítások, 143
Townson, Robert, 103–4
trade unions, 228, 254, 264–5
Trajan, Emperor, 18
Treaty of Pressburg, 54
Treaty of Trianon, 268–70, 274,
    277, 281, 294, 336, 376
Trefort, Ágoston, 7, 232
Triple Alliance, 241
Triple Entente, 244, 255, 263, 276

Truman, Harry S., 290
Turkish baths, 66–7, 69, 103
Twelve Points of 1848, 137, 347

Újházi, Ede, 202n
Ullmann, Móric, 172
underground railway, 6, 200
Ungars (Onogurs), 26
unification, of Buda and Pest,
    117–19, 155, 196–9
    rescinded by Austrians, 161,
    196–7
United Lamp Factory, 350
universal suffrage, 137, 228–9,
    247, 321
Uprising of 1956, 3, 41, 344–64,
    375
USS Missouri, 162

Vajdahunyad castle, 7
Valerius Corvinus, 50
Valéry, Paul, 230
Vandals, 25
Vásárhelyi, Miklós, 350, 369
Vaszary, Kolos, 9
Vázsonyi, Vilmos, 273
Vazul, 32–3
Veesenmayer, Edmund, 289, 294,
    297, 307
Verdi, Giuseppe, 161, 202
Vérmező, see Field of Blood
Verolino, Archbishop Gennaro,
    303
Veszprém, Battle of, 31
Victoria, Queen, 137n, 140
Vienna, siege of, 65, 78
Vienna Awards, 277–8

Vienna Gate, 70, 80
Vigadó Concert Hall, 4, 162, 298
Vilag (World), 119, 240
Villa, Pancho, 256n
Vincent IV, Pope, 41
Vindobona, 18, 19n
Visegrád palace, 55–6
Visigoths, 25
Vizinczey, Stephen, 351
Volner, Hernamm, 215
Voltaire, 38, 101, 107
Voroshilov, Kliment, 321–2, 374
Vörösmarty, Mihály, 127, 130,
    149, 159
Vyx, Fernand, 250

Wagner, Otto, 167n
Wagner, Richard, 202
Wahrmann, Moritz, 198
Walko, Éva, 340, 356
Wallenberg, Raoul, 306–7
war criminals, executions of,
    325–6
War of Independence, *see*
    Revolution of 1848 and War
    of Independence
War of the Austrian Succession,
    100
Warner, Jack, 211n
Warsaw Pact, 356, 360, 372
Washington, George, 163
water supplies, 102
Waugh, Evelyn, 2
Weiss, Manfréd, 13, 217, 316
Weisz, Richárd, 213n
Wekerle, Sándor, 227n
Welch, Raquel, 364

Wellington, Duke of, 120
Wesselényi, Baron Miklós, 125,
    127n, 146
White Russians, 303n
White Terror, 263–4, 267, 274,
    310
Wiener Zeitung, 155
Wiesel, Elie, 279
Wigner, Eugene, 209, 266n
Wilhelm I, Elector of Hesse-
    Kassel, 160
Wilhelm I, Kaiser, 174, 178
Wilhelm II, Kaiser, 241, 244
William IV, King of Great
    Britain, 120
Wilson, Woodrow, 248
Windisch-Grätz, Field Marshal
    Prince Alfred, 154
windows, Soviet-era, 363
wine production, increase in, 132
Władysław I Łokietek, King of
    Poland, 45
Wodianer, Samuel, 118
Wohl, Janka and Stefánia, 208n
women
    and coffee houses, 210, 213–14
    and Magyar raiding parties, 27
    raped by Soviets, 313–16, 324
Woriadner, Mór, 172
working class, rise of, 228–9

Yalta Conference, 310, 321
Ybl, Miklós, 201, 225
Yiddish, 114, 169–70

Zách, Klára, 45
Zala, György, 195n

Zápolya, János, 59, 65
Zhukov, Marshal Georgy, 353
Zichy, Count Géza, 203–4
Zichy, Count Ödön, 176
Zichy, Countess, 120
Zita, Empress, 246

Zöld, Sándor, 338–9
Zrínyi, Miklós, 75
Zsindely, Agnés, 298
Zsindely, Sándor, 329, 339, 362
Zukor, Adolph, 211n
Zweig, Stefan, 12, 14